REGINO OF PRÜM

Two Books on Synodal Causes and Ecclesiastical Disciplines

Regino of Prüm (ca. 840–915), after being deposed as abbot of Prüm, became a notable musical theorist, historical chronicler, and student of the canons. His *Two Books on Synodal Causes and Ecclesiastical Disciplines* have generally been seen as practical handbooks to be used in the decision of synodal cases. Although they may have been used in the course of episcopal visitations, they are not to be read as limited to such use. They are to be regarded primarily as a pedagogical tool, intended to remedy an ignorance of the canonical tradition by the clerics in his part of the world. They are intended to be of use to all who have some position of responsibility within the Church and, ultimately, to every member of the Church. They are meant to help form every Christian, but particularly those clerics who have the responsibility to issue judgments and hear confessions in the Church, and to develop in them a disciplined discernment and a habit of addressing issues as they arise in personal and community life in the light of Scripture and of the long experience of the Church. They are brilliantly arranged around the device of questionnaires which fosters a case-based and tentative approach to the resolution of problems while avoiding abstraction and striving to mitigate legalism. The work was influential in its own region, but obtained much greater resonance through its eventual absorption into the *Decretum* of Burchard of Worms, thus affecting the whole Western canonical tradition.

St Michael's College Mediaeval Translations

Edited by

JOSEPH GOERING, *University of Toronto*
GIULIO SILANO, *University of Toronto*

Mediaeval Sources in Translation 60

REGINO OF PRÜM

Two Books on Synodal Causes and Ecclesiastical Disciplines

Translated with an Introduction by
GIULIO SILANO

PIMS PONTIFICAL INSTITUTE OF MEDIAEVAL STUDIES
Toronto

Library and Archives Canada Cataloguing in Publication

Title: Two books on synodal causes and ecclesiastical disciplines / Regino of Prüm ; translated with an introduction by Giulio Silano.

Other titles: Libri duo de synodalibus causis et disciplinis ecclesiasticis. English

Names: Regino, of Prüm, approximately 840–915, author. | Silano, Giulio, 1955– translator, writer of introduction. | Pontifical Institute of Mediaeval Studies, publisher.

Series: Saint Michael's College mediaeval translations. | Mediaeval sources in translation ; 60.

Description: Series statement: Mediaeval sources in translation ; 60 | Saint Michael's College mediaeval translations | Translation of: Libri duo de synodalibus causis et disciplinis ecclesiasticis. | Includes bibliographical references and indexes.

Identifiers: Canadiana (print) 20210254335 | Canadiana (ebook) 20210254890 | ISBN 9780888443106 (softcover) | ISBN 9781771104166 (PDF)

Subjects: LCSH: Catholic Church – Discipline – Early works to 1800. | LCSH: Canon law – Early works to 1800. | LCSH: Canon law – History – To 1500 – Sources.

Classification: LCC BX1800 .R44 2021 | DDC 262.9/2–dc23

Pontifical Institute of Mediaeval Studies
59 Queen's Park Crescent East
Toronto, Ontario M5S 2C4
Canada
www.pims.ca

PRINTED IN CANADA

To

Joe Goering

Il miglior fabbro

Contents

Introduction

Canon law

Regino of Prüm's *Two Books on Synodal Causes and Ecclesiastical Disciplines* is usually described as a canon law collection composed by a Carolingian churchman in the first decade of the tenth century to aid bishops in carrying out their work of oversight over their clergy and people. Clear as that may sound, it still remains somewhat challenging to decide where to start in telling inexpert readers of such a text what it is that they may be reading and why they ought to make the effort.

Canon law, for quite some time now, has not been thriving. Familiarity with the expression does not dispel the sense that it denotes something esoteric and out of its time. Even in the Catholic Church, it appears to have long since yielded its primacy to theological opinion; to read the news is to become quickly aware that bishops and priests do not feel bound by it in any significant way and that an active effort has been made to purify the collective memory from those ages when the Church strove to be, among other things, a society ruled by law. As a consequence, it requires an enormous imaginative effort to consider that canon law – the oldest continuous juridical order in the West and its associated traditions of reflection – was of central importance for many centuries and constituted the forge in which many of our public and private institutions, political and ecclesiological doctrines, and even anthropologies, in the Church and out of it, were shaped.[1] The reasons for this state of things are complex and manifold and to outline them

1. For a short and clear introduction to the history of canon law in the Middle Ages, see James A. Brundage, *Medieval Canon Law* (London and New York: Routledge, 2013). Paolo Grossi, *A History of European Law*, tr. Laurence Hooper (Chichester: Wiley-Blackwell, 2010), p. 17, assesses the place of canon law in the history of the medieval West in the following terms: "The Church of Rome is the pre-eminent figure at every level of medieval culture: religious, cultural, socio-economic, political and legal. Indeed, one could say that medieval culture is, for the most part, a creation of the Church. The history of the Roman Catholic Church is of particular interest to the legal historian because it is the only religious denomination which takes it upon itself to create its own original body of law, drawing its authority directly

all goes beyond our brief. But it may be necessary to touch upon some of them, if we are to try to aid our mythical inexpert reader to approach the text here offered in translation with some degree of confidence and understanding.

The expression itself, canon law, is not free of difficulty and may easily cause misunderstanding. Any dictionary will convey its meaning as law of the Church, particularly in the Catholic tradition. But living as we do within juridical orders in which positive legislation has formally triumphed, we will almost unavoidably construe the expression to indicate positive legislation passed by the Church to regulate its social life. Just as it would be very reductive to think of the English common law as consisting exclusively of statutes passed by Parliament, so it would be reductive to think of canon law as consisting only of written law as promulgated by popes and bishops. In either case, we would be canonizing a specific moment in the long history of a juridical order as constituting the whole. In English, this difficulty is compounded by the cumbersomeness and imprecision with which we can currently render the distinction between *ius* and *lex*, a distinction which in other European languages is preserved by the juxtaposition of analogues of "right" and law.[2] Canon law translates the expression *ius canonicum*, or "canonical right," as it were, but we are tempted to understand it as if it translated *lex canonica*, an expression which is almost wholly foreign to canon law until recent times.[3] Even the first expression, *ius canonicum*, is not used in the first mil-

---

from that of Christ as divine legislator, rather than from any temporal political system. This body of law develops into a unique legal system: canon law. Canon law is by no means the discipline of an isolated priestly caste: in a historical context such as that of the Middle Ages, where Heaven and Earth meet, sacred and secular intermingle, and the citizen and the believer join in one complete unity, canon law cannot but be integrated into the medieval legal order and, indeed, it makes a significant contribution to the shape of that order as we find it." The argument for the centrality of canon law to the whole Western juridical tradition has been set forth most compellingly and successfully by Harold Berman, *Law and Revolution: The Formation of the Western Legal Tradition* (Cambridge, MA: Harvard University Press, 1983). For a careful and shrewd assessment of the early reception of Berman's argument, see R.H. Helmholz, "Harold Berman's Accomplishment as a Legal Historian," *Emory Law Journal* 42 (1993): 475–96.

2. Somewhat analogous reflections on the difficulties presented by the dominance of "law" in English juristic language are presented by Patrick Wormald, *Legal Culture in the Early Medieval West: Law as Text, Image and Experience* (London, Rio Grande: Hambledon Press, 1999), p. 179, where he notes that "English-language scholars need to be aware that they are handicapped by a linguistic muddle when it comes to distinguishing, as early medievalists must, between (say) *underlying* and enacted law."

3. Brundage, *Medieval Canon Law*, p. 60, notes that "Canonists prior to the late thirteenth century usually refrained from using the term 'law' (*lex*) to describe the material of their discipline. 'Law' comes into general use to describe the canons only after the Council of Trent in the mid-sixteenth century." For further reflection on this, Brundage refers to Stephan

lennium. And if we have recourse to a quaint word like right, it is because it would not be good to see the alternative to positive law as being merely unwritten law. Certainly, *ius* is capable of bearing that meaning, but it also, and perhaps more relevantly for our purposes, points to traditions of reflection and practice that do not rely primarily on positive law-making as the obvious way to develop and enforce norms for a common life. In the foundational case of Roman law, *ius* points both to the institutions inherited from the past (*mos maiorum*) and to the contribution made by magistrates and jurists to the development of the complex and rich Roman legal order. These elements may be the ones most fruitfully kept in mind in striving to understand canon law before the so-called classical age (1140–1378), when positive legislation first came to characterize it in a big way.

For the first thousand years of its existence, then, what we call canon law carefully avoids referring to itself as law. As one would expect, the word law is well-known, but it is used almost exclusively to refer to the Law of the Old Testament, or the Mosaic law, and to the legislation of secular governments. One probable reason for what looks very much like a deliberate choice to avoid applying the term law to the standards devised for the disciplining of Church life is the way in which law is treated in some of the Christian Gospels.[4] Law can be a pitfall and legalism may be antithetical to the aims that Christianity pursues. The Church, being also a human society, cannot live its social life without norms, but it cannot be satisfied with pursuing and achieving a merely external submission on the part of its members. The particularity of the Christian vision of law as it applies to the body of believers that is the Church finds a durable expression in the adoption of the term "canon" to mark a norm that is thought to be relevant to Christian social life.

The adoption of canons as the preferred appellation for the Church's legal norms is sometimes treated as if it were a distinction without a difference. In such

---

Kuttner, "Some Considerations on the Role of Secular Law and Institutions in the History of Canon Law," in *Scritti di sociologia e politica, in onore di Luigi Sturzo* (Bologna: Zanichelli, 1953), vol. 2, pp. 351–62, and "Reflections on Gospel and Law in the History of the Church," in *Liber amicorum Monseigneur Onclin*, Bibliotheca ephemeridum theologicarum Lovaniensium 42 (Gembloux: Duculot, 1976), pp. 199–209, both reprinted in Kuttner's *Studies in the History of Medieval Canon Law* (Aldershot: Ashgate, 1990). Also Gérard Fransen, "De analogia legis apud canonistas," *Periodica de re morali, canonica, liturgica* 66 (1977): 535–47.

4. The Gospels of Mark and Matthew are particularly scathing on the problems that can arise from adhering to a legalistic vision of life and the deformations that can occur from lawyers being let loose on the social body. For a recent and thorough consideration of the Gospel evidence, see John P. Meier, *A Marginal Jew: Rethinking the Historical Jesus*: Volume IV: *Law and Love* (New Haven: Yale University Press, 2009). For an earlier consideration by the greatest historian of canon law in our time, see Stephan Kuttner, "Reflections on Gospel and Law in the History of the Church."

a view, the Church may have started off with some aversion to law, but then, faced by the necessity of making provisions to regulate its life, it freely adopts laws, but calls them something else in order to avoid or mitigate the embarrassment of violating its founding principles.[5] This view fits well with certain confessional traditions regarding Church history and can be particularly plausible if one begins an assessment of the canonical tradition from the classical period, when canonists took particular pleasure in pointing out the analogies between Roman and canon law and did not dwell unduly on the particularity of the latter. However, to be convinced by such a view, one needs to disregard the extent to which even the canonists of the classical age regarded their discipline as being concerned with more than peace, order, and good government or the fact that the analogies that most interested them and which were most creative in their own work were those with Roman *ius*, rather than with Roman *lex*.

The canons must and do include provisions to pursue the usual ends of law, namely peace, order, and good government within the community, but they also include many other provisions which can seem rather distant from, if not contradictory with, such aims. It may be difficult to understand this paradox, if one does not keep in mind that the purposes of a legal order strive to be congruent with the way in which the human person and the purposes of human life and action are perceived by the participants in such an order. For Christianity, the human person is a flawed divine creation. Created in freedom and for freedom, human beings fell from participation in the divine life by the sinful choice of their progenitors. They are the heirs and bear the consequences of this original sinful choice, most notably in their inability to pursue fruitfully the good which they weakly perceive. Mercifully, God, in the person of Jesus, man and Word of God, came, lived, and

5. Robert Somerville and Bruce C. Brasington, *Prefaces to Canon Law Books in Latin Christianity. Selected Translations, 500–1245* (New Haven and London: Yale University Press, 1998), p. 2, say that the expression canon law is "etymologically perhaps a redundancy." Brundage, *Medieval Canon Law*, p. 5, thoughtfully outlines the problem in these terms: "Christians have from the beginning felt ambivalent about the proper role of law in religious life. Jesus expressed grave reservations about the Mosaic law as a source of spiritual guidance and enlightenment, although he denied that he wished to abolish the law [cf. Mt. 5:17–20 and Mt. 23:23]. The ambivalence was even more marked in St Paul's letters. Some Pauline passages strongly hinted that law was an altogether inappropriate mechanism for defining the spiritual goals of Christian believers, although elsewhere Paul described the Law of Moses as sacred, just, and good [cf. Rom. 7:12 with Rom. 10:4, Gal. 3:10–13, and Col. 2:14]. Despite the evident reservations of its founder and early teachers about the place of law in Christian life, the church soon began to develop its own legal system, for its leaders quickly discovered that a viable community not only needed goodwill and fraternal love, but also required some rules and regulations for the orderly conduct of its business, to define the functions of its officers, and to govern relationships among its members."

died to offer redemption to fallen human beings. That offer of redemption, which must be freely accepted to be fruitful, continues through the Church, instituted by Christ himself to continue his redemptive presence and work in history. This presence and work summon human beings to rediscover their original nature, to repent of their shortcomings, and to live in a way that is congruent with their nature, that is to say, to live in adherence to God's original design for humankind. This process of discernment and change is called conversion, a process, usually gradual, of turning toward God in love which, with extremely rare exceptions, is never perfectly achieved in this life.[6] If the Church were to achieve in its members perfect conformity of outward behaviour with its requirements, it would be perfectly successful in achieving what legal orders usually set out to achieve, and it would fail perfectly when measured by its own premises regarding its reasons for being. Any account of the canons that fails to take notice of this paradox is bound to be a misleading description of their nature and purposes.

Canon is a Greek term, usually translated as rule. It is a difficulty that, in our current usage, rule is often used as a synonym for law. This may lead us to conclude uncritically that canon is also a synonym for law and so to read canons as written laws. This is not a conclusion which the least familiarity with the Latin jurisprudential tradition ought to allow.

The Roman precedent

The claim may at first seem preposterous that jurisprudence, or legal science, is the particular creation of Rome, and only comes into existence in cultures which encounter the Roman jurisprudential tradition.[7] Obviously, this does not and cannot mean that law is not a ubiquitous phenomenon. What it does mean is that legal cultures unconnected with the Roman one do not usually allow themselves the luxury of a body of learning whose purpose is to examine the law critically, and of a body of learners whose purpose is to cultivate "the art of goodness

6. Two articles by Gerhart B. Ladner remain beautiful reflections on the particularity and fruitfulness of Christian anthropology in the Middle Ages: "Homo Viator: Mediaeval Ideas on Alienation and Order," *Speculum* 42 (1967): 233–59; "Greatness in Mediaeval History," *The Catholic Historical Review* 50 (1964): 1–26.

7. The claim is made eloquently and convincingly by Carlo Augusto Cannata, *Per una storia della scienza giuridica europea. 1. Dalle origini all'opera di Labeone* (Turin: G. Giappichelli Editore, 1997), pp. 17–18. In this part, I take up again some of the arguments made in Giulio Silano, "The *regulae iuris* and the Jurists. Reflections in Margin to *Liber Sextus* 5.13," in *Rule Makers and Rule Breakers*, ed. J. Goering, F. Guardiani, G. Silano (New York, Ottawa, Toronto: Legas, 2006), pp. 171–92.

and fairness."[8] The jurists themselves, members of this body, would recount the history of their role and discipline by pointing back to an ancient and odd priestly body which had existed in Rome almost from its origins, namely the college of pontiffs. This body is odd in the sense that its role is not the more usual priestly one of divination and the performance of religious rituals; other priestly bodies did this in Rome, while the pontiffs were established as expert consultants to advise citizens about the proper performance of any action that might be relevant in the eyes of the gods.[9] Given that a number of legal acts are not devoid of a sacred or religious dimension (e.g. adoption, involving the rejection of the gods of one's family of origin and the assumption of the obligation to venerate the gods of the adoptive family),[10] it is perhaps not surprising that the consulting function of the pontiffs should have extended also to the proper forms to be used for the performance of legal transactions. Certainly, the jurist Pomponius, in recounting the origin of Roman jurisprudence, squarely associates it with pontifical activity.[11] For Pomponius, the *interpretandi scientia* was born almost at the

8. *Digest* 1.1.1: "Ulpian, *Institutes, book 1*: A law student at the outset of his studies ought first to know the derivation of the word *jus*. Its derivation is from *justitia*. For, in terms of Celsus' elegant definition, the law is the art of goodness and fairness. 1. Of that art we [jurists] are deservedly called the priests. For we cultivate the virtue of justice and claim awareness of what is good and fair, discriminating between fair and unfair, distinguishing lawful from unlawful, aiming to make men good not only through fear of penalties but also indeed from allurement of rewards, and affecting a philosophy which, if I am not deceived, is genuine, not a sham." Here and below, we quote from the Alan Watson translation, *The Digest of Justinian*, 4 voll. rev. ed. (Philadelphia: University of Pennsylvania Press, 1998).

9. Livy, *The History of Rome*, tr. William Masfen Roberts, 6 voll. (London: J.M. Dent, 1912), vol. 1, p. 20. Livy described the functions of the pontiff in these terms: "He [King Numa] placed all other sacred functions, both public and private, under the supervision of the Pontifex, in order that there might be an authority for the people to consult, and so all trouble and confusion arising through foreign rites being adopted and their ancestral ones neglected might be avoided. Nor were his functions confined to directing the worship of the celestial gods; he was to instruct the people how to conduct funerals and appease the spirits of the departed, and what prodigies sent by lightning or in any other way were to be attended to and expiated."

10. For this and other instances of intersection between legal activities and the sacred, see Mario Bretone, *Storia del diritto romano*, 7th ed. (Bari: Editori Laterza, 2000), pp. 111–12.

11. *Digest* 1.2.2.6: "Then about the same time actions-at-law whereby people could litigate among themselves were composed out of these statutes [the laws of the *Twelve Tables*]. To prevent the citizenry from initiating litigation any old how, the lawmakers' will was that the actions-at-law be in fixed and solemn terms. This branch of law has the name *legis actiones*, that is, statutory actions-at-law. And so these three branches of law came into being at almost the same time: once the statute law of the *Twelve Tables* was passed, the *jus civile* started to emerge from them, and *legis actiones* were put together from the same source. In relation to all these statutes, however, knowledge of their authoritative interpretation and conduct of the actions at law belonged to the College of Priests, one of whom was appointed each year to preside over private matters."

same time as the law itself. This same science, together with the function of free consultation, by stages which are hard to trace, would eventually be "laicized," and claimed as their prerogative by the jurists.[12] They would also claim as their burden the duty to provide education in the law – a claim which the same Pomponius would trace to the beginning of the third century B.C.[13]

The attachment of the function of teaching to the more ancient one of consultation may have served as a spur to reflection about whether there was not a need to arrange legal learning in a form that revealed its underlying assumptions to the student. A development of this sort appears to be what Pomponius credits to Quintus Mucius, of whom he says: "... Quintus Mucius, son of Publius and a *pontifex maximus,* became the first man to produce a general compendium of the civil law by arranging it into eighteen books."[14] This same Quintus Mucius, here described as the first to produce a compendium of the law *per genera,* was also the first jurist to write a book of definitions. These developments have been read as testifying to the attentiveness of the Roman jurists to Greek notions of what constitutes a science and to their willingness to "set out to discover the peculiar principles of their law and formulate them into propositions."[15]

Cicero saw in these efforts of Quintus Mucius a small beginning of the development of jurisprudence as a science, but he was convinced that this was only a beginning, and that jurists ought to undertake more seriously and thoroughly the task of showing forth the systematic nature of their science. To this end, he composed a little work, which does not survive, on the reduction of the civil law to an art.[16] But the need for jurists to learn from the practitioners of geometry, astronomy, and grammar how to reduce their own learning to scientific form was also expressed by Cicero in the *De Oratore.* His proposal was that the whole of Roman legal learning ought to be distinguished into some general classes, further subdivided into members to be clearly defined.[17] This would be sufficient,

12. For a plausible description of the process by which to jurists came to replace the pontiffs in the function of consultation, see Cannata, *Per una storia,* pp. 89–206; the transition is described very economically by Bretone, *Storia del diritto romano,* pp. 153–56.

13. *Digest* 1.2.2.35.

14. *Digest* 1.2.2.41.

15. Peter Stein, *Regulae iuris. From Juristic Rules to Legal Maxims* (Edinburgh: University Press, 1966), p. 36; Stein provides examples of Mucius' work on pp. 36–41.

16. On Cicero's *De iure civili in artem redigendo,* see Cannata, *Per una storia,* pp. 289–90, who disagrees with the view, expressed among others by Stein, *Regulae iuris,* p. 41, that the lost work was an attempt, rather than a proposal of the desirability, to produce a systematic outline of Roman law.

17. Cicero, *De Oratore,* bk. 1.190, tr. E.N.P. Moor (London: Methuen and Co., 1892): "As it is, I will state in one sentence the object I have in view. If I am allowed to carry out a long-cherished purpose, or if someone else forestalls me owing to my many engagements, or com-

he was convinced, to transform a difficult and obscure branch of learning into a perfect science. The jurists never took Cicero up on his invitation. And yet they had taken the lessons of the grammarians to heart, hence their propensity to frame rules; this task of rule-framing is, in a sense, the jurists' crowning achievement in the practice of their art.[18]

Canons as rules, canonists as jurists

Our brief tracing of the classical jurists' move toward the ordering of their learning, and their concurrent resistance to accepting invitations such as Cicero's to move whole hog into the effort to apply dialectics to the task of making their discipline easily apprehensible, is intended to suggest that the framers of canons, at least in the first millennium, may have been moved by concerns and interests similar to those of the grammarians and jurists, with which they were not entirely unfamiliar. The latter ultimately resist Cicero's efforts because of the essentially casuistic nature of their own efforts and the deep conviction that to yield to Cicero's chimeric proposals would require a degree of abstraction that was wholly undesirable within the ambit of jurisprudence. Their interest, in the framing of their own rules, is in retaining a provisional and problematic character in their formulation of the principles that appear to underlie cases.[19] Perhaps we ought to consider that the canons, too, are intended to be read as rules which are provisional and problematic in character rather than as restatements of legislation, and that this is the case even when the canon in question may originally have been a legislative enactment.

Let us use an example relevant to our text below. Many of the chapters of Regino's work consist of the canons of various Councils which had been held at various times in different parts of the world (e.g. Africa, Spain, Italy, etc.). In later terms, it has certainly proved possible to conceive of these texts as written

---

pletes the work in event of my death – if, I mean, he makes a digest, first of all, of the civil law according to the different classes of case (which are really very few), then distinguishes the different organic divisions, so to speak, of these classes, adding, finally, the definition significant of the exact nature of each class or division, then you will have a complete system of civil law, whose difficulty and obscurity will be nothing compared with the magnitude and wealth of its utility."

18. The tracing of the origin and development of this practice and its long life in the history of Western jurisprudence is the task brilliantly carried out in Peter Stein, *Regulae iuris*.

19. On these aspects of classical jurisprudence, illuminating remarks are those of Bretone, *Storia del diritto romano*, pp. 303–14.

law intended to bind those who were subject to their original authors. But even by those terms, Regino and his readers were not among those who were so subject; they did not live in those places and were not subject to the authors of those texts or to their successors. So, what can it mean for them to "canonize" such texts? It is surely plausible to suggest that such "canonization" both raises and lowers the status of these texts. It lowers them, if that is the right term, in the sense that they cease to be texts which one is bound to observe literally since one is not subject to the jurisdiction of their authors, that is to say, one is not within the class of persons for whom the original authors were stating the law; it raises them because they are taken to contain something which is valuable and instructive beyond the place, time, and circumstances in which they were originally conceived.

If we backtrack to the original framers of the canons which Regino collects, we may find that our excursus into the Roman jurists may still not be without relevance. They, too, in their approach to problems and in the solutions which they propose, seem to us predominantly closer to the jurists than to positive lawmakers. Their texts hardly ever speak in terms of commands; they often take the form of recognition that a problem has emerged and that it requires resolution by reflecting on Scripture and the past experience of the Church as it is expressed in the canons. Their approach is better seen as driven by a desire to elicit and convey rules from, and regarding the circumstances of, particular cases than as being concerned with devising any sort of chimerical systematic body of positive law. Their aim is usually as much to instruct and move to conversion as to compel observance.

Monks as canonists

These sorts of concerns and attitudes may have been especially powerful for those who were the principal cultivators of canonical learning in the first half of the Latin Middle Ages, namely the monks.[20] If a canon is a rule, then surely those who lived their whole lives under a Rule may very well have approached the canons as if they were in some way the same sort of document as their Rule. Most of the monks who gathered canons, like our very own author, lived their lives

20. A wonderfully graceful presentation of the role of monasteries in the cultivation of canon law is Abigail Firey, "How Carolingians Learned Canon Law," in *Proceedings of the Fourteenth International Congress of Medieval Canon Law, Toronto, 5–11 August 2012*, ed. J. Goering, S. Dusil, and A. Thier (Vatican City: Biblioteca Apostolica Vaticana, 2016), pp. 355–68.

under the Rule of St. Benedict.[21] The nature and purpose of this document may easily be gathered from the opening lines of its prologue: "Listen carefully, my child, to your master's precepts, and incline the ear of your heart (Prov. 4:20). Receive willingly and carry out effectively your loving father's advice, that by the labor of obedience you may return to Him from whom you had departed by the sloth of disobedience." The text professes to have as its author someone with experience of the monastic life (hence master) who has taken the trouble to isolate some of the precepts that underlie it and wishes to convey them to those who believe that they can profit from such an exercise. This set of precepts may become the law under which the disciples live their whole lives, but only if they choose it. That life will not be fruitful, unless they incline the ear of their heart to its precepts; a merely external conformity to the prescriptions of the Rule will make for good order in the monastery, but it will not result in the monk's return to God, which is the purpose of the monastic life. The monastic life is to be a lifelong exercise of the free choice to become more and more faithfully and consciously subject to what the Rule prescribes so that the original flaw of sinful human nature, best expressed by the term disobedience, may be curbed and the converted person may participate more fully in the divine life.

Benedict's Rule is full of "laws," that is, of definite and possibly binding prescriptions about the monastery, its officers, and their respective discipline, from the election and obligations of the abbot to the quantity of wine that the monks may drink. But its overall framework is one of a "canon" and not one of a written law. The author does not have any more authority than those who pick up his Rule are willing to grant to him, and his claim to insight is grounded in his experience and reflection, and not in any sort of public or institutional power. Like a jurist, he has pondered the life of a monk in its specific difficulties and has formulated possible solutions to those difficulties. Like a jurist, he has accepted a responsibility to educate, and he does so by reducing his experience and reflections to a set of rules within the Rule which often provide the reasoning on which a provision is based. From beginning to end, the desire to inform and to educate is at least as prominent as any desire to obtain observance of what he is prescribing. Nor is he afraid to make prescriptions which might easily be perceived to be contradictory, as, for example, in setting out how an abbot is to be chosen.[22] Election by the whole community (clearly to be preferred), or by a small

21. An easily accessible English version of the Rule, from which we cite, can be found at http://www.archive.osb.org/rb/text/toc.html#toc. For reflections on the juridical dimension of the Rule, see Lawrin Armstrong, "Rule-Maker or Law-Giver? Legal Forms in the *Regula Benedicti*," in *Rule Makers and Rule Breakers*, pp. 7–15.

22. (c. 64): "In the constituting of an Abbot let this plan always be followed, that the office be conferred on the one who is chosen either by the whole community unanimously in

more qualified group, or even intervention by outsiders are all contemplated as possibilities, if the case should warrant it. Even on something as crucial as this, there is no anxiety to have the sort of clarity for which the written law usually strives; any one of the solutions proposed may be acceptable, so long as, in the specific circumstances, it results in the best possible choice of an abbot and keeps the community faithful to its purposes.

Canon law and philology

A final preliminary consideration ought to be entertained before we address our text specifically, and that concerns the relationship between canon law and philology. Modern philology emerges in the course of the Renaissance; one of its signal early achievements is the finding that the Donation of Constantine, considered by some to be a canonical text, is a forgery. The divisions of the Protestant Reformation fruitfully pick up this line of enquiry and strive to show that many of the documents on which the Roman Church founded its claims to authority were equally unreliable.[23] The upshot is that the philological treatment of canon law texts at times seems more concerned with putting them on trial than with restoring them to the form in which they left their authors' hand. As a consequence, a philologically sound edition of a canonical text often is one which strives to show how its author mishandled, mangled, or forged texts. This involves the risk that the reader is invited to consider more how such a text ought to have been composed than to attend to what was actually composed. It also involves premises about the nature and purposes of a canonical work which may not be those that moved the author (e.g. that such a work *ought* to be an anthology of legislative provisions and patristic authorities which the author *ought* to convey with as great a fidelity to their originals as possible) and which may prejudge the

---

the fear of God or else by a part of the community, however small, if its counsel is more wholesome. Merit of life and wisdom of doctrine should determine the choice of the one to be constituted, even if he be the last in the order of the community. But if (which God forbid) the whole community should agree to choose a person who will acquiesce in their vices, and if those vices somehow become known to the Bishop to whose diocese the place belongs, or to the Abbots or to the faithful of the vicinity, let them prevent the success of this conspiracy of the wicked, and set a worthy steward over the house of God. They may be sure that they will receive a good reward for this action if they do it with a pure intention and out of zeal for God; as, on the contrary, they will sin if they fail to do it."

23. For a brief examination of instances of this process in the 16th and 17th centuries, see Giulio Silano, "Paolo Sarpi and Canon Law," in *Going for Baroque. Cultural Transformations 1550–1650*, ed. Francesco Guardiani (New York, Ottawa, Toronto: Legas, 1999), pp. 93–110.

reading of the actual text. What the philologist tells us about the sources of a particular text and the permutations which those sources have undergone at the hands of our author or of others can be of great interest and utility in reconstructing the settings in which such texts were composed and makes an important contribution to our knowledge of many topics of historical relevance. What it does not do is to enable us to read the text as the author intended it to be read. It has been our intent, in producing this translation, to place the modern reader roughly in a position similar to that of its medieval reader. To that end, the translation does not reproduce the information about sources which its nineteenth-century editor provides.[24]

Because philology tends to treat the author of canonical collections simply as a compiler, it judges him on the degree to which he is faithful to his sources. In this regard, it is customary to distinguish between material and formal sources. Material source designates the original source from which a text purports to come; formal source indicates the collection or work from which the compiler has actually drawn his text. An author is likely to be chastised for being unfaithful to either of these, although in most instances he was unlikely to look beyond his formal source, so that, if he is faithless, it is with this latter source that he fails to keep faith. But the question ought to be asked: what faith does he owe to such a source? Here, too, we are likely to be caught in the presupposition that these compilers are conveying legislative texts and ought to treat them with the deference that such important texts seem to us to deserve. If we consider that the compilers might believe instead that they are compiling rules and framing them for pedagogical effectiveness, it is possible that our judgment will be less lapidary.

It is worth pointing out that compilers of canonical materials generally did not carry out philological analyses of their formal sources. Even when their libraries contained volumes which would have allowed them to do so, they did not go back to the material sources in order to correct what we have come to regard as errors, or worse, in the transmission of those texts. It seems noteworthy, for example, that Regino – a Benedictine monk and abbot who had lived his life under, and instructed his monks in, the Rule of Benedict, in including selec-

24. Regino of Prüm, *Libri duo de synodalibus causis et disciplinis ecclesiasticis*, ed. F.G.A. Wasserschleben (Leipzig: Engelmann, 1840), repr. with some corrections and partial German translation in Wilfried Hartmann, *Das Sendhandbuch des Regino von Prüm* (Darmstadt: Wissenschaftliche Buchgesellschaft, 2004). The Wasserschleben text is easily available on the Internet; hence readers with a basic knowledge of Latin may easily consult its notes on each chapter. An examination of sources is best conducted on the Latin texts and is not easily served by a translation, but, for those interested, the tracing of the fate of each of Regino's chapters in earlier and subsequent canon law collections, found in Wasserschleben's synoptic tables on pp. 497–516, is instructive.

tions from the Rule in his collection, does not go beyond what earlier collections had already excerpted from it, making no selections of his own. It seems too easy to hold that this failure, if such it is, is due to laziness. It seems more plausible to hold that compilers expect, and even value the fact, that their predecessors in the compilation of the canons have exercised a useful discretion and freedom in their choice and presentation of those texts. Perhaps they are even endowing these earlier collections with a "magisterial" authority which ought to be appreciated and gratefully received. Exactly because they are compiling rules, and not laws, they are expected to present them in a form that makes them more accessible, understandable, attractive, relevant, and useful to their audiences. This is a freedom which they will then exercise themselves in the compilation of their own works, even as they usually preserve the changes made by their predecessors. It does not seem far-fetched to suggest that a compiler of canons may be regarded somewhat like Benedict in the compilation of the Rule. At the most basic level, it will never be his aim to gather all the canons he can possibly get his hands on. Such a compiler is implicitly making a claim to a mastery of his material which allows him some latitude in its reshaping, a claim, in other words, to the prerogative to decide which canons one ought to read and which ones one is free to forget, based on the assumption of some competence in doing so (tested, of course, by the usefulness of the work). In the face of such a power to accept or reject, the practice of silent correction, emendation, or addition seems remarkably mild. And yet the users of these works were clearly grateful for the efforts of earlier compilers to make the whole massive tradition more manageable by their work of selection and presentation.

This freedom in selection and presentation seems to confirm the contention that the compilers of canonical works did not regard themselves as being the transmitters of legislative texts. If they had so regarded themselves, they ought to have felt bound to transmit all the canons of the various Councils and other authorities from which they cull their texts, since they are all formally the same sort of text. As we will see Regino doing, these authors claim for themselves the right to choose which of these texts are instructive and relevant in the present moment, so that there is an explicit or implicit premise that the compiler is making a judgment as to what the current problems of the Church in a specific place and time are and what bits from the rich canonical tradition may provide instruction and solutions in the present circumstances. Indeed, it is precisely this nature of the canonical compilations as thoughtful and educated judgments about the state of Church and society at a given time and place that can make them still interesting even to those who have no other reasons to be interested in them. Apart from serving as barometers of the state of legal, theological, and sociopolitical reflection, they constitute uniquely valuable windows into the problems of life as they were considered by often thoughtful and engaged observers and provide materials which those observers regarded as possibly useful for their solution. It is for the reader to judge whether Regino's work meets this test.

Regino of Prüm

One of Regino's most recent students has rightly pointed out that "[t]he career, mental world and writings of Regino ... were all defined by the Carolingian empire and, more particularly, by its end."[25] Regino himself, in his capacity as a chronicler, was aware of living at the end of an age.[26]

A late Prüm tradition gives Altrip near Speyer as Regino's birthplace and describes his family as noble.[27] At some unspecified date, he had become a monk at Prüm, an important abbey with close links to the Carolingian dynasty. Women of the dynasty had founded it, and King Pippin had refounded and richly endowed it. Emperor Lothar I was also one of its patrons; he became one of its monks, shortly before his death, and was buried there.[28] Within this community, Regino rose steadily to positions of responsibility. In 892, Abbot Farabert resigned, perhaps exhausted by the vicissitudes to which the community had been subject due to repeated Viking incursions. Pursuant to a royal privilege allowing the community to elect its own abbot, the monks chose Regino. As abbot, Regino saw to the completion of a survey of the properties of the monastery as they had been left after the Viking attacks. He also became the keeper of Hugh, the blinded rebellious son of Lothar II.

25. Simon MacLean, *History and Politics in Late Carolingian and Ottonian Europe: The Chronicle of Regino of Prüm and Adalbert of Magdeburg* (Manchester: Manchester University Press, 2009), p. 1; although MacLean has nothing to say regarding Regino as a cultivator of the canons, his reading of Regino's life and experiences within the dissolution of the Empire is masterful. For a brief restatement of the known facts regarding Regino's life and works, see Wilfried Hartmann, "Regino von Prüm," in *Neue deutsche Biographie* 21 (2003), pp. 269–70. The most recent discussion of Regino and his canonical work is to be found in Greta Austin, "*Regino of Prüm,*" in *Great Christian Jurists and Legal Collections in the First Millennium*, ed. Philip L. Reynolds (Cambridge: Cambridge University Press, 2019), pp. 444–57

26. See Simon MacLean, "Insinuation, Censorship and the Struggle for Late Carolingian Lotharingia in Regino of Prüm's *Chronicle*," *The English Historical Review* 124 (2009): 1–28, at p. 3 and passim.

27. The tradition seems plausible because a local monastic cell had become a dependency of Prüm; see F. Kurze, ed., *Reginonis abbatis Prumiensis Chronicon cum continuatione Treverensi*, MGH Scriptores Rerum Germanicarum in usum scholarum separatim editi 50 (Hanover, 1890), p. v.

28. MacLean, *History*, pp. 5–8, presents more fully what we know of Regino's biography.

Regino was to remain in office until 899; in that year, the very importance of the abbey in the roiling politics of the age made for his ejection from the abbacy. He found refuge in Trier, where he enjoyed the friendship and patronage of Archbishop Ratbod, who entrusted him with the care of the abbey of St. Martin, also destroyed by the Vikings. Far from living out his final years peacefully licking his wounds, Regino, among other things, turned to literary activities, becoming in turn the first chronicler of the demise of the Carolingian empire, an important contributor to musical theory, and the author of the canonical work which is of special interest to us.[29] According to a tomb inscription discovered at St. Maximin of Trier, Regino died in 915 and was there buried.[30]

The *Two Books on Synodal Causes and Ecclesiastical Disciplines*

Wasserschleben published his edition of Regino's canon law work under the above title because that expression is used in the description of the work in its prologue.[31] He regarded it as not superfluous to edit Regino's work since its

29. Regino's chronicle was last edited by Kurze in the work cited above, at n. 27; it was translated by MacLean in *History*, where the work is intriguingly assessed at pp. 8–28. On his musical work, see M.P. LeRoux, "The *De harmonica institutione* and *Tonarius* of Regino of Prüm," Catholic University of America, Ph.D. thesis, 1965. The texts of these works, as edited by LeRoux, can also be found at http://www.chmtl.indiana.edu/tml/9th-11th/REGDHI and http://www.chmtl.indiana.edu/tml/9th-11th/REGTONA. An Italian translation with commentary was produced by Alessandra Fiori, *Music: Ubaldo di Saint-Amand. Epistola de harmonica institutione: Reginone di Prüm; introduzione, traduzione e commento* (Florence: Edizioni del Galluzzo, 2010). Regino seems to have thought rather highly of his contribution to the restoration of sound singing practices, if it is true that he compared himself to Gregory the Great and the institution of Gregorian chant: see Warren Sanderson, "Archbishop Radbod, Regino of Prüm and Late Carolingian Art and Music in Trier," *Jahrbuch der Berliner Museen* 24 (1982): 41–61.

30. The inscription is reported by Wasserschleben, p. ix.

31. For a listing of the manuscripts (including those not known to Wasserschleben) and editions of, and bibliography on, Regino's work, see Lotte Kéry, *Canonical Collections of the Early Middle Ages (ca. 400–1140): A Bibliographical Guide to the Manuscripts and Literature* (Washington, D.C.: Catholic University of America Press, c1999), pp. 128–33. To the editions and literature there listed are to be added Wilfried Hartmann's contributions, namely, *Das Sendhandbuch des Regino von Prüm*: "Die *Capita incerta* im Sendhandbuch Reginos von Prüm," in *Scientia veritatis. Festschrift für Hubert Mordek zum 65. Geburtstag*, ed. O. Münsch, Th. Zotz (Ostfildern: Jan Vorbecke Verlag, 2004), pp. 207–26; "Zu Effektivität und Aktualität von Reginos Sendhandbuch," in *Medieval Church Law and the Origins of the Western Legal Tradition: A Tribute to Kenneth Pennington*, ed. W.P. Müller, M.E. Sommar (Washington, D.C.: Catholic University of America Press, 2006), pp. 33–49.

importance and authority is clear to all, given the extent to which it would influence later and sometimes less worthy collections; more importantly, it provides a true and sincere image of the disciplines and customs that were at work in those times and instructs us as to the manner of proceeding in synodal causes, so that it is the principal source for knowing the practice of tribunals in ecclesiastical matters. The authority of the work is increased by the fidelity, care, and diligence with which the author gathered his sources.[32] That Regino's work was destined for court use is clear, Wasserschleben believes, from Archbishop Ratbod's mandate, from the preface addressed to Archbishop Hatto, and from the very nature and condition of the collection. Hence the division in two books, of which the first concerns clerics and ecclesiastical matters, the second lay people and their crimes. Hence also the instructions set out before each book, and the formulae of inquisition that the bishop or his vicar could use at a synod and the samples of oaths to be sworn there, taken from the practice of the diocese of Trier, as also the examples of *epistolae formatae*, the formed letters of reference inscribed in the name of Ratbod, Trier's archbishop.[33]

The editor is clear and succinct in outlining the sources of the chapters of both books: they are taken from the canons of Councils, the decretals of popes, the capitularies of Frankish kings, Roman law, the writings of Church Fathers, and penitential books. But distinctions are in order. The Greek, African, Gallic, and Spanish conciliar canons and the papal decretals which are contained in the *Dionysio-Hadriana* and in the *Hispana* were not drawn directly from those collections, but from some intermediate ones such as a Vatican collection, the *Dacheriana*, and Halitgar's compilation. Citations from the Church Fathers, the bits from the Rule of Benedict, excepting the fragments from the works of Ambrose, Jerome, and Ferrandus, are taken from the Vatican collection. The canons of the more recent Councils of Germany and Gaul, which provided abundant material for Regino, appear to have been taken from their several documents, as also the fragments of the decretals of Pope Nicholas I. The capitularies of the kings of the Franks are from the works of Ansegisus. The source for the Roman law is the *Breviarium Alaricianum*. The penitential canons are from the Vatican collection, Halitgar's collection, Rabanus' works, and a penitential in a Darmstadt manuscript. The formulae are taken from practice. Regino handled his sources with care and diligence; that not a few inscriptions are false or lacking is due for the most part to his sources.[34] As for the

32. Wasserschleben, p. v.

33. Wasserschleben, p. ix.

34. Wasserschleben, pp. ix–xiii. For the various canonical collections mentioned here, see Lotte Kéry, *Canonical Collections of the Early Middle Ages*. The Vatican collection has been

three appendices – evidence of interest in and study of Regino's collection in the decades after its composition – Wasserschleben dates the first to shortly after Regino's composition of the work, the second to sometime after 952, and the third to Regino's own time.[35] Apart from the appendices, Regino's work survives in two recensions because some unknown critic decided to rearrange some of Regino's chapters in a different order; Wasserschleben's edition restores the original order.[36]

Many of the conclusions reached by Wasserschleben have remained largely uncontested in the intervening decades. They were thoroughly tested, largely approved, and greatly expanded by Paul Fournier.[37] For Fournier, Regino's work is a notable product and expression of the Carolingian ideals of Church reform for which the institution of the synod as an investigative and judicial body was pivotal. It is also a necessary tool to inform the bishops who preside over the synod so that they may function effectively.[38] Regino's simple plan for this tool divided his material into two books covering the types of matters that might come before the synod: the first deals with cases involving the clergy, the second with those of the laity. Since the synod proceeded chiefly by investigation through the questioning of synodal witnesses, Regino provides two model questionnaires to be used. The materials are then arranged in each book according to the order in which problems are raised in the questionnaires, expressing the rule at issue, and providing indications for the punishments that might follow a finding of infringe-

---

identified as the so-called *Quadripartitus,* see Franz Kerff, *Der Quadripartitus. Ein Handbuch der karolingischen Kirchenreform. Überlieferung, Quellen und Rezeption* (Sigmaringen: Jan Thorbecke Verlag, 1982), p. 7. See Gerhard Schmitz, "Ansegis und Regino. Die Rezeption der Kapitularien in den Libri duo de synodalibus causis," *Zeitschrift der Savigny-Stiftung für Rechtsgeschichte, Kanonistische Abteilung* 74 (1988): 95–132, who argues convincingly that Regino only used Ansegisus for the capitularies. The Darmstadt source has been identified as Cologne, Dombibliothek, Cod. 118 (Darmst. 2117) containing the *Paenitentiale Pseudo Bedae-Egberti mixtum,* see Reinhold Haggenmüller, *Die Überlieferung der Beda und Egbert zugeschriebenen Bußbücher* (Frankfurt am Main: Lang, 1991), p. 67.

35. Wasserschleben, pp. xiii–xiv.

36. Wasserschleben, pp. xiv–xv.

37. The fundamental study is Paul Fournier, "L'œuvre canonique de Réginon de Prüm," *Bibliothèque de l'École des chartes* 81 (1920): 5–44; the conclusions of the study were republished, with slight changes and less detail, in Paul Fournier and Gabriel Le Bras, *Histoire des collections canoniques en Occident dépuis les fausses décrétales jusqu'au Décret de Gratien* (Paris: Sirey, 1931), vol. 1, pp. 244–68.

38. Fournier, "L'œuvre," pp. 5–7. Fournier ties Regino's work to the Council of Tribur of 895 as an important summation of the Carolingian ideals of reform; the same Ratbod, who was to be Regino's patron and at whose command Regino claimed he had composed his canonical work, had been present at the Council, and Hatto, the archbishop of Mainz to whom Regino dedicates his work, had presided over it.

ment of a rule. Some forms are added for the swearing in of witnesses, the proclamation of excommunication, and the issuing of absolution.[39]

Rich as Regino's collection is, it should not be thought of as containing the whole of the Church's legislation. Fournier claims that it limits itself to matters of morality and discipline as they arise from the questioning of the synodal witnesses.[40] He also points out that Regino does not only collect texts; if rarely, he intervenes in the first person to explain what he is doing, to explain reservations about the bearing of a rule which he has presented, or to show the utility of some of his texts.[41] Fournier's tally of the sorts of texts collected by Regino, even if more detailed than Wasserschleben's, does not much differ from it, although his analysis of Regino's use of the Tribur canons was ground-breaking.[42] Regarding the three appendices, on the grounds that chapters 1–28 of the first one come from the same sources as Regino's work, he is not averse to regarding Regino as their compiler. The other two appendices he judges to be quite removed from Regino's time.[43] Usefully, he points out that, in quoting from Roman law, if Regino has a choice between a legislative text and its interpretation, he unfailingly chooses to reproduce the latter.[44] This practice seems like a small, if telling, confirmation of Regino's distinct preference for rules over laws. Fournier summarizes his conclusions about the sources used by Regino as follows:

> In sum, Regino's work is composed by fusing texts of Roman origin with texts that were characteristic of the reforming work undertaken by Charlemagne and pursued with more or less zeal under the rule of his successors: canons of Carolingian Councils, fragments of capitularies, penitential canons in use in the ninth century in the Frankish lands. The Church whose features this collection reveals is truly the Frankish Church, regenerated, at the beginning of the Carolingian age, by Roman influence, but allowing, to a certain degree, institutions foreign to the Roman world, such as synodical jurisdiction, compurgators, ordeals.[45]

39. Fournier, "L'œuvre," p. 8.

40. Fournier, "L'œuvre," p. 9.

41. Fournier, "L'œuvre," p. 9, n. 1, in which Fournier points to examples of each of the types of first-person exchanges in which Regino has engaged.

42. Fournier, "L'œuvre," p. 10; the use by Regino of the Tribur canons in a version other than the Council's official one constituted the subject of the whole second part of – indeed of a separate second study in – Fournier's essay, at pp. 30–44.

43. Fournier, "L'œuvre," pp. 7–8.

44. Fournier, "L'œuvre," p. 11.

45. Fournier, "L'œuvre," p. 12.

Fournier's somewhat more detailed investigations, in part made possible by work done by others in the intervening decades and in part from his own profound knowledge of the relevant manuscripts, confirm the broad conclusions reached by Wasserschleben regarding the formal sources used by Regino.[46] As to Regino's being a faithful transmitter of the sources which he uses, Fournier is far less convinced than Wasserschleben; on this topic, Fournier concludes that "one would deceive oneself greatly, if one were to attribute to Regino the respect for texts which characterizes modern jurists. He does not hesitate to retouch them, sometimes to harmonize them with supervening changes in laws or customs, more often to render them more intelligible or even to give them a more elegant form."[47]

Fournier is most illuminating on a question which Wasserschleben never quite formulated, perhaps due to his valuing Regino's work primarily as one addressed to the practice of tribunals, namely that of how binding Regino expected the pronouncements which he had collected to be. Rightly, Fournier insists that it was not Regino's purpose to define a rigid code to be imposed on the judge. According to him, the collection is intended instead to guide ecclesiastical superiors as they take into account the circumstances of each case. That is why Regino places side by side pronouncements which impose different penalties on the same offense. It remains the judge's role to decide which one to follow.[48]

On balance, Fournier and subsequent scholars had been satisfied with Wasserschleben's edition of Regino's work.[49] But, of late, philology has been raising its ugly head to query this judgment and to insist on the need for a new edition.[50] Although it is granted that the text would not change very much,[51] it is

46. Fournier, "L'œuvre," pp. 13–17.

47. Fournier, "L'œuvre," p. 19. Fournier, at p. 24, concludes his close analysis of Regino's handling of his sources with this wonderfully contorted judgment: "Now that we know that Regino retouched his texts ..., we cannot help but think that, among the uncertain Chapters, there are some which may be his own work. ... In any case, I do not believe it temerarious to conclude that Regino knew the art of accommodating texts and made use of it, in truth, with much greater discretion than Burchard of Worms would do later."

48. Fournier, "L'œuvre," p. 25.

49. Not long ago, Giorgio Picasso, *Sacri canones et monastica regula. Disciplina canonica e vita monastica nella società medievale* (Milan: Vita e Pensiero, 2006), p. 313, described Regino's work as a "systematic canonical collection of the end of the tenth century, ... a collection that is well-known and even fortunate because, already in 1840, it was edited in an entirely satisfactory manner (a privilege still rare today in canonistic literature) by Wasserschleben."

50. Most recently and fully in Wilfried Hartmann, "Neue Erkenntnisse aus der Arbeit an der Edition des Sendhanduchs Reginos von Prum," *Bulletin of Medieval Canon Law* (n.s.) 34 (2017): 33–59.

51. Hartmann, "Neue Erkenntnisse," p. 38.

felt that a new edition would handle the manuscript evidence (which has grown since Wasserschleben's day) more fully and more adequately; in particular, it would do a much better and more complete job of presenting the relationship between Regino's work and its material sources. For reasons expounded earlier, it does not seem that for our purposes the eventual publication of a new edition is worth the wait. If our object is to make Regino's work available as he intended it to be read, Wasserschleben's text continues to be satisfactory, and we remain grateful for his efforts.

Visitation book?

As we have seen, Wasserschleben and subsequent scholars have been particularly taken by the notion that Regino's *Two Books on Synodal Causes and Ecclesiastical Disciplines* was closely tied to contemporary practices, as it arose from practice and was intended to be used in the course of actual visitations by the archbishop of Mainz, to whom it was dedicated. This seems to remain the consensus.[52] The notion of having such a direct window on practice is an attractive one and is charmingly proposed in the prologue with which the work opens, although it may be worth pointing out that Wasserschleben found the prologue in only one of his manuscripts.[53] In the absence of the prologue, and despite the arrangement of the work in terms of the two sets of questions to be posed at a visitation, the copyists of the other manuscripts of the work were not tempted to call it a visitation book; indeed, they all agree in calling it something else, namely "a little book on ecclesiastical disciplines and the Christian religion, gathered at the command of the lord metropolitan Ratbod, bishop of the city of Trier, by Regino, formerly abbot of the monastery of Prüm, from the Councils of diverse holy Fathers and the decrees of the Roman pontiffs, happily in God's name. Amen."[54] Despite lacking the prologue, the manuscripts bearing this title show familiarity

52. Recent expressions of this consensus are Rob Meens, *Penance in Medieval Europe, 600–1200* (Cambridge: Cambridge University Press, 2014), pp. 141–48; Sarah Hamilton, *The Practice of Penance, 900–1050* (London: Royal Historical Society; Woodbridge, Suffolk: Boydell Press, 2001), pp. 27–30; Sarah Hamilton, *Church and People in the Medieval West, 900–1200* (London: Routledge, 2013), pp. 11–15; Greta Austin, *Shaping Church Law Around the Year 1000: The Decretum of Burchard of Worms* (Aldershot: Ashgate, 2008), pp. 39–41 and passim. This last makes sustained use of Regino's work as a source and term of comparison for Burchard's much larger and more influential work.

53. Wasserschleben, p. 1, n.

54. Wasserschleben, p. 19, n. 1. The editor, in the same place, states that he has declined to use this title because it was clearly added after Regino.

with its claim that Ratbod had asked for the work and, in their choice of title, take up what forms the second half of the title which Wasserschleben preferred, namely the matter of ecclesiastical disciplines. To it, they add the notion that the book is about the Christian religion.

It must be acknowledged that Wasserschleben, in his enthusiasm for the idea that Regino's work was a document concerned with practice, paid no attention to the second half of the title which he had chosen for the work. This is something that Meens instead tacitly does by noting that Regino "collected sentences from various councils and decrees of the holy fathers, in order to inform bishops in a convenient way about the proper rules for Christian life. ... Regino placed himself in the Carolingian tradition of providing authoritative ecclesiastical rules for a Christian life."[55] In addition, Meens asks himself how the book might actually have been used in the course of a visitation and provides a fascinating answer by examining the report of a visitation in the Life of Ulrich, bishop of Augsburg from 923 to 973.[56] The Life confirms a procedure like the one Regino's work describes, the carrying out of an enquiry into the religious life of the community through an examination of jurors. If breaches of the rules were found, the bishop strove to bring the offenders to repentance through the judgment of his clerics. If a case proved difficult, the bishop himself would discuss it with all his companions. If an offender would not accept the sentence so reached, the case might extend into the night "and the person contesting his judgment was silenced by the reading of ecclesiastical regulations (*regulas canonicas*)."[57] A book like Regino's would have been perfect for this effort to silence the refractory by means of an incantatory reading of the rules convicting him or her. Is this what makes it a visitation book?

We have had occasion to note the argument that Regino's work contains documents of practice and therefore must have been meant for practice. Does this argument compel, if one adds that documents which might be described as being tied to practice (e.g. commendatory letters and forms of oaths) constitute no more than one or two percent of the material in the book? Furthermore, as we have noted, the fiction of the prologue seems to be that the work is being sent for use by the archbishop of Mainz, but the letters at the end of book 1 that contain mentions of a bishop uniformly refer to the archbishop of Trier, and scholars agree that the penitential usages which Regino describes are to be referred to the

55. Rob Meens, *Penance in Medieval Europe*, p. 141.

56. Rob Meens, *Penance in Medieval Europe*, pp. 143–45. His source for the discussion is *Vita sancti Oudalrici episcopi Augustani auctore Gerhardo*, c. 6, ed. G. Waitz, in *Lebensbeschreibungen einiger Bischöfe des 10.–12. Jahrhunderts*, tr. Hatto Kallfelz, 2nd ed. (Darmstadt: Wissenschaftliche Buchgesellschaft, 1986), pp. 78–80.

57. Rob Meens, *Penance in Medieval Europe*, p. 144.

Church of Trier.[58] Does this not put in doubt the notion that the book was really put together for use by the archbishop of Mainz in the visitation of his diocese?

The prologue

Perhaps a reading of the prologue will help to clarify some of these issues. It is addressed to Hatto, bishop of Mainz and primate of all Germany, whose most devoted and humble client Regino professes to be. The bishop is busy both with the care of his ecclesiastical province, "in accordance with the provisions of the sacred canons," but also with matters useful to the whole kingdom, hence Regino has sent to him "a little book on synodal causes and ecclesiastical disciplines." At the mandate and exhortation of Archbishop Ratbod of Trier, Regino had "gathered it and brought it together with the greatest effort from different Councils and decrees of the holy Fathers." The book is not meant to add anything to what Hatto already has in his well-stocked library or to what he already knows, since he alone presents "to us in this decayed age the genius of those philosophers in whom that sagacious antiquity of the Latins found its glory."[59] This manual is merely meant to avert the need for Hatto to go about with the many large volumes from his library containing the Councils because he will find all that he needs for actual ecclesiastical business in this little book.

The criteria by which Regino has chosen his "examples" from Councils may seem questionable to some because he has privileged "our Councils, that is, the Councils of the Gauls and Germany." His *responsum* (a juridically redolent expression!) is that "I took care to insert those in particular which I knew to be more necessary for these dangerous times of ours and which appear to be pertinent to the business of the cause I have taken up." Furthermore, "many kinds of crimes have been and are being perpetrated in this worst of times in the Church that were unheard of in ancient times because they were not done then and so were not written down and condemned with fixed sentences, which have been and are condemned every day by the modern rules of the Fathers." It is also the case that "as the different nations of people diverge among themselves as to kind, customs, language, and laws, so the holy universal Church spread throughout

58. Sarah Hamilton, *The Practice of Penance*, p. 36: "It is likely, but we cannot be certain, given Regino's reliance elsewhere on Carolingian precedents, that this chapter is a description of local practice in early tenth-century Trier; it cannot be accepted as evidence of practice in early eleventh-century Worms or beyond."

59. One cannot help but wonder whether the philosophy of the Latins here mentioned is not to be identified with jurisprudence, that "philosophy which, if I am not deceived, is genuine, not a sham," as we saw Ulpian describe it, above, n. 8.

the world, although joined in the unity of faith, yet has differences from place to place in ecclesiastical customs." Moreover, "Scripture admonishes that the bounds, that is, the laws and decrees, which our Fathers set down are to be observed in every way, nor are they ever to be transgressed by a bold presumption. For this reason, following the footsteps of our predecessors, I digested in order the diverse statutes of the diverse Fathers. I leave it to the judgment of the reader which above all he prefers to choose and approve."

Although it has become customary to say that Regino dedicated his book to Hatto, our reading has not revealed any words of dedication, but only words of presentation. It seems possible that the prologue is describing a two-stage process: 1) mandate and encouragement by Ratbod to produce the work for use in his own diocese and province, hence the choice to include forms and practices from Trier; 2) eventual decision to present it also to Hatto in his capacity as primate. This may explain why almost all the manuscripts omit the prologue; interesting as it may be to know that the book was presented to Hatto, that presentation is not taken to be decisive regarding the nature and purposes of the book.

Discussions of this matter do not seem to have considered the possibility that we are here faced by *topoi*. No writer of the age – indeed, no writer for many centuries to come – wished to present his work as proceeding from his own desire for fame or some other disreputable motive, hence the practice of claiming that the irresistible pressure of friends, superiors, students had compelled one to take on the burden of authorship and to produce the humble thing now being presented. In Regino's case, the concurrent claims that Ratbod had requested and commanded him to compose, and that Hatto had received a copy of, his work had the effect of associating his work with the metropolitan and primatial authority of two of the foremost ecclesiastics of his time and place. If one were to ask why any attention should be paid to the canonical lucubrations of a dispossessed abbot, it might be good to be able to answer that one should do so because Archbishop Ratbod and Primate Hatto had already done so, particularly in view of the rather bold claims which Regino was making for his little enchiridion.

He claims no less than that his reading of the situation and needs of the Church in the present degenerate age and place was so clear, and his selection of materials that might help to resolve its problems was so shrewd, that one would not need to refer to other books in addressing them. Indeed, one could do so quickly and effectively because his choice had been governed by actual local and contemporary needs, and so he had privileged the examples and rules of Fathers and Councils close to his own time and place. He had not neglected antiquity, but he had wished especially to present to his reader those materials which would enable him to judge cases likely to arise in his own situation in accordance with the customs of his own Church and the laws of his own ancestors. Indeed, Regino nowhere claims that he is limiting himself to collecting canons, even though the canons of Councils have the pre-eminent place in his collection; he is also concerned with presenting opinions, customs, and laws which may be relevant in forming judgments regarding the wrongs of all sorts likely to be encountered in his time and place. It will be left to others (primarily Burchard of Worms) to decide that almost everything which Regino collects, apart from the strictly royal provisions, is to be regarded as canonical. In that way, perhaps, Regino indirectly contributes to a broadening of the meaning of the term canon, which earlier may not have included what are better regarded as sentences, opinions, or customs.

It is difficult to say in what sense and to what degree Regino is presenting his materials as being binding on his reader. This fortunate person is encouraged both to exercise his own judgment and not to trust his own judgment alone. Because other collections had not included the rules of more recent Fathers and Councils, Regino's reader had been left without guidance as to the penalties to be exacted from those who committed wrongs which had not been considered by the Fathers of antiquity. His collection is intended to remedy this difficulty. But there is no attempt on Regino's part to present the reader with a single rule or opinion to be followed in each instance. The reader's freedom is to be disciplined and enriched, but not abolished; indeed, the success of the work will lie in engaging and educating that freedom. It does not seem implausible that Regino intends his entire collection to be read in the same way in which he expects his order of penance to be used by priests with the authority to absolve; he says to them:

> We excerpted these things on the remedies of sins from the monuments of our predecessors; yet, in all these things, we made use not of the authority of the censor, but rather of the counsel of a fellow sufferer. We admonish energetically each learned priest of Christ that in all that he finds noted here he is to distinguish attentively as to the sex, age, condition, state, person, understanding, and the very heart of the penitent; he is to judge each matter in accordance with these and as seems best to him. It is necessary to correct all errors by doing what pertains to the purgation of sins, for some by abstinence from foods, for others by giving alms, for a few by frequent kneeling, or standing as on a cross. All of these must depend on the examination of the discreet judge.[60]

Regino's collection as a whole shares the character of excerpts from his predecessors' remedies for wrongs, instructive "examples" he had culled in the course

60. 1.304, below.

of "digesting" his materials. Example, we may note, can bear the meaning of precedent. And the use of the verb "digesting," even if it were not read as an echo of the most challenging and rule-framing part of Justinian's compilation, surely claims a degree of authorial autonomy for Regino that goes beyond the task of mere faithful reporting of authorities. The prospective judge will form his own judgment as to how well Regino has shaped examples and digested materials as he ponders all these excerpts and so informs and forms his conscience, but the conscience so informed and formed must then exercise the necessary discernment to further the correction or conversion of everyone involved, for the judge is always as much on trial as the party before him.

Regino's reader and the purposes of his work

The inclusion in Regino's work of a form of penance with a questionnaire to be used by priests in hearing confessions again raises the question of whether we can still simply hold that his work is literally intended for the bishop carrying out his visitation. It is difficult to see where, in the course of a visitation, the need arises for an order of penance. It is equally difficult to see how the bulk of the material presented in the collection could be used in a practical way during a visitation. Sufficient indications have been provided for scepticism regarding such a straightforward reading of this work. It is our contention that Regino intended to produce an essential canonical guide to everything that each person needed to know in order to live out the requirements of Christianity in an ever more conscious and deliberate way appropriate to the circumstances of a specific place and time.

To suggest that an overarching desire to foster conversion at all levels of his society is what drives Regino's effort is not to diminish the relevance and usefulness – indeed, the brilliance – of using the prospect of a visitation as the organizing principle of his collection. It is customary to refer to canonical collections as either chronological or systematic. Chronological collections, as their name implies, collect and arrange materials in chronological order. Systematic collections arrange the same material topically in separate books and titles. Chronological collections require the reader to look in many different places to find material regarding a specific issue or topic. Systematic collections risk ending up being used as mere reference works for the resolution of specific issues. If one were interested in a pedagogical program that might remedy a perceived deficiency in the apprehension of the canonical tradition as a whole, each of the traditional arrangements had drawbacks. It was no less than brilliant for Regino to tie his presentation to the series of cases that might arise in the course of a visitation, for in effect each of his questions sets forth a hypothetical case. The arrangement almost required his reader to make his way through the whole book and ponder the whole gamut of ways in which clergy and laity might fail to live up to their vocation and might be assisted to undertake a path of conversion.

In the Life of Ulric, we saw the expectation that the vast majority of cases that might arise in the course of a visitation were to be decided by the clerics who accompanied the bishop. We also saw that harder cases might be decided by the discussion of the bishop and the clerics accompanying him. Both these possibilities presume not that the bishop and clerics will sit down with the book in order to decide the cases now before them, but that they have already made their way through it in preparation for these activities. The book is the instrument by whose study these clerics could make themselves ready for any case that might arise and could contribute intelligently to the discussion and decision of even the most difficult cases. Since they could not tell ahead of time what cases might arise in the course of the visitation, they could only prepare themselves by reading and mastering the whole book. Something analogous must also be postulated of the jurors who are to answer the questions posed by the synodal investigators. These questions cover the whole range of requirements for a decent Christian life, both clerical and lay. It seems most implausible that lay jurors could have kept track of all that the questions cover, if there had not been a prior effort to educate them in the requirements of both clerical and lay life and to keep their eyes open for transgressions of those requirements. If this seems sensible, if not obvious, then the sets of questions and the authorities collected under them serve also as a pedagogical program for the laity, perhaps to be carried out primarily by preaching.

With regard to his arrangement of the materials, Regino would not soon find imitators. The much larger collections by Burchard of Worms and Ivo of Chartres, although they take over much of Regino's material, reject his manner of organization. Both of them produce systematic collections divided in books and titles. But Gratian, the most consequential successor of all, even though he did not use Regino's work directly for his own collection of canons, rejected the chronological and systematic approaches and arranged the bulk of his material around a series of hypothetical cases that might arise in an ecclesiastical court. What one might call the casuistic approach to legal education has never looked back and still characterizes legal training in our day in our part of the world. Chronological collections may be more attractive to those with an historical sense, and systematic collections may serve very well for the stating of what one might call black-letter law, but both have generally not been regarded as the most effective means for the formation of people who can think juridically. It does not seem far-fetched to suggest that Regino is the first explicit proponent of the casuistic method in the long history of canonical education and that his aim is no less than that of training as many people as possible to think juridically. For him, as for Gratian, this is entirely congruent with the pursuit of Christian perfection which must begin with each person acting as the judge of his or her own choices and actions. The practice of discernment that characterizes the good judge begins in the practice of discernment that characterizes every decent person; *mutatis mutandis,* each of them is called to navigate the tension between learning and abiding by the rules and taking the necessary risks that go with the necessary exercise of the freedom that characterizes the human person.

Apart from the book itself, is there any other evidence that Regino cared about the form of law books and the state of canonical learning in his region? There are two moments in Regino's *Chronicle* which may help to illuminate these matters. As to the first, there is his entry regarding Emperor Justinian, the great codifier of Roman law. There, after noting military achievements against the Persians, in Africa, and in Italy, Regino added: "Also, he shortened the Roman laws, whose prolixity was burdensome, and corrected their useless dissonances with an admirable brevity."[61] The note is very (fittingly?) brief, but it conveys effectively the sense that a collection of laws ought to be as short as possible, avoiding uselessly contradictory material, yet preserving useful contradictions. As we have seen from the prologue and the instructions to priests called to administer penance, these are exactly the features which Regino has pursued in his own canonical work. The book is no more than a *libellus* or very little book, which purports to make redundant the recourse to much more prolix and burdensome works. It also strives to strike a balance between the extremes of providing a single course of action for its judicious reader and leaving him without the guide of precedents in framing judgments about cases. No doubt, we recognize in this our own continuing dilemma about the judicial function: should it be hemmed in by laws or should it exercise unbridled discretion? Heirs as we are to the tradition which Regino helps to shape, we recognize that ultimately we find any solution unsatisfactory that wishes to avoid the placing of our trust in the disciplined discernment of the person vested with the judicial function, even as we know that such discernment is fallible and bound to disappoint in some cases.

As the reader has no doubt guessed, Regino in his *Chronicle* also had things to report about the state of canonical learning in his region. The comments occur in the course of the many pages which Regino devotes to recounting the events surrounding the marriage difficulties of Emperor Lothar and his wife

61. Kurze, ed., *Reginonis abbatis Prumiensis Chronicon,* p. 20: "Leges quoque Romanas, quarum prolixitas gravabat, minoravit et inutiles dissonantias mirabili brevitate correxit."

Theutberga.[62] In outlining the beginning of the dispute, Regino identifies as a villain Gunther, bishop of Cologne and royal arch-chaplain, who led the initial campaign to convince the bishops that Lothar had grounds to divorce his wife and marry his concubine, as he wished to do. Among the bishops to be convinced was Theutgaud, archbishop of Trier. Gunther approached him and, "knowing him to be a simple man, not very learned in the divine Scriptures, nor practiced in the canonical provisions, he read to him some sentences from the pages of both Testaments; interpreting these otherwise than the ecclesiastical rule teaches, he drew the improvident man with himself into the pit, as the blind led the blind."[63] That ignorance of canonical matters was not limited to Theutgaud is made clear when some avaricious papal legates, having come to adjudicate the dispute with great profit to themselves, upon returning to Rome, reported to the pope that, "in Lothar's kingdom, they had not found a single wise bishop who was clearly instructed in the canonical disciplines."[64]

62. On this famous dispute, which did much to elicit disputation and clarification regarding a number of canonical topics, both procedural and substantive, see Abigail Firey, *A Contrite Heart: Prosecution and Redemption in the Carolingian Empire* (Leiden: Brill, 2009), pp. 13–60 and passim; Stuart Airlie, "Private Bodies and the Body Politic in the Divorce Case of Lothar II," *Past and Present* 161 (1998): 3–38; Karl Heidecker, *The Divorce of Lothar II: Christian Marriage and Political Power in the Carolingian World*, tr. T.M. Guest (Ithaca: Cornell University Press, 2010). On Regino's linking of the divorce case and the troubles of the Empire, see MacLean, *History*, pp. 43–47. The relentless pursuit of brevity which characterizes the *Chronicle* is abandoned in the report of this case, which clearly was of great interest to Regino as symptomatic of many of the ills for which, among other things, he himself had paid a very personal price in his expulsion from his abbacy. The main narrative is found in Kurze, ed., *Reginonis abbatis Prumiensis Chronicon*, pp. 80–90; it concludes with this apology (pp. 89–90): "See, we have taken care to note a few things from the many, so that they may be partially known to those who do not know them and yet may not be entirely burdensome to those who already know them. As will become clear in what follows, the often-mentioned most holy pope, inspired by the Holy Spirit, had rightly foretold what evil outcome the curse of this pestilential illness would bring about because of the refusal to be healed by the apostolic remedy and how many losses would be caused to the kingdom by this deadly contagion."

63. Kurze, ed., *Reginonis abbatis Prumiensis Chronicon*, p. 81: "Rursus idem Guntarius Thietgaudum archiepiscopum Treverensem hac de causa alloquitur et, sciens esse virum simplicem nec adeo in divinis scripturis eruditum canonicisque sanctionibus exercitatum, ex utriusque testamenti paginis quasdam sententias profert, quas aliter, quam ecclesiastica regula docet, edisserens virum improvidum secum in foveam trahit, caecus caeco ducatum prestans." Regino reports that, for his improvident agreement with Gunther, Theutgaud, too, incurred a sentence of deposition, which he bore patiently and obediently (pp. 83–84).

64. Kurze, ed., *Reginonis abbatis Prumiensis Chronicon*, pp. 82–83: "Legati inmensis ditati opibus Romam regressi sunt nunciaveruntque presuli, quae in Galliis viderant et audierant, adicientes se nullum sapientem episcopum in regno Lotharii invenisse, qui ad liquidum canonicis esset institutus disciplinis."

Regino's whole narrative of Lothar's divorce case, among other things, seems designed to confirm this judgment of the legates, almost as if it were intended to justify in turn Regino's effort to compose the *Two Books* as a remedy to the widespread ignorance of the canonical tradition that had caused so much harm to the Church and the body politic in his region of the world. The transition from ignorance of the canonical disciplines to the need for a little book on ecclesiastical disciplines does not seem difficult to make, if we are not misled by the reference to synodal causes. If we had missed this pointer, Regino is kind enough to provide another one. Although, as has been stated, the chapters of the *Two Books* are broadly arranged to correspond to the questions set out in the questionnaires that preface each of the books, this is not true for the initial chapters of the first book. The first thirteen of these chapters are designed to outline the relationship between the bishop and the churches subject to him and to define the responsibilities which the bishop has in regard to those same churches. The very first of these chapters reads: "The statutes of the canons are to be kept by all without prejudice, and no one is to judge in ecclesiastical actions or judgments by his own sense, but each is to be led by the authority of the same statutes. Also, in expounding or preaching the divine Scriptures, each is to follow the sense of the holy Catholic and most proven Fathers, in whose writings, as St. Jerome says, the truth of faith does not waver."[65] It is as if, belatedly, Regino wished to instruct Theutgaud in the very things whose ignorance had led Ratbod's predecessor to his ruin.

To summarize: it is our view that the *Two Books*, although they may have been used in the course of episcopal visitations, are not to be read as limited to such use. They are to be regarded primarily as a pedagogical tool, intended to remedy an ignorance of the canonical tradition which had proven disastrous not many years before their composition. They are intended to be of use to all who have some position of responsibility within the Church and, ultimately, to every member of the Church. They are meant to help form every Christian, but particularly those clerics who have the responsibility to issue judgments in the Church, and to develop a disciplined discernment and a habit of addressing issues as they arise in personal and community life in the light of Scripture and of the long experience of the Church. They are brilliantly arranged around the device of questionnaires which fosters a case-based and tentative approach to the resolution of problems while avoiding abstraction and striving to mitigate legalism.

65. Below, 1.1.

The appendices

Mention has already been made of the three appendices which Wasserschleben decided to include in his edition. It should be clear to the reader that these are not appendices in the ordinary sense of the term, that is, they were not included by the author in order to provide subsidiary evidence. The decision to include them in the translation is moved by the thought that they might be considered as evidence of three critical readings of Regino's work at disparate times in the course of the tenth century. The reader who does not lack time and patience has, in the appendices, three implicit perspectives on Regino's work, so they can serve as a testing ground for hypotheses about the nature of the work as perceived by tenth-century readers. All three reveal that later readers found the work engaging and useful enough to take the time to improve it according to their own reading of needs, times, and circumstances. All three reveal that the desirability of not leaving canonical learning to the Italians had not fallen on deaf ears.

The translation

A word should be said about the translation. The temper of our times is averse to both literalism and Latinism. This translation tends to cultivate both. The translator's laziness and cowardice may not be the only reasons for this tendency. If canon law is indeed a privileged locus of the elaboration of the public language of Western Christendom, then the tracing of the development of such a language would be made difficult by a translation that recast the words and phrases evolved and honed in this process for the sake of mere ease of reading. This case for Latinism, or preference for Latinate forms, seems strengthened by the consideration that so many of these words and phrases are still in effective use in their Latinate forms in the various juridical orders of the Western world and their ancestry might be obscured by rendering them by other sorts of expressions.

If the argument for using Latinate forms is grounded in the long stability eventually achieved by the terms of art of the canonical tradition, the argument for literalism is based on the desirability of being able to trace the changes and fluctuations which precede that stability. By the mid-thirteenth century, reflection on the canonical materials had developed so richly and fruitfully that its panoply of words, expressions, forms, and concepts, with hardly any addition, if with many subtractions, proved sufficient to serve the needs of the Church and of many other components of Western Christendom into the twentieth century. So impressive is the achievement of those centuries that one is tempted to backdate it and impose the same clarity and stability on materials from earlier centuries. It is to avoid this sort of misapprehension that literalism has been preferred in translating materials which are quite disparate in time and origin and do not yet possess, and whose authors perhaps would not have desired, the sophistication and homogeneity of the scholastic rendering of the canonical tradition.

Before allowing Regino to speak for himself, the sweet obligation remains to thank once more Jean Hoff and Fred Unwalla, of the PIMS Department of Publications. They have lavished their gifts as unstintingly on this most recent project of mine as they did on several past ones. Their expert discernment and prudent encouragement have kept the thing going through a few trials, saving me from many errors and improving markedly the legibility of the text. Megan Jones, of the same Department, has brought her own energy and meticulousness to the task of improving this work to make it more useful to the reader. Professor Robert Sweetman inimitably brought and found joy to and in the reading of Regino and so confirmed how well-rooted is our friendship of several decades.

The possibility that one might read Regino with joy is not one that I would have found plausible at one time. I happen to remember vividly my first encounter, while a graduate student, with this seemingly arid text in the PL edition. Taken as I was and remain with the wonders of the high jurisprudence of later centuries, I was then not curious enough to wonder about the origins and earlier developments of the more attractive and specific features of the canonical tradition. That I find my openness to such questions so different now seems to me to be a good thing. In no small part, I think I must give credit for this and many other positive developments in my thought regarding this and many other issues to the steadfast friendship of Professor Joseph W. Goering and to the seemingly endless dialogue in which he and I have engaged spiritedly over the last forty years. Joe and I came together under the aegis of our lord and master, Fr. Leonard E. Boyle, O.P. A shared impish piety toward Fr. Boyle became the sturdy foundation of a friendship and intellectual exchange that has felt like one of the greater gifts that our supervisor left to us and a living out in our own way of the human and scholarly virtues that he had exemplified for us. The dedication of this book to Joe is a very small token of the affection and gratitude that I am glad to owe to him for the unreserved generosity of his long friendship.

Giulio Silano
St. Michael's College, Toronto
Holy Monday, 2021

REGINO OF PRÜM

Two Books on Synodal Causes and Ecclesiastical Disciplines

Parenthetical references to the Bible, as well as parenthetical cross-references to other chapters, are drawn from Regino of Prüm, *Libri duo de synodalibus causis et disciplinis ecclesiasticis*, ed. F.G.A. Wasserschleben (Leipzig: Engelmann, 1840). Parentheses are also used to present the original when the translation is uncertain. Square brackets indicate editorial insertions.

Here begins the Preface
of the work that follows.

To Hatto, bishop of the holy see of Mainz and primate of all Germany, Regino, most devoted and humble client of your Sublimity, prays for your prosperity in this life and the glory of future blessedness. Knowing that the greatness of your Prudence not only bears the responsibility for the whole province, in accordance with the provisions of the sacred canons, but also labours mightily with vigilant care for the usefulness of the whole kingdom, I sent to your Excellency a little book on synodal causes and ecclesiastical disciplines. At the mandate and exhortation of the Lord and of the most reverend Archbishop Ratbod, I gathered it and brought it together with the greatest effort from different Councils and decrees of the holy Fathers. Not that I rashly believed that something might be lacking out of the abundance of your library, or that anything is hidden from the prudence of your excellent intelligence – you who adorn the place entrusted to your Excellency by heaven through the dignity of your nobility and your celebrated praiseworthy acts, you who are so great in every kind of philosophy that alone you present to us in this decayed age the genius of those philosophers in whom that sagacious antiquity of the Latins found its glory. But because your wise and pre-eminent Excellency is so assiduously engaged in the disposition of public business, perhaps it would seem onerous if you had always to carry about with yourself back and forth the many volumes of the Councils. Hence, I sent to your Lordship this handy little book, so that you may use it as an enchiridion, if at any time all your books are not available to you. But if anyone is troubled by my having chosen more frequently examples from our Councils, that is, the Councils of the Gauls and Germany, let him receive the response and know that I took care to insert those in particular which I knew to be more necessary for these dangerous times of ours and which appear to be pertinent to the business of the cause I have taken up. It is also to be added that many kinds of crimes have been and are being perpetrated in this worst of times in the Church that were unheard of in ancient times because they were not done then and so were not written down and condemned with fixed sentences, which have been and are condemned every day by the modern rules of the Fathers. It is also to be known that, as the different nations of people diverge among themselves as to kind, customs, language, and laws, so the holy universal Church spread throughout the world, although joined in the unity of faith, yet has differences from place to place in ecclesiastical customs. Some customs as to ecclesiastical offices are found in the kingdoms of the Gauls and Germany, others in the kingdoms of the East and in the regions across the seas. Furthermore, Scripture admonishes that the bounds, that is, the laws and decrees which our Fathers set down are to be observed in every way, nor are they ever to be transgressed by a bold presumption. For this reason, following the footsteps of our predecessors, I digested in order the diverse statutes of the diverse Fathers. I leave it to the judgment of the reader which above all he prefers to choose and approve. Hence, may your Grace receive this very trifling gift with a benignity equal to the devotion with which it is sent by my littleness. May the glory of your Beatitude be well now and in the future. Amen.

Here ends the Preface
of the work that follows.

HERE BEGIN THE CHAPTERS OF THE FIRST BOOK

1 That the statutes of the canons be kept by all without prejudice.
2–3 What sort of minister a bishop is to keep with himself.
4 That it is to be asked of the king that bishops, at the suitable time, have the opportunity to carry out the ministry entrusted to them.
5 Lest the bishops neglect the people entrusted to them for the sake of their own quiet.
6 Of bishops who rarely or never visit personally the peoples entrusted to them.
7 That the bishop walk through his diocese.
8 That the bishop go about his parish with a few people.
9 That if a bishop is unable to fulfil this, he is to send his vicars.
10 That bishops visit their diocese.
11 That a bishop is to receive only two shillings from the priest when he goes around his diocese.
12–13 On bishops who require the price of service from parishes which they have not visited.
14 On the immunity of churches.
15 That all parishes are to be within the power of the bishops.
16 On parishes.
17 What sorts of ministers bishops are to leave in their cities.
18 On thirty-year prescription.
19 On things possessed for thirty years.
20–22 On the inscription of times.
23 On consecrating a church.
24 On the liberty of churches.
25 On the boundary of churches.
26–27 On new churches.
28–29 On the manse of the church.
30 On the privilege of churches.
31 On churches or doubtful altars, and that superfluous altars be thrown out of a church.
32 On ecclesiastical honour.
33 That the endowments of all churches pertain to the bishop.
34–35 That churches are to be restored and show obedience to the bishop.
36 On the honour of God's church.
37–38 Also, on the restoration of God's churches.
39 On formerly sacred places.
40–42 On destroyed churches.
43–44 On tithes.
44b–52 When someone has worked new land.
53–55 That no hay or wheat or wine is to be deposited in the church.

56–57 That no one presume to hold banquets in a church.
58–59 That no one presume to sell wine in church.
60 That the altars be covered with the cleanest linens.
61 That priests preach to women to provide the linens from which the altar may be clothed.
62 That no priest receive another's parishioner at mass.
63 On the offerings of the faithful at the altar.
64 That nothing else is to be offered in the Lord's sacrifice apart from what the Lord established.
65 What sorts of things are to be offered at the altar, and not for the sacrifice.
66 That those things which cannot be offered in churches are to be brought by the faithful to the house of the priest.
67 What is to be offered at the Lord's sacrifice.
68 On the Lord's chalice.
69 On the Lord's corporal.
70–71 On the Eucharist.
72 On the offerings, that they be renewed from Saturday to Saturday.
73 That the chrism be always under lock.
74 If the priest has given the chrism for the subversion of judgment.
75 That no priest give any gift for the chrism.
76 That each priest bring two ampoules to the city on Holy Thursday.
77 On priests who are far away, that one out of eight or ten come on Holy Thursday, who may bring the chrism to the others.
78 That no priest is to receive another bishop's chrism.
79 That no minister go about without chrism.
80 On sacred fonts.
81 That no priest presume to sing mass without priestly vestment.
82 That sacred vessels or vestments not be given as pledges.
83 That the bishop and priest have a little dwelling not far from the church.
84 That priests not at all be allowed to be hosted anywhere.
85–100 On the incontinence of priests.
101 Which women may live in the houses of clerics.
102 Lest maidservants or freedwomen keep the cellar of clerics or extend secret service.
103–5 On the familiarity of strange women.
106 That the sick are to be visited by the priest.
107 On the sick who confess their sins and ask to be reconciled.
108–11 On reconciling the infirm.
112–14 On those who become mute before the priest comes to them.
115 On the penitents who have died suddenly.
116 Of those deprived of communion who have died in this state.

209 Admonition to the bishops.
210 That each priest who holds a church is to have a cleric.
211 That each priest fulfil the canonical hours solemnly.
212 That the priest take care of guests.
213–14 On making blessed water.
215 On priests who remain silent regarding the faults of sinners, or bring to reconciliation those who are less worthily penitent.
216 On priests who are invited to dinner by the faithful.
217 On the brawls and fights of priests.
218 On the banquet of priests.
219 On the kalends.
220–22 Of those who have nothing when they are ordained.
223 On the income or offering of the church.
224–27 On usuries.
228–35 That clerics not engage in usury under another's name.
236–40 Of those who have been ordained for money.
241 That a gift is also by the tongue.
242 Lest priests give gifts to obtain churches.
243–44 That no one is to place a priest in a church or cast him out.
245–46 On churches which are divided among coheirs.
247 That several priests are not to be established in one church.
248–50 That laymen must not hold churches, nor receive tithes.
251–54 On those who abandon the churches to which they have been promoted and pass to others.
255 On clerics who are set over hospices.
256–57 That a priest have not more than one church.
258–60 That no priest receive another's parishioner.
261 That a bishop is not to do an ordination in another bishop's parish.
262 That no priest or layman is to invite a penitent to drink wine or eat meat.
263 That no priest write charters.
264 That no one, contemning a lesser church, aspire to a better one.
265–69 On baptism, and at what time it is to be celebrated.
270 On the baptized who die without confirmation.
271–73 On the rebaptized.
274 On sacred fonts.
275 That each priest teach the Creed and the Lord's Prayer to his parishioners.
276 Of those priests or clerics who steal or subvert the churches or benefices of other priests for money.
277 That each priest be content with one church.
278 That a priest not take a church through money.
279 On the greater litany.
280 On the fast of the Rogations.

281 On the fast of the Ember Days.
282 On fasting on the vigils of the saints.
283–87 On a prescribed fast.
288–88 What is usury.
290–91 What is a loan.
292 On confession and penance.
293–95 On penitents.
296 On assigning penance.
297–98 How bishops or priests are to receive a penitent.
299 That no one presume to give penance to another or hear confession, except for a bishop or priest.
300 That a deacon, if it is necessary, receive the confession.
301–2 Also, on receiving confession.
303 Prayer.
304 Order for the giving of penance.
305–6 On penitents.
307–12 That penance be assigned to the married with their consent.
313 That no bishop receive a penitent of another city or parish, or reconcile him without the testimony of the bishop or priest.
314 That hands be not imposed on priests and deacons as they are on penitents.
315 That penance not be denied to clerics.
316 How priests and deacons do penance.
317 That penitents are to abstain from trade.
326 What disposition the penitent is to have.
327 What is true penance.
328 How we are to be toward the impenitent.
329–30 On sacred communion.
331–33 On diligence as to the body of the Lord.
334 That laymen communicate three times each year.
335–37 That clerics not be present at weddings.
338–39 On the times at which married men are to contain themselves from their wives.
340 On Lent.
341 That married persons are to abstain before communion.
342 On the blessed bread to be given to the people by priests.
343–44 That priests go about with their stole.
345–47 That clerics not dress in lay garb.
348 On wine, that it is not to be offered pure at the sacrifice, but mixed with water.
349–50 That priests not obtain a church for a price.
351 That the sacrifice is not to be offered everywhere.
352 Where mass is to be celebrated.
353 If four portions are made of the tithes.

354 If a bishop or priest has presumed to alienate a possession of the church by whatever device.

355 That it is not lawful for any bishop to alienate in perpetuity any possession, large or small, of the Church.

356–58 On houses.

359–61 That priests not sell a possession of the church in which they are established.

362 What is to be done by the relatives of one who has enriched a church with his goods, if they perceive that something of the goods conferred has been defrauded.

363 On scanty bits of land and vineyard belonging to a Church.

364 That fugitive slaves are permitted to be sold.

365 If someone has dared to suppress royal charters or precepts or has handed them over to adversaries.

366 On the testament of a bishop, how it is to be valid.

367–69 On manumissions in the Church.

370 On the freedmen of the Church.

371 On ecclesiastical treasures.

372 That no one presume to alienate an immovable good of a church.

373 If the prince wishes to make a commutation with a church.

377 That royal precepts not be issued as to leases.

378 That leases be renewed every five years.

379 On commutations.

380 Also, that no precepts be issued as to ecclesiastical benefices or leases.

381–82 That no commutations be done regarding ecclesiastical possessions without the king's consent, and that ecclesiastical slaves not be exchanged, unless into freedom.

383 On the Lord's day.

384 What may be done licitly on Sundays.

385 Also, on the Lord's day.

386–87 That no market be held on the Lord's day.

388–89 On the feasts of the year.

390–91 On not bending the knee on feast days.

392–93 That unseemly songs be forbidden to the peoples.

394–95 That a bishop is not at all to ordain the clerics of another parish.

396 That no bishop, or any of lower rank, presume to judge causes on the Lord's day.

397 That it is not opportune for ordinations to be done absolutely.

398 Lest diabolical verses be sung at nighttime over the bodies of the dead.

399 Also, that none be ordained absolutely.

400–401 On the examination before ordination.

402 That the ordained receive letters from their ordainers.

403–4 That no one presume to ordain another's slave.

HERE BEGIN THE CHAPTERS OF THE SECOND BOOK

263 Also, on the copulation of the faithful.
264 Lest adulteries be perpetrated in the houses of the faithful.
265 Also, on incests.
266–77 On theft and rapine.
278 On a criminal cause.
279–88 On rapine and violence.
289 On those who breach sacred places.
290 How the bishop is to call plunderers to the synod.
291–93 On those who are another's parishioners.
294 If a bishop does not excommunicate plunderers.
295 Also, on the rapacious.
296 That bishops must protect and defend the people.
297–302 Also, on malefactors.
303 If a man is accused and has denied it.
304–5 Lest anyone usurp another's parish.
306–10 That none excommunicate another's parishioner.
311–13 That a bishop not excommunicate anyone quickly and moved by anger.
314 That no one presume to remit a sin that another has committed against the Lord.
315–20 On perjury.
321 That a bishop not swear on sacred objects.
322 Also, on perjury.
323 At what time oaths are sworn.
324–25 That oaths not be sworn on the Wednesday before Lent.
326 On a cleric, if he has perjured himself.
327 On those who bind themselves by oath not to return to peace.
328–38 Also, on perjury.
339–50 On false witness.
351–53 On one who has stolen a man.
354–65 On enchanters.
366–68 On trees, springs, and stones consecrated to demons.
369–70 On menstrual blood.
371 On the women who say that they go riding with demons at nighttime.
372 On the observance of months and days.
373 That Christians not observe the traditions of the gentiles.
374 On the gathering of herbs.
375 On women's wool-workings.
376 On dead animals.
377 On a liquid.
378 On blood.
379 Also, that no one is to eat blood.

380–85 On those in discord.
386 On the judgment of God.
387–89 On the offerings of the dead.
390 On communion.
391–94 That the principal festivities be celebrated in the cities.
395 On the deans to be sent through the parishes.
396–406 On excommunicates.
407 On those condemned by a synod.
408 On the same matter.
409–10 If a bishop wishes to banish a cleric from the Church.
411 On an accused priest.
412 How a bishop is to excommunicate the faithless.
413 Excommunication.
414 Also, another allocution of excommunication.
415 Excommunication.
416 Also, another and more fearful excommunication.
417 Also, a brief excommunication.
418 How a bishop may reconcile or receive an excommunicate.
419 On one who dishonors his father or mother.
420 On oxherds and swineherds.
421 What priests must do on Sundays.
422 On one who remains silent as to his brother's sin.
423–24 On the poor, how they are to be fed.
425 Of one who gives slight weight to the ban of the bishop or priest.
426 On a priest who has been demoted.
427–28 That no one deny hospitality to a traveler.
429 On one who dishonors a priest.
430–31 On godfathers or godsons.
432 If anyone opposes a bishop as to the flogging of serfs with rods for crimes.
433–34 On foreigners who are unjustly reduced to servitude.
435–36 That the measures be just.
437–40 On conspiracies.
441 On confraternities or associations.
442 That if a priest has died, a neighboring priest is never to obtain the church before the secular lord.
443 Of the liquid into which a mouse has fallen.
444 If anyone has violated a tomb.
445 If anyone has died while excommunicate.
446 On the price of redemption.
447 What is to be done for one month.
448 What for one week.

First Book

List of what the bishop or his ministers must ask diligently at their synod in all the public villages and estates and the parishes of his diocese.

1. First, it is to be asked in the honour of which saint the basilica is consecrated, and by whom it was consecrated. After this, let the church be looked over: Whether it is well covered and constructed so that no doves or other birds make their nests there because of the messiness of their excrement and the inopportunity of their restlessness?

2. Of what metal are the bells of the same church?

3. Whether hay, wheat, or any such is kept in the church?

4. Then it is necessary to approach the altar and examine how its cloths are: How many new, and how many old, and how clean?

5. With what metal are the reliquaries and crosses covered, and whether the relics are diligently stored within the altar, and are the same reliquaries protected with locks and key?

6. Of what metal is the chalice and paten, and whether it is clean from all filth, and where is it kept?

7. Whether the corporal is of the cleanest and purest linen, and where is it kept?

8. Whether there is a place prepared in the sacristy or near the altar where the water can be poured out when these things are washed, and whether a vessel hangs there where the priest may wash his hands after the reception of the body and blood of the Lord, and the priest, deacon, or subdeacon may first wash the corporal there?

9. It is to be inquired whether the pyx is always on the altar with the sacred Host as a viaticum for the infirm?

10. Whether the church has a full missal, a lectionary, and an antiphonary? Indeed, without these, mass is not celebrated perfectly.

11. It is also to be seen how many other books are there, and whether they are well read?

12. How many and which priestly vestments are there, and whether they are clean and kept in a clean place?

13. It is to be asked concerning the lamps of the same church, and how many wax-lights it has?

14. It is to be investigated whether the said church has a manse of twelve bunders, apart from the cemetery and courtyard where the church and priest's house are contained, and whether it has four slaves?

15. How many manses does it have consisting of freeborn men, and how many of servile ones, and tenants from which the tithe is rendered?

16. It is also to be considered whether the forecourt of the church is frequently secured so that it is not polluted by any uncleanness?

On the life and bearing of the priest.

17. It is to be inquired whether the priest has a cottage near the church, and whether there are suspicious little gates around?

18. Whether he is under suspicion as regards some woman, or has some woman whom he secretly brings into his house?

19. Whether he visits the sick, reconciles them, anoints them with holy oil according to the Apostle, gives communion to them with his own hand, and not through some layman, or whether he gives the communion to a layman or woman to be brought to the sick, which is an offence against divine law?

20. Whether he demands payment or a gift for baptizing infants, or reconciling the sick, or burying the dead?

21. This, above all things, is to be investigated: Whether, by the priest's negligence, some infant in the parish has died without baptism?

22. Whether he sings mass in houses outside the church?

23. Whether he is prone to drunkenness and litigiousness?

24. Whether he bears arms in fights?

25. Whether he engages in past-times involving dogs and birds?

26. Whether he drinks in taverns?

27. Whether he has a cleric to read the Epistle or the lesson, and to respond at mass, and to sing the psalms with him?

28. Whether he arises each night in the night hours to perform lauds?

29. Whether he announces prime, terce, sext, and none at a certain time with the church bell, and sings the due office?

30. Whether the solemn observance of mass is not celebrated before the third hour?

31. Whether the priest (far be it!) presumes to celebrate mass after he has taken food or drink?

32. Whether he has a thurible, and offers incense in the sacrifice of the Lord?

33. Whether he announces the Lord's word to the people?

34. Whether he celebrates mass at the appointed time, that is, around the third hour of the day, and whether after this he fasts until the middle of the day, so that, if it were necessary, he could sing mass for guests and arriving travellers?

35. Whether he takes care of the poor and pilgrims and orphans, and invites them to his meal insofar as possible?

36. Whether, on each Sunday before the solemnities of mass, he makes blessed water in a clean vessel suitable for such a mystery, with which the people may be sprinkled as they enter the church?

37. Whether he presumes to give as pledge to a tavern-keeper or merchant the chalice, or paten, or priestly vestment, or book?

38. Whether he accepts a bribe or any temporal emolument (or rather spiritual detriment) from anyone who sins publicly or commits incest in order to keep silent before the bishop or his ministers regarding the donor's sin?

39. Whether, for the sake of favour, or familiarity, or consanguinity, he has brought to reconciliation a less than worthy penitent and has given him testimony of reconciliation?

40. Whether, when he is called to a thirtieth, seventh, or third anniversary of a deceased person, he presumes to get drunk, and to ask to drink to the love of the saints or drink to the deceased's soul, and compel others to drink, or gorge himself at another's invitation, or break into disorderly noise and laughter, or join in shameful games and indecent songs?

41. If he had no patrimony when he was promoted to his ecclesiastical dignity, and afterwards he bought property, to whose right does it belong?

42. Whether he exacts usuries, and is his lord's money lender?

43. Whether he sings mass without taking communion?

44. Whether he allows a woman to approach the altar and, as is not licit, to touch the Lord's chalice?

45. Whether he was ordained for money, or has obtained for a price the church in which he sings?

46. Whether he had another church and, having left it, moved to another one for the sake of gain?

47. Whether he holds several churches without the aid of other priests?

48. Whether he receives to mass another's parishioner, unless the latter is travelling?

49. Whether he sings mass in another's parish without the consent and request of his fellow priest?

50. Whether he receives the tithe that pertains to another?

51. Whether he invites a penitent to eat meat and drink wine, unless the latter has now given alms for it?

52. Whether he writes charters, or is his lord's money lender?

53. Whether he baptizes carelessly?

54. If he does not have stone fonts, whether he has another vessel ready for this purpose, in which nothing else is done?

55. Whether he has taught the Lord's Prayer and the Creed to all his parishioners?

56. On the greater Litany.

57. On the Rogations.

58. Whether he announces to his people that the fast of the Ember Days must be observed in every way?

59. Whether, on the Wednesday before Lent, he invites the people entrusted to him to confession, and enjoins penance according to the quality of the wrong, not from his own heart, but as it is written in the Penitential?

60. Whether he admonishes all the faithful to approach the communion of the body and blood of the Lord three times a year, that is, the Lord's Nativity, Easter, and Pentecost?

61. Whether he also admonishes about the times when married men are to abstain from their wives?

62. That no cleric go to marriage feasts.

63. Whether he offers blessed bread (*eulogiae*) at the end of the mass from the offerings which are made by the people on Sundays and feast-days?

64. Whether he goes travelling without a stole or scarf?

65. Whether, setting aside clerical vestments, he wears lay clothing?

66. Whether he mixes water with the wine at the Lord's sacrifice?

67. Whether, at the end of the mass, the priest himself, with fear and reverence, consumes what is left of the body and blood of the Lord and, if he does not have a deacon or subdeacon, does he wash or clean the chalice and paten with his own hand?

68. Whether he presumes to sing mass without an alb, or in the alb which he uses in his everyday activities?

69. Whether four portions are made of the tithes?

70. Whether he has presumed to sell, exchange, or alienate by any device a thing, or possession, or slave of the Church?

71. Whether he teaches that Sundays and other feast-days are to be celebrated without servile work from vespers to vespers?

72. Whether he admonishes the people that women are never to sing or dance in the forecourt of the church, but are to enter the church to hear the word of God in silence?

73. Whether he forbids, under the invocation of almighty God as his witness, those diabolical verses which the infamous rabble are accustomed to sing over the dead in the night hours, and the laughter in which they engage?

74. Whether he instructs those making the offering that they are to offer the candle, or whatever else it pleases them to bring to the altar, before the mass, or before the Gospel is read?

75. Does each person offer only one offering at the offertory for himself and all his own?

WHAT IS TO BE ASKED OF THE PRIEST?

After all these things have been diligently investigated, then the priest himself is to be questioned by the bishop or his vicar:

76. Whether he was born of free parents, or he is of a servile condition?

77. Whether he was born or ordained in the same parish or another?

78. If he is from the same parish, it is inquired by which bishop he was ordained, and to which place he had been given title?

79. If he was of servile condition, he is to show his charter of freedom.

80. If he is from another parish, he is to show the commendatory letters, which they call formed (*formata*).

81. If he lacks any part of his body, whether he mutilated himself?

After these things, there is to be inquiry into the ministry committed to him.

82. Whether he has in his possession a written exposition of the Creed and of the Lord's Prayer according to the tradition of the orthodox Fathers, and does he understand it fully, and does he diligently in his preaching from it instruct the people entrusted to him?

83. Whether he understands well the prayers of the mass, the preface of the canon, and the canon itself, and is he able to say them clearly from memory?

84. Whether he is able to read the Epistle and Gospel well, and whether he can make manifest at least their literal sense?

85. Whether he knows how to recite by heart the words of the psalms with their pauses according to the accepted procedures and with the customary canticles?

86. Whether he knows by heart the sermon of Bishop Athanasius on faith in the Holy Trinity, whose beginning is "Whoever wishes to be saved," and understands its sense, and knows how to explain it in common words?

87. Whether he is able to utter clearly and reasonably the exorcisms and prayers for the making of a catechumen, and for the consecration of the font, and the other prayers to be said over male and female, and in the plural and the singular?

88. Similarly, with regard to the order of baptizing and bringing succor to the sick.

89. Also, whether he knows how to read well and say from memory the order of reconciliation according to the manner reserved to him canonically, and of anointing the sick, and the prayers suitable for that need?

90. Similarly, the order and prayers for a funeral and other things to be done for the deceased.

91. Whether he has committed to memory the exorcisms and blessings of salt and water?

92. Whether he knows the chant appropriate for night and for daytime?

93. Whether he knows the lesser computus, that is, the epacts, the concurrents, regulars, the dates within which Easter falls, and the rest?

94. Whether he has a Martyrology, from which on certain days he will announce the birthdays of the saints to the people?

95. Whether he has the forty homilies of Gregory, and reads them studiously and understands them? And if he is unable to have them, at least does he have the sermon of the same doctor on the seventy disciples sent by the Lord to preach, and does he read it diligently and understand it, and does he know that he has been promoted to the ecclesiastical ministry on the model of the seventy disciples?

96. Whether he has the Roman Penitential, or the one published by Bishop Theodore, or the one by the venerable Bede, so that he may question one confessing and impose the manner of penance on one who has confessed according to what is written there?

END OF THE INVESTIGATION.

It is fitting that these things, which as we explained above must be summarily investigated, be strengthened by canonical authority.

C. 1. THAT THE STATUTES OF THE CANONS BE KEPT BY ALL WITHOUT PREJUDICE.
From the Council of Meaux, which was held in the times of Charles the Younger, in the year of the Lord's Incarnation 845, 5 days before the Kalends of July, Indiction 10, tit. 10.

That the statutes of the canons are to be kept by all without prejudice, and no one is to judge in ecclesiastical actions or judgments by his own sense, but each is to be led by the authority of the same statutes. Also, in expounding or preaching the divine Scriptures, each is to follow the sense of the holy Catholic and most proven Fathers, in whose writings, as St. Jerome says, the truth of faith does not waver.

C. 2. WHAT SORT OF MINISTER A BISHOP IS TO KEEP NEAR HIMSELF.
From the same Council, tit. 11.

That each bishop to the best of his ability is to strive to have near himself such a man as may assiduously instruct and inform the priests of the people in faith and in the observance of God's mandates, as also in the doctrine of preaching, according to a most sincere and pure sense of the Catholic Fathers, lest the house of the living God, which is the Church, remain without the lamp of God's word. But let him also be such as is not troubled by the love of money, or whose wicked conduct and reprehensible way of life render him contemptible. So it is that, when Moses lodged the complaint in the sight of God that he could not bear so great a burden as had been imposed on him, he heard from the Lord: "Gather for me seventy men from the elders of Israel, men already known to you as elders and teachers of the people, and I will take away some of your spirit and give it to them instead, so that they may bear with you the burden of the people, and not you alone be burdened (cf. Num. 11:16–17)." What do we accept in Moses, if not the highest priesthood? What in the seventy men, if not the priests? And what the Lord takes from the spirit of Moses and gives to them shows manifestly that those who are called by the bishop in the sight of God to bear with him the burden of the people must feel the same as the bishop and want the same things and cooperate with their whole strength in bearing the burden shared out to them. Indeed, this is what it means to say that they receive not another spirit, but that of Moses himself.

C. 3. ON THE SAME MATTER.
From the synodal Chapters of Emperor Charles, tit. 103.

And so, we admonish the bishops that, either personally, or through their vicars, they proclaim persistently the nourishment of the divine word to the people. As Blessed Gregory says, a priest arouses the wrath of the hidden Judge against himself, if he proceeds without the sound of preaching.

C. 4. THAT IT IS TO BE ASKED OF THE KING THAT BISHOPS, AT A SUITABLE TIME, MAY BE FREE TO APPLY THEMSELVES TO THE MINISTRY ENTRUSTED TO THEM.
From the aforesaid Council.

That the royal magnificence may grant a more unrestricted liberty to bishops to carry out their ministry within the parishes than they had formerly because of the various troubles. But the same bishops are not to turn this free time conceded to them to their own pleasures, but to divine and useful business, so that, as they apply themselves to preaching, correction, and confirmation, what had been formerly neglected throughout the parishes may in the future be emended with care.

c. 5. THAT THE BISHOPS ARE NOT TO NEGLECT THE PEOPLE ENTRUSTED TO THEM FOR THE SAKE OF THEIR OWN TRANQUILITY.
From the same Council.

Care is to be taken in advance that bishops do not, for the sake of their own tranquility, withdraw to more remote places, neglecting their ministry, and abandoning their cities. Instead, either they are to travel around their parishes and exercise their office efficaciously, or they are to reside conscientiously in accordance with the canons in their cities with their spiritual children. They are also to compel the priests entrusted to them to be equipped, in accordance with their ministry, with doctrine, chastity, sobriety, and hospitality.

c. 6. OF BISHOPS WHO RARELY OR NEVER VISIT PERSONALLY THE PEOPLE ENTRUSTED TO THEM.
From the same Council.

That the reprehensible – indeed, damnable – custom of some bishops be entirely corrected, who rarely or never visit the people entrusted to them personally, in accordance with the evangelical, apostolic, and canonical order, since the Lord says: "I have made you a watchman to the house of Israel: and you shall hear the word out of my mouth, and shall tell it to them from me (Ez. 3:17)," and the rest that the divine speech comprises.

c. 7. THAT THE BISHOP WALK THROUGH HIS DIOCESE.
From the Council of Braga.

It pleased all bishops and was agreed that, as bishops go about their several churches and dioceses, they first examine how the clerics perform the order of baptism and of the mass, and how they carry out all the offices in church. And if they find that they are rightly done, let them give thanks to God; if that is not the case, they are to teach the ignorant and enjoin this in every way that, as the ancient canons command, twenty days before baptism, catechumens are to have recourse to the purgation of exorcism; in those twenty days, they are to be taught especially the Creed, which is "I believe in God."

WHAT IT IS NECESSARY TO TEACH TO LAY PEOPLE.

And so, after the bishops have examined or taught their priests, on another day, after summoning the people of the same church, they are to teach them to flee the error of idols, or diverse crimes, that is, homicide, adultery, perjury, false witnesses, and the other death-dealing sins, and that they are not to do unto others what they do not wish to be done to themselves, and to believe in the resurrection of all men and the day of Judgment, on which each will receive according to his works. And so afterwards, let the bishop proceed from that church to another one.

c. 8. THAT THE BISHOP GO ABOUT HIS PARISH WITH A FEW PEOPLE.
From the Council of Toledo, c. 5.

When a bishop visits his diocese, let him be burdensome to none because of the multitude, nor let him travel with a retinue of more than fifty people, nor have license to remain in each basilica more than one day.

c. 9. THAT IF A BISHOP IS UNABLE TO FULFIL THIS, HE IS TO SEND HIS VICARS.
From the same Council, c. 6.

But if a bishop should be unable to carry this out, either due to illness, or because of the press of other business, he is to send priests or deacons of proven life, who may inquire into the income of the basilicas, and their repairs, and the manner of life of those who minister in them.

c. 10. THAT BISHOPS VISIT THEIR DIOCESE.
From the synodal Chapters of Emperor Charles.

That bishops are to go around the parishes entrusted to them and there make careful effort to inquire regarding incest, parricides, adulteries, and other evils which are contrary to God and which Christians are to avoid. They are also to take care to emend the churches that require it within their parishes. They are to do this with the greatest care both with regard to the churches given by us as benefice and in those of others.

c. 11. THAT A BISHOP IS TO RECEIVE ONLY TWO SHILLINGS WHEN HE GOES AROUND HIS PARISH.
From the Council of Braga.

It pleased that none of the bishops, as he visits his diocese, take anything from the churches apart from the mark of esteem for his chair, that is, two shillings. He must not require the third part of any offering of the people in parish churches, but that third part is to be kept for the lamps of the church or its upkeep, and an account is to be made for it to the bishop every year. For if the bishop takes that third part, he is stealing the church's lights and mended roofs.

c. 12. ON BISHOPS WHO REQUIRE PAYMENT FOR SERVICE FROM PARISHES WHICH THEY HAVE NOT VISITED.

From the Council held at Tribur, in the times of King Arnulf, c. 26.

The complaint of the people has been reported before the holy Synod that there are some bishops who are unwilling to go around their parishes throughout the year preaching and confirming, but who yet require that those who are obliged to make ready the lodgings, which they would have used if they had come, pay some other sum. This double infamy, of negligence and avarice, greatly horrified the holy Synod. And so, they established that no one exercise any further this device of cupidity, and that bishops be more solicitous about visiting their flocks.

c. 13. ON THE SAME MATTER.

From the synodal Chapters of Emperor Charles, c. 94.

Having been admonished by us not to be a burden to the people by occasion of their preaching or confirming, the bishops promised that they were willing to avoid this henceforth, and that, insofar as the possibility offers itself, they would carry out their ministry at a time when their coming, insofar as they can, will not be inopportune or burdensome to those to whom they can be of use.

c. 14. ON THE IMMUNITY OF CHURCHES.

From the same Capitulary, tit. 103.

It is to be announced to all, and to be ordained by our envoys, that all churches and priests are to remain under the immunity, privilege, ordinance, and disposition of the bishops of the several parishes within which they lie, in accordance with canonical authority.

c. 15. THAT ALL PARISHES ARE WITHIN THE POWER OF THE BISHOPS.

From the Council of Orléans, tit. 13.

It has pleased that all basilicas, which have been built in the different places or are daily being built, according to the rule of the earlier canons, are to lie in the power of the bishop in whose territory they are placed.

c. 16. ON PARISHES.

From the Council of Chalcedon, c. 17.

The rural parishes and property of each Church shall remain firmly with those bishops who are known to hold them, particularly if the bishops obtained them without violence and have ruled them under their governance for thirty years. But if within thirty years there has been, or is, any altercation concerning them, it is licit for those who assert that they are harmed by this to move a suit before the Synod of the province.

c. 17. WHAT SORTS OF MINISTERS BISHOPS ARE TO LEAVE BEHIND IN CITIES.
From the Capitularies of Charles the Younger, tit. 7.

Because bishops, who are busy with our and their own common needs of the Church and the whole kingdom, are not able by themselves to look after all that is perpetrated within the bounds of their parish, we establish that, whenever bishops leave their city, each is to leave behind in his city helpers who may do all these things most prudently in their city, so that the poor redeemed by Christ's blood may always find someone present in the city from whom to receive a response and consolation. But in villages and vills far removed from the city, let each bishop establish priests who are respected, cautious, and prudently temperate in their manner of life, who may carry out in his stead what is established above, and to whom other junior and less cautious priests may refer their cause.

c. 18. ON THE THIRTY-YEAR PRESCRIPTION.
From the letter of Gelasius.

It also pleased that it be added that if any bishops claim at law (far be it!) the properties of the Church and even dioceses which are in the possession of other bishops, the thirty-years law has excluded their claim, because the authority of the princes our sons has decreed that it is not licit for anyone to appeal for that which the legally prescribed time has precluded.

c. 19. ON GOODS POSSESSED FOR THIRTY YEARS.
From the Capitularies of Emperor Louis, tit. 7.

As for the goods of churches, which have been in their possession for a period of thirty years without any challenge, testimonies are not to be received, but they are to be held in the same way as goods belonging to the lord's treasury are held.

c. 20. ON THE ATTESTATION OF TIMES.
From the same, c. 9.

If someone says and proves that land has been violently taken from him by another before the period of thirty years is complete and demonstrates that the property was seized, and is able to make his claim, let it be restored to the party of the claimant. But if thirty years have gone by since it was said to have been seized by anyone, and its restitution was not sought earlier, let him know that nothing is to be restored to him. And after a few words:

c. 21. ALSO, ON THE SAME MATTER.

And because it is suitable that the law provide for all those things that pertain to the tranquility of all, it will not be licit henceforth for anyone to move any suits whatsoever regarding any matters which were not decided within thirty years. It is clear to all that the said number of years can suffice for anyone to claim and receive what was due to him.

c. 22. ALSO, ON THE SAME MATTER.

If anyone has had someone else's tenant in his possession for thirty years, he can claim him as his own. If he has been found within thirty years, he is to be reclaimed by his master with the children due to him and all his personal property. But if he has died, the master is to receive his personal property. On a female tenant. But if a female tenant has remained within another's possession for twenty years, she is not to be claimed by her former master. Two thirds of the offspring are to follow the male tenant, one third the female. But if the offspring were born within the twenty years when the tenant still belonged to her master, they are not to be denied to the claimants, because so it is provided in the modern laws. Reasonably, so that there be no break-up of a marriage, we command that the master of the male tenant not refuse a substitute woman with a third part of her offspring.

c. 23. ON THE CONSECRATION OF A CHURCH.
From the Council of Worms.

It has pleased that, whenever a bishop is invited by any of the faithful to consecrate churches, he is not to require any gift from the founder as if his due. But if the latter should offer something of his own wish, let it not be rejected. And yet, let each bishop remember not to dedicate a church, unless he first receive an endowment of the basilica and service for it, confirmed by a charter of donation. Indeed, this temerity is not a light fault, if a church is consecrated as if it were a private house without [provision for] lamps, or without the material sustenance of those who are to serve there.

c. 24. ON THE LIBERTY OF CHURCHES.
From the Capitularies, tit. 85.

It has been ordered that an entire manse is to be granted to each church without any servitude. The priests established in these churches are not to perform any service, apart from the ecclesiastical one, for their tithes, or the offerings of the faithful, or the houses, or forecourts, or gardens situated near the church, nor for the aforesaid manse. If the priests have anything more, let them provide the due service to their superiors for it.

c. 25. ON THE TERRITORY OF CHURCHES.
From the same Capitulary, c. 117.

That each church is to have a territory from whose villages it receives tithes.

c. 26. ON NEW CHURCHES.
Cap. 87.

It has been established regarding new villages and new churches, that is, those newly constituted in them, that the tithes from the same villages be conferred on the same churches.

c. 27. ALSO.
From the same, c. 5.

Anyone who should wish to build a church on his property is to have license to do so if he has the consent and will of the bishop. And yet, provisions are to be made most thoroughly that the other older churches do not lose their right or tithe for this reason, but that it is always paid to the older churches.

c. 28. ALSO, ON THE MANSE OF THE CHURCH.
From the same Capitulary.

As to the one manse given to the church, from which, against the statutes, some men exact service, the count or the envoys, by their law, are to make whoever has been accused for this cause return whatever has been taken from the priests.

c. 29. ON THE SAME MATTER.
Also, from the Synod of Meaux, c. 63.

That, according to canonical authority and the constitution of the lord Emperor Louis as to a church's field, manse, and slaves, which he established in his own Capitularies, if anyone has granted something to a church for a place of burial, he is not to compel any of the priests to pay any rent from the tithes and offerings of the faithful, nor is anyone of any order or dignity to take anything from it or exact any temporal restitution. If he has done this, he is to be deprived of communion until satisfaction, and he is to be compelled by the royal power to make reparation lawfully for this.

c. 30. ALSO, ON THE PRIVILEGE OF CHURCHES.

Anciently established churches are not to be deprived of tithes, or of any possession, so that these may be given to new oratories.

c. 31. ON DOUBTFUL CHURCHES OR ALTARS, AND THAT SUPERFLUOUS ALTARS BE THROWN OUT OF A CHURCH.

Cap. 65.

That churches or altars whose consecration is doubtful are to be consecrated, and superfluous altars are to be destroyed in the church.

c. 32. ON ECCLESIASTICAL HONOUR.

Cap. 142.

That bishops are to define what honour priests are to give to their [secular] superiors for their churches.

c. 33. THAT THE ENDOWMENTS OF ALL CHURCHES PERTAIN TO THE BISHOP.

From the Council of Toledo, c. 19.

Many people, against the provisions of the canons, demand that the churches which they have built be consecrated in such a manner that the endowment which they have conferred on the same church not be thought to pertain to the bishop's disposition. That this has been done in the past is displeasing, and it is forbidden to be done in the future, but everything is to pertain to the bishop's disposition and power, according to the ancient custom.

c. 34. THAT CHURCHES ARE TO BE RESTORED AND SHOW OBEDIENCE TO THE BISHOP.

From the letter of Pope Gelasius.

It is fitting to make four portions from both the income and the offerings of the faithful, insofar as the capability of each church allows, as was formerly and reasonably decreed. The first of these is for the bishop, the second for the clerics, the third for the poor, and the fourth is to be applied to the fabric. Concerning these, just as it is in the bishop's interest to expend the entire mentioned amount on the ministers of the church, so a cleric knows that he is not to ask with insolence for an amount greater than has been allotted to him. As for the resources which are to be dedicated to ecclesiastical buildings, let the manifest restoration of holy places teach that it has been truly expended to this end, since it would be an offence against divine law if, while the sacred buildings remain destitute, the bishop should convert the funds meant for this purpose to his own gain.

c. 35. ON THE SAME MATTER.
From the letter of Pope Simplicius, c. 2.

From the income of the church and the offerings of the faithful, only one portion of these is to be remitted to the bishop; two are to be given to the church's fabric and for alms to pilgrims and the poor; and the last is to be shared among clerics according to the merits of each.

c. 36. ON THE HONOUR OF GOD'S CHURCH.
From the synodal Chapters, tit. 68.

It has pleased us to admonish that each bishop see to it, within his parish, that the Church of God have its honour, and altars are venerated according to their dignity, and the house of God and the sacred altars are not accessible to dogs; and that vessels consecrated to God are held in great veneration; and that the sanctified sacrifices are gathered with great diligence by those who are worthy.

c. 37. ALSO, ON THE RESTORATION OF CHURCHES.
From the Capitularies of Emperor Louis, c. 40.

As to work on, or the restoration of, churches, the count and bishop or abbot, together with our envoy, whom they have chosen for this, are to consider that each of them accept only as much to work and restore as he is known to have of the possessions of the churches. Similarly, our vassals either are to accept in common as much of the work as they have of ecclesiastical possessions, or each of them severally according to the quantity which he holds, or, if it has been agreed among them that they give silver for the work to be done, they are to pay in silver according to the estimate of the work, with which payment the rector of the church may hire workers and buy the materials for the said restoration. And he who has neglected to give ninths and tenths, first he must restore them with his law, and, in addition, he is to pay our ban, so that, so chastised, let him beware lest, by frequent repetition, he lose his benefice.

c. 38. ON THE SAME MATTER.
Also, from the Capitulary, tit. 22.

As to the works for the restoration of churches, whether in doing it or contracting for it, let the episcopal will be followed. Yet, let it remain firm that, as it has often been commanded by us, in no wise is the one or the other to be paid out of the portions of the churches. And let it be known to all that whoever has acted negligently in this matter, and is found to be negligent in this before us, we will that he undergo all that we ordained in our Capitulary on this matter with the common counsel of our faithful subjects.

c. 39. ON PLACES FORMERLY SACRED.
From the same, c. 54.

As to the places that were formerly sacred and which now are filthy with dirt, let them be restored to their ancient state insofar as possible.

c. 40. ON CHURCHES THAT HAVE BEEN DESTROYED.
Also, c. 3.

As to churches that have been destroyed, let the bishops and our envoys make inquisition as to whether they were destroyed by negligence or impossibility [of supporting them]; and where negligence has been found, those who ought to have restored them are to be compelled by episcopal authority to make amends. But if it has happened by impossibility, so that either there are more than are needed, or they were of greater size than can be restored from the possessions pertaining to them, let the bishop find a way as to how they may be suitably repaired and continue to exist.

c. 41. ON THE SAME MATTER.
From the synodal Chapters of Charles the Younger, c. 62.

As for the slaves of churches, to whatever powers they may be subject (regarding whom there is no better custom or more devout provision from the time and command of the Lord Louis, or certainly of Lord Charles, or even of Pepin), they are to be allowed without trouble to serve the said church for at least twenty days each year to rebuild its ruins. But where there is a broader provision or a better custom as to this, it is not to fail because of this consideration of necessity of ours.

c. 42. ON THE SAME MATTER.
Also, from the Chapters of Louis, Admonition to the bishops, c. 5.

Your Solicitude is likewise to be vigilant lest the churches entrusted to priests be neglected by them as to their repairs and lamps according to the resources available. And just as you forbid others to take anything from the manses given for the lamps of a church, so you and your archdeacons are to provide an example for others by taking nothing from the same manses. But let them rather be allowed to serve that for which they were given, so that all, as we said, may by your authority and effort go to the restoration of churches and to their lamps.

c. 43. ON TITHES.
Capitularies, c. 142.

That how tithes are spent by priests be in the power of the bishop.

c. 44. ON NINTHS AND TENTHS.
From c. 157.

That those who hold benefices of churches are to give a ninth and a tenth from them to the church whose possessions they are; those who hold such a benefice are to work it for a share of the fruits and must give tithes from their portion to their proper priest.

c. 44b. WHEN SOMEONE HAS WORKED NEW LAND TWO, THREE, OR FOUR MILES INTO UNTILLED LAND.

That new fields, which are made near cultivated fields, are to pay tithe to the ancient church. And if any worthy person has worked some new land more than four or five miles into untilled land, and he has built a church there with his bishop's consent, after the consecration of the church, he is to provide a priest, and he is to confer the tithe from the work there on the same church for the support of the priest.

c. 45. ALSO, ON TITHES.
From the same, c. 37.

Those who, after the very frequent admonition and preaching of priests, have neglected to give their tithes are to be excommunicated. But we do not wish them to be bound by oath because of the danger of perjury.

c. 46. Also, on ninths and tenths.
From the same, c. 21.

As to ninths and tenths, regarding which both our progenitor and we have made admonition frequently and in diverse assemblies and have ordained by our Capitularies how these are to be observed, we will and command that a ninth and a tenth be paid faithfully and fully by all on all produce, and on wine and hay. But as to the tithe on fodder, the custom that formerly obtained is to be observed by all. Yet, if there is any bishop who wishes to accept silver for this, let it remain in his power according to any agreement reached between him and the one who has to pay it.

c. 47. ALSO, ON NINTHS AND TENTHS.
From the same, c. 5, bk. 5.

As for those who already for many years have neglected to pay ninths and tens in part or in total, we will that they be constrained by our envoys, according to the earlier custom, to pay the ninth and tenth of one year with their law, and, additionally, our ban. And let this be announced to them, that whoever repeats this negligence is to know that he will lose the benefice from which he is obliged to have paid this ninth and tenth.

c. 48. ALSO, ON THE SAME MATTER.
Cap. 6.

Whoever has appropriated a tithe from the church to which by justice it is to be given, and has presumptuously given it to another church either for gifts, or friendship, or any other reason, is to be distrained by the count or our envoy so that he restores the amount of the same tithe with his law.

c. 49. ALSO, ON THE SAME MATTER.
Cap. 7.

As to the tithes which the people are unwilling to give unless they are bought off from it in some way, it is to be forbidden by bishops that this be done. If any contemner has been found, who is willing to hear neither the bishop, nor the count, and he is our man, he is to be compelled to come into our presence; but the others are to be distrained so that they return to the Church unwillingly what they neglected to give willingly.

c. 50. ALSO, ON THE SAME MATTER.
Cap. 9

As for those who have neglected to cultivate the fields of the demesne so as not to pay the ninth and tenth from them, and for this reason accept another's lands for cultivation, we will that they pay the fruits of three years with their law. And if anyone has been a contemner of the count or our envoys in this matter, he is to be compelled by sureties to come to the palace.

c. 51. ALSO, ON THE SAME MATTER.
From the Council of Meaux, c. 62.

Those who are obliged to pay the ninths and tenths from ecclesiastical possessions and to restore and repair the roof of a church according to ancient authority and custom, and not only neglect this, but also dismiss it in contempt and permit the clerics to be reduced to nothing from hunger and penury and church buildings to fall into dissolution, are to be severed from ecclesiastical communion until they strive to emend with diligence what they neglected through inaction. If they repeat this again, after satisfaction for excommunication, compelled by royal power, in accordance with the ancient pronouncement of the law: He who neglects the rent is to lose the field.

c. 52. ALSO, ON TITHES.
From the Chapters of Charles.

As to the tithes, where baptismal churches were established in ancient times and devotion was done, they are to be given in every way in accordance with what the bishop of the same parish has ordained. And if, by the donations of kings and other good God-fearing men, other possessions have been given to episcopates or monasteries, and from such possessions tithes were given in ancient times to those same prior churches, that ancient donation or offering is to remain firm and stable. Yet, as we said above, the one who appears to be in the possession of such properties is to pay the tithes as to them.

c. 53. tHAT NO HAY OR WHEAT OR WINE IS TO BE DEPOSITED IN THE CHURCH.
From the same, c. 144.

That no priest presume to deposit wheat or hay in the church.

c. 54. ON THE SAME MATTER.
From the sayings of St. Augustine, bishop.

In an oratory, no one is to do anything other than what it was made for and from which it took its name. And if perhaps, even apart from the established hours, there are people who have time and wish to pray in it, those who believe that it should be used for some other purpose are not to be an impediment to them.

c. 54b. THE SAME, ELSEWHERE.

In the oratory, nothing at all is to be done, except for what pertains to the practice of prayer and psalmody in the worship of God so that the activities carried out there will accord entirely with the name of the place.

c. 55. ALSO, ON THE SAME MATTER.
From the sayings of St. Benedict.

An oratory is to be that which it is called, nor is anything else to be done or performed in it.

c. 56. THAT NO ONE PRESUME TO HOLD BANQUETS IN A CHURCH.
From the Council of Carthage.

That no bishops or clerics are to hold banquets in a church, except perhaps if, by necessity of hospitality, those passing through a community take a meal there; as far as possible, people are to be forbidden from this kind of banquet.

c. 57. AS ABOVE.
From the Council of Laodicea.

It is not suitable to hold love-feasts in domiciles or churches, nor to eat within them or set up couches.

c. 58. THAT NO ONE PRESUME TO SELL WINE IN CHURCH.
From the Council of Tours.

It has been reported to the holy Synod that some priests establish taverns in the churches entrusted to them, which is an offence against divine law. Through tradesmen, they sell wine in them, or allow others to do so, and where only prayers, the divine word, and the praise of God ought to resound, there revelries and drunkenness occur, there laughter, clapping, and shameful words, there brawls and contentions result. How contrary this is to God, the Lord Jesus shows, who, when he found buyers, sellers, and moneychangers sitting in the Temple, made a whip out of cords and expelled them all from the Temple (cf. Jn. 2:13–17). Indeed, if he cast outside those things which were seen to be sold lawfully within the Temple and were bought so that they might be offered to the Lord in the same Temple, what do you think he would do as to such a pestiferous presumption and contempt for God? And if not the priests alone, but also all clerics, are instructed not to enter taverns, who can bear to hear that the churches of God are made into taverns? Hence, the Synod entirely forbids that henceforth this be done in any way. If it is done, the priest is to be deposed, and laymen are to be deprived of communion and expelled from the Church, which they have dishonoured.

c. 59. MEANWHILE IT IS NOT TO BE TAKEN LIGHTLY THAT THE LORD SAYS: "MY HOUSE IS A HOUSE OF PRAYER (IS. 56:7; MT. 21:13)."

For if the house of God is called a house of prayer, then it must be what it is called, nor is anything else to be done or stored in there. Indeed, where the body of the Lord is consecrated, where it is not doubted that the angels are present, where the relics of the saints are stored and venerated, let nothing dishonourable be seen, which may offend the eyes of those who come to pray. Let nothing be seen there which pertains to temporal gain, but all things are to be holy and pure and pertaining only to the ministry of the Church.

c. 60. THAT THE ALTARS ARE TO BE COVERED WITH THE CLEANEST LINENS.
From the Council of Reims, c. 5.

It is to be observed that Christ's table, that is, the altar, where the body of the Lord is consecrated, where his blood is shed, where the relics of the saints are stored, where the prayers and vows of the people are offered by the priest in the sight of God, is to be honoured with all veneration. It is to be covered with the cleanest linens and palls, and nothing is to be placed on it apart from the reliquaries with the relics of the saints and the four Gospels. At the end of the mass, the chalice and the book of the sacraments and the priestly vestments are to be stored in a clean place under lock and key.

c. 61. ON PREPARING THE ALTAR LINENS.
From the Capitularies.

That priests are to make known to the women throughout their parishes that they are to prepare the linens for the altar.

c. 62. THAT NO PRIEST RECEIVE ANOTHER'S PARISHIONER AT MASS.
From the Capitularies.

That no priest is to dare to receive at mass another's parishioner, unless he is travelling, or he has a legal proceeding there. (As to another's parishioner, see bk. 2, c. 421.)

c. 63. ON THE OFFERINGS OF THE FAITHFUL AT THE ALTAR.
From the Capitulary mentioned above.

If the faithful offer something at the altar, it is to be received by the minister and placed behind the altar.

c. 64. THAT NOTHING ELSE IS TO BE OFFERED IN THE LORD'S SACRIFICE APART FROM WHAT THE LORD ESTABLISHED.
In the Canons of the Apostles, tit. 3.

If any bishop or priest offers on the altar in the sacrifice anything other than what the Lord ordained, that is, either honey, or milk, or beer instead of wine, or some sorts of confections, or birds, or any animals, or pulses, he is to be deposed from his degree as one who acts against the Lord's constitution.

c. 65. WHAT SORTS OF THINGS ARE TO BE OFFERED AT THE ALTAR, NOT FOR THE SACRIFICE, BUT FOR SIMPLE BLESSING.
In the Canons of the Apostles, tit. 4.

It is not licit to offer anything at the altar other than new ears of wheat, and grapes, and oil, and thymiama, that is, incense, at the time when the oblation is celebrated.

c. 66. THAT THOSE THINGS WHICH CANNOT BE OFFERED IN CHURCHES ARE TO BE BROUGHT BY THE FAITHFUL TO THE HOUSES OF PRIESTS.
As above, c. 5.

All other fruits or first-fruits are to be sent to the house of the bishop or priest, nor are they to be offered at the altar. But it is established that they are to be divided among bishops, priests, deacons, and other clerics.

c. 67. WHAT IS TO BE OFFERED AT THE LORD'S SACRIFICE.
From the Council of Worms, c. 39.

When the Master of Truth commended to his disciples the true sacrifice of our salvation, we know that he only offered bread and the chalice in this sacrament, and so nothing else is to be offered, apart from bread and wine mixed with water. Indeed, the Lord's chalice is to be offered mixed with wine and water because we see that in the water the people are understood, but the blood of Christ is understood in the wine. Hence, when the water is mixed with the wine, the people are gathered into one with Christ, and the community of believers is connected to and joined with him in whom it believes. This connection and joining of water and wine is so mixed in the Lord's chalice that the mixture can never be separated. For if one offers only the wine, the blood of Christ begins to be without us. But if the water is alone, the people begin to be without Christ. Indeed, the Lord's chalice cannot consist in water only or in wine only, but each is to be mixed with the other. (See c. 348.)

c. 68. ON THE LORD'S CHALICE.
From the Council of Reims, tit. 8.

That the Lord's chalice along with the paten, if not from gold, is to be made at least from silver. Nor are priests to allow their avarice to persuade them to plead poverty or impossibility, since one part of all things pertaining to a church is to be spent on the fabric of the same church. The people are also to be admonished to offer something as gifts to the Lord (cf. Num. 31:50), as we read that the ancient people did under Moses in the Lord's tabernacle. But if someone is so very poor, he is to have at least a chalice made of tin. But the chalice is not to be made from copper or brass, because on account of the property of wine these produce rust, which provokes vomit. But no one is to presume to sing [mass] with a wooden chalice.

c. 69. ON THE LORD'S CORPORAL.
From the Council as above.

The corporal, on which the sacred victim is immolated, is to be of the cleanest and purest linen, nor is a more or less precious material of another kind to be mixed with it because the Lord's body in the tomb was not wrapped in silks, but only in a clean shroud. The corporal is never to remain on the altar, but let it be kept either in the book of the sacraments, or stored with the chalice and paten in the cleanest of places. When it is washed by the priest, deacon, or subdeacon, first, let it be washed in church, in a place and vessel prepared for the purpose, since it was filled with the body and blood of the Lord. Afterwards, let it be prepared by the launderer in a clean place.

c. 70. ON THE EUCHARIST.
From the synodal Chapters, c. 155.

That the priest always have the Eucharist ready so that, if anyone becomes ill, or a child is ill, he may immediately give him communion, lest he die without communion.

c. 71. ON THE SAME MATTER.
From the Council of Tours.

That each priest is to have a pyx, or a vessel worthy of such a great sacrament, where the body of the Lord may be diligently reserved as a viaticum for those who are departing the world. The sacred oblation is to be dipped into the blood of Christ, so that the priest may say truly to the infirm, "May the body and blood of Christ be of profit to you." It is to be always kept locked on the altar because of mice and nefarious men, and it is always to be changed from third day to third day, that is, it is to be received by the priest, and another one, consecrated on that day, is to be put in its place, lest perhaps it become mouldy (far be it!), if it is reserved too long.

c. 72. ON THE OFFERINGS, THAT THEY BE RENEWED FROM SATURDAY TO SATURDAY.
Also, as above.

It has also seemed fitting to add that the oblations which are offered on the altar be always renewed from Saturday to Saturday because the loaves of proposition which used to be placed on the Lord's table were always changed from Sabbath to Sabbath (cf. Lev. 24:8–9).

c. 73. THAT THE CHRISM BE ALWAYS UNDER LOCK AND KEY.
Also, from the same.

Furthermore, it is also to be observed in every way that the sacred chrism and the consecrated oil be always kept under lock and key, lest that by which we are incorporated into Christ, and with which all the faithful are sanctified, and with which kings and priests are anointed, be touched by some faithless or unclean person, or some perfidious person steal it to subvert the judgment of God, which we know from experience to have occurred.

c. 74. IF THE PRIEST HAS GIVEN THE CHRISM FOR THE SUBVERSION OF JUDGMENT.
From the Capitularies, tit. 55.

That a priest who has given chrism for the subversion of judgment, after he has been deposed from his degree, is to lose a hand.

c. 75. THAT NO PRIEST GIVE ANY GIFT FOR THE CHRISM.
From the Council of Meaux, c. 45.

That none of the bishops, or any ecclesiastical minister, accept any gift for the sacred chrism, neither money, nor trifling presents, which are exacted against all order from priests by the bishops' servants. Yet it is fitting for priests at an appropriate time to visit and show reverence to their bishops with voluntary gifts.

c. 76. THAT EACH PRIEST BRING TWO AMPOULES TO THE CITY ON HOLY THURSDAY.
From the Chapters, tit. 156.

That a priest, on Holy Thursday, is to bring with himself two ampoules, one for chrism, another for the oil to anoint the catechumens or the sick, according to the Apostle's statement, that "when someone becomes ill, let him bring in the Church's priests (Jas. 5:14)."

c. 77. ON PRIESTS WHO ARE FAR AWAY, THAT ONE OUT OF EIGHT OR TEN COME ON HOLY THURSDAY, WHO MAY BRING THE CHRISM TO THE OTHERS.
Also, as above, c. 93.

As for the priests who were accustomed to come to the cities on Holy Thursday in order to receive the chrism, it is approved that, of those who are far away, one out of eight or ten be chosen by the bishop who will receive the chrism and bring it diligently to his associates. But those who dwell no more than four or five miles from the city are to come to receive the chrism personally in the usual way.

But for the sake of learning, let them be summoned to the city at another non-Lenten time for the benefit of the people entrusted to them.

c. 78. THAT NO PRIEST IS TO RECEIVE THE CHRISM FROM ANOTHER BISHOP.
From the Council of Vaison, c. 3.

Throughout the several territories, priests or ministers, as the solemnity of Easter approaches, are to seek the chrism each year from their own bishops, and not from closer ones as it pleases them, and not through any ecclesiastic whatsoever, but, if, by any chance, the ministers have some necessity or business, through a subdeacon, because it is dishonourable to entrust the highest things to inferiors. But it is best that he receive it who is going to use it by administering it, but if something stands in the way, at least the one whose office it is to set the sanctuary in order and receive the sacramental objects.

c. 79. THAT NO MINISTER GO OUT WITHOUT CHRISM.

None of the priests who has received the office of baptizing must ever go forth without chrism, because among us it has pleased to be anointed with chrism once in baptism. But as for him who, in baptism, because of any necessity, was not anointed with chrism, the bishop will be reminded at confirmation.

c. 80. ON SACRED FONTS.
As above.

A priest, who has been unable to have stone fonts, is to have a suitable vessel exclusively for the administration of baptism, which is never to be taken outside the church. Similarly, for the washing of the corporal and altar palls, let there be appropriate vessels in which nothing else is done.

c. 81. THAT NO PRIEST EVER PRESUME TO SING MASS WITHOUT PRIESTLY VESTMENTS.
From the Council of Reims.

That no priest presume to celebrate mass without amice, alb, stole, fanon, and chasuble. These sacred vestments are to be absolutely clean and are to be kept in a clean place within the church, and a priest is never to exit the church wearing these because it is forbidden by divine law.

c. 82. THAT SACRED VESSELS OR VESTMENTS NOT BE GIVEN AS PLEDGES.
As above, c. 11.

That no priest presume to give a chalice, or paten, or altar pall, or priestly vestment, or a book as a pledge to a tavern-keeper or tradesman, or to any lay man or woman, unless for a most just and pressing necessity. Such is the holiness of the holy ministry that, with regard to an understanding of the deeper mystery, the Lord through the Prophet even forbade that the priest proceed among the people in his vestments, but, as he returns from speaking with God, he must leave them within those sacred places (cf. Ez. 44:19). And how much less ought he, to whom it is forbidden by the sacred canons to enter taverns to drink or to defile things sanctified to the sacred ministry by contact with unclean things, to offer them in pledge? Thus, the holy pope and martyr Stephen taught St. Hilary in his decretals.

FROM HERE ON THE LIFE OF THE PRIEST.

c. 83. THAT THE BISHOP HAVE A LITTLE DWELLING NOT FAR FROM THE CHURCH.
From the Council of Carthage.

That the bishop have a little dwelling not far from the church.

c. 84. ON THE SAME MATTER, THAT PRIESTS NOT AT ALL BE ALLOWED TO LODGE AS GUESTS ANYWHERE.
From the Council of Meaux, c. 36.

That priests not at all be allowed, or in any way are they themselves to presume, to lodge as guests anywhere, but they are to see that they are assiduously near their churches in order to perform the sacred mysteries or ministries for the faithful. Hence, they are not to be permitted to live elsewhere. Neither are women to have any dwelling whatsoever in those places to which the priests have any recourse. If they give little weight to observing this, they are to be judged as if transgressors and as having acted against these prohibitions.

c. 85. ON THE INCONTINENCE OF PRIESTS.
From the Council of Neocaesarea, c. 1.

If a priest takes a wife, he is to be removed from his order; but if he commits fornication or adultery, he is to be struck even further and brought to penance. In a similar way, a deacon, too, if he has succumbed to the same sin, is to be withdrawn from the order of ministry.

c. 86. ON THE SAME MATTER.
From the same Council.

If a priest had committed a carnal sin and has confessed that he had sinned before his ordination, he is not to consecrate the oblations, but he may remain in his other functions on account of the usefulness of his zeal. But if he has not confessed and cannot be openly charged, he is to be left to the power of his own judgment.

c. 87. ON THE SAME MATTER.
In the Canon of the Apostles.

A priest or deacon who is caught in fornication, or perjury, or theft, or homicide is to be deposed, but he is not to be deprived of communion. As Scripture says: "The Lord does not judge twice in the same matter (Nahum 1:9)."

c. 88. ALSO, ON THE SAME MATTER.

The priests of the Lord and the deacons, or those who handle the sacraments, as keepers of chastity, are to abstain from their wives.

c. 89. ON THE SAME MATTER.

Moreover, the Church in every respect is to hold what is worthy, chaste, and honourable so that priests and deacons not have intercourse with their wives because they are busy with the needs of their daily ministry. For it is written: "Be holy, as I, the Lord your God, am holy (Lev. 11:44–45)."

c. 90. ALSO, ON THE SAME MATTER.

As to priests and deacons, it is the discipline of the divine laws that incontinent persons placed in such offices are to be deprived of all ecclesiastical honour, nor are they to be admitted to such ministry, which continence alone can suitably fulfil.

c. 91. ALSO, ON THE SAME MATTER.
From the Council of Nicaea, c. 3.

The great Synod has entirely forbidden any bishop, priest, deacon, or anyone of the clergy whatever, to be allowed to have a woman living with him, unless perhaps a mother, or sister, or aunt, or only such persons who are beyond all suspicion.

c. 92. ON THE SAME MATTER.
From the decrees of Pope Siricius, tit. 12.

We do not suffer any other women to be in the houses of clerics, other than those only whom the Synod of Nicaea allowed to live with them for the sake of necessity.

c. 93. ON THE SAME MATTER.
From the Council of Carthage, c. 25.

Bishop Aurelius said: We add, dearest brothers, furthermore, that, since it has been reported about the incontinence of certain clerics, even though lectors, toward their wives, it has pleased that, in accordance with what has been affirmed by different Councils, subdeacons, who handle the sacred mysteries, as also deacons, priests, not to mention bishops, in accordance with their own statutes, abstain from their wives and appear to be as if they did not have them; unless they do this, they are to be removed from ecclesiastical office. But other clerics are not to be compelled to this, except at a more mature age.

c. 94. ON THE SAME MATTER.
From the decrees of Pope Siricius, c. 7.

We have learned that many priests of Christ and deacons, long after the times of their consecration, have procreated offspring both from their own spouses and even from shameful joinings. They defend their crime with the excuse that it is read in the Old Testament that the dispensation of generating was granted to priests and ministers. Let him tell me now, whoever he may be, this supporter of lusts and teacher of vices, if he adjudges that in different places in the Law of Moses the bridles of lust are relaxed by our Lord for sacred orders, why does he warn in advance those to whom the Holy of Holies was entrusted, saying: "Be holy, because I, the Lord your God, am holy (Lev. 11:44)"? And why were priests commanded to live in the temple and away from their homes, in the year of their office? Indeed, for this reason, lest they be able to engage in carnal intercourse even with their wives, so that shining in integrity of conscience they might offer an acceptable service to God. Even when the period of their service had been fulfilled, the use of their wives was allowed to them only for the sake of succession, because none had been commanded to be admitted to God's ministry from any other tribe than that of Levi.

c. 95. ON THE SAME MATTER.
Cap. 92.

It has been established by the bishops as to priests who permit women to dwell with them indiscriminately, and for this are marked by the suspicion of a bad reputation, that, if they have not corrected themselves after admonition, they are to be struck down with the canonical invective as contemners of the sacred canons.

c. 96. ON THE SAME MATTER.
From the Council of Worms, c. 38.

It pleased that bishops, priests, deacons, and subdeacons abstain from their spouses, so that they do not generate offspring. If they have violated this decree, they are to be expelled from the honour of the clergy.

c. 97. ON THE SAME MATTER.
From the decrees of Pope Leo.

The law of continence is the same for the ministers of the altar as for bishops and priests, who, when they were laymen or lectors, could lawfully marry and have offspring. But when they reached the said degrees, what was before lawful began to be unlawful for them. Thus, in order that their carnal marriage may become spiritual, it is fitting that they not send away their wives, but have them as though they had them not (1 Cor. 7:29), so that the affection for their wives may be retained and the labours of marriage cease.

c. 98. ON THE SAME MATTER.
From the sayings of Pope Gregory.

They who dedicate their body to chastity are not to permit women to live with them.

c. 99. ON THE SAME MATTER.
Also, St. Augustine.

I do not wish my sister to be with me because those who are with my sister are not my sisters.

c. 100. ON THE SAME MATTER.
From the Council of Worms, c. 9.

Priests, therefore, if they have fallen into the snare of fornication, and the act of the crime is manifest or clear, cannot have the honour of the priesthood according to the authority of the canonical instruction.

c. 101. WHICH WOMEN ARE TO LIVE IN THE HOUSES OF CLERICS.
From the Council of Agde.

In order to preserve their life and reputation, we also command by a special ordinance that no cleric be joined in solace or familiarity with any woman not related to him. Not only is such a woman not to go into his house, but neither is he to have the power to go into the house of such a woman. But he is to enjoy free power to live with his mother, sister, daughter, or niece alone, if he has them and wishes to do so, of which names it is evil to suspect anything other than what nature has established.

c. 102. THAT MAIDSERVANTS OR FREEDWOMEN NOT OCCUPY THE PANTRY OF CLERICS OR PROVIDE PRIVATE SERVICE TO THEM.
From the Council of Agde.

It has pleased that maidservants or freedwomen be removed from the pantry, or the back rooms, or even the house itself in which a cleric lives.

c. 103. ON FAMILIARITY WITH WOMEN WHO ARE NOT RELATED.
From the Council of Orléans.

And so, we establish that none of the bishops or clerics have license to have any person within his house other than the female relatives of whom the earlier canons speak. As to whom, it is especially enjoined that, if any cleric has incurred any adverse suspicion or popular reproach because of some woman, he is to cast her out immediately, if he has her within his house. If she is not a relative and not subject to anyone, he is to see to it that he casts her out under all circumstances, so that the infamy which has arisen may be abrogated. If any of the bishops or clerics is unwilling to avoid what is written above, he is to be punished with an excommunication of three years for his disobedience. If the commission of adultery is proved, the statutes of the canons with regard to the loss of his prior honours are to be observed.

c. 104. AS ABOVE.
From the Council of Tours.

And because it is fitting to give no room to the devil, we decreed that this especially is to be observed, that clerics have no familiarity with women not their relatives, nor give occasion to men to speak or feel any ill, because frequently by this indecent occurrence it happens that the devil, who lies in ambush like a lion in his lair, leaps and causes the ruin of the servants of God. But if any cleric, after the prohibition of his bishop, has presumed to persist in illicit familiarity with such women, he is to be regarded as alien from communion.

c. 105. ON THE SAME MATTER.
From the Council of Nantes, c. 6.

It is to be forbidden and in every way prohibited for any priest to have within his house those persons of women, as are mentioned in the canon, regarding whom suspicion may arise, but not even those whom the canons allow, namely mother, aunt, sister (because, at the instigation of the devil, even with these it is frequently found that a wrong is perpetrated, or even with their female attendants). But if any of these are in such unyielding need that the priest's support is necessary, then let him keep them in the village or on the estate far from where the priest resides, and there provide them with what they need. But according to the authority of the canons, this too is in every way to be forbidden, that any woman presume to approach the altar, or minister to the priest, or to stand or sit within the chancel.

c. 106. THAT THE SICK ARE TO BE VISITED BY THE PRIEST.
As above.

When a priest has heard that someone in his parish has become sick, he is to go to him as quickly as possible. Entering his bedroom, he is to sprinkle holy water over him and over the whole room, with the antiphon, "Sprinkle me, Lord," and the verse, "May God arise." Then, he is to say the prayer: "God, who granted to your priests before all others such grace." Then, he is to sing the seven psalms with the prayers for the sick. After these things, he is to command all to leave the room, and approaching the bed on which the sick person lies, he is to tell him soothingly and gently to place all his hope in God, bear patiently God's scourge, believe that all these things come for his purgation and chastisement, confess his sins, promise emendation if the Lord should grant him life, promise penance for the faults he has committed, make disposition of his wealth while he still has sense and reason, redeem his sins with alms, forgive those who have sinned against him, hold right faith and belief, and never despair of God's mercy. When the mind of the sick person has been relieved by these and like consolations, after giving him the blessing, the priest is to withdraw for a time, to return after a short while, and give an opportunity to the sick person to consider his sins.

c. 107. ON THE SICK WHO CONFESS THEIR SINS AND ASK TO BE RECONCILED.
As above.

A sick man, who confesses his sins under the pressing necessity of death, is to be reconciled by the priest under the same condition that, if God grant him life and restore his health, he is to do penance in every way according to the quality of his wrong.

c. 108. ON RECONCILING THE SICK.
From the Council of Nicaea.

As for those who are coming to their end, the ancient and regular law will be observed even now, so that, if someone is withdrawing from his body, he is not to be deprived of the final and necessary viaticum. But if someone who had been despaired of has received communion and been made a participant in the oblation should revive, he is to remain among those who communicate only in prayer. Indeed, generally, in the case of all those who have come to their end and ask that the grace of communion be given to them, the bishop shall fittingly have to give them of the oblation.

c. 109. ON THE SAME MATTER.
From the letter of Pope Leo.

But to those who in time of need and in the urgency of pressing danger implore the protection of penitence, and then of reconciliation, satisfaction is not to be forbidden, nor reconciliation to be denied, because we can neither place limits on, nor define the times of, God's mercy, before whom conversion suffers no delay of forgiveness, as the Spirit of God says through the Prophet: "As soon as you moan in your conversion, then you shall be saved (cf. Is. 30:15)." And elsewhere: "Tell first your iniquities, that you may be justified (cf. Is. 43:26)." Also: "With the Lord there is mercy, and abundant is redemption before him (Ps. 130:7)." And so, we must not be difficult in dispensing God's gifts, nor neglect the groans and tears of those who accuse themselves, since we believe that the very emotion of repentance is conceived from God's inspiration so that they may escape from the snares of the devil by which they are held prisoners to his will (cf. 2 Tim. 2:25–26).

c. 110. ON THE SAME MATTER.
From the African Council.

Bishop Aurelius said: If anyone finds himself in danger and has requested to be reconciled to the divine altars, if the bishop is absent, the priest is obliged to consult the bishop and so reconcile the one in danger at the bishop's command. We ought to strengthen this matter by our salubrious counsel.

c. 111. ON THE SAME MATTER.
From the letter of Pope Celestine.

Hence, true conversion to God is to be weighed more as to the mind of those in their final moments than as to its time, as the Prophet asserts: "Whenever you groan in conversion, you will be saved (cf. Is. 30:15)." Since, therefore, the Lord is the inspector of the heart, penance is not to be denied at any time to one who seeks it, since he binds himself to that Judge to whom he knows all hidden things are revealed.

c. 112. ON THOSE WHO BECOME MUTE BEFORE THE PRIEST COMES TO THEM.
From the letter of Pope Leo.

Hence, aid is to be extended to the need of such people, so that neither the action of penance, nor the grace of communion, is to be denied to them, if it is proved that they ask for it by the signs of an unimpaired sense, even if they have lost the power of speech. But if they are so burdened by some illness that they are no longer able to signify in the present that which a little earlier they were asking for, the testimonies of the faithful around them are to be of aid. They are to receive penance and the benefit of reconciliation at the same time.

c. 113. ON THE SAME MATTER.
From the Council of Carthage.

Those penitents who during their illness received the viaticum of the Eucharist are not to believe themselves absolved without imposition of hand, if they survive.

c. 114. ON THE SAME MATTER.
From the letter of Pope Siricius.

We will that those who fell through the fragility of the flesh, as they begin their journey toward God, are to be aided by the grace of communion with the gift of the viaticum.

c. 115. ON PENITENTS WHO HAVE DIED SUDDENLY.
From the Council of Vaison, c. 15.

As for those who die suddenly without communion after receiving penance while they were still in good health, their offering is to be received, and their funerals and later memorial are to be carried out with ecclesiastical devotion.

c. 116. ON THOSE DEPRIVED OF COMMUNION WHO HAVE DIED IN THIS STATE.
From the letter of Pope Leo.

Their cause is to be reserved to God's judgment, in whose hand it was that the death of such persons was not delayed until the remedy of communion. But we cannot be in communion with those who are dead whom we were not in communion with while they were alive.

c. 117. ON ANOINTING THE SICK.
From the Council of Tours.

After the sick person has been relieved of the burden of his sins through confession and has been reconciled by the priest, he is to be anointed in God's name with sanctified oil, first on the breast, then between the shoulders, with the prayers pertaining to this holy anointing, so that, according to the Apostle, prayer offered in faith may save the sick man (Jas. 5:15), etc.

c. 118. ON THE SAME MATTER.
From the letter of Pope Innocent, c. 377.

For the blessed James the Apostle wrote in his letter: "Is one of you sick? Let him bring in the priests of the Church, and let them pray over him, anointing him with oil in the Lord's name. Prayer offered in faith will save the sick man, and the Lord will relieve him and, if he is in sins, they shall be forgiven him (Jas. 5:14–15)." It is not doubtful that this is to be taken or understood of those of the faithful who are ill, that they can be anointed with holy oil, which, confected by the bishop, is not only licit for priests, but for all Christians, to make use of, anointing according to their need and that of their own. Furthermore, we consider the addition superfluous to doubt as to the bishop that which is not doubted to be licit for priests. For the reason for its being said to priests is that bishops, impeded by their business, cannot go to all the sick. But if the bishop can, or deems it worthy, to visit someone himself and to bless and touch him with chrism, without doubt he to whom it pertains to confect the chrism can do so. This cannot be poured over penitents because it is a kind of sacrament. How can it be held that one kind of sacrament can be granted to those to whom the rest of the sacraments are denied?

c. 119. ON THE SAME MATTER.
From the sayings of the priest Bede.

"Is one of you sick? Let him bring in the priests of the Church, and let them pray over him, anointing him with oil in the Lord's name. Prayer offered in faith will save the sick man (Jas. 5:14–15)." We read in the Gospel that the Apostles did this, and now the Church's custom holds that the infirm be anointed by the priests with consecrated oil and, with prayer accompanying, they may be healed. Not only to priests, but, as Pope Innocent writes, it is also licit for all Christians to use the same oil, anointing according to their own need and that of their own. Yet, it is not licit for the oil to be confected by anyone other than the bishops. For when he says, "oil in the Lord's name," it signifies the oil consecrated in the name of the Lord, or certainly because also, when they anoint the infirm, they are to invoke the Lord's name over him. "And if he has committed sins, they shall be forgiven him." Many are struck with infirmity, or even the death of the body, because of the sins committed against the soul. Hence, the Apostle says to the Corinthians, who were accustomed to receive the body of the Lord unworthily:

"That is why many of you are weak and infirm, and many sleep (1 Cor. 11:30)." Hence, if the infirm are in sin, and they have confessed their sins to the Church's priests, and they have striven with perfect heart to abandon and correct them, it shall be forgiven them. Nor, indeed, can sins be forgiven without confession of amendment; hence, it is rightly added: "Confess your sins to one another, and pray for one another, that you may be saved (Jas. 5:16)."

C. 120. ON SACRED COMMUNION.
As above.

After the ill person has been anointed with the sacred anointing, he is to be restored immediately with the body and blood of the Lord, so that, even as his bodily life is despaired of, he may be vivified in his soul and merit eternal life. Indeed, the Lord says: "He who eats my flesh and drinks my blood has eternal life (Jn. 6:55)." And: "Unless you eat, you will not have life in you (Jn. 6:54)." So it is that the holy canons instruct that communion is not to be denied to any of the faithful at the point of death.

C. 121. THAT A PRIEST NOT GIVE COMMUNION TO A LAYMAN TO DELIVER.
From the Council of Reims.

It has come to our notice that some priests hold the divine mysteries in so little regard that they give the sacred body of the Lord to a lay man or woman to be brought to the sick; the holy of holies is entrusted to those to whom it is forbidden to enter the sacristy, or to approach the altar. The prudence of all religious persons knows how horrible and detestable this is. And so, the Synod forbids in every way that such temerarious presumption occur henceforth; the priest is to administer communion to the sick wholly by himself. If he has done otherwise, he shall be subject to the risk of his degree

C. 122. THAT NO PAYMENTS BE REQUIRED OF THOSE TO BE BAPTIZED.
From the letter of Pope Gelasius.

They are not to set any prices on the faithful to be baptized or anointed with the sign of the cross, nor let them wish to disturb the reborn by the imposition of any payments, because what we freely receive, we are commanded to give freely (Mt. 10:8). And so, let them not endeavour to exact anything from the aforesaid, as a result of which they may decline to approach the causes of their redemption either because they are deterred by pressing poverty, or held back by their indignation. Let them be certain that those who are caught infringing these prohibitions, or do not freely correct what they have done, will suffer the loss of their honour.

c. 123. THAT NO ONE EXACT ANYTHING FOR BURIAL.
From the letter of Pope Gregory.

It is very grave and far from a priest's office to seek payment for land granted to putrefaction and to wish to make a profit from another's mourning. We ourselves, after we had by God's permission acceded to the honour of the episcopate, forbade this abuse entirely in our Church, and never allowed this evil custom to be taken up again, remembering that, when Abraham for a price begged for land for a tomb for the burial of his wife's body from the sons of Ephron, that is, from the son of Seor, the latter refused to accept payment, lest he should appear to have made profit out of a corpse (Gen. 23:1–11). If, then, a pagan man proved to be of such great consideration, how much more ought we, who are called priests, not to do this thing? And so, I admonish you that this abuse of avarice be not further attempted, even in the case of strangers. But, if at any time you grant that anyone be buried in your church, and the parents, relations, or heirs of such person should freely wish to offer something for lamps, we do not forbid its acceptance. But we entirely forbid that anything be asked for or exacted, lest (what is a very irreligious thing) either the Church be called venal (far be it!), or you should seem to rejoice in human deaths, if you strive in any way to seek profit from their corpses.

c. 124. ON THE SAME MATTER.
From the Council of Meaux, c. 72.

That no one is to presume to bury any dead person in a church, as if by hereditary right, except one whom the bishop or priest has deemed worthy by the quality of his bearing and life. Neither let anyone eject the bones of any dead person from his sepulcher, or violate in any way with a temerarious boldness anyone's burial, but allow each one to await the coming of his Judge in the place prepared and granted to him by God, particularly as not only the divine laws, but also human ones, adjudge as worthy of death before the human commonwealth those who violate sepulchers. But neither is anyone to try to seek payment for a place of burial, or, to use St. Gregory's words, from land granted to putrefaction, or to wish to make a profit from another's mourning. But if at any time the relatives or heirs wish to offer freely something in the church as alms for the deceased, we do not forbid its acceptance. But we entirely forbid that anything be asked for or exacted, lest (what is a very irreligious thing) either the Church be called venal (far be it!), or we should seem to rejoice in human deaths, if we strive in any way to seek profit therefrom.

c. 125. THAT NO ONE BURY A DEAD PERSON IN A CHURCH.

From the synodal Chapters, tit. 153.

That no one henceforth bury a dead person in a church.

c. 126. ALSO, ON THE SAME MATTER.

Cap. 46.

That, regarding the burial of the dead in basilicas, that constitution which was established by the ancient Fathers is to be observed.

c. 127. ON THE SAME MATTER.

From the Council of Nantes.

According to the authority of the canons, it is to be commanded that they exact no gifts for tombs or the burials of men, unless perhaps the one to be buried, in life, had commanded that some of his possessions be given to the church in whose forecourt he is buried, or even after his death those who have been entrusted to give alms should freely wish to give some of his possessions. And yet, nothing at all is to be exacted by the church's priests, or by those who preside over the places and settlements. According to the statutes of our ancestors, it is also to be forbidden that there be burials within the church, but only in its forecourt, or in its portico, or in the church's exedra. But no one at all is to have license to be buried within the church or near the altar, where the body and blood of the Lord are confected.

c. 128. ON THE SAME MATTER.

Also, from the Council of Tribur.

That, if it can be done, the dead not be buried elsewhere than near the church, and henceforth nothing is to be exacted as payment for the burial.

c. 129. ON THE SAME MATTER.

Also, from the same.

It has been said that, in some places, it is customary for money to be given for the reception of the chrism, as also for baptism and communion. The holy Synod has expressed detestation for and anathematized this seed of the simoniacal heresy, so that henceforth nothing be exacted for ordination, or burial, or communion, but that Christ's free gifts are to be given freely.

c. 130. ON INFANTS WHO, THROUGH NEGLIGENCE, DIE UNBAPTIZED.

From a Penitential, c. 17.

A woman who gives birth, and whose child has died unbaptized through negligence, is to do penance for one year, and she is never to be without some penance. If the priest to whom this pertained was called to baptize the child, and neglected to come, he is to be chastised at the discretion of the bishop to the damnation of his soul. But it is licit for all the faithful – indeed, it is commanded them – where they perhaps find unbaptized persons who are about to die, to snatch all souls away from the devil by baptism, that is, by water blessed simply in the Lord's name, and to baptize them in the name of the Father, and Son, and Holy Spirit, by intinction or sprinkling with the water. Hence, it is fitting that those who can, if they are of the faithful, and especially monks, have knowledge of baptizing, and, if they are going out very far, they are to have the Eucharist always with them.

c. 131. ON THE SAME MATTER.

Let priests ponder how dangerous it is for the souls of innocents to be excluded from the kingdom of God by their negligence. For if there is joy in heaven over one sinner doing penance, how much wrath and indignation will there be over him who, by his negligence, closes the gates of paradise to the innocent? And so, let priests beware with the highest diligence lest souls for which Christ's blood has been shed be separated from heavenly blessedness because of their carelessness. But if (far be it!) it has happened, let the one by whose neglect it happened submit himself to the deep mourning of penance all the days of his life.

c. 132. ON THE SAME MATTER.
Also, as above.

One whose child has died without baptism through negligence is to do penance for three years, the first of which at bread and water.

c. 133. THAT OBLATIONS NOT BE OFFERED IN HOUSES.
From the Council of Laodicea.

That it is not fitting for oblations to be celebrated in houses by bishops or priests.

c. 134. MASSES ARE NOT TO BE SUNG OUTSIDE A CHURCH.
Also, as above.

We have heard that some laymen command their priests to celebrate masses in their houses, and that the mysteries of holiness are polluted rather than consecrated among the running about of dogs and flocks of prostitutes. Hence, we instruct that no priest is to presume to sing mass outside a church, unless perhaps the necessity of travel requires it, when we permit the celebration of masses in a tent or under the sky, in a clean place, and removed far from every uncleanness, and this never without a consecrated table.

C. 135. ON DRUNKEN CLERICS.
From the Council of Agde.

Accordingly, we decree that anyone who it is established has been drunk, insofar as his order allows, is to be removed from communion for the space of thirty days or subjected to corporal punishment.

C. 136. ALSO, ON THE SAME MATTER.
Bishop Fructuosus.

If anyone endowed with ecclesiastical ordination, or a monk, is found to be drunk, he is to do penance at bread and water for three months.

C. 137. ALSO, ON THE SAME MATTER.
From the sayings of Blessed Ferreolus.

As to drunkenness, I believe it superfluous that a monk be admonished since, if he takes even a little wine, he has deviated from his proposed contrition of body. And so, if it ever happens that a monk is seen to be drunk (which it is an offence against divine law to say), filled with zealous wrath, I instruct him to be suspended for thirty days from drinking wine, so that during this period his soul may be voided of its fullness by being allowed digestion.

C. 138. ON CLERICS GIVEN TO DRUNKENNESS.

If any bishop, or anyone ordained, is habitually drunk, he must either cease, or be deposed.

C. 139. ALSO, ON DRUNKEN LAYMEN.

If a layman has been drunk, he is to do penance for three days at bread and water.

C. 140. GENERAL SENTENCE REGARDING DRUNKS AND WINE TIPPLERS OF JEROME THE PRIEST AND EPHREM THE DEACON.

Flee wine as a poison, lest drunkenness overcome you and leave you despoiled of your virtues and naked. For wine, as holy Scripture says, causes even the wise to fall (cf. Sir. 19:2). Note how Noah, a wise and holy man, was left naked and sleeping by drunkenness (Gen. 9). Note how the patriarch Lot shamelessly joined with his daughters because of drunkenness (Gen. 19). Hence, Blessed Basil says: "Many have been caught by demons through drunkenness, nor is drunkenness other than a most manifest demon." Hence, the Prophet says: "Fornication and drunkenness take away the heart (cf. Hos. 4:11)." Indeed, drunkenness causes confusion of mind and arouses the flame and madness of lust, as the Apostle attests: "Do not become drunk with wine, in which lies lust (Eph. 5:18)." If anyone has acted against these statutes of the saints, he is to do long and worthy penance, because it is one of those sins which separate man from the kingdom of God, as the Apostle Paul says: "Nor will the drunk possess the kingdom of God (1 Cor. 6:10)."

c. 141. ALSO, ON THE SAME MATTER.
From the sayings of St. Benedict.

Nothing is so pernicious to a Christian man as crapulousness, as the Lord says in the Gospel: "See that your hearts are not burdened by crapulousness and drunkenness (Lk. 21:34)."

c. 142. ALSO, ON THE SAME MATTER.
From the Capitularies, tit. 161.

As to drunkenness, that, first of all, the elders beware of it in themselves and show a good example of sobriety to their juniors.

c. 143. ALSO, ON THE SAME MATTER.
From bk. 3, c. 38.

That no drunken person is to presume to pursue his cause in judicial assembly, nor give testimony, nor is the count to hold a plea, unless fasting.

c. 144. ON THE SAME MATTER.
Also, from the same, c. 72.

That, while in the army, no one is to ask an equal or any other man to drink, and whoever is found drunk in the army is to be so excommunicated that he is to drink water exclusively until he acknowledges that he did wrong.

c. 145. ON THE SAME MATTER.
Also, from the Capitulary, bk. 1, tit. 138.

That it is licit for no one to compel another to drink.

c. 146. ON THE SAME MATTER.
In the Canons of the Apostles, tit. 42.

A bishop, priest, or deacon who is devoted to dice or drunkenness is either to stop or certainly be condemned. A subdeacon, or lector, or cantor who does the same things is either to stop or be deprived of communion; similarly also, a layman.

c. 147. ON THE SAME MATTER.
From a Penitential, c. 19.

One who vomits because of drunkenness, if he is a priest or deacon, is to do penance for forty days; thirty days if a monk; twenty days if a cleric; fifteen days if a layman.

c. 148. ON THE SAME MATTER.
From the Canons.

If any bishop, or anyone ordained, has the vice of drunkenness, he is either to cease, or be deposed.

c. 149. ON THE SAME MATTER.
Also, from another Penitential.

A layman, if he has been drunk to the point of vomiting, is to abstain for three days from meat, wine, and beer.

c. 150. ALSO, ON THE SAME MATTER.

If someone, through his wickedness, makes another drunk, he is to do penance for forty days.

c. 151. ON THOSE WHO VOMIT THE EUCHARIST.

If anyone has vomited the Eucharist because of drunkenness or voracity, he is to do penance for forty days; clerics, monks, or deacons are to do penance for forty days; priests, for seventy days; bishops, for ninety. If he has vomited because of illness, he is to do penance for seven days.

c. 152. ON CLERICS WHO SING AT BANQUETS.
From the African Council.

Clerics who sing at banquets are to be removed from their office.

c. 153. ON THE SAME MATTER.
Also, from the same.

If any cleric or monk speaks scurrilous words that move to jocularity and laughter, he is to be corrected most harshly.

c. 154. ON THE SAME MATTER.
Also, from the same.

Clerics who are buffoons and jesters using obscene language are to be removed from office.

c. 155. ALSO, ON CLERICS WHO SPEAK ILL.

A cleric who speaks ill (particularly against priests) is to be compelled to seek forgiveness; if he refuses, he is to be demoted, nor is he ever to be re-established in office without making satisfaction.

c. 156. ON CLERICS WHO SWEAR.

Clerics who swear are to be excommunicated.

c. 157. ON THE SAME MATTER.
Also, as above.

A cleric who swears by creatures is to be rebuked severely. If he persists in this vice, he is to be excommunicated.

c. 158. ALSO, OF THOSE WHO INSULT AND SPEAK ILL.

If anyone has harmed another by insult, abuse, or even the suggestion of a crime, he is to be purged with the most worthy satisfaction. If he has repeated this vice, he is to be made to expiate it by a most just penance according to the manner of his fault.

c. 159. ON THE SAME MATTER.
As above.

The Apostle says: "Neither will slanderers possess the kingdom of God (cf. 1 Cor. 6:10)." If anyone has committed this sin, let him repent as greatly as the crime he committed is great, which separates him from the kingdom of God.

c. 160. ALSO, ON DETRACTION.

If anyone is prompt and easy to engage in detraction and to say what is not true, he is to do penance at bread and water for seven days in separation from the brotherly fellowship.

c. 161. ON CONTENTIONS OR BRAWLS AND INSULTS.

If anyone has loved contentions or brawls, or has inflicted manifest insult on his brother, let it be expiated by a long penance according to the discretion of his superior and the manner of the sin.

c. 162. ON THE SAME MATTER.
As above.

He who has been contentious or a murmurer is to do penance according to the discretion of his prior for as long as the quality of his fault endures.

c. 163. ON THE SAME MATTER.
As above.

If anyone is seen to be contentious, as the Apostle says: "We have no such custom among us, nor does God's Church (1 Cor. 11:16)"; if anyone does this, he is to be stigmatized until he is corrected.

c. 164. ON THE LASCIVIOUS AND THE PROUD.

Anyone who has been lascivious and proud is to do penance for three days at bread and water.

c. 165. ON THE SAME MATTER.
As above.

If anyone has been lascivious of tongue, it is to be expiated by a penance of three days.

c. 166. ON MURMURERS.

The Apostle says: "Do all things without murmuring (Phil. 2:14)." Let the one who murmurs be alien from the unity of the brethren, and let his work be cast out.

c. 167. ON THE SAME MATTER.
As above.

If anyone is a murmurer, may he not incur the penalty of those who murmur, of which the Apostle says: "Neither do you murmur, as some of them murmured and perished by the destroyer (1 Cor. 10:10)." According to the measure and work of his sin (which is made clear more fully in this decision of the Apostle), let the sinner do penance at the judgment of the priest.

c. 168. ON CLERICS WHO DISPARAGE.
From the sayings of St. Basil.

If anyone disparages the one who presides over him, severed for seven days from the Church's assembly, he is to do penance like Mary, Aaron's sister, who disparaged Moses (cf. Num. 12:1–15).

c. 169. ON SEDITIOUS CLERICS.
From the Council of Toledo.

As for clerics who took up arms in sedition, after the loss of the degree of their order, they are to be confined in a monastery for punishment.

c. 170. ON CLERICS WHO BREAK OUT INTO MUTUAL KILLING.
From the Council of Lérida.

If any clerics have broken out into mutual killing, to the extent that the dignity of their offices has suffered contumely in such an excess, it is to be more strictly punished by the pontiff.

c. 171. AS ABOVE.

If a brother has dared to lay hands on his brother, he is to receive lawful discipline.

c. 172. ON THE SAME MATTER.
From the sayings of St. Ferreolus.

A cleric or monk, enflamed against another (which is most shameful), is not to presume to lay hands on him, apart from those to whom correction pertains. If anyone has transgressed these things, he shall be subject to the canonical disciplines.

c. 173. ON THE SAME MATTER.
From the Council of Agde.

The seditious are never to be ordained as clerics, as neither usurers nor those who avenge their own injuries.

c. 174. AS ABOVE.

If anyone consecrated in any ecclesiastical degree has been an assailant, he is to be corrected most harshly. If he does not amend, he is to do penance for three months at bread and water.

c. 175. ON THE SAME MATTER.
In the Canons of the Apostles.

We command that a bishop, or priest, or deacon who strikes the faithful who do wrong or the faithless who act wickedly, wishing to be feared in this manner, is to be deposed from his office, because the Lord never taught us this; on the contrary, when he was struck, he did not strike back.

c. 176. THAT CLERICS NOT BEAR ARMS.
From the Capitularies, bk. 1, tit. 67.

It is to be said in every way to priests and deacons that they not bear arms, but entrust themselves more to God's defense than to arms.

c. 177. ON THE SAME MATTER.
From the Council of Meaux.

Any who appear to be from the clergy are not to take up military arms, nor to go about armed, but are to show forth the title of their profession by a religious mode of life and religious habit. If they have contemned to do this, they are to be punished as contemners of the sacred canons and profaners of ecclesiastical holiness with the loss of their degree, because they cannot serve both in God's ranks and in the world's.

c. 178. THAT A BISHOP, PRIEST, OR DEACON IS NOT TO HAVE HUNTING DOGS.

It is not to be licit for a bishop, priest, or deacon to have hunting dogs or hawks. If any of this sort of person is detected in this disposition, a bishop is to suspend himself from communion for three months, a priest for two months and a deacon one from any office and communion.

c. 179. THAT CLERICS ARE NOT TO ENTER TAVERNS.
From the Council of Laodicea.

That clerics are not to enter taverns for the sake of food or drink, unless compelled by the necessity of travelling.

c. 180. ALSO, ON THE SAME MATTER.
From the Council as above.

It is not fitting for those dedicated to the sacred ministry, from priests to deacons and the rest of the ecclesiastical order (that is, subdeacons, lectors, cantors, exorcists, door-keepers, and psalmists), and from the number of those who have vowed continence and monks, to enter taverns.

c. 181. AS ABOVE.
From the decrees of Augustine.

As the provisions of the canons forbid, none of the clerics is to dare to enter taverns in order to take food or drink. If anyone has violated these prohibitions, he is to be corrected with the harshest discipline as a contemner of the holy canons.

c. 182. ON THE SAME MATTER.
From the Council of Carthage.

A cleric who goes about fairs or the market square not for the sake of purchasing anything is to be demoted from his office.

c. 183. ON CLERICS WHO ARE ABSENT FROM THE VIGILS.
From the Council of Carthage.

A cleric who, without indisposition of body, is absent from the vigils, having been deprived of his stipend, is to be excommunicated. (See bk. 2, c. 393.)

c. 184. ON THE SAME MATTER.
From the Council of Toledo.

That a priest, or deacon, or subdeacon, or any cleric deputed to the Church, if he is within a city, or in a place in which there is a church, or in a castle, or in a village, or on an estate, if he does not come to the church for the daily sacrifice, is not to be regarded as a cleric if, after chastisement, he has not amended.

c. 185. ON THE SAME MATTER.
From the Council of Vannes.

A cleric who dwells within the walls of the city and, on any day when he is not ill, has been absent from the morning hymns is to be kept from communion for seven days.

c. 186. ON THE SAME MATTER.
From the Council of Agde.

As for clerics who have neglected to frequent the church, or to fulfil their office, the peregrine communion is to be allotted to them.

c. 187. ON THE SAME MATTER.
From the decrees of St. Benedict.

As the Prophet says: "Seven times a day I have given praise to you (Ps. 118:164)." This seven-fold sacred number shall be fulfilled by us, if we fulfil the offices of our servitude at the time of matins, prime, tierce, sext, none, vespers, and compline, because it was of these that the Prophet spoke. Indeed, of the night vigils, the same Prophet said: "I rose at midnight to give praise to you (Ps. 118:62)," etc. And so, at these times, let us give praises to our Creator for the judgments of his justice.

c. 188. THAT MASSES NOT BE CELEBRATED BEFORE THE THIRD HOUR.
From the letter of Pope Telesphorus.

Except on the night of the holy Nativity, the celebrations of mass are not to be held before the third hour of the day (because it was at that same time that the Lord was crucified [Mk. 15:25], and that the Holy Spirit is said to have descended over the Apostles [Act. 2:15]).

c. 189. THAT THE FAITHFUL ARE NOT TO EAT BEFORE THE THIRD HOUR.
From the Council of Carthage.

It is not fitting for clerics or religious laymen to begin banquets before the sacred third hour of the day. Clerics are never to eat bread without first saying a hymn and, after their food, they must give thanks to God, its Maker.

c. 190. THAT THE SACRAMENTS OF THE ALTAR BE CELEBRATED WHILE FASTING.
From the African Council.

That the sacraments of the altar are to be celebrated only by those who are fasting, except for the anniversary day on which the Lord's Supper is celebrated. Indeed, if the commendation of deceased persons, whether bishops or others, is to be done in the afternoon, it is to be done with prayers alone, if those who do it have already eaten.

c. 191. THAT AFTER THE BISHOP'S ADDRESS AT THE SOLEMNITIES OF MASS, THE PEOPLE BE INVITED TO PRAYER.
From the Council of Laodicea.

It is fitting that, after the address of bishops, the prayer over the catechumens be made and, after the catechumens have exited, prayer be made over those who are in penance. After these have approached the hand of the priest and left, three prayers of the faithful are to be completed, in such a way that the first is done silently, but the second and third with the usual exclamations.

c. 192. ON THE SAME MATTER.

It is fitting that, on Sundays or feast-days, after the sermon preached to the people within the solemnities of the mass, the priest admonish all, in accordance with the apostolic instruction, to pray in common to the Lord for diverse needs, for kings and the rulers of churches, for peace, for the plague, for the ill who lie in bed in their very parish, for the recently deceased, as to which the people are to say singly and silently the Lord's Prayer. The priest is to conclude the prayers pertaining to these matters solemnly with several admonitions. After these things, the sacred oblation is to be celebrated, for the Apostle says: "This, first of all, I ask, that petition, prayer, entreaty, and thanksgiving be done (1 Tim. 2:1)."

C. 193. THAT NO PRIEST PRESUME TO SING MASS ALONE.
From the Council of Nantes.

The holy Council has pronounced definitively that no priest is to presume to sing mass while he is alone. Indeed, to whom does he say, "The Lord be with you," or "Let us lift up our hearts," or "Let us give thanks to the Lord our God," when there is no one to answer? Or to mention in the canon "all who are present," when there is no one? Or whom does he invite to prayer, when he says, "Let us pray," when there is no one who may pray with him? Hence, either such things are to be omitted entirely, and then not only will the sacrifice not be perfect, but also, whoever he is, he will incur that terrible sentence: "If anyone has taken anything from this, may God take away his share from the book of life (Apoc. 22:19)," or, if he whispers these things to walls and partitions, [the sacrifice] will be ridiculous. Hence, this dangerous superstition is to be cast out especially from the monasteries of monks. Let prelates see to it that priests in monasteries have helpers in the celebration of masses. If anyone has transgressed these things, he is to be suspended from office.

C. 194. ON PRIESTS WHO, HAVING CELEBRATED MASS, DO NOT TAKE COMMUNION.
From the Canons of the Apostles.

If any bishop, priest, deacon, or anyone from the priestly roster, does not communicate after making the oblation, either he is to state the cause and, if it is reasonable, receive indulgence, or, if he fails to state it, be deprived of communion as one who has been a cause of harm to the people.

C. 195. THAT THE LAY FAITHFUL ARE TO RECEIVE COMMUNION.
As above.

All faithful Christians who enter a church on Sunday and hear the Scriptures of the Apostles and the Gospel, but do not persevere in prayer until the mass is completed nor receive holy communion, it is suitable that they be deprived of communion as persons who cause disturbance to the Church.

C. 196. AS ABOVE.
From the Council of Antioch.

All Christians, who enter God's church and hear the sacred Scriptures, but do not communicate in prayer with the people and turn away from the reception of holy communion for some intemperance, are to be removed from the Church until, through confession, they show fruits of penance.

c. 197. ON THE SAME MATTER.
From the Capitularies, bk. 1, tit. 6.

It has come to our hearing that some priests celebrate mass, and do not communicate, which we read is entirely forbidden in the Canons of the Apostles. But, if he has not taken communion, how can he rightly say: "We have received, Lord, the sacraments," etc.?

c. 198. THAT THE PEOPLE NOT EXIT THE CHURCH BEFORE MASS IS FINISHED.
From the Council of Arles.

When a gathering is made to celebrate mass in God's name, people are not to leave before the solemnity of mass is complete; where the bishop is not present, the people are to receive the priest's blessing.

c. 199. ALSO, ON THE SAME MATTER.
From the Council of Carthage.

While the priest is speaking in church, he who has left the audience is to be excommunicated.

c. 200. THAT WOMEN ARE NOT TO ENTER THE SANCTUARY.
From the Council of Laodicea.

That it is not fitting for women to approach the altar and touch those things which have been deputed to the offices of men.

c. 201. ON THE SAME MATTER.
From the letter of Pope Leo.

We have heard with some impatience that the scorn for divine things has gone so far that women are allowed to minister at the sacred altars, and that the sex to which it does not belong performs all the things which have been deputed to the exclusive service of men

c. 202. ON THE SAME MATTER.
From the Council of Rouen.

It has been reported to us that some priests at the celebration of mass refuse to receive the divine mysteries which they have consecrated. They give the Lord's chalice to common women who offer it at mass, or to some laymen who do not know what to make of the body of the Lord, that is, how to discern between spiritual and carnal food. The piety of the faithful knows to what degree this is contrary to all ecclesiastical religion. Hence, we forbid all priests that any of them do this henceforth, but either he is to receive with reverence, or give the rest for gathering by the deacon or subdeacon, who are ministers of the altar. He is also to see to it that he gives communion to them with his own hand. He is not to put the Eucharist in the hands of any lay man or woman, but only in their mouth, as he says these words: "May the body and blood of the Lord be of aid to you for the remission of sins and eternal life." If anyone has transgressed against these things, because he contemns almighty God and dishonours him insofar as he can, he is to be removed from the altar.

c. 203. THAT EVERY PRIEST WHO HOLDS A CHURCH IS TO HAVE A THURIBLE AND INCENSE.

As above.

That, at the time when the Gospel is read and when the offertory is finished, he is to place incense over the oblation, namely, at the death of our Redeemer.

c. 204. ON THE PREACHING OF PRIESTS.

From the Capitularies, bk. 1, tit. 76.

Most beloved and venerable shepherds of God's churches, it is for each of you to see to it that the priests whom you send throughout your parishes to rule and preach in all the churches to the people of God preach decently; do not allow any of them to make up and preach to the people new and uncanonical things from their own understanding and not according to the sacred Scriptures. But you yourselves preach decently and rightly useful things which lead to eternal life; also, instruct others to preach these same things.

c. 205. WHAT IS TO BE PREACHED BY THE PRIESTS.

First of all, it is to be preached to all generally that they believe the Father, and the Son, and the Holy Spirit to be one almighty God, who made all things, and that there is one Godhead, and substance, and majesty in the three persons of Father, Son, and Holy Spirit.

On the incarnation. Also, it is to be preached how the Son of God became incarnate of the Holy Spirit and Mary ever Virgin, suffered for the salvation of humankind, was buried, rose on the third day, and ascended into heaven, that he is coming at the end of the world to judge all men according to their own deeds, and how the impious will be sent into the eternal fire with the devil, and the just will be in eternal life with Christ.

Also, it is to be preached that all men will rise again in their own flesh

Also, it is to be preached for what crimes men are consigned to the same lot as the devil, which the Apostle enumerates as follows: Fornication, uncleanness, lust, idolatry, witchcraft, etc. (cf. Gal. 5:19–20). Those who do such things will not obtain the kingdom of God, and so let them be forbidden with every effort.

Also, it is to be preached about the love of God and neighbour, about faith and hope in God, about humility, patience, chastity, benignity, mercy, about alms, about confession, that we forgive our brothers from the heart. Those who do these and like things will obtain the kingdom of God.

c. 206. ALSO, ON THE SAME MATTER.
From the same, bk. 1, c. 154.

That each priest is to have the chapters regarding the greater and lesser vices, by which he may know and preach to his subjects to beware of the wiles of the devil.

c. 207. ALSO, ON THE SAME MATTER.
From the same, c. 159.

That priests admonish the people to give alms and offer prayers for the different plagues which we suffer continuously for our sins.

c. 208. ON THE SAME MATTER.
From c. 160.

That the priests themselves, each according to his order, strive to preach to and teach the people entrusted to them.

c. 209. ADMONITION TO BISHOPS.
Also, from bk. 2, c. 5.

As for the priests pertaining to your care, apply great effort so that they are instructed and admonished by you with great care as to how they ought to live, and how they are to be of profit by example and word to the people allotted to their care, and that they are constrained by your authority to be zealous in doing this.

c. 210. THAT EACH PRIEST WHO HOLDS A CHURCH IS TO HAVE A CLERIC.
From the Council of Nantes.

That each priest who has charge of people is to have a cleric who sings and reads the Epistle and the lesson, and who can keep the school; he is to admonish his parishioners to send their children to church to learn the faith, and he is to instruct them in all chastity.

c. 211. THAT EACH PRIEST FULFIL THE CANONICAL HOURS SOLEMNLY.
From the same, c. 19.

In the morning, the priest, after completing the morning office, is to fulfil the burden of his servitude by singing prime, tierce, sext, and none, but in such way that afterwards they be completed publicly, insofar as possible, by himself or by his young assistants (*scholares*). After mass has been performed and the sick have been visited, he is to go out to work in the fields while still fasting, so that he may again assist the needs of pilgrims and guests, or others who come by, and also of the sick and the dead, until the appointed hour in accordance with the quality of time and opportunity.

c. 212. THAT THE PRIEST TAKE CARE OF GUESTS.
As above.

That the priest is to take care of guests, especially the poor and the weak, as also orphans and pilgrims; he is to call them to his meal each day insofar as possible and give them a place to rest. (See bk. 2, c. 428.)

c. 213. ON MAKING BLESSED WATER.
From the letter of Pope Alexander.

We bless water mixed with salt for the people, so that all sprinkled with it be sanctified, and we command that this be done by all priests. For if the sprinkled ashes of a heifer sanctified and cleansed the people, how much more does water which is sprinkled with salt and consecrated by divine prayers sanctify and cleanse the people (Heb. 9:13–14)? And if the sterility of the water was healed by the salt sprinkled by the Prophet Eliseus (2 Kings 2:19–22), how much more does water consecrated with divine prayers take away the sterility from human things, sanctify and purge those who are polluted, multiply other goods, turn aside the wiles of the devil, and defend men from the craftiness of phantasms?

c. 214. ON THE SAME MATTER.
From the above-mentioned Council [of Nantes], c. 5.

That every Sunday each priest in his church before the solemnities of mass is to make holy water in a vessel which is clean and suitable for such a mystery from which the people may sprinkle themselves as they enter the church. Whoever wishes may take from the same water in their own little containers and sprinkle their houses, fields, vineyards, as also their sheep and their pasturage, as also their own food and drink.

c. 215. ON PRIESTS WHO REMAIN SILENT REGARDING THE FAULTS OF SINNERS, OR BRING TO RECONCILIATION THOSE WHO ARE LESS WORTHILY PENITENT.

As above.

That none of the priests is to accept a bribe or any temporal emolument (or rather spiritual detriment) from anyone who sins publicly or commits incest in order to remain silent before the bishop or his ministers regarding the donor's sin. Neither is he, participating in other's sins out of respect for some person, or consanguinity, or familiarity, to fail to report this to the bishop. Nor is he, by reason of grace or favour, to presume to receive a gift from any penitent in order to bring to reconciliation anyone who has done less than worthy penance, or give to him testimony of reconciliation, or, by reason of any spite, remove from reconciliation any worthier penitent, because this is simoniacal and contrary to both God and men. (See bk. 2, c. 422.)

c. 216. ON PRIESTS WHO ARE INVITED TO DINNER BY THE FAITHFUL.

As above, c. 14.

That none of the priests is to presume to get drunk when priests come together for the thirtieth, seventh, or third anniversary of a deceased person or to a meeting at anyone's summons. Nor is he to presume to ask to drink to the love of the saints or drink to the deceased's soul, or compel others to drink, or gorge himself at another's invitation, sing, or tell silly tales, or make disorderly noises and laughter, or join in shameful games with a bear or dancers. And he is not to allow demonic masks (which are called *talamascas* in the vernacular) to be brought before him because this is diabolical and forbidden by the sacred canons.

c. 217. ON THE BRAWLS AND FIGHTS OF PRIESTS.

Most especially, let each priest beware, as he wants to be in possession of his status, that he not on any occasion irritate or provoke his equal or anyone else to wrath and brawl, much less to fight or kill, by some word; nor if provoked, let any spring forward to take part because the devil always mixes himself into such revelries and drinking parties.

c. 218. ON THE BANQUET OF PRIESTS.

And when priests come together for some banquet, let the dean or one of their leaders begin the prayer before the meal and bless the food. Then, let them take their places according to their order, each showing honour to the other, and let each in turn bless the food and drink, and let one of their clerics read something from holy Scripture. In the same way, after they have eaten, let them sing a holy hymn, according to the Lord's example, as it is read that he did at the supper (Mt. 26:30). Let all priests so control themselves, especially on such occasions, that our ministry is not maligned.

c. 219. ON THE KALENDS.
As above, c. 16.

When priests come together for the required meal on the kalends, after the performance of the divine mystery and the necessary discussion, let them not take their places at table as if for a meal and burden one another with such unsuitable banquets because it is indecent and oppressive. For it often happens that, returning late to their churches, they derive from criticism and incur from mutual intoxication greater harm than they gain profit from participating in such events. Paul reproved the Corinthians about this type of meeting because they came together in an unsuitable manner to eat the Lord's Supper (1 Cor. 11:17–34). So it is that those who come together for the Lord's Supper, on the pretext, that is, of feeding upon the word, but in truth do so in order to fill their bellies, are considered reprehensible before God and men. And so, when all things are done, let those who might wish to do so break bread with charity in their brother's house with their brothers and let them accept individual drinks. Without touching drink more than three times, let them then return to their churches.

c. 220. OF THOSE WHO HAVE NOTHING WHEN THEY ARE ORDAINED.
From the Council of Carthage.

It pleased that bishops, priests, deacons, or any clerics, who have nothing when they are ordained, and who in the time of their episcopate or clerical tenure purchase fields or any farms in their own name, are to be held guilty of the crime of unlawful seizure of the Lord's possessions, unless, having been admonished, they confer those possessions upon the Church.

c. 221. ON THE SAME MATTER.
From the Capitularies, bk. 1, c. 150.

That each priest is to leave to his church those things which he acquired after the day of his consecration.

c. 222. ON THE SAME MATTER.
From the Council of Reims.

If a priest who had no patrimony when he was promoted to the ecclesiastical order afterwards bought farms, it is to be investigated to whose right they belong, because according to canonical authority they ought to belong to the church to which he was promoted from having nothing.

c. 223. ON THE REVENUES OR OFFERING OF A CHURCH.

It is to be investigated whether, with regard to this preceding chapter, any priest has used the revenues of his church, or the offerings and vows of the faithful, to acquire possessions under another's name, and to build structures there, or has placed things there which pertained to the Church, and permitted the frequent presence of women there or (what is more shameful) kept such women there to work with wool and take care of the house, and the priest frequently comes there to stay. This evil is done against the decrees of the canons because, just as a priest must not engage in usury in his own name, so neither in another's, and much less commit fraud against ecclesiastical resources since this is sacrilege and an equal crime to that of the thief Judas, who took away and stole the sacred offerings.

c. 224. ON USURIES.

In the Canons of the Apostles.

A bishop, priest, or deacon who exacts usuries from his debtors either must cease, or he is certainly to be condemned.

c. 225. ON THE SAME MATTER.

From the Council of Nicaea.

Because many who are set under a rule pursue avarice and unlawful gains, having forgotten the Scripture, which says: "He has not given his money at usury (Ps. 14:5)," in lending money ask for the hundredth, the holy and great Synod has justly adjudged that, if anyone is found to lend money at interest, either by demanding *hemiola* (that is, the one and one half), or by contemplating any other means for the sake of shameful gain, he is to be cast out from the clergy and no longer remain under the rule.

c. 226. ON THE SAME MATTER.

From the Council of Laodicea.

It is not fitting for priests and clerics to lend or receive at usury, nor to receive those gains which are called one and one half, that is, the principal and a half.

c. 227. ON THE SAME MATTER.

From the letter of Leo.

Nor have we also thought it to be passed over that some people, seized with lust for shameful gain, lend out their money at interest, and wish to become rich by usury. We deplore that this occurs not only among those who hold a clerical office, but also among laymen who desire to be called Christians.

c. 228. THAT CLERICS NOT ENGAGE IN USURY UNDER ANOTHER'S NAME.
From the same letter.

We were also led to admonish that no cleric is to attempt to engage in usury, just as not in his own name, so also not in another's.

c. 229. ON THE SAME MATTER.
From the Council of Tarragona.

Whoever wishes to be in the clergy is not to strive to profit by purchasing more cheaply or selling more dearly.

c. 230. ON THE SAME MATTER.
From the Council of Elvira.

Bishops, priests, and deacons are not to leave their places for the sake of trade; they are not to go around the provinces, attending fairs. In order to acquire their food, let them send their son, or freedman, or employee, or friend. And if they wish to trade, let them do so within the province.

c. 231. ON THE SAME MATTER.
From the Council of Carthage.

It has pleased that bishops, priests, and deacons are not to be agents or stewards, nor are they to seek their livelihood by any shameful or indecent business, because it is written: "No man, being a soldier of God, entangles himself with secular businesses (2 Tim. 2:4)."

c. 232. ON THE SAME MATTER.
From the same Council.

Also, it has pleased that if a cleric lent money, let him receive money, and if in kind, then, in the same kind let him receive as much as he gave.

c. 233. ON THE SAME MATTER.
From the Capitularies, bk. 2, c. 36.

That priests not only themselves are to abstain from shameful gains and usuries, but are even to instruct the people subject to them also to abstain.

c. 234. ON THE SAME MATTER.
From the Council of Chalcedon.

It has come to the attention of the holy Synod that some of those who appear to have been chosen for the clergy, for the sake of shameful gain, have become agents for other men's possessions and take up secular business under their care, giving little thought to God's ministry. They also run to the houses of secular people and, by reason of their greed, they take on the management of the estates of such people. And so, this holy Council has decreed that henceforth none of these, no bishop, cleric, or monk, is to manage possessions, or become involved in secular business, apart from the management of ecclesiastical properties.

c. 235. ON THE SAME MATTER.
From the Council of Meaux, c. 49.

That no layman is to involve the priests of his churches in the shameful management of farms and, according to the Apostle, in secular and dishonourable business (cf. 2 Tim. 2:4), nor presume to take them elsewhere with him against authority, whereby they are compelled to neglect the ministry entrusted to them. If he has presumed to do so against this interdiction, he is to be excommunicated.

c. 236. OF THOSE WHO HAVE BEEN ORDAINED FOR MONEY.
In the Canons of the Apostles.

If any bishop, or priest, or deacon has obtained this dignity for money, he and the one who ordained him are to be deposed and cut off from communion in every way, as Simon Magus was by Peter (cf. Act. 8:14–24).

c. 237. ON THE SAME MATTER.
From the Council of Chalcedon.

If any bishop should perform an ordination for money, and reduce to a price the grace of the Holy Spirit, which cannot be sold, and for money ordain a bishop, or a priest, or a deacon, let him be subject to the loss of his rank. As for him who is ordained, let him gain no profit from this ordination, but let him be alien from the dignity. And if anyone was an intermediary in what was given or received, let him also, if he is a cleric, fall from his degree, and if he is a monk or layman, let him be anathematized. (See bk. 1, c. 402.)

c. 238. ON THE SAME MATTER.
From the letter of Pope Gelasius.

It is fitting that those who, unworthy by their merits, are established to have purchased a sacred dignity for a price, upon their conviction should be kept at a distance because the condemnation of Simon, which is attested by the sacred text (Act. 8:20–23), binds both the giver and the taker.

c. 239. ON THE SAME MATTER.
From the letter of Pope Hormisdas.

This too we add to what precedes, that the blessing by the imposition of hands, which is believed to be from God, is not to be purchased for a price, because Simon, who wished to buy the Holy Spirit with a bribe, was struck by the curse of the Apostle (Act. 8:20–23).

c. 240. ON THE SAME MATTER.
From the Council of Meaux, c. 43.

The warning is to be repeated over and over again, and so, by the power of Christ's blood, it is to be forbidden to bishops and kings and all the more lofty powers, and to all supporters and electors of anyone, as also to those who consent to them or who ordain them in ecclesiastical degrees, that no one is to obtain a place of rule by the simoniacal heresy, by any deed, craftiness, promise, or benefit, or gift, either personally or through an intermediary. Among other attestations, the Holy Spirit says through the mouth of Gregory: "Why does he not understand that the blessing is turned into a curse for him?" And elsewhere he says: "With sorrow I say it, with groans I announce it: The priesthood which among you has fallen internally cannot long stand externally."

c. 241. THAT A GIFT IS ALSO BY THE TONGUE.
From the sayings of Pope Gregory.

There are some who do not accept payment of money for ordination, yet they bestow sacred orders for some human favour. These certainly do not give freely what they freely receive, since they expect the coin of approval for granting an office of holiness. Hence, Isaiah described the just man, saying: "He is the one who keeps his hand from every kind of gift (Is. 33:15)." For one gift is by deference, another by the hand, another by the tongue. A gift by deference is one of undue submissiveness; a gift by the hand is money; a gift by the tongue is approval. Therefore, he who bestows sacred orders then keeps his hands from all gifts when in divine matters he seeks not only no money, but also no human favour.

c. 242. THAT PRIESTS NOT GIVE GIFTS TO OBTAIN CHURCHES.
From the Capitularies, bk. 1.

That no priest is to give bribes at his entry into a church. (See bk. 1, c. 276.)

c. 243. THAT NO ONE IS TO PLACE A PRIEST IN A CHURCH OR CAST HIM OUT.
From the same Capitulary, c. 41.

That no layman is to presume to place a priest in a church or cast him out, unless by the consent of the bishop.

c. 244. ON THE SAME MATTER.
From the same.

As for those who, without the bishop's consent, establish priests in their churches, or cast them out of the churches, and are unwilling to obey when admonished by the bishop or any of his envoys, they are to be compelled to give pledge for our ban and are ordered with their sureties to come to our palace, and we may then decree whether it pleases us that they pay the ban, or bear some other greater fine.

c. 245. ON CHURCHES WHICH ARE DIVIDED AMONG COHEIRS.
From the same.

As for churches which are divided among coheirs, if, in conformity with the providence and admonition of the bishop, the same coheirs wish to keep and honour them, consideration has been given as to what extent they are to do so. But if they dispute this, it is to remain in the bishop's power whether he permit the churches to remain unchanged there or take the relics out of them.

c. 246. ON THE SAME MATTER.
From the Council of Tribur.

If several heirs have been contending as to a common church, the bishop is to command that the sacred relics be taken from there and the church be closed until, by common consent, they establish a priest there and provide for his living.

c. 247. THAT SEVERAL PRIESTS ARE NOT TO BE ESTABLISHED IN ONE CHURCH.
From the Council of Reims, c. 8.

Just as there ought to be a priest in each church, so also a church, which is called his bride or wife, cannot be divided among several priests, but shall have only one priest, who will rule her chastely and sincerely. And so, we forbid that anyone presume to divide one church between two or more, because Christ's Church ought to be a wife and bride, and not a harlot, as Pope Callixtus attests. (See bk. 1, c. 277.)

c. 248. THAT LAYMEN MUST NOT HOLD CHURCHES, NOR RECEIVE TITHES.
From the Council of Meaux, c. 65.

It is very unworthy that you, who, by God's authority, in your royal dignity excel the rest of the Church's children, seem to carry out more negligently matters which are God's. Hence, it was worthy that you not entrust the chapels of your villages to laymen, but rather to those who would treat those same consecrated places more religiously and would extend to you the due respect. And so, we admonish and exhort you lest (far be it!) you incur the danger of anathema from the presumptuous appropriation of tithes, that you strive to correct this.

C. 249. ON THE SAME MATTER.
Also, from the same.

If you have given your chapels to priests or ecclesiastical men, and they have received the Lord's tithes, from these they are to make suitable provision for repairs to the roof of the church and for lamps; the priests are to receive the parish tithes and duly look after the needs of the people.

C. 250. ON THE SAME MATTER.
Also, from the same.

But if laymen have possession of your chapels, it is alien from reason and authority that they receive tithes, and from them feed their dogs and courtesans. Rather, the priests of the churches are to receive them, and from them support the churches' restoration, and lamps, and the reception of guests and of the poor, and zealously implore the mercy of God for you and the state of your kingdom.

C. 251. ON THOSE WHO ABANDON THE CHURCHES TO WHICH THEY HAVE BEEN PROMOTED AND PASS TO OTHERS.
From the Council of Nicaea.

If any persons temerariously and wrongly, not having the fear of God before their eyes, nor observing the ecclesiastical rule, withdraw from their church, whether they be priest, deacon, or belong to any other rule, they are not to be received in another church. It is agreed that every necessity be imposed upon them to return to their parishes, and, if they do not do so, it is fitting that they be deprived of communion. (See bk. 1, c. 261.)

C. 252. ON THE SAME MATTER.
From the Council of Chalcedon, c. 10.

It is not licit for a cleric to be at the same time enrolled in the churches of two cities, both in the one where from the first he was ordained, and one to which he fled as if to a greater one, out of the desire for vainglory. Those who do this are to be recalled to their church in which they were first ordained, and minister there only.

c. 253. ON THE SAME MATTER.
From the Council of Antioch.

A bishop is not to migrate from one parish to another, neither by intruding himself by his own will, nor under violent compulsion by the people. He is to remain in the Church which God allotted to him from the beginning and is not to move elsewhere from it.

c. 254. ON THE SAME MATTER.
From the decrees of Pope Callixtus.

Just as the wife of one man is not permitted to be approached adulterously by another, or judged, or overseen by him, but only by her own husband while he lives, so the wife of a bishop or priest, which undoubtedly his Church or parish is understood to be, is not permitted to be given to another to judge, or to oversee, or to enjoy in his bed, while he lives. And so, the Apostle says: "A woman is bound by the law while her husband lives, but she is freed from the law of her husband, after he has died (1 Cor. 7:39)." In the same way, a church, which is said to be the spouse of the priest, is bound to him while he lives; but after he has died, let her marry in the Lord, that is, in accordance with the rules. But if she should have married another while he was alive, she shall be judged an adulteress. (See bk. 2, c. 304.)

c. 255. ON CLERICS WHO ARE SET OVER HOSPICES.
From the Council of Chalcedon.

Clerics who are set over hospices, or who are ordained in monasteries and the basilicas of martyrs, are to remain in the power of the bishops who are in each city according to the traditions of the holy Fathers, nor are they to depart from their bishop through contumacy. Those who dare to upset this provision and are not subject to their own bishop, if they are clerics, they shall be subject to the corrections of the canons; if they are laymen or monks, they are to be deprived of communion.

c. 256. THAT A PRIEST HAVE NOT MORE THAN ONE CHURCH.
From the Capitularies, bk. 1, c. 86.

It has been established that each church have its own priest at the provision of the bishop, where resources allow it.

c. 257. ON THE SAME MATTER.
From the Council of Nantes.

Indeed, just as a bishop cannot have more than one city, and a husband one wife, so a priest only one church. Hence, no priest is to presume to have several churches, unless perhaps he have other priests under himself in each of them, who may fulfil the night and day office solemnly and carry out the celebrations of mass with daily ceremonies.

c. 258. THAT NO PRIEST RECEIVE ANOTHER'S PARISHIONER.
From the Capitularies, bk. 1, tit. 148.

That no priest receive at mass another's parishioner, unless he is travelling, or he has a legal proceeding there.

c. 259. ON THE SAME MATTER.
From the Council of Carthage.

Bishop Cassian said: May your Gravity establish that each cleric or layman is not to receive communion in another congregation without the letters of his bishop.

c. 260. ON THE SAME MATTER.
From the Capitularies, bk. 1, tit. 188.

That no priest is to presume to sing mass in another's parish, unless he is travelling, nor dare to receive the tithe which pertains to another.

c. 261. THAT A BISHOP IS NOT TO PERFORM AN ORDINATION IN ANOTHER BISHOP'S PARISH.
From the Council of Antioch.

A bishop is not to visit a strange city, which is not subject to him, nor go into a possession which does not pertain to him, nor presume to perform an ordination there, unless perhaps with the counsel and will of the bishop of the region.

c. 262. THAT NO PRIEST OR LAYMAN IS TO INVITE A PENITENT TO DRINK WINE OR EAT MEAT.
From the Capitulary, bk. 1, tit. 151.

That no priest or layman is to invite a penitent to drink wine or eat meat, unless he has given presently for him one or two pennies according to the quality of his penance.

c. 263. THAT NO PRIEST WRITE A CHARTER.
Also, from the same.

That no priest write a charter, or to be an agent of his [secular] superior.

c. 264. THAT NO ONE, CONTEMNING A LESSER CHURCH, ASPIRE TO A BETTER ONE.
From the Synod of Meaux.

If anyone from the priestly order, out of contempt for a lesser church, evilly and out of ambition, has aspired to a better one, let the canonical pronouncement be observed regarding him.

c. 265. ON BAPTISM, AND AT WHAT TIME IT IS TO BE CELEBRATED.
From the Canon of the Apostles.

If any bishop or priest has not baptized in accordance with the Lord's commandment in the name of the Father, the Son, and the Holy Spirit, but in three beginning-less beginnings, or in three sons, or in three paracletes, let him be cast out.

c. 266. ON THE SAME MATTER.
From the same.

If any bishop or priest does not celebrate the threefold immersion of the one mystery, but immerses only once in baptism (which seems by some to be given in the death of the Lord), let him be deposed. For the Lord did not say: Baptize in my death; but: "Going therefore, teach you all nations; baptizing them in the name of the Father, and of the Son, and of the Holy Spirit (Mt. 28:19)."

c. 267. THAT BAPTISM IS TO BE DONE AT EASTER AND PENTECOST.
From the letter of Pope Leo.

Hence, because it is most manifestly clear that these two times, that is, Easter and Pentecost, are lawful for baptizing those who have been chosen in the Church, we admonish your Dilection that you add no other days to this observance. Because even if there are other feasts on which much reverence is due in God's honour, nevertheless, the mystical and reasonable exemplary role of our principal and greatest sacrament is to be kept by us, without denying that license by which help is given in providing baptism at any time to those who are in danger. We delay the free vows of those who are healthy and in the safety of peace to these two connected and cognate feasts in such a way that at no time do we deny this singular stronghold of true salvation to anyone in danger of death, in the difficulties of a siege, in the anguish of persecution, in fear of shipwreck.

c. 268. ON BAPTIZING PREGNANT WOMEN.
From the Council of Neocaesarea.

It is fitting to baptize a pregnant woman whenever she wishes. For she communicates nothing of this to the unborn child, since the intent of each person is declared by confession.

c. 269. ON THE SAME MATTER.
From the Council of Carthage.

It has also pleased, concerning infants, whenever very certain witnesses are not found who may attest without doubt that they were baptized, and who are not fit themselves by reason of age to answer as to the sacraments they may have received, that they be baptized without any scruple.

c. 270. ON THE BAPTIZED WHO DIE WITHOUT CONFIRMATION.
From the Council of Elvira.

If any deacon ruling a congregation without a bishop or priest has baptized some persons, the bishop is obliged to perfect them by a blessing. If they have already departed this world, each one can be righteous by the faith which he has.

c. 271. ON THE REBAPTIZED.
From the Council of Lérida.

As to those who have been rebaptized in apostasy, without any necessity or torture, it pleased that the statutes of the Synod of Nicaea about them be observed, that is, that they pray for seven years among the catechumens, and for two among Catholics, and afterwards communicate with the faithful in the offering and Eucharist.

c. 272. AS ABOVE.
From the Council of Worms.

Each of the faithful is to know that the sacrament of most holy baptism is not to be conferred other than on the feast of Easter or Pentecost, except for those whom it is fitting to aid with such remedies, lest they perish eternally because of the pressing danger of death.

c. 273. ON THE SAME MATTER.
From the Council of Meaux, c. 48.

None of the priests is to presume to baptize other than in the villages and baptismal churches and at the established times, except for reason of illness or certain necessity, and those villages are to retain their due authority and privileges.

c. 274. ON SACRED FONTS.
As above.

Each priest, who has been unable to have stone fonts, is to have a suitable vessel exclusively for the administration of baptism. Similarly, for the washing of the corporal and altar palls, let there be appropriate vessels in which nothing else is done.

c. 275. THAT EACH PRIEST TEACH THE CREED AND THE LORD'S PRAYER TO HIS PARISHIONERS.

From the Council of Reims, tit. 20.

That each priest is to teach, or enjoin others to do so, all his parishioners the Creed and the Lord's Prayer. And, when they come to confession in the Lenten season, he is to have these recited from memory to him by each of them, nor is he to give communion to anyone if the person does not know how to say these by heart, if, indeed, without knowledge of these, no one can be saved. For in the first is contained the Christian faith and belief, and in the second is expressed what we must pray for and seek from God. That no one can be saved without faith, the Lord shows when he says: "He who believes and is baptized will be saved (Mk. 16:16)." But no one can believe what he does not know and has not heard, as Paul says: "And how are they to believe in him, until they have heard him (Rom. 10:14)?" Nor does it suffice only to have faith in the heart, unless it is also enunciated in words, as the same Apostle testifies: "The heart has only to believe, if we are to be justified; the lips have only to make confession, if we are to be saved (Rom. 10:10)." Let no one plead stolidity of feeling, or weakness of intelligence, because these things are so short that there is no one, no matter how dull and barbaric he may be, who cannot learn this and state it in common words. And yet these are so great that anyone who can take in knowledge of them fully may well believe it suffices him for eternal salvation. It is also to be observed that no one is to receive an infant at baptism from the sacred font before he recites the Creed and the Lord's Prayer before the priest; and that the priest announce to all godparents that they owe it to their godchildren to teach them these things when they come to an age of understanding. (See bk. 2, c. 428.)

c. 276. OF THOSE PRIESTS OR CLERICS WHO STEAL OR SUBVERT THE CHURCHES OR BENEFICES OF OTHER PRIESTS FOR MONEY.

It has been decreed and in all ways prohibited that, if any priest should be caught giving or having given gifts to any cleric or layman, or conferring any money in order to take away another priest's church, for this cupidity, or theft for the sake of shameful gain, he is to be cast out of the clergy and is to be alien from its rule. If out of mercy it should please the bishop to place him who repents what he has done in the tribulation of jail for a long time, there to be detained until satisfaction, and afterwards, if he has corrected himself and has promised not to do such things henceforth, then the bishop may act more humanely toward him, if he wishes and the priest has been found worthy.

c. 277. THAT EACH PRIEST BE CONTENT WITH ONE CHURCH.
From the Council as above.

Each priest is to be content with the one church to which he has been ordained, and no one is to presume to minister in two churches. (See bk. 1, c. 247.)

c. 278. THAT A PRIEST NOT RECEIVE A CHURCH THROUGH MONEY.
As above.

That no one become a supplanter of another priest secretly by some device or manifestly, and if a priest has acquired another's church for a price or for money by the simoniacal heresy, he is to be deposed in every way.

ON THE FAST.

c. 279. ON THE GREATER LITANY.
From the Council of Mainz, c. 16.

It pleased us that the greater litany be observed by all Christians on one day, on the seventh day before the Kalends of May, as we found in our reading and as our holy Fathers established; they are not to ride horses, or wear precious garments, but are to cover themselves in ashes and wear sackcloth, unless infirmity impedes them.

c. 280. ON THE FAST OF THE ROGATIONS.

When, for their sins, the people of the Gauls were being killed fiercely by the rage of wolves, nor was it possible to find a remedy to this scourge, the bishops of the Gauls are said to have met in the city of Vienne, and they established in common that they would do a three-day fast. And when the Lord mercifully took the plague away, those days became a customary annual celebration to be held throughout the provinces of the Gauls before the day of the Ascension of the Lord. Let us see to it that we too keep these days with the highest reverence and devotion, with abstinence of the flesh and humility of heart, not to escape the rage of visible wolves, but of the invisible ones, that is, that we be able to overcome the temptations of unclean spirits. On those days, let none wear precious clothing, because we must lament in sackcloth and ashes. Let drunkenness and revelries be forbidden. Let no one presume to ride horses then, but let all walk barefoot. Women are not to dance, but all in common are to sing "Lord, have mercy" and, with contrition of heart, beseech God's mercy for sins, for peace, for the plague, for the preservation of the harvest, and for other necessities. For these are days of abstinence, not of rejoicing.

c. 281. ON THE FAST OF THE EMBER DAYS.
From the Council of Mainz.

We establish that four times of the year be observed by all with a fast, that is, in March, the first week; in June, the second; in September, the third; in December, the week which shall be complete before the vigil of the Lord's Nativity. That is, on Wednesday, Friday, and Saturday, let all come to the church at the ninth hour for the solemnities of mass with the litanies.

c. 282. ON FASTING ON THE VIGILS OF THE SAINTS.

As priests announce the sacred feasts to the people, they are also to admonish them to observe the fast of the vigils in every way.

c. 283. ON A PRESCRIBED FAST.
From the Council of Mainz.

If anyone, in his pride, has contemned to keep a prescribed fast and has been unwilling to observe it with other Christians, it is prescribed in the Council of Gangra that he be anathematized.

c. 284. ON THE SAME MATTER.
From the Council of Gangra.

If anyone of those who pursue continence becomes insolent and, without bodily necessity, dissolves the fasts held in common and kept by the Church driven on by the goad of his own judgment, let him be anathema.

c. 285. ALSO, ON THE SAME MATTER.

Those who violate a prescribed fast without grave necessity ought to remember Jonathan, the son of King Saul, who gave little weight to his father's curse and ate a little honey at the tip of his staff and so merited a sentence of death (cf. 1 Sam. 14:24–30).

c. 286. ON THE SAME MATTER.
Also, from the Capitularies, bk. 1, c. 48.

That the fasts prescribed in the Church not be broken by priests without a reasonable necessity.

c. 287. ON THE SAME MATTER.

As to this, if famine, pestilence, unseasonable weather, or any other tribulation has come, do not await our edict, but let the Lord's mercy be begged immediately.

c. 288. WHAT IS USURY.

From the Capitularies.

It is usury, where more is required than is given. For example, if you gave ten shillings, and you asked for more back, or if you gave one measure of wheat, and you exact something above that.

c. 289. ON THE SAME MATTER.

Also, c. 123.

They acquire a shameful gain who, by various devious devices intended to generate gains, dishonestly strive to amass any goods.

c. 290. WHAT IS A LOAN.

A loan consists in someone lending something. A loan is just when one does not require more than one lent.

c. 291. ON THE SAME MATTER.

In the same place, c. 125.

Whoever, at the time of harvest or grape-gathering, buys wheat or wine, not by any need, but out of cupidity, so that, for example, he buys a measure for two pennies and keeps it until it is sold for four, or six, or more pennies, we call this a shameful gain.

c. 292. ON CONFESSION AND PENANCE.

Priests are to admonish the people subject to them that anyone who feels himself wounded with the wound of death-dealing sin, on the Wednesday before Lent is in all haste to have recourse to the vivifying Mother Church. There, after confessing simply, with all humility and contrition of heart, what he has evilly committed, he is to receive the remedies of penance according to the manner set forth by canonical authorities, and he is to be handed over to Satan for the destruction of his flesh, so that his spirit might be saved in the day of the Lord (1 Cor. 5:5). Not only he who has committed some mortal sin, but also any man at all who recognizes that he has polluted with the stain of sin Christ's immaculate robe, which he received at baptism, is to hurry to his own priest. In purity of mind, he is to confess humbly all transgressions, all sins by which he is mindful that he incurred God's offense. He is to follow diligently and fulfil most carefully whatever is enjoined upon him by the priest, as if it had issued from the mouth of almighty God himself.

C. 293. ON PENITENTS.
From the African Council.

If the crime of a penitent is public and so very widely known as to have moved the whole Church, a hand is to be imposed upon him before the apse.

C. 294. ON THE SAME MATTER.
From the Council of Agde.

The penitents, when they seek penance, are to receive from the priest the imposition of hands and the sackcloth over their heads, in the manner established everywhere. They are to be turned away if they do not cut off their hair or change their dress.

C. 295. ALSO, AS ABOVE.

At the beginning of Lent, all the penitents who have or had received public penance are to present themselves to the bishop of the city before the doors of the church. They are to be dressed in sackcloth, with bare feet, their glance turned to the ground, proclaiming themselves guilty by their very dress and attitude. The deans are to be present there, namely the archpriests of the parishes, with the witnesses, that is, the penitents' priests, who are to examine carefully the penitents' manner of life. [The bishop] is to impose penance in accordance with the measure of the fault and the above-stated criteria. Afterwards, let him lead the penitents into the church and, prostrated on the ground, with the whole clergy tearfully sing the seven penitential psalms to obtain their absolution. Then, rising from this prayer, in accordance with what the canons prescribe, he is to place his hands on them, sprinkle them with holy water, mark them with ashes, and cover their heads with sackcloth. And, with groans and frequent sighs, he is to tell them that, as Adam was cast out of paradise, so are they too now cast out from the Church for their sins. Then he will command his ministers to take the penitents outside the doors of the church, while the clergy accompanies them with the responsory: "By the sweat of your brow you shall eat your bread (Gen. 3:19)," so that the penitents, seeing Holy Church to be filled with fear and sadness for their sins, will not approach their penance lightly. On Holy Thursday, they will again be presented by their deans and priests at the entrance of the church.

c. 296. ON ASSIGNING PENANCE.
From the Council of Mainz.

The manner and time of penance is to be imposed by priests on those who confess their sins either by the instruction of the ancient canons, or by the authority of the holy Scriptures, or by an approved ecclesiastical custom. For those who impose unaccustomed and light manners of penance for grave sins, according to the Prophet's words, "stitch an elbow-cushion for every comer, make a soft pillow for the heads of young and old to capture souls (Ez. 13:18)." But a distinction is to be preserved between those who do penance publicly and hiddenly. For it is fitting that he who sins publicly be punished with public penance and, according to the order of the canons, he is to be excommunicated as he deserves and to be reconciled.

c. 297. HOW BISHOPS OR PRIESTS ARE TO RECEIVE A PENITENT.
From the Roman Penitential.

As often as Christians come to penance, we enjoin fasts; and we ought to share in their fast for one or two weeks, or as much as we can, so it is not said to us what the Lord said to the priests of the Jews: "Woe to you, experts in the law, who burden men and place heavy and unbearable burdens on their shoulders, while you yourselves do not touch their load with one of your fingers (cf. Mt. 23:4)."

c. 298. ALSO, AFTER A FEW WORDS.

And as often as you give counsel to a sinner, give him a penance immediately as to how much he is to fast, or redeem his sins with alms, lest you perhaps forget what he has already told you and it be necessary for you to question him again, and perhaps he would blush to confess again, and be judged more broadly.

c. 299. THAT NO ONE ELSE PRESUME TO GIVE PENANCE TO ANOTHER OR HEAR CONFESSION, EXCEPT A BISHOP OR PRIEST.
From the same.

Just as none but bishops and priests, to whom the keys of the kingdom of heaven have been entrusted, are to offer the sacrifice, so also neither are others to usurp the judgments of penitents.

c. 300. THAT A DEACON, IF IT IS NECESSARY, RECEIVE THE CONFESSION.
Also.

But if necessity occurs, and the priest is not present, a deacon may receive a penitent to holy communion.

c. 301. ALSO, ON RECEIVING CONFESSION.
From the Penitential of Archbishop Theodore, or Bede the priest.

Bishops or priests, when they receive the confessions of the faithful, are to humble themselves and pray with groans of sadness and tears, not only for their own wrongs, but also for the fall of their brother. For the Apostle says: "Who is weak, and I am not weak (2 Cor. 11:29)?"

c. 302. ON THE SAME MATTER.
Also, as above.

Hence, when someone has come to the priest to confess his sins, let the priest command him to wait a little time until he enters the church, or his chamber, to pray. But if the place is not suitable for this, let him say this prayer in his heart:

c. 303. PRAYER.

Lord, almighty God, be propitious to me, a sinner, that I may worthily give you thanks for making my unworthy self, out of your mercy, a minister of the priestly office. You established me as the poor and humble mediator to pray and intercede before our Lord Jesus Christ, your Son, for sinners and for those returning to penance. And so, Lord and Ruler, who wish all men to be saved and to come to the knowledge of truth, and wish not for the death of sinners, but that they convert and live, receive my prayer, which I pour out before your clemency, for your male and female servants who have come to penance, that you may give them the spirit of compunction, and that they may recover from the snares of the devil, by which they are kept bound, and return to you by worthy satisfaction. Through the same, etc.

As the one who comes to penance sees the priest sad and tearful over his wrongs, he is struck all the more with the fear of God and is further saddened and feels horror for his sins.

c. 304. ORDER FOR THE GIVING OF PENANCE.
As above.

Then, ask him soothingly and mildly:

Do you believe in God the Father, Son, and Holy Spirit?

Resp. I believe.

Do you believe that these three persons is one God?

Resp. I believe.

Do you believe that in this very flesh in which you now are you are to rise again on the day of Judgment, and receive the good or the evil which you have done?

Resp. I believe.

Are you willing to forgive the sins of those who have sinned against you, with the Lord saying: "If you do not forgive your fellow men their sins, neither will your Father forgive your sins (cf. Mt. 6:14–15)"?

Resp. I am.

And ask him diligently whether he is incestuous, or faithless to his superior; and if he is not willing to set aside his incest, you cannot give him a penance; but if he is willing, you can. After these things have been done, the priest is to speak affectionately to the penitent in these words:

Brother, do not be ashamed to confess your sins, for I too am a sinner, and perhaps I have done worse things than you have. But I make these admonitions because it is the customary vice of humankind, as Blessed Gregory says, to commit sin by falling, and not to reveal what has been committed by confessing, but to defend it by denying, and convicted to multiply it by defending. Even as we did not fear, at the devil's instigation, to perpetrate nefarious crimes, these very same things, which we did without any shame in deed, at the persuasion of the same, we blush to confess even in words. We are ashamed to say before a man who is like us, and perhaps subject to the same passions, those greatly detestable things which we did not fear to do without any blushing of our mind before God, who sees all things. Hence, let us confess freely what we committed under no one's coercion. But if we have hidden our crimes, they shall be revealed by the one who is both accuser and encourager of sin. Indeed, he instigates us to sin, and he accuses us when we have sinned; hence, if we forestall him in this life and become the accusers of our own crime, we will escape the malice of the devil, our enemy and accuser, as Paul attests, saying: "If we were to judge ourselves, we would not at all be judged (1 Cor. 11:31)."

As the priest sees him blushing, let him continue again: "Perhaps, most beloved, not all things that you have done now come into your memory. I will question you. Beware lest, at the persuasion of the devil, you presume to hide anything." And then let him question him in an orderly manner.

Did you commit a homicide either by accident, or voluntarily or involuntarily, or to avenge relatives, or at your lord's command, or in a public war? If you did it voluntarily, you must do penance for seven years; if involuntarily or by accident, for five years. If to avenge a relative, one year, and three forty-day fasts and lawfully prescribed days for the next two years. If at war, forty days. If you are free, and you killed an innocent slave at your lord's command, one year, with three forty-day fasts and lawfully prescribed days for two further years. If the slave deserved death, then do penance for forty days.

Q. Did you cut off the hands or feet, or rip out a man's eyes, or did you wound a man? For the mutilation, you are to do penance for one year; for the wounding, forty days.

Q. Did you commit perjury, either out of worldly cupidity, or coerced and out of necessity either for your life or that of your relatives, or unknowingly, or did you induce others into perjury knowingly? If you perjured yourself knowingly and induced others into perjury, you are to do penance for seven years. If unknowingly, one year and three forty-day fasts. If for life or limbs, three forty-day fasts.

Q. Did you commit theft, or sacrilege, or break-ins, or rapine, taking what was not yours? If you broke into houses by night and took away four-footed animals, or a more valuable thing worth forty shillings, you are to do penance for one year and repay the price. If you do not repay it, you are to do penance for two years. If you committed a greater theft, you are to do penance for three years, and if you did it often, seven years. For a small theft, twenty days; children, ten days. If you took something from a church, which is sacrilege, you are to do penance for seven years.

Q. Did you commit adultery with another's wife or betrothed, or did you corrupt a virgin, or with a nun or a woman dedicated to God, or with an unbound woman, that is, without a husband, or with your own maidservant? If you are an adulterer with another's wife or with a nun, you are to do penance for seven years; if with a virgin, two years; if with a widow, one year. If you dismissed your wife and joined with another woman, you are to do penance for seven years; if with an unbound woman, three forty-day fasts and lawfully prescribed days; if with your own maidservant, you are to do penance for forty days.

Q. Did you have intercourse with your wife or maidservant from behind? If you did it, you are to do penance for forty days.

Q. Did you have intercourse with your wife forty days before she gave birth? You are to do penance for forty days.

Q. Did you have intercourse on Sunday? You are to do penance for three days.

Q. Did you abduct a virgin or a widow? You are to do penance for three years.

Q. Did you commit fornication as the men of Sodom did, or with animals, or with your mother or sister? You are to do penance for fifteen or twelve years.

Q. Did you defile yourself with your wife in Lent? If you did this, you are to do penance for one year, or give twenty-six shillings in alms. If it happened because of drunkenness, you are to do penance for forty days. One must also beware of this, that a husband is to be continent toward his wife for twenty days before the Lord's Nativity and Pentecost, and every Sunday, and after conception has become manifest.

Q. Did you give false testimony out of cupidity or unknowingly? You are to do penance for one year.

Q. Did you cut off any limb? You are to do penance for three years.

Q. Did you hate your brother? For as long as you remained in that hate, for so long you are to do penance at bread and water.

Q. Did you disparage any man before a superior or peers out of envy? You are to do penance for forty days.

Q. Did you violate a tomb for theft? You are to do penance for two years.

Q. Did any negligence concerning the Lord's sacrifice happen to you? You are to do penance for a hundred or forty days.

Q. Did you consult magicians, or diviners, or sorcerers, or soothsayers, or did you make the vows which are done at trees or springs, or cast lots? You are to do penance for three years.

Q. Did you take any money from a church? Either restore it fourfold or do penance for three years.

Q. Did you destroy anyone by an unjust accusation? You are to do penance for three years.

Q. Did you lead or send any Christian man into captivity? You are to do penance for three years.

Q. Did you burn another's house or threshing-floor? You are to do penance for three years.

Q. Did you vomit for drunkenness? You are to do penance for fifteen days. If in a contest, forty days. If unknowingly, you are to do penance for seven days.

Q. Did you eat animals that were dead or torn by beasts? You are to do penance for forty days. Similarly, if you ate blood.

Q. Did you drink any liquid in which a dead mouse or weasel had been found? You are to do penance for forty days.

Q. Did you contemn a fast prescribed in the Church or the decrees of your superiors? You are to do penance for forty days. If in Lent, one year.

Q. Did you crush your infant? You are to do penance for five years or for three years.

Q. Did you drink anything made by witchcraft, that is, herbs or other things, so as to be unable to have children, or did you give it to another, or did you wish to kill a man with a deadly potion, or did you teach another to do this, or did you taste your husband's semen so he would burn with love for you, or did you drink chrism or give it to another to subvert God's judgment? If you have done any of these, you are to do penance for seven years.

Q. Did you kill willingly your offspring? You are to do penance for ten years. And if you killed your son or daughter, twelve years. And if in the uterus before quickening, one year. If after quickening, three years. If your infant, by your negligence, has died without baptism, you are to do penance for one year, and you are never to be without some penance.

Q. Did you do anything which the pagans do on the Kalends of January, with a stag or calf? You are to do penance for three years.

Q. Did you do or say anything at the beginning or in the course of any work by way of the soothsayer's or magician's art? You are to do penance for one year.

Q. Did you place your child on the roof or on the stove for some cure, or did you burn grains where a dead man lay? You are to do penance for five years.

Q. Did you sing diabolical verses over the dead? You are to do penance for twenty days.

Q. Did you join with your wife during her menstrual period? You are to do penance for forty days.

Q. Did you have intercourse with your wife after she gave birth and before forty days were completed? You are to do penance for thirty days.

Q. Did you take communion from the Lord's sacrifice, without first abstaining from your wife's embrace for five or seven days? You are to do penance for twenty days.

Q. Did you do any work on Sunday? You are to do penance for seven days.

Q. Did you disparage or curse someone out of envy? You are to do penance for seven days.

Now, I will explain to you the eight principal vices, that is, pride, vainglory, envy, wrath, melancholy, avarice, gluttony, lust. If you are aware of being guilty of any of these, take up penance, because from these all vices arise.

From pride, which is the beginning of all sin and the queen of all evils, is born all disobedience, all presumption, and all stubbornness, contentions, heresies, arrogance.

From vainglory arise disobedience, boasting, hypocrisy, contentions, stubbornness, discords, the presumptions of novelties.

From envy is born hate, whispering, disparagement, exultation in a neighbour's adversities, affliction in his prosperity.

From wrath arise quarrels, swelling of the mind, insults, clamour, indignation, blasphemies.

From melancholy is born malice, rancour, pusillanimity, despair, torpor, wandering of the mind.

From avarice arise betrayal, fraud, deceit, perjury, restlessness, and hardening of heart against mercy.

From gluttony is propagated unseemly joy, scurrility, uncleanness, excessive talking, dullness of the senses.

From lust is generated blindness of mind, lack of consideration, inconstancy, precipitousness, love of self, hate for God, fondness for the present world, horror and despair as to the future.

ADDRESS.

Hence, if you were proud until now, humble yourself in the sight of God. If you have loved vainglory, consider whether you do not lose an eternal reward for the sake of transitory praise. If the rust of envy has consumed you until now (and this is the worst of sins and detestable above all, because an envious person is compared to the devil, who envied what was given to the first man that he himself had lost by his own fault), then do penance and count the profit of others as your own. If melancholy overcomes you, ponder patience and longanimity. If the illness of avarice burdens you, consider that it is the root of all evils, and that it is compared to idolatry, and so it is fitting that you be generous. If wrath vexes you, which rests in the bosom of the foolish, you must rule your own spirit and make it flee from you by the tranquility of your mind. If gluttony draws you to devour, follow sobriety. If you lust, vow chastity.

Then the penitent casts himself upon the ground and says in tears: "In these and in the other vices by which human fragility can sin against its God and Creator in thought, speech, deed, delight, and desire, I confess that I have sinned in all, and I acknowledge and confess that I am guilty more than all men in God's sight. I beseech you humbly, priest of God, to intercede for me and for my sins before our Lord and Creator that I may merit to receive forgiveness and indulgence for these and all my wrongs."

Then the priest is to rise and sing Psalm 37, followed by Psalms 50 and 53. Then he is to prostrate himself on the ground and say the following prayer:

PRAYER

I pray, Lord, your clemency, mercy, and majesty that you deign to grant forgiveness to your servant N., who has confessed his sins and crimes, and to forgive the guilt of his past deeds; you, Lord, who brought back the lost sheep on your shoulders and were placated by the prayers and confession of the publican, deign to be favourably disposed also to this servant of yours. Assist his prayers with benignity, so that he may remain acceptable in confession. May his tears and prayer gain speedily your perpetual clemency, and, restored to the holy altars, may he be granted eternal hope and heavenly glory. You who live, etc.

Then, let it be added:

May almighty God be your help and protection, and may he grant you forgiveness for your sins, past, present, and future.

We excerpted these things on the remedies of sins from the monuments of our predecessors; yet, in all these things, we made use not of the authority of the censor, but rather of the counsel of a fellow sufferer. We admonish energetically each learned priest of Christ that in all that he finds noted here he is to distinguish attentively as to the sex, age, condition, state, person, understanding, and the very heart of the penitent; he is to judge each matter in accordance with these as seems best to him. It is necessary to correct all errors by doing what pertains to the purgation of sins, for some by abstinence from foods, for others by giving alms, for a few by frequent kneeling, or standing as on a cross. All of these must depend on the examination of the discreet judge.

c. 305. ON PENITENTS.
From the African Council.

The times of penance are to be decreed at the bishop's discretion according to the difference of sins.

c. 306. ON THE SAME MATTER.
From the same.

That a priest is to enjoin the laws of penance without acception of persons upon one who implores penance.

c. 307. THAT PENANCE BE ASSIGNED TO THE MARRIED WITH THEIR CONSENT.
From the Council of Arles.

Penance is not to be assigned to the married other than with their consent.

c. 308. ON THE SAME MATTER.
From the Council of Laodicea.

As for those who have sinned by diverse crimes and shown perfect conversion from their evils by persevering in their prayer and penance, after a time of penance has been imposed on them according to the quality of their wrong, out of God's mercy and goodness, communion is to be granted to them.

c. 309. ON THE SAME MATTER.
From a Penitential.

If you see any one of the men approaching penance remain at it assiduously and fiercely, immediately act more leniently toward him.

c. 310. ON THE SAME MATTER.
From the African Council.

That a priest must not reconcile a penitent without consulting the bishop, unless necessity compel in the bishop's absence.

c. 311. ON THE SAME MATTER.
From a letter of Pope Innocent.

As for penitents who are under the obligation of penance, whether for graver sins, or for lighter ones, if there is no intervening illness, the custom of the Roman Church shows that they are to receive remission on the Thursday before Easter. Indeed, if anyone has fallen into illness and has come to the point of despair, remission is to be granted him before the time of Easter.

c. 312. ON THE SAME MATTER.
From the Council of Carthage.

That negligent penitents are to be received later.

c. 313. THAT NO PRIEST RECEIVE A PENITENT OF ANOTHER'S CITY OR PARISH, OR RECONCILE HIM WITHOUT THE TESTIMONY OF THE BISHOP OR PRIEST.
From the letter of Pope Felix.

The greatest care is to be taken lest any of our brothers and fellow bishops, or even priests, receive a penitent in another's city or diocese, or anyone placed under the hand of a priest, or someone who says that he has been reconciled, without the testimony and letters of the bishop or priest to whose parish he pertains.

c. 314. THAT A HAND BE NOT IMPOSED ON PRIESTS AND DEACONS AS THEY ARE ON PENITENTS.
From the Council of Carthage.

It is confirmed that, if priests or deacons have been convicted of some grave fault which requires their removal from the ministry, a hand is not to be imposed on them as is done for penitents or the lay faithful.

c. 315. THAT PENANCE NOT BE DENIED TO CLERICS.
From the Council of Arles.

Penance is not to be denied to the clerics who desire it.

c. 316. HOW PRIESTS AND DEACONS DO PENANCE.
From the letter of Pope Leo.

It is foreign from the custom of the Church that those who have been consecrated to the honour of the priesthood or the degree of the diaconate should receive the remedy of penance by the imposition of hand for any crime, according to what is written: "If a priest shall have sinned, who shall pray for him (1 Sam. 2:25)?" Hence, by those who have lapsed in this way, a private withdrawal must be sought to earn God's mercy, where their atonement, if it is worthy, may also be fruitful.

c. 317. THAT PENITENTS ARE TO ABSTAIN FROM TRADE.
From the letter of Pope Leo.

The quality of his gain either excuses, or condemns a trader, because there is an honourable and a shameful profit. And yet, for a penitent, it is more useful even to suffer losses than to be bound by the dangers of trade, because it is difficult for sin not to intervene in the commerce between buyer and seller.

c. 318. THAT A PENITENT WHO HAS LAID DOWN HIS BELT IS NOT TO RETURN TO THE WORLDLY ARMY.
From the same.

It is entirely contrary to ecclesiastical rules to return to the worldly army after the performance of penance, since the Apostle says: "No man, being a soldier to God, entangles himself with secular businesses (2 Tim. 2:4)." Hence, he is not free from the devil's snares who wishes to entangle himself in the worldly army.

c. 319. ON THE SAME MATTER.
From the Council of Arles.

Those who abandon the purpose of holy religion and return to the world and do not afterwards seek the remedies of penance are not to receive communion without penance. We also order that they be not admitted to clerical office.

c. 320. ON THE SAME MATTER.
Also, from the same.

Whoever presumes to wear secular attire is to be expelled from the Church.

c. 321. ON THE SAME MATTER.
From the Council of Toledo.

As for those who, after penance, return to their former sins, the Councils of the ancient Fathers decree that those who, after penance, return as dogs and swine to their former vomits and wallowing pits, until they have recourse to the remedies of penance and return to the order they have abandoned, are to be treated as excommunicate and condemned by an anathema.

c. 322. ON THE SAME MATTER.
From the sayings of Gregory.

He who remembers that he committed illicit things is to see to it that he abstains even from licit ones so far as to make satisfaction to his Creator, that having committed forbidden things he must cut off from himself even the ones that are allowed.

c. 323. ON THE SAME MATTER.
From the letter of Leo.

It is fitting that he who seeks forgiveness for illicit things abstain even from licit ones, as the Apostle says: "All things are lawful, but not all things are expedient (1 Cor. 6:12)."

c. 324. ON THE SAME MATTER.
From the Council of Toledo.

Those things which are repeated by frequent transgression are condemned also with a frequent sentence.

c. 325. ON THE SAME MATTER.
From the sayings of Bishop Basil.

It is fitting that he who is penitent from the heart be received as the Lord shows, when he says: "He called together his friends and neighbours, saying: 'Rejoice with me, for I have found my sheep that I had lost' (Lk. 15:6)."

c. 326. WHAT DISPOSITION THE PENITENT IS TO HAVE.
As above.

The penitent is to receive within himself the same disposition as that person had who said: "I have hated and abhorred iniquity (Ps. 118:163)."

C. 327. WHAT IS TRUE PENANCE.
From the sayings of Augustine.

Nothing makes a penance certain other than hatred for sin and love of God. When you so repent that what used to be sweet in life tastes bitter to your spirit, and what used to delight you in your body now tortures you in your heart, then you are truly penitent.

C. 328. HOW WE ARE TO BE TOWARD THE IMPENITENT.
As above.

Toward him who does not repent of his sin, we must be such as the Lord commanded, saying: "Let him be to you as a heathen and a publican (Mt. 18:17)," and as the Apostle commands: "Withdraw yourselves from every brother walking disorderly, and not according to the tradition which we gave you (2 Thess. 3:6)."

C. 329. ON SACRED COMMUNION.
(*From the Canon of the Apostles*: All faithful Christians. *Also*: All who enter church. See above, cc. 195 and 196: On priests who do not communicate).
From the Definition of Ecclesiastical Teachings.

I neither praise, nor condemn daily reception of the Eucharist, but I exhort all to communicate every Sunday. But if the mind has the will to sin, I say that the reception of the Eucharist rather burdens than purifies. And so, although one is vexed by sin, if he does not have the wish to sin in the future, let him make satisfaction with tears and prayers, and confiding in the mercy of the Lord, let him approach the Eucharist fearlessly and securely. But I say this of one whom mortal sins do not burden.

C. 330. ON THE SAME MATTER.
Also, Augustine to Januarius.

One person has said that the Eucharist is not to be received every day, another affirms that it is; let each of them do what he piously believes is to be done according to his faith. Indeed, they did not fight among themselves, nor did one of them set himself above the other, Zacchaeus and that centurion, when one of them received the Lord in his house with rejoicing (Lk. 19:6), and the other said: "I am not worthy that you enter under my roof (Mt. 8:8)." Both honoured the Saviour, although not in the same way. Both were miserable in their sins; both received mercy. It is relevant to this that each one tasted the manna in his own mouth according to his own will.

C. 331. ON DILIGENCE AS TO THE BODY OF THE LORD.
From the letter of Pope Clement.

Certainly, so many holocausts are to be offered at the altar as must suffice for the people. And if they should be left over, let them not be reserved for the following day, but let them be consumed with fear and trembling by the clerics' diligence. But those who consume the remains of the Lord's body which have been left in the sacristy are not to proceed immediately to consume common foods nor are they to believe the holy food is mixed with the food which is digested in the intestines and expelled in private. Hence, if it is offered on Sunday morning, let the ministers who have consumed it fast until the sixth hour; and if they received it at the third or fourth hour, let them fast until vespers. In this way, the eternal sacraments are to be kept with a secret sanctification.

C. 332. ON THE SAME MATTER.
From the Capitularies, bk. 1, c. 32.

That all the faithful receive communion, and that they remain at mass until the final prayer.

C. 333. ON THE SAME MATTER.
Also, from bk. 2, c. 37.

Great discretion is to be exercised in the reception of the body and blood of the Lord. There is to be care lest, if one delays it too long, it result in ruin to the soul, as the Lord says: "Unless you eat of the flesh of the son of man and drink of his blood, you will not have life in you (Jn. 6:54)." But if it is received without discretion, that is to be feared which the Apostle says: "For he who eats and drinks the body and blood of the Lord unworthily is eating and drinking his own judgment (1 Cor. 11:29)." According to the statement of the same Apostle, a man is to test himself, and then so eat of that bread that he prepare himself for the reception of such a great sacrament, namely by abstaining for some days from the works of the flesh and purifying his body and soul. Such was the example of David, who, if he had not confessed that he had abstained from conjugal union for a day or two, would not have accepted the loaves of proposition from the priest (cf. 1 Sam. 21:1–6).

C. 334. THAT LAYMEN COMMUNICATE THREE TIMES EACH YEAR.
From the same book, c. 43.

That, if not more frequently and, except perhaps for anyone who is impeded by any of the major crimes, laymen receive communion at least three times a year, that is, at Easter, the Lord's Nativity, and Pentecost.

c. 335. THAT CLERICS NOT BE PRESENT AT MARRIAGE FEASTS.

Priests, deacons, subdeacons, and others who do not have license to take wives are also to avoid the marriage feasts of others, nor are they to mix in gatherings where lewd and indecent songs are sung or obscene bodily movements are shown in leaping and dances, lest hearing and sight which has been deputed to the sacred mysteries be polluted by the contagion of indecent spectacles and words.

c. 336. ON THE SAME MATTER.

From the Council of Mainz, c. 39.

Those who do not have license to take wives are to avoid the marriage feasts of others.

c. 337. ON THE SAME MATTER.

From the decrees of Pope Martin.

It is not licit for priests or clerics to be spectators at certain spectacles at marriage feasts or at banquets, but it is fitting that they rise and depart from them before those spectacles begin.

c. 338. ON THE TIMES AT WHICH MARRIED MEN ARE TO CONTAIN THEMSELVES FROM THEIR WIVES.

From the Council of Elvira.

The Synod of Elvira says: Married men are to contain themselves from their wives during the three forty-day fasts of the year, and on Sunday, Wednesday, and Friday. Also, they are not to become joined on these particular days: As long as the wife is pregnant, that is, from the day on which the child moves in the womb until the birth, and for thirty-three days after the birth in the case of a son, and fifty-six days in the case of a daughter.

c. 339. ON THE SAME MATTER.

From a Penitential.

That a married man is to contain himself for forty days before Easter and Pentecost, or before the Lord's Nativity, and every Sunday, Wednesday, and Friday night, and from manifest conception until the birth of offspring, and abstain from church for thirty days, if it is a son, and forty days if a daughter. The woman is to abstain from her husband for three months before the birth and forty days afterwards. Whoever has intercourse on these days is to do penance for twenty days.

c. 340. ON LENT.

He who has intercourse with his wife during Lent before Easter, and is not willing to abstain from her, is to do penance for one year, or pay to the Church his price, namely twenty-six shillings, or distribute it to the poor. If it happened because of drunkenness and it is not his custom, he is to do penance for forty days.

c. 341. THAT MARRIED PERSONS ARE TO ABSTAIN BEFORE COMMUNION.

Each man before sacred communion is to abstain from his wife for three, or five, or seven days.

c. 342. ON THE BLESSED BREAD (*EULOGIAE*) TO BE GIVEN TO THE PEOPLE BY PRIESTS.
From the Council of Nantes.

That from the oblations which are offered by the people and which are left over from consecration, or from the loaves which the faithful offer to the church, or certainly from his own, a priest is to place in a clean container suitably cut portions so that, after the solemnities of mass, those who were not ready to communicate may take blessed bread (*eulogiae*) from it on every Sunday and feast-day. With the words that follow, the priest is to bless beforehand that which he will distribute as blessed bread.

PRAYER.

Holy Lord, almighty Father, eternal God, deign to bless this bread with your holy and spiritual blessing, so that it may be to all health in mind and body, and protection against all illness and all the wiles of the enemy. By our Lord Jesus Christ, your Son, bread of life, who comes down from heaven and gives life and health to the world, and lives and reigns with you.

Care is to be taken that crumbs do not spill incautiously.

c. 343. THAT PRIESTS GO ABOUT WITH THEIR STOLE.
From the Synod of Tribur.

That priests are not to go about, unless wearing a stole or scarf. And if priests are robbed, or wounded, or killed while travelling while not clothed in their stole, a simple fine is to be paid, but if with the stole, a threefold one.

c. 344. ON THE SAME MATTER.
From the Council of Mainz.

Priests are always to make use of their stoles for the distinction of the priestly dignity.

c. 345. THAT CLERICS NOT DRESS IN LAY GARB.
From the Council as above.

That clerics are not to use lay clothing, that is, mantle or cloak without a cape, nor precious and unsuitable shoes, and other novel vanities, but let them go about wearing a religious and decent habit.

c. 346. ON THE SAME MATTER.
From the Council at Rispach in Bavaria, c. 41.

That no cleric is to wear lay garments, nor is he to presume to bear arms, except insofar as it befits his religion.

c. 347. ON THE SAME MATTER.
From the Council of Carthage.

Let a cleric prove his profession even in his habit and bearing, and not seek adornment in dress and shoes.

c. 348. ON WINE, THAT IT IS NOT TO BE OFFERED PURE AT THE SACRIFICE, BUT MIXED WITH WATER.
(If the priest mixes water with wine at the sacrifice. *From the Council of Worms*: see above, c. 67: WHAT IS TO BE OFFERED IN THE LORD'S SACRIFICE.)
From the Ecclesiastical Definition.

In the Eucharist, pure water must not be offered, as some are mistaken in doing for the sake of sobriety, but wine mixed with water, because the wine too was in the mystery of our redemption, as he says: "I will not drink of this fruit of the vine (Mk. 26:29)," and mixed with water, which he gave after the supper. But even the water that issued from his side with the blood shows the wine that issued with water from the true vine of his flesh.

c. 349. THAT PRIESTS NOT OBTAIN CHURCHES FOR A PRICE.
From the Council of Mainz, tit. 12.

Any priest who has acquired a church for a price is to be deposed in every way because he who has by money expelled another priest legitimately ordained to a church, and has in such manner claimed it for himself, is acknowledged to have acted against the discipline of ecclesiastical rule.

c. 350. ON THE SAME MATTER.
From the same.

Also, it seems that it is to be forbidden to clerics or laymen lest anyone presume to give a church to any priest without the license and consent of his bishop. (See above, c. 244.)

c. 351. THAT THE SACRIFICE IS NOT TO BE OFFERED EVERYWHERE.
From the letter of Pope Anacletus.

Priests, when they sacrifice, must not do this alone, but they are to have witnesses present so that they may be proved to sacrifice perfectly to God in places consecrated to the Lord. For the authority of the divine Law says: "See that you do not present your holocausts in every place you see, but in the place which the Lord your God has chosen (cf. Deut. 12:13–14)."

c. 352. WHERE MASS IS TO BE CELEBRATED.
From the canons of St. Sylvester.

That no priest presume to celebrate mass other than in places consecrated by the bishop, if he wishes henceforth to be in a state of piety and the priesthood.

c. 353. IF FOUR PORTIONS ARE MADE OF THE TITHES.
From the Council of Nantes.

Priests are to be both instructed and admonished to acknowledge that tithes and the oblations which they receive from the faithful are stipends for the poor, guests, and strangers; they are not to be treated as theirs, but as entrusted to them. They are to know that they will have to render an account as to all of them in the sight of God and that, unless they administer them faithfully to the poor and to those mentioned earlier, they will suffer much harm. As to how they are to be dispensed, the holy canons establish that four parts be made of them, one for restoring the fabric of the church, another to be distributed to the poor, a third to be had by the priest and his clerics, and the fourth to be reserved to the bishop so that whatever he commands as to it may be done with prudent counsel.

c. 354. IF A BISHOP OR PRIEST HAS PRESUMED TO ALIENATE A POSSESSION OF THE CHURCH BY WHATEVER DEVICE.
From the Council of Braga.

If a priest or deacon has been found to have sold anything out of the ministries of the Church, because he has committed sacrilege, it has pleased that he is not to be counted within the order of the Church. And yet, it is to be left to the discretion of the bishop whether such a one is worthy or not of being received in his degree.

c. 355. THAT IT IS NOT LICIT FOR ANY BISHOP TO ALIENATE IN PERPETUITY ANY POSSESSION, LARGE OR SMALL, FROM THE CHURCH.
From the decrees of Pope Symmachus.

That it not be licit for any bishop of the Apostolic See to transfer into anyone's rights under a perpetual alienation or commutation a rustic estate, whatever its largeness or smallness.

c. 356. ON HOUSES.
From the same.

Houses situated in any cities, whose state requires more than moderate expenses to maintain, if accepted (if they happen to be offered), are to be turned into rental property with a just valuation and in fear of the divine judgment.

c. 357. ON THE SAME MATTER.
From the same.

Any priest who has attempted to alienate in perpetuity in any way anything from the right of his title, besides gold, silver, or gems, also clothing if there is any, or if there happen to be any movable properties which do not pertain to divine ornaments, whether as donor, or alienator, or seller, is to be punished with the loss of his honour.

c. 358. ON THE SAME MATTER.
From the same, c. 6.

Moreover, he who has sought and accepted a possession of the Church, or any of the priests, or deacons, or defenders who has given his approval to giving it, is to be struck by the anathema with which God strikes souls in his wrath.

c. 359. THAT PRIESTS NOT SELL A POSSESSION OF THE CHURCH IN WHICH THEY ARE ESTABLISHED.
From the Council of Carthage.

Also, it pleased that priests, without the knowledge of their bishops, not sell a possession of the church in which they are established; in the same way, neither is it to be licit for bishops to sell the estates of the Church, without the knowledge of the Council or his priests. If there is no necessity, it is not licit for the bishop to usurp a possession of Mother Church, nor for a priest a possession of his title.

c. 360. ON THE SAME MATTER.
From the same.

It pleased that no one sell a possession of the Church. But if he has no income and some great necessity compels, this is to be made known to the primate of his province so that what is to be done may be decided by the established number of bishops. If he has not done this, the vendor, having lost his honour, is to be held guilty before God and the Council.

C. 361. ON THE SAME MATTER.
From the decrees of Pope Martin.

If any bishop, compelled by no need of ecclesiastical requirement, without the knowledge of his clergy, or perhaps where there is no priest, has presumed to sell anything from ecclesiastical properties, he is to be compelled to restore the same properties to his Church and, after being heard, he is to be deposed in the judgment of bishops, and deprived of his honour as one guilty of theft and rapine.

C. 362. WHAT IT IS FITTING FOR THE RELATIVES OF ONE WHO HAS ENRICHED A CHURCH WITH HIS PROPERTIES TO DO IF THEY SEE THAT SOME OF WHAT HAD BEEN CONFERRED HAS BEEN TAKEN BY FRAUD.
From the Council of Toledo.

Every amount of ecclesiastical property, just as it provides a remedy of forgiveness to the one who confers it, so it rightly prepares harm for its defrauder. And so, no priest or minister is to take anything from the properties of the Church which in any places are bestowed by the faithful and transfer it to his own right or to the unity of his chair. In order that the solidity of this matter may be greater, it has been licit for the relatives of him who built or enriched a church to have this care of his good intention so that, if they see a priest or minister take by fraud some of what was conferred, either they constrain him by an honourable summons of admonition, or denounce such things to a bishop or judge for correction. If a bishop attempts to do such things, let them see to it that they inform his metropolitan of this. If the metropolitan does such things, let them not delay to report such things to the king's ear. But it is not licit for the heirs themselves in the same matters to exhibit as if the power of their own right, and engage in rapine or fraud or presume any sort of violence. If anyone has presumed to act temerariously against these admonitions, he will restore with shame what he has wickedly taken and bear the sentence of excommunication for a year.

C. 363. ON SCANTY BITS OF LAND AND INSIGNIFICANT VINEYARDS BELONGING TO A CHURCH.
From the Council of Agde.

A bishop is to have the power to sell, without the counsel of his brethren, if there should be need, scanty bits of land and vineyards which are insignificant and less useful to the Church, or are too distant and small.

C. 364. THAT FUGITIVE SLAVES OF THE CHURCH ARE PERMITTED TO BE SOLD.
From the same Council.

By a similar reasoning, fugitive slaves who desert their houses or households and who, even if they are recalled, cannot be detained, may be sold by the bishop, if he wishes or if they have deserved it.

c. 365. IF SOMEONE HAS DARED TO SUPPRESS ROYAL CHARTERS OR DOCUMENTS OR HAS HANDED THEM OVER TO ADVERSARIES.
From the Council of Agde.

If any of the clerics presume to suppress or refuse to provide documents by which a church's possession is confirmed, or perhaps by a damnable and punishable obstinacy hand them over to adversaries, he is to compensate the church out of his own resources for whatever damage has been inflicted upon it by the absence of the documents, and he is to be deprived of communion. But those who have impiously, to a church's harm, solicited and received the documents of Holy Church from the betrayers are to be punished by an equal sentence.

c. 366. ON THE TESTAMENT OF A BISHOP, HOW IT IS TO BE VALID.
From the same.

If any bishop, in making his will, has bequeathed something from a property which by right belongs to the Church, it will not be valid, unless he has supplied as much from the resources which by right are his own.

c. 367. ON MANUMISSIONS IN THE CHURCH.
From the same.

It is not licit for slaves given to monks to be manumitted by the abbot. Indeed, it is unjust that, as monks engage in daily work in the fields, their slaves enjoy the leisure of liberty.

c. 368. ON THE SAME MATTER.
From the Council of Toledo.

Bishops, who have conferred nothing of their own on Christ's Church, are not to presume, to their own condemnation, to make slaves from the Church's households into freedmen. Indeed, it is impious that he who did not confer his goods on Christ's Church should inflict harm on it. Therefore, the bishop who succeeds him will recall such freedmen to the right of the Church without any opposition.

c. 369. ON THE SAME MATTER.
From the same Council.

The bishop who desires to manumit a slave of the right of the Church without retaining ecclesiastical protection is to offer by way of commutation two slaves of the same worth and their personal property before the Council of the Church over which he presides, to the priests who subscribe to it so that the transaction of the exchanger may be found approved and just. But permission is to be denied to this freedman to accuse or testify against the Church to whose right he had pertained. If he should presume to do this, it pleases that, while the exchange remains in force, he be recalled to the servitude of his Church.

C. 370. ON THE FREEDMEN OF THE CHURCH.
From the same Council.

Freedmen, who have been manumitted by anyone and have been entrusted to the protection of the Church, are to be protected by priestly defence from anyone's insolence, whether in regard to the state of their freedom or the personal property which they are known to have.

C. 371. ON ECCLESIASTICAL TREASURES.
From the Capitularies, bk. 1, tit. 117.

That the several bishops, abbots, and abbesses diligently take care of ecclesiastical treasures, lest, because of the perfidy or negligence of the custodians, something be lost of the gems, or vessels, or any other treasure.

C. 372. THAT NO ONE PRESUME TO ALIENATE AN IMMOVABLE PROPERTY OF A CHURCH.
From bk. 2, c. 19.

It is not licit for anyone to alienate an immovable property of a church, whether a house, or a field, or a garden, or a rustic property, or rents paid in kind, nor to bind them to creditors by title of a special mortgage. The term alienation is to include rental, donation, exchange, and a perpetual contract of emphyteusis. But all priests are to abstain entirely from this sort of alienation, fearing the penalties which Leo's constitution threatens.

C. 373. IF THE PRINCE WISHES TO MAKE A COMMUTATION WITH A CHURCH.
From the same, c. 30.

If the prince wishes to give an immovable property to holy places and receive another immovable in return, and so contract an exchange in that way, let it be licit for him to do so by a divine pragmatic sanction promulgated by him.

C. 374. ON THE LEASES (*PRECARIAE*) OF CHURCHES.
From the Council at Beauvais.

Leases and exchanges while Churches were vacant made by those who occupied the places of bishops are to be rescinded, and if they ought to be made, they are to be made with ecclesiastical or civil authority.

c. 375. ON THE SAME MATTER.
Also, c. 22.

Leases are not to be presumed to be made for ecclesiastical possessions by anyone, unless double the amount is received from the Church's property as is given from the lessee's own property and of suitable quality, and in the donor's name only, if he wishes to hold in usufruct his own possessions and those of the Church. But if he immediately surrenders his own property, he may, in his own name only, hold in usufruct ecclesiastical possessions worth three times the value, because it is fitting that each one treat such property as if he were a steward of another's goods, and not the liberal giver of what is his own.

c. 376. ON THE SAME MATTER.
From the same.

No one is to be compelled by any power to lease possessions dedicated to God and his saints, since reason and usage obtain that no one make a benefice out of his own property against usefulness and reason to someone to whom he does not wish to do so.

c. 377. THAT ROYAL PRECEPTS NOT BE ISSUED AS TO LEASES.
From the same Chapter.

Neither reason allows, nor authority in any way permits, that royal precepts be issued as to ecclesiastical leases, since it is necessary that the royal Majesty adjudge it unworthy to confirm such precepts at ecclesiastical law, unless they be sought by the ecclesiastical ruler. But the same keeper of the Church is to beware most carefully lest, perhaps forgetful of his order and the Church's communion, against authority, he petition for a royal precept to be made for any assent. If he has done so, he is not to be heard. But if he has obtained this, then the same is to be rescinded by royal discretion and episcopal judgment, and the unjust petitioner is to be corrected worthily for his unjust request to the prince.

c. 378. THAT LEASES BE RENEWED EVERY FIVE YEARS.
From the same.

That leases, according to ancient custom and authority, are to be renewed every five years.

c. 379. ON COMMUTATIONS.
From the same, c. 23.

That commutations of ecclesiastical possessions are much to be avoided, and, if they are to be done in some way, they are to be inspected most carefully. According to the canonical decree of Pope Hilary, those which have been done recklessly and which the previous bishop allowed illicitly, or have been made illicitly by others, are to be emended by his successor.

c. 380. ALSO, THAT NO PRECEPTS BE ISSUED AS TO ECCLESIASTICAL BENEFICES OR LEASES.
From the Council at Saint-Médard, c. 11.

Let our faithful subjects know that we have granted to the venerable bishops in Synod that we will in no way grant precepts of our confirmation regarding ecclesiastical benefices or leases, even if any prelate of monasteries has unreasonably sought them. Hence, let each restrain himself from an unreasonable petition.

c. 381. THAT NO COMMUTATIONS BE MADE REGARDING ECCLESIASTICAL POSSESSIONS WITHOUT THE KING'S CONSENT, AND THAT ECCLESIASTICAL SLAVES NOT BE COMMUTED, UNLESS INTO FREEDOM.
From the same, c. 12.

That our legates are to announce to all throughout the area of their legation that no prelate is to presume to make commutations of ecclesiastical goods and slaves without our license and consent. Nor is anyone to commute ecclesiastical slaves, unless into freedom, namely that slaves which will be given for the benefit of a man of the Church are to remain in the servitude of the Church, and a man of the Church who is commuted is to enjoy perpetual liberty. Indeed, what has once been consecrated to the Lord cannot ever be transferred to human uses. For the Law says: "If one has exchanged, then what was exchanged and what was taken in exchange shall be sanctified to the Lord (cf. Lev. 27:10)."

c. 382. ON THE SAME MATTER.
Also, from the Chapters at Quierzy.

It seems unjust and impious that slaves, whom faithful men and women have consecrated to God and his saints for the remedy of their soul, should again be reduced to worldly servitude in exchange for some gift, payment, or commutation, since canonical authority allows only fugitive slaves to be sold. And so, all the rulers of churches are to be greatly careful lest one person's alms should become another person's sin. For just as it is unseemly that a free man be made into a slave, so it is absurd that a slave should fall from ecclesiastical dignity and become bound to human servitude.

c. 383. ON THE LORD'S DAY.
From the Chapters of Charles.

We also establish, in accordance with what the Lord commanded in the Law, that no servile work be done on Sundays; as my father commanded in his synodal edicts, men must not do rural work, nor cultivate their vineyards, nor plough their fields, or harvest wheat, or cut hay, or plant hedges, or clear forests, or cut trees, or quarry stones, nor build houses, nor work in the garden, nor are they to meet for pleas, nor hold a market, nor hunt.

c. 384. WHAT MAY BE DONE LICITLY ON SUNDAYS.
From the same.

It is licit to do three types of carting work on Sundays, that is, to carry for the army (*hostilicia*), to carry victuals, or as a service due (*angaria*) and, perhaps, if it is necessary, to bring someone's body to the tomb.

c. 385. ALSO, ON THE LORD'S DAY.

Also, on the Lord's day, women must not do weaving work, or cut out or sew clothing, or card wool. It is not licit to dress flax, or wash clothing in public, nor shear sheep, so that the honour and rest of the Lord's day may be satisfied fully. They are to come together from everywhere for the solemnities of mass, and praise God for all the goods which he has deigned to confer on us on that day.

c. 386. THAT NO MARKET BE HELD ON THE LORD'S DAY.
From a Council.

We have decreed that all observe Sundays with all veneration and abstain from illicit work, and that no market happen on those days, nor any plea be held where anyone can be condemned to death or punishment, nor are oaths to be sworn.

c. 387. ON THE SAME MATTER.
From the Capitularies, bk. 1, c. 139.

That on the Lord's day, a market is not to be held in any place.

c. 388. ON THE FEASTS OF THE YEAR.
From the Capitularies, bk. 2, c. 33.

We ordain that feast-days be celebrated throughout the year, that is, the Sunday of Easter with the whole week, the day of the Lord's Ascension, and Pentecost in the same way as on Easter, the one day of the Apostles Peter and Paul, the Nativity of St. John the Baptist, the Assumption of St. Mary, St. Michael, St. Remi, St. Martin, St. Andrew, four days for the Lord's Nativity, the Lord's octave, the Lord's Epiphany, the Purification of St. Mary; we also decree that the feasts of martyrs or confessors be observed in each parish in which their bodies rest.

c. 389. ON THE SAME MATTER.
From the Council at Rispach.

We ordain that feasts be celebrated, that is, the day of Easter, as also the Monday, Tuesday, Wednesday, and Thursday. Before mass, there is to be license to plough and sow, to tend the garden or vineyard, and to enclose a hedge. But we decree that other work cease, and there is to be no work after mass. Pentecost is to be observed in the same way as Easter, and the feast of St. Lawrence, All Saints on 1 November, and similarly the dedications of churches.

c. 390. ON NOT BENDING THE KNEE ON FEAST-DAYS.
From the Council of Nicaea.

Because there are some who bend their knees on Sunday and during the days of Pentecost, it has pleased the holy Council (so that all things may be observed consonantly in the diverse places) that we render our vows to the Lord at prayer while standing.

c. 391. ON THE SAME MATTER.
As above.

That priests are to announce to the people that only in Lent and during the fast of the Ember Days, at the deacon's injunction, must they bend their knees during the solemnities of mass. To the contrary, on Sundays and other feast-days, from vespers to vespers, they are not to kneel, but pray bending while standing. Nor is anyone to presume to pray with one knee bent to the ground, as we read that the Jews did in deriding the Lord during his Passion, but let each put both knees firmly on the ground. For the Apostle says: "I bend my knees to the Father of our Lord Jesus Christ (Eph. 3:14)."

c. 392. THAT UNSEEMLY SONGS BE FORBIDDEN TO THE PEOPLE.
From the Council of Arles.

That irreligious custom is entirely to be removed which the rabble has been accustomed to follow on the solemnities of the saints, that the people who ought to attend the divine offices are intent upon unseemly dances and songs, not only doing harm to themselves, but also causing a din during the offices of the religious. Hence, the holy Council commits to the care of priests and judges that this be removed from all Spain.

c. 393. AS ABOVE.

We entirely forbid that shameful and lascivious songs be sung near churches, which ought to be avoided everywhere.

c. 394. THAT A BISHOP IS NOT AT ALL TO ORDAIN THE CLERICS OF ANOTHER'S PARISH.
From the Council of Antioch.

A bishop is not to establish priests or deacons subject to another bishop, unless perhaps with the counsel and will of the bishop of the region. But if anyone has attempted to do this, his ordination is to be without force, and he is to be corrected by the Synod.

c. 395. ON THE SAME MATTER.
From the African Council.

Also, it pleased that anyone who once read in one Church not be bound to the clerical state by another Church.

c. 396. THAT NO BISHOP, OR ANY OF LOWER DEGREE, PRESUME TO JUDGE CAUSES ON THE LORD'S DAY.
From the Council of Tarragona.

That none of the bishops, priests, or clerics are to dare to judge on the Lord's day any legal claim proposed in any cause, except only this: To ensure that the solemnities established as due to God be done.

c. 397. THAT IT NOT BE FITTING FOR ORDINATIONS TO BE DONE ABSOLUTELY.
From the Council of Chalcedon.

No one is to be ordained absolutely a priest, a deacon, or anyone in an ecclesiastical degree, unless the person to be ordained is specifically appointed to a church of a city, or of a possession, or the shrine of a martyr, or a monastery. As for those who are ordained absolutely, the holy Synod has decreed that the imposition of hands of this sort is void, and they may never minister, to the detriment of the one who ordained them.

c. 398. THAT DIABOLICAL VERSES NOT BE SUNG AT NIGHTTIME OVER THE BODIES OF THE DEAD.
From the Council as above.

Lay persons who keep funeral wakes are to do this with fear and trembling and reverence. No one is to presume to sing diabolical songs there and engage in those jokes and dances which the pagans devised at the devil's instruction. Indeed, who does not know that it is diabolical, and not only alien from the Christian religion, but also contrary to human nature, to rejoice there, sing, become drunk, and for the mouths to dissolve into laughter, and setting aside all piety and feeling of charity, exult, as it were, in their brother's death, where weeping and wailing ought to resound with tearful voices for the loss of a dear brother. Indeed, we read in many places that the Fathers of the Old and New Testament bemoaned the deaths of holy men, but in no place that they exulted at their departure from this world. For the whole of Egypt mourned the patriarch Jacob for seventy days (Gen. 50:3). And Joseph and his brothers, when they brought their father for burial into the land of Canaan, celebrated his funeral at the threshing-floor of Atad, which is situated across the Jordan, and they filled seven days with their great and vehement wailing. Such was their wailing that the place itself took its name from it (Gen. 50:10–11). And regarding the blessed Stephen, we read that devout men took care of, or buried, him, and they mourned greatly over him (Act. 8:2). And so, such unsuitable rejoicing and pestiferous singing are to be utterly forbidden by God's authority. If anyone wishes to sing, let him sing "Lord, have mercy," or otherwise be completely silent. But if he is not willing to keep silent, let him be so adjured and disciplined by all that he no longer has God's permission to remain there, but let him return to his own dwelling. On the next day, let him be constrained in such a way that the rest may be afraid.

c. 399. ALSO, THAT NO ONE BE ORDAINED ABSOLUTELY.
From the Capitularies, bk. 1, c. 25.

That no one be ordained absolutely and without public proclamation of the stability of the place to which he is ordained.

c. 400. ON THE EXAMINATION BEFORE ORDINATION.
From the same, c. 136.

That priests not be ordained before they are examined.

c. 401. ON THE SAME MATTER.
From the Council of Meaux, c. 52.

Those from our parishes who petition for ordination either to a title or absolutely are not at all to be ordained, unless they have dwelled either in a certain and religious place, or even in the city, at least for a year, so that certain knowledge may be had of their life, conduct, and learning. And let no one presume to ordain anyone absolutely, as the holy canons have confirmed.

c. 402. THAT THE ORDAINED RECEIVE LETTERS FROM THEIR ORDAINERS.
From the African Council.

It pleased that whoever henceforth are ordained throughout the African provinces are to receive letters from their ordainers, signed in their own hand, containing the consul and the day, so that no altercation may arise as to who is later or earlier.

c. 403. THAT NO ONE PRESUME TO ORDAIN ANOTHER'S SLAVE.
From the letter of Pope Leo.

Men are here and there admitted to the sacred order who are not supported by any dignity of birth or manners; even some who have been unable to obtain their liberty from their masters are raised to the eminence of the priesthood, as if vile slavery could rightfully receive that honour, and it is believed that he is approvable to God who was not even able to prove himself to his lord. (And after a few words:) For he who is to be added to the divine army must be free from others so that he be not taken away from the Lord's encampment, in which his name is enrolled, by any other bonds of necessity.

c. 404. ON THE SAME MATTER.
From the Council of Mainz, c. 36.

If a slave, in his master's absence or ignorance, but with the bishop's knowledge, has been ordained as a deacon or a priest, he is to remain in his clerical office, and the bishop is to make compensation for him by paying double his price to his master. But if the bishop did not know that he was a slave, then those who gave testimony, or made supplication that he should be ordained, are held liable for the same recompensation.

c. 405. THAT NONE OF THE MINISTERS IS TO INTRODUCE FURTIVELY A CLERIC OF ANOTHER'S PARISH FOR ORDINATION.
From the Council of Nantes.

We forbid all ministers of ecclesiastical dignity that any of them, corrupted by any sort of gift or favour, presume to introduce into an ordination, openly or furtively, a cleric of another's parish. If he has done this, according to the decree of Chalcedon, the one who has been ordained is to lose the gift of the Holy Spirit, which he attempted to steal; the one who has been a mediator, if he is a cleric, is to fall from his degree, if he is a layman or monk, he is to be anathematized. (See above, c. 237.)

c. 406. ALSO, ON ORDAINING SLAVES.
From the Council of Toledo.

Those who so receive freedom from their masters that the patron retains no right of obedience over them, if they are without crime, may be admitted to the clerical order freely, because they are known to be freed by direct manumission. But those who have been manumitted with the retention of obedience, because they are still bound in service to their patrons, are not at all to be promoted to the ecclesiastical order, lest, whenever it please their lords, from clerics they should become slaves.

c. 407. ON THE SAME MATTER.
From the Capitularies, tit. 84.

If laymen have offered clerics of approved life and doctrine to bishops for consecration and establishment in their churches, they are not to reject them for any reason.

c. 408. ON THE ORDINATION OF SLAVES.
From the same, c. 82.

As to the ordination of slaves, who here and there are indiscriminately promoted to the ecclesiastical degrees, it has pleased all that it should be in concordance with the sacred canons. It has been established that none of the bishops henceforth presume to promote them to sacred orders, unless first they have received freedom from their own masters. And if any slave, fleeing his master or hiding, has come to ecclesiastical degrees by bribing witnesses with gifts or corrupting them, or by any cunning or fraud, it has been decreed that he be deposed and that his master should take him back. But if a grandfather or father, migrating from one fatherland to another, has had a child in the latter province, and that son has been there educated and promoted to ecclesiastical degrees, and it is unknown whether he is a slave, and his master afterwards comes and acquires him in accordance with the laws, then it is decreed that, if his master should wish to grant him liberty, he may remain in his degree. But if he should wish to take him away from the Lord's encampments by the chain of servitude, then he is to lose his degree because, according to the sacred canons, one who remains a base person cannot exercise the dignity of the priesthood.

c. 409. ON THE PERSONAL PROPERTY OF SLAVES.

As to the goods and personal possessions of those who are freed by their masters so that they may be promoted by right to ecclesiastical degrees, it has been established that it be within their masters' power whether to grant such things to them or claim them for themselves.

c. 410. ON THE PERSONAL PROPERTY OF THE ORDAINED.

Furthermore, if he has acquired something after his ordination, that must be observed which has been established in the canons as to consecrated persons who had nothing.

c. 411. ON THE SLAVES OF CHURCHES.

As to the slaves of Churches, it has been decreed by a common judgment that the archbishops established through the several provinces have our authoritative pronouncement and their suffragans keep a copy with themselves. And, whenever someone is found in the ecclesiastical household whom it would be useful to ordain, that pronouncement is to be read at the ambo before the people, and before the priests and the whole clergy before the horn of the altar, as is contained in our pronouncement. With every wile removed, let him receive his freedom and then be promoted to the ecclesiastical degrees.

c. 412. ON THE HOUSEHOLDS OF MONASTERIES.

It is also to be done similarly with regard to those whom laymen wish to promote to sacred orders from the households of Churches. Furthermore, the same form is to be observed with regard to those whom the superiors of canons or monks seek to have ordained.

c. 413. THE EXEMPLAR OF FREEDOM MENTIONED ABOVE.

Ecclesiastical authority patently admonishes, and moreover the royal majesty gives its assent to canonical religion, that whomever any Church has chosen to promote to sacred orders from its own household be confirmed solemnly by a charter of liberty with the subscription and manumission of the one to whom he was subject in the presence of the priests, canons, and noble laymen. Hence, I, in God's name bishop, or abbot, or anyone else, with Christ's approval rector of such and such a Church, at the horn of the altar and in the presence of noble men, establish by this authoritative charter that a certain servant of our Church, named such and such, who has been offered to sacred orders, is to possess free status from this day forward and to remain secure from any bond of servitude, as if he had been engendered or born of freeborn parents, and may proceed to any place he freely chooses, so long as it is canonical; that henceforth he owes no service flowing from servile condition to us or to our successors, but, by this title of manumission and freedom, he may live always securely and well as a freeborn person all the days of his life in the fullest and certain freedom, like other Roman citizens. As for his personal property which he already has, or which he may acquire hereafter or henceforth, he may freely do whatever he pleases with it in accordance with canonical authority. In order that this charter of freedom may remain inviolable, we confirmed it by our own hand.

C. 414. EXEMPLAR OF FREEDOM OF ONE'S OWN SLAVE.

Anyone who releases an obligation due to him and a service that pertains to him will not doubt that he will receive a reward for it in the future before the Lord. Hence, I, so-and-so, in God's name, for the remedy of my soul or eternal reward, in the church of St. Peter, or of St. so-and-so, in the presence of the bishop, and of the priests there gathered and of noble laymen, before the horn of the altar of this church, by this charter of absolution and freedom, free my slave so-and-so from every bond of servitude, so that from this day forward he possess freeborn status, and remain freeborn, as if he had been engendered and born of freeborn parents. Let him proceed to any place he prefers, or that canonical authority allows him, and let him lead a free life like other Roman citizens. He is not to render any debt of servitude or enfranchisement to any of my heirs or their representatives, or to any other person other than God alone, to whom all things are subject, and for whose love I vowed and offered him to his service. As for his personal property which his master gave him, and which he may acquire henceforth by his labour with God's help, let it be granted to him in perpetuity to do with as he pleases, according to the ecclesiastical provisions. But if anyone (which I do not believe will happen) or I myself, or any of my heirs, or any opposed person, should strive to go against this charter of freedom, or wish to infringe it in any way, first, let him incur the wrath of God and be made a stranger from the bounds of God's Holy Church; furthermore, let him pay sixty shillings to the person against whom he brought suit, and let him fail in his claim, but this present charter, strengthened by my hand or that of other good men, and its attached stipulation are to remain undisputed for all time.

The charters of the abovementioned freedom are to contain not only the name of the one who asks that this be done, but also the names of the priests and noble laymen who were there, arranged in order, with the seals impressed by their own hands. Indeed, without the confirmation by these things, the charter, deprived of witnesses, will be regarded as null. It is also fitting that, at the end or in the margin, they contain a note of the place, day, year, consul, and indiction in this form: Done in such-and-such a city, in the house of St. Peter, on the Kalends of N, in the year of the Lord's Incarnation N, under the reign of king N, with bishop N ruling and presiding over the chair of the abovementioned city, or in such-and-such a monastery, at Indiction N, in God's name happily. Amen. Indeed, Roman authority says: "Whatever laws have been issued without day and consul are not valid."

c. 415. THAT MANUMISSION IS TO BE DONE IN CHURCH.
As above.

Furthermore, laymen are to be instructed so as to know that they cannot manumit their own slaves whom they have decreed to be added into the Lord's army otherwise than in a most holy church by the procedure noted above. For how can clerics, who are strangers to the world's law, acquire their freedom outside the Church? And how will they, to whom it is forbidden to proceed to a secular judgment, be freed from the yoke of servitude by a secular judgment? But perhaps someone will say: He is not permitted to become a cleric, unless he enjoys the dignity of free birth status before he received the clerical office. Indeed, he speaks the truth, and yet we must avoid what can be rendered void or censured.

c. 416. ON THE SAME MATTER.
As above.

It is not only those who are to be promoted to the clerical order that are to be manumitted in a church, but also those whom someone wishes to emancipate for the good of one's soul according to the law of the world are to be freed in a church and to be commended to the patronage of that same church. Indeed, it is written in the Pact of the Franks:

c. 417. ON THE SAME MATTER.
From the Pact.

We also will this, that any Ripuarian Frank who, for the remedy of his soul, wishes to free his slave according to the Roman law is to deliver him with a written document in the bishop's hand in a church before the priests, deacons, or the whole clergy and people. The bishop is to command the archdeacon that he draft a document for him according to the Roman law, by which the Churches live, that both he and all his issue are to remain free and stand under the protection of the Church; they are to pay to the Church all the income of their status, and they are to come to judgment nowhere other than in the church where they have been freed. And if they have died without issue, they are not to leave any other heir than the Church.

c. 418. ON THE SAME MATTER.
From the Roman law.

Emperor Constantine Augustus to Hosius, bishop of Cordoba: If anyone has the will to manumit in the most Holy Church, it suffices that he wishes to free his slaves in the presence of the priests to know that they are Roman citizens in the liberty they have received. For if clerics wish to grant freedom to their slaves, even if they do so outside the sight of priests, or if they were freed by words alone and without writing, their whole and full liberty will stand, as with Roman citizens.

c. 419. THAT THE CHARTER OF LIBERTY IS TO BE READ AT THE AMBO.
From the Council of Tribur.

That no men of servile condition are to be promoted to sacred orders, unless they first receive lawful freedom from their masters; their charter of freedom is to be read publicly at the ambo before their ordination and, if none contradicts, then they will be properly consecrated. Furthermore, if afterwards he has fallen from his degree, he is to be of the same condition as he was before his promotion.

c. 420. THAT NO ONE ORDAIN ANOTHER'S CLERIC.
From the Council of Nicaea.

If any bishop has boldly attempted to take a cleric pertaining to another and ordain him in his own Church, without the consent of the bishop from whom he has withdrawn, let such an ordination be acknowledged to be void. (See above, c. 394.)

c. 421. ALSO, ON ORDINATION.
From the Council of Neocaesarea.

No one at all is to be ordained a priest before the thirtieth year of his age. This time is to be observed, even if he is very worthy, for our Lord was baptized in his thirtieth year.

c. 422. ON DEACONS.
From the Council of Carthage.

Also, it has pleased that, before the twenty-fifth year of age, neither deacons are to be ordained, nor virgins to be consecrated.

c. 423. HE WHO CUT OFF A PART OF HIS OWN FINGER MUST NOT BE A CLERIC.
From the letter of Pope Felix.

The canons do not admit to the clergy anyone who has wilfully cut away part of any of his fingers. But if it happened to some by chance, they can be made clerics, and if they were already to be found in the clergy, they are not to be cast out.

c. 424. ON ILLITERATE PRIESTS.
From the letter of Pope Gelasius.

No one is to presume to promote to the clergy the illiterate or those who are diminished in any part of their bodies because one who is lacking in learning cannot be suitable for sacred functions, and the precepts of the Law sanctioned that nothing defective was ever to be offered to God (Lev. 22:20–21). The same is the case with those who have mutilated themselves.

c. 425. THAT CRIMINALS ARE NOT TO BE ADMITTED INTO THE CLERGY.
From the same letter.

For the Apostle says: "Do not impose your hands lightly upon any man, neither be a partaker of another's sins (1 Tim. 5:22)."

c. 426. THAT THOSE WHO ARE AFFLICTED BY DEMONS AND SIMILAR AILMENTS MUST NOT HANDLE THE SACRED MYSTERIES.
From the same letter.

It is our certain knowledge that unlawful acts have become so common that it is allowed for those who are afflicted by demons or similar ailments to handle the most holy mysteries. (And after a few words:) If divine law prohibits even one who is weak or wounded in his body (cf. Lev. 21:16–21) to touch holy things, how much more is it not fitting that the dispensers of the heavenly gift should be afflicted in the mind, which is worse?

c. 427. OF THE CHILDREN OF CONCUBINES, THAT THEY ARE NOT TO BE ADMITTED TO THE CLERGY.
From the Council of Orléans, c. 10.

As for those who have children from their concubines, and had lawful wives and, at the death of their wives, join publicly with the concubines, we have adjudged it be observed that, just as we do not remove those who have already been ordained clerics in ignorance, so we establish that they are no longer to be ordained.

c. 428. ON THE SAME MATTER.
From the Council of Meaux, c. 64.

The ravishers of virgins and widows are to be subject to public penance, even if afterwards they have taken them in marriage under title of a dowry with the consent of their parents, as if they had espoused them. Lest they sink into worse things, after their public penance, they are to come together again and make it their business to devote themselves to alms and all the other actions that pertain to a saving manner of life and to abstain from conjugal intercourse for as long as they are able to do so by mutual consent. As for the children procreated from this sort of blameworthy joining before their less than praiseworthy marriage, they are not to be promoted to an ecclesiastical dignity, nor are those engendered in such a marriage to be admitted to ecclesiastical orders, unless perhaps the very great utility or necessity of the Church or the clear prerogative of their merits commends them.

C. 429. ON THE SAME MATTER.
From the Roman law.

If one has entered into incestuous or nefarious nuptials, he is seen to have neither a wife nor children. Indeed, those who have been born from this sort of conception, although they are seen to be born, are regarded as having no father at all, and are treated as if they had been conceived in adultery. Hence, the ecclesiastical dignity does not at all receive those whom the public laws do not admit but reject as stained by the marks of infamy and look down upon as if degenerate, especially because nothing that is stained may be properly offered to God or applied to his service.

C. 430. THAT NO ONE RECEIVE ANOTHER'S CLERIC.
In the Canons of the Apostles.

A bishop in whose region it has been established that another's clerics reside, if he has regarded as nothing a decree of withdrawal against them and has perhaps received them as his own clerics, is to be deprived of communion as a master of disquietude.

C. 431. ON THE SAME MATTER.
From the letter of Pope Innocent.

That no bishop is to dare to ordain a cleric from another Church, unless he has done this at the request of the other bishop, or the other bishop has been willing to grant it upon being requested. The Synod of Nicaea also established this, that another Church not receive a cleric who has been cast out by another bishop.

C. 432. ON THE SAME MATTER.
From the decrees of Pope Leo.

No one is to receive another's cleric against his bishop's will, nor to solicit such a one, unless perhaps out of a loving agreement such a thing is agreed between giver and receiver. Indeed, he is guilty of a grave injury who dares to cast out or retain from his brother's Church that which is more useful or more precious.

c. 433. ON CLERICS WHO HAVE DESERTED.

Accordingly, if the matter has arisen within the province, the metropolitan shall compel the cleric who has deserted to return to his Church. But if he has withdrawn farther away, he shall be recalled by the authority of your command.

c. 434. AS ABOVE.

It has pleased to recall a fugitive cleric, or a monk who has abandoned his discipline, as one guilty of contempt.

c. 435. ON THE SAME MATTER.
From the sayings of Bishop Basil.

If anyone has not immediately handed over someone who admitted he was contemplating flight because he could not bear ecclesiastical austerity, let him not doubt that he is a sharer in the other's perdition; and he is to be severed from the assembly of the brethren until the other can be recalled.

c. 436. THAT CLERICS GO FORTH WITH THE LETTERS OF THEIR BISHOP.
In the Canons of the Apostles.

If any cleric or lay person goes to another city, and is received without commendatory letters, both the one who received and the one who was received are to be deprived of communion.

c. 437. ON THE SAME MATTER.
From the Council of Antioch.

No strangers are to be received without peaceful, that is, commendatory letters.

c. 438. ON THE SAME MATTER.
From the Council of Chalcedon.

Travelling clerics and lectors must never minister in another city without commendatory letters from their bishop.

c. 439. ON THE SAME MATTER.
From the Council of Agde.

A priest, or deacon, or cleric travelling without the letters of his bishop, no one is to give him communion.

c. 440. ON THE SAME MATTER.
From the Council of Chalcedon.

We have decreed to commend all the poor and those in need of ecclesiastical help, as they travel, only by proof of a letter or by ecclesiastical letters of peace, and not by commendatory ones, since it is meet that commendatory letters be granted only to more honoured persons.

c. 441. ON THE SAME MATTER.
From the same Council.

There is to be no license to wander for clerics without commendatory letters of their bishop; the form of this present sentence is to be observed also in the case of monks.

c. 442. ON THE SAME MATTER.
From the Council of Sardica.

Bishop Januarius said: Let your Holiness also establish that it be licit for no bishop to solicit an ecclesiastical minister of a bishop of another city and ordain him in his own parishes.

c. 443. ON THE SAME MATTER.
From the same Council.

Bishop Hosius said: And we all establish this that, if anyone should wish to ordain an alien minister from another parish without the consent and will of his own bishop, his ordination is not to be valid.

c. 444. AS ABOVE.
In the Canons of the Apostles.

No foreign bishop, priest, or deacon is to be received without commendatory letters; when they have submitted these writings, these are to be examined diligently, and so let them be received.

c. 445. ON THE SAME MATTER.
From the Council of Laodicea.

That it is not fitting for a priest or cleric to travel without canonical letters.

c. 446. ON THE SAME MATTER.
From the Council of Meaux, c. 50.

That priests, or any clerics, are not to be received or accepted into another's parish without a formed letter, nor are they to be allowed to minister. Those accused of this are to be rejected by all and are to be cast out of the parishes in which they are hiding until they are returned to that bishop from whom they are known to have fled.

c. 447. ON THE SAME MATTER.
From the same Council, c. 51.

Those who come into our provinces with their superiors from other provinces are not to be allowed to minister without formed letters; even if they bring them and are found suitable for ministry, let them be instructed on how to perform their sacred ministry religiously and studiously, and in which places they are not to do it.

c. 448. ON CLERICS.
From the same.

But if clerics are offered for ordination by such men, they must be instructed to send them to the bishops from whose parishes they have been taken, and either be ordained there, or bring canonical letters from the bishop to whose diocese they belong, as canonical authority teaches.

c. 449. THE NICENE SYNOD INSTITUTED THIS ORDER TO BE PRESERVED IN WRITING LETTERS BETWEEN BISHOPS.

No one who has even slight knowledge of Greek speech does not know that the letters of the Greek alphabet also express numbers. Therefore, lest any fraudulent act of falsehood be temerariously presumed in the composition of canonical letters, which Latin custom calls formed, what follows was most salubriously devised and established by the 318 Fathers gathered at Nicaea, that formed letters have this rationale of calculation or reckoning, namely that the first letters of Father, Son, and Holy Spirit in Greek, which are Π, Υ, Α, are adopted in the reckoning; these letters signify the numbers 80, 400, and 1. Also, the first letter of the Apostle Peter, that is, Π, which signifies the number 80; the first letter of him who is writing; the second letter of the one to whom it is written; the third letter of the one receiving it; the fourth letter of the city from which it is being written; and the number of the indiction is to be taken, whatever it is at the time. And so, the letter is to contain the single sum which has been collected together of the numbers which all these Greek letters, as we have said, express. Moreover, the writer is to add separately in the letter also the number 99, which, according to the Greek letters, signifies ΑΜΗΝ [Amen]. Thus, the three above-mentioned Greek letters, that is, Π, Υ, Α, and the first letter from Peter's name, that is, Π, make 561. For Π, which is the first letter in the name of the highest Father, makes

80; Υ, which is first in the name of the Son, makes 400; A, which is first in the name of the Holy Spirit, indicates 1. If you add Π, which is first in Peter's name, that is, 80, you will have 561. AMHN, which is written at the end of the abovesaid letter, indicates 99; for A is 1, M 40, H 8, N 50, which make 99. If you add together the whole sum, then the letter has 660.

But for the sake of the less learned, it seems good to set out the Greek letters themselves with their proper numbers: 1. A. 2. B. 3. Γ. 4. Δ. 5. E. 6. Ϛ. 7. Z. 8. H. 9. Θ. 10. I. 20. K. 30. Λ. 40. M. 50. N. 60. Ξ. 70. O. 80. Π. 90. Σ. 100. P. 200. Σ. 300. T. 400. Υ. 500. Φ. 600. X. 700. Ψ. 800. Ω. 900.

C. 450. EXEMPLAR OF A FORMED LETTER.

In the name of the Father, Π, and of the Son, Γ, and of the Holy Spirit, A. Ratbod, humble servant of the holy Church of Trier and its people, to Rotbert, bishop of the reverend holy Church of Metz, [sends] glory in Christ, prince of shepherds, and that it ever remain with the joy of prosperity and lastingness. Observing the most salubrious decrees of the 318 holy Fathers gathered at Nicaea, we canonically approach your worthy and pious Fraternity in God, and by way of a formed letter we come reverently to your Holiness, namely to inform you that we have given these dimissory letters to the presentee, our priest, Gislemarus by name, who was educated in accordance with ecclesiastical discipline in our diocese and whom we promoted from the clerical order to the degree of the priesthood so that, furnished with these canonical letters and with our license, it may be licit for him to dwell in your parish under the protection and rule of your dear Dilection, and we entrust him to you to protect and rule canonically in the bosom of Holy Mother Church. Hence, we decreed that this letter be furnished with Greek letters here and there, and we saw fit to seal it with a bull by the ring of our Church. May Christ, prince of shepherds, at the intercession of Blessed Peter, to whom the Lord's flock has been especially entrusted, long keep your Fraternity safe to us for the custody of his flock. Amen. Π. Υ. A. Ω. P. O. C. Υ. Θ. AMHN. The sum of these is 1,539. Given at Trier, on the Ides of October, in the year of the Lord's Incarnation 906, in the ninth Indiction.

C. 451. ALSO, ANOTHER LETTER.

To the most reverend and holy Ratbod, archbishop of the holy Church of Trier, Dado, devoted servant of Christ's flock in the holy Church of Verdun, [sends] the blessedness of the highest happiness in the Lord, our true King. Since the holy Catholic Church is prompt to follow the Gospel words, which say: "He that receives a prophet in the name of a prophet, shall receive the reward of a prophet: and he that receives a just man (Mt. 10:41–42)," etc., and the Apostle commands to extend hospitality and communicate to the necessities of holy men (cf. Rom. 12:13), yet there are those who have a cauterized conscience (cf. 1 Tim. 4:2). They say that they are simple, when they are full of diabolical cunning; they say that they go from place to place for a work of piety, when they are fugitives by their own malice. They say that they are enrolled in the sacred ministry, when such is not the case. It was established by the holy Fathers that no alien and unknown cleric is to be received by any bishop and enthroned in his Church, unless he have a letter from his own bishop, which in the canons is termed formed. And so, we make known to your Paternity that our present brother, bearer of these letters, who is called Adruinus, has not been sent away from us for his wickedness; at the request of our brethren, because he was a member of our household, we granted him liberty canonically at the horn of the altar and ordained him to the degree of the priesthood. We have also drawn up these dimissory or commendatory letters, and we direct him to your beloved Fraternity, so that he may remain in your parish under your sacred rule and defense. And so, in the name Π of the Father, and Υ of the Son, and Α of the Holy Spirit, and in the unity of holy Church, in which the right to bind and to loose is granted to Peter, I, Dado, humble bishop, do release the priest Adruinus from the city of Verdun, in the ninth Indiction, and grant to you, venerable Archbishop Ratbod, license to enthrone him in whatever church you wish within your own parish. May almighty God deign to preserve your beloved Paternity distinguished by the flowers of virtues. Amen. Π. Υ. Α. Π. Δ. Α. Π. Δ. Θ. 778. Given on the fifth day before the Ides of May, in the year of the Lord's Incarnation 906, Indiction 9.

c. 452. ON ORDINATION.
From the letter of Pope Gelasius.

Know that the ordinations of priests and deacons, which must not be done other than at certain times and days, are to be celebrated at the fast of the fourth and seventh and tenth month, as also at the fast at the beginning of Lent and on the middle day of Lent, on the Saturday fast, around vespers; nor is anyone to presume, by reason of any utility, to set a priest or deacon ahead of those who were ordained before them.

c. 453. HOW A BISHOP IS TO PERFORM AN ORDINATION.
From the Council of Nantes.

When the bishop makes ready to confer ordinations, all those who wish to proceed to the sacred ministry are to be called to the city on the Wednesday before the ordination, together with the archpriests who must present them. The bishop must then choose priests from his household and other prudent men, knowledgeable in the divine law and practiced in the ecclesiastical ordinances, who will diligently inquire regarding those to be ordained as to their manner of life, kin, provenance, age, institution, the place where they have been educated, whether they are sufficiently literate and instructed in the Lord's law, and, above all, whether they hold firmly the Catholic faith and are able to state it in simple words. Those to whom this is entrusted are to beware lest they depart from the truth due to the blandishments of favour or desire for any gifts, so as to bring to the bishop's hands or the reception of the sacred degrees one who is unworthy and less than suitable. If they should have done this, both the one who approached unworthily will be removed from the altar, and those who attempted to sell the gift of the Holy Spirit, already condemned before God, shall be deprived of ecclesiastical dignity. Therefore, let them be examined diligently for three continuous days so that, on the Saturday, those who have been found acceptable may be presented to the bishop.

c. 454. ON THE SAME MATTER.
From the Council of Meaux

Those who are asked to be ordained are not at all to be ordained, unless they live for at least a year in a certain and religious place, or even in the city, in order that certainty may be reached as to their life, conduct, and their learning.

c. 455. HOW ONE TO BE ORDAINED A BISHOP SHALL BE EXAMINED.
From the Council of Carthage.

He who is to be ordained bishop must first be examined as to whether he is by nature prudent, teachable, temperate in manners, of chaste life, serious, always careful in his affairs, humble, affable, merciful, literate, learned in the Lord's law, cautious in interpreting the senses of the Scriptures, well-trained in ecclesiastical doctrine. And, above all, whether he asserts in simple words the teachings of the faith, confirming that the Father, Son, and Holy Spirit is one God, preaching that the whole Godhead of the Trinity is of the same essence and substance, co-eternal and co-omnipotent, and that each of the persons of the Trinity is fully God and all three persons one God. Whether he believes that the divine Incarnation occurred neither in the Father, nor in the Holy Spirit, but in the Son alone, so that he who was the Son of God the Father according to divinity became his human mother's son according to humanity, true God from the Father, true man from the mother, taking flesh from his mother's body and a rational human soul, of both natures at the same time, divine and human, one person, one Son, one Christ, one Lord, of all creatures that exist both the Maker, Lord, and Ruler, with the Father and the Holy Spirit. Who suffered true suffering of the flesh, died a true death of his body, rose again by the true resurrection or resumption of his flesh, in which he shall come to judge the living and the dead. He is also to be asked by him whether he believes that one and the same God is the author of the New and Old Testaments, that is, of the Law, the Prophets, and the Apostles; whether the devil became evil by his own choice and not by his condition. He is also to be asked whether he believes in the resurrection of this flesh which we bear, and not of another, and whether he believes in a future judgment and that each will receive either punishment or reward for what he has done while in the flesh. Whether he does not disapprove of marriage; whether he does not condemn second marriages; whether he does not fault the eating of meat; whether he shares communion with reconciled penitents; whether in baptism all sins, both the original one and those wilfully committed, are remitted; whether no one is saved outside the Catholic Church. After he has been examined on these matters, if he is found fully instructed, then he is to be ordained bishop.

How priests or deacons are examined before or after their ordination, or how they are assessed as to their ministry, has been sufficiently expressed at the beginning of this little book, where is written what is to be required of a priest. And so, it seems superfluous to repeat anew what has already been clearly set down.

END OF THE FIRST BOOKLET

Second Book

In the previous booklet, we noted in part what the bishop or his ministers are to do and examine in his synod with regard to ecclesiastical men. Let us now quickly run through what is to be done, or may be opportune to do, as the Lord may grant, with regard to lay and secular persons.

C. 1. HOW THE BISHOP IS TO MAKE A CIRCUIT OF HIS PARISH.
From the Council of Rouen.

As the bishop goes around his diocese, the archdeacon or archpriest is to go before him by a day or two through the parishes which he will visit. After convoking the people, he is to announce the coming of their shepherd and instruct them fully, by the authority of the holy canons, that all are to come without fail on the stated day to the bishop's synod, and he is to announce with threats that, if anyone should be absent without grave necessity, he is undoubtedly to be excluded from the Christian communion. Then, after summoning to himself the priests who must exhibit service to the bishop in that place, he is to strive to emend whatever he can correct of the lesser and lighter causes, so that the pontiff, in coming, is not burdened at all with the easier matters, or it become necessary for him to stay there longer than the expenses suffice. For concerning such collaborators, the Lord says to Moses: "so that they may bear with you the burden of the people, and not you alone be burdened (cf. Num. 11:17)." And the blessed John the Baptist, as he ran ahead of the Lord's coming, preached and said: "Repent (Mt. 3:2)," etc. And also: "Make ready the way of the Lord (Mt. 3:3)." Since indeed the bishop is seen to act in the place of Christ, he is to be received by the peoples subject to him with joy, fear, and the highest reverence, so that it may be said to them with praise what the Apostle says to his disciples: "I give you a testimony that you received me as an angel of God, as the Lord Jesus (cf. Gal. 4:14–15)."

c. 2. ON THE JURORS OF THE SYNOD.

As above.

The bishop, as he sits in synod, after a suitable allocution, must call out seven men from the people of the same parish, or more or less, as he may deem expedient, of the more mature, honourable, and truthful among them; bringing forth the relics of the saints, he is to bind each of them by the oath that follows.

c. 3. SYNOD OATH.

From this moment forward, whatever you know, or have heard, or will afterwards learn to have been done, or to be about to be done, in this parish, against the will of God and right Christianity, if it happens in your lifetime, provided only that it come to your knowledge in whatever manner, if you know, or if it is indicated to you, that it is a synodal cause and pertains to the bishop's ministry, without regard to love, fear, reward, or kinship, you shall not hide it in any respect whatsoever from the archbishop of Trier, or his envoy whom he has commanded to inquire into this, whenever he interrogates you in regard to the matter. So help you God and these relics of the saints.

THE REST ARE TO SWEAR AS FOLLOWS:

This oath, which this man has sworn as to a synodal cause, you shall observe it, insofar as you know, or have heard, or will learn from this day forward. So help you God.

c. 4. AFTER THE GIVING OF THE OATH, THE BISHOP IS TO ADDRESS THE JURORS AS FOLLOWS:

Observe, brethren, that you render your oaths to the Lord, for you did not swear to a man, but to God, your Creator. We, who are his ministers, do not lust after your earthly wealth, but seek the salvation of your souls. Beware not to hide anything and bring about your own damnation from another's sin.

c. 5. AFTER THESE THINGS, LET HIM QUESTION THEM IN THE FOLLOWING ORDER:

1. Is there in this parish a homicide, who has killed a man either by his own spontaneous will, or out of cupidity or rapacity, or by chance, or unwillingly, or coerced, or to avenge relatives, which we call a feud (*faida*), or in war, or at his lord's command, or has killed his own slave?

2. Is there any parricide, or fratricide, who has killed father, mother, sister, brother, uncle or any relative?

3. Is there anyone who has killed a priest, or deacon, or any cleric, or cut off any of their limbs?

4. Is there any man or woman who has crushed his or her own child, or suffocated it with the weight of clothing? And if this was done, before baptism or after baptism; or if an ill child died without baptism because of parental negligence?

5. Is there any man or woman who has forced the ejection of another's offspring, or if a woman has by her own will ejected her offspring, and caused an abortion?

6. Is there any woman who, after conceiving in fornication and fearing it would be made public, either cast her child into water, or hid it in the earth, which they call *morth*?

7. Is there anyone who, without law or certain proof, has killed his wife?

8. Is there any woman who has killed her husband or some other man with poisonous herbs or death-dealing potions, or who has taught someone else to do this?

9. Is there any man or woman who has brought it about, or who has taught someone to bring it about, that a man cannot engender or a woman conceive?

10. Is there any man who, without judicial process, has killed his own slave, and any woman who has killed her maidservant, burning with jealous anger?

11. Is there anyone who, at the impulse of the devil, has killed himself?

12. If there is anyone who, in a war, has wounded men, and does not know whether anyone has perished from that wounding? And if it is imputed to anyone that he killed a man, and he denies it?

13. If there is anyone who counselled the killing of a man, and was not in on the deed, and yet the man was killed by his counsel and exhortation?

14. Is there anyone who has cut off the hands, feet, tongue, and testicles, and has ripped out the eyes of another?

THEN, THERE IS TO BE QUESTIONING AS TO ADULTERIES AND FORNICATIONS.

15. If any married man has committed adultery with another's wife, or any wife with another's husband?

16. If any man who has a wife has simultaneously kept a concubine, either his maidservant or some other woman?

17. If any man has dismissed his lawful wife and taken another woman in marriage?

18. If any woman has dismissed her husband and joined herself to another man?

19. If any who, having divorced, are separated from each other and remain that way?

20. If any man, without his wife's consent, has abandoned his lawful marriage and entered a monastery?

21. If any man has abandoned his wife, although she was guilty, without the bishop's judgment?

22. If any woman, with her husband's knowledge, has committed fornication?

23. If any man who, not having a wife of his own, has committed fornication with another's wife? Or any woman who, not having a husband, did so with another's husband?

24. If any man who, not having a wife of his own, has fornicated with a woman who has no husband?

25. If a lay virgin has committed fornication with an adolescent?

26. If any man has not married the girl whom he had espoused, and has broken the faith of their espousal?

27. If any man has seized another's betrothed and joined her to himself?

28. If any man has taken by seizure any woman, virgin, or widow, and joined her to himself in marriage; and if there are any, who consented and assisted him in this?

29. If any man has committed adultery with a Jewess, or, if he is a Jew or pagan, with a Christian woman?

30. If any man has seized a nun or a widow dedicated to God, and taken her in marriage, or has fornicated with them with their consent?

31. If any man who, while her husband lived, is accused of having committed adultery with that man's wife, and is known to have married the same woman soon after her husband's death?

32. If any woman says that her husband is unable to have intercourse with her and, for this cause, seeks a divorce, and wishes to take another husband?

33. If any man has committed adultery with his spiritual godmother, or taken her in marriage, or similarly with a goddaughter whom he received from the sacred font, or held before the bishop?

34. If any man has taken in marriage his relative and blood-kin, or has fornicated with her?

35. If any man irrationally, that is, against nature, has joined with males or dumb beasts?

36. If any woman has engaged in procuring?

37. If any man is party to adulteries being perpetrated in his house with his maidservants or women working in the women's quarters?

ON THEFT AND SACRILEGE.

38. It is to be asked whether there is any thief or sacrilegious person who has broken into God's churches, or stolen anything from a church, or has done public plunder, or stolen something secretly, or if someone has been rapacious and a thief and plunderer of God's Church? For although these things are to be corrected and punished according to human law, yet penance [for them] pertains to the bishop.

ON PERJURY.

39. It is to be asked whether anyone is a perjurer and if he perjured himself knowingly and out of cupidity for earthly things. And if unknowingly, either if coerced at the command of his superior, or to redeem his life or limbs; or if someone not only perjured himself knowingly, but also led others into perjury?

ON FALSE TESTIMONY.

40. It is to be asked whether anyone has knowingly borne false witness against anyone (for this is a capital crime), and what harm did someone suffer by this attestation?

41. It is to be asked whether anyone has stolen a free man, or another's slave, or a pilgrim, or a stranger, or seduced him with blandishments and sold him, or sent him into captivity outside his country; or if anyone has sold a Christian slave to a Jew or a pagan, or if the same Jews sell Christian slaves?

ON ENCHANTERS AND SOOTHSAYERS.

42. It is to be asked whether anyone is a magician, a fortune-teller or an enchanter, a diviner or a soothsayer?

43. If anyone makes vows to trees, or springs, or stones as if at altars, or brings a candle or some gift there, as if there were some numinous presence there which can bring about something good or evil?

44. It is to be investigated whether any swineherd, or oxherd, or hunter, or any others of this sort, says diabolical verses over bread or herbs, or over some nefarious charms, and hides these in a tree or throws them at the crossings of two or three roads in order to free his own animals from plague or harm and destroy those of another? None of the faithful doubts that such things are idolatry and so entirely to be rooted out.

45. It is to be investigated whether there is any woman who, by some sorcery and enchantments, claims that she can change the minds of men, that is, change them from hate to love, or from love to hate, or harm or take away men's goods? And if there is any woman who claims that on certain nights she goes riding on

some beasts with a crowd of demons who have taken female aspect, and that she is numbered in their fellowship, such a woman is entirely to be cast out of the parish.

ON BLOOD AND DEAD ANIMALS

46. It is to be asked whether anyone has eaten blood, a dead animal, or one torn apart by beasts?

47. If anyone does not return to peace because of hate, or who has sworn, which is contrary to God, never to reconcile with a brother, which is a sin unto death?

48. If anyone drinks a liquid into which a weasel, or a mouse, or some unclean animal has drowned?

49. If anyone has not observed the Lenten fast, or the fast of the Ember Days, or the greater litany, or of Rogationtide, or a fast proclaimed by the bishop for any plague?

50. If there is anyone who drinks, or eats, or carries about with him anything which he believes could pervert God's judgment?

51. If anyone does anything on the Kalends of January which was devised by the pagans, and practices the observance of days, moon, and months, and hopes that, by the effective power of these things, something is changed for better or worse?

52. If anyone, in beginning any work, says anything there, or does anything by any magical art, other than, as the Apostle teaches, that all things are to be done in the name of the Lord? Indeed, we must not invoke demons to our aid, but God. Similarly, in gathering medicinal herbs, it is fitting to say the Creed and the Lord's Prayer and nothing else.

53. It is also to be asked whether women, in working wool and weaving cloth, say or observe anything other than, as was said above, all things in the name of the Lord?

54. If anyone retains unjustly the offerings, that is, the alms of their dead parents?

55. If anyone, in the night hours, sings diabolical verses over a dead person, and eats and drinks there, as if he were glad for the person's death, and whether the dead are kept elsewhere than in a church for night vigils?

56. If there is anyone who does not take communion at least three times a year, that is, at Easter, Pentecost, and the Nativity of the Lord, unless he has been removed from communion for death-dealing sins by the judgment of the bishop or priests?

57. Is there anyone who, on Sunday or on the principal feast-days, does some sort of work, and whether on those days all come unfailingly to matins, and to mass, and to vespers?

58. If any excommunicate has treated excommunication as nothing, and whether anyone has had dealings with an excommunicate?

59. If anyone has not observed the manner of penance enjoined upon him?

60. If anyone has dishonoured, or struck, or cursed his father or mother?

61. If anyone has vomited out of drunkenness after receiving the Eucharist?

62. If there is anyone who has withheld his tithe from God and His saints?

63. If there is anyone so perverse and alien from God that he does not come to church at least on Sunday?

64. If swineherds and other shepherds come to church on Sunday, and hear mass, and similarly on other feast-days?

65. If there is anyone who does not come to confession at least once a year, that is, at the beginning of Lent, and does not receive penance for his sins?

66. If there is anyone who pursues continuous drunkenness? For drunkards will not possess the kingdom of God (cf. 1 Cor. 6:9–10).

67. If there is anyone who, contemning his own priest, goes to church in another parish, and receives communion and gives his tithe there?

68. It is to be investigated regarding the beggars who roam through the country (*per patrias*), and whether each person supports a poor person out of his own household.

69. Whether tithingmen have been appointed in each parish throughout the vills, truthful and God-fearing men who may admonish the others to go to church for matins, mass, and vespers, and to do no work on feast-days; and if anyone of these has transgressed, they are to announce it to the priest immediately, as also with regard to lust and every depraved act?

70. If there is anyone who gives slight weight to the ban of his bishop or priest, as also to excommunication, so treating them as nothing?

71. If parishioners show due honour to their priest, or if there is anyone who dishonours him in word or deed, and spurns his admonitions?

72. If there is anyone who has refused hospitality to a pilgrim or traveller?

73. It is to be investigated what feast-days they keep.

74. If godparents teach, or have others teach, their godchildren the Creed and the Lord's Prayer?

75. If four or five or more people killed a man?

76. If there is anyone who speaks against the bishop or his ministers as to not striking naked tenants or slaves with rods for the crimes they have committed?

77. It is to be asked if anyone wishes to treat as his slave, and presumes to sell or give to someone else, a stranger who has fled his country because of the inva-

sion of pagans, or persecution, on the grounds that he stayed in his house, and served him for days or years as a hireling?

78. If there is anyone who sells his grain or wine with an unjust measure, when the Lord says: "Let the bushel be just, and the sextary equal (Lev. 19:36)?"

79. It is also to be denounced how great a crime it is to exact usury, and to wish to be enriched on another's interest payments, and that the sacred canons instruct that such people are to be ejected from the Church.

80. If anyone has killed a Jew or a pagan out of cupidity?

81. If anyone has killed a man while insane?

82. If anyone cut down a tree and, while he applies himself to the necessary task, another man, coming under the tree, is unexpectedly crushed?

83. If anyone pursues plots and conspiracies?

84. If anyone presumes to harass the Church or a cleric?

85. It is to be investigated regarding fugitive and faith-breaking laymen.

86. There is to be strict questioning regarding the manner in which confraternities and fraternal societies in the parish are operated.

87. If anyone presumes to sing shameful songs that move to laughter near a church?

88. If anyone, entering a church, is accustomed to engage in chatting and does not diligently listen to the divine words, and whether he exits the church before the end of the mass?

89. If men and women offer the oblation at mass, that is, the bread and wine, and if the husbands do not do so, wives are to make the offering for them, for themselves and all of theirs, as is contained in the canon.

It is fitting that these articles, which we have noted in order, be strengthened by canonical decrees.

ON THE PENANCE OF HOMICIDES

c. 6. THAT PENANCE FOR HOMICIDES NOT BE DONE DIFFERENTLY, AS BEFORE, BUT IN THE SAME WAY THROUGHOUT THE SEVERAL EPISCOPATES.

From the Council of Tribur.

If anyone, at the devil's instigation, has perpetrated a homicide by his own free will, according to the provisions of the canons and the judgment of the bishops, he must accept such a penance: First, that he not have license to enter the church for the next forty days; he is to go about barefoot, and make use of no vehicle. He is to wear woolen clothing with no breeches; he is not to bear arms, is to eat nothing in these forty days apart from only bread and salt, and he is to drink pure water. He is to have no communion in food and drink with other Christians, nor with another penitent, until the forty days have expired. No one else is to eat from the food that he takes. But out of consideration for the quality of the person, or his infirmity, for the sake of mercy and as seems proper, especially if he committed the homicide under coercion and not willingly, he may be allowed some fruit and vegetables or legumes. By canonical authority, for those days, he is to be forbidden in any way to have intercourse with any woman, nor is he to approach his own wife, nor to sleep with any man. He is to be near the church, before whose doors he is to bemoan his sins night and day, and he is not to wander from place to place, but to be in one place for these forty days. And if perhaps he has people who threaten his life, let his penance be delayed until the bishop obtains peace for him from his enemies, and if he is constrained by infirmity, so that he cannot worthily do penance, let the penance be delayed until he is restored to health. But if he is constrained by a long illness, it shall pertain to the bishop's judgment to make disposition as to how to heal the guilty and ill man. After the forty days are completed, he may wash in water, put on again the clothing and shoes which he had put aside, and cut his hair.

c. 7. WHAT MUST HE OBSERVE IN THE FIRST YEAR?

In the first year after the forty days, for that whole year, he is to abstain from wine, mead, and honeyed beer, from meat, cheese, and fat fishes, except on the feast-days which are celebrated by the whole people within that episcopate. And unless perhaps he is on a long journey, or in the army, or for a lengthy stay at his lord's court, or if he is constrained by infirmity; in those cases, it is licit for him for one penny, or the price of one penny, or by feeding three poor people, to redeem Tuesday, Thursday, and Saturday, but in such way that he make use of only one of these three things. After he has returned home, or has been restored to health, he is to have no license to redeem.

c. 8. WHAT MUST HE OBSERVE IN THE NEXT TWO YEARS?

After the course of the year has been completed, he is to enter the church, and the kiss of peace is to be granted to him. In the second and third year, he is to fast in a similar manner, except that he has the power to redeem Tuesday, Thursday, and Saturday wherever he is. Let him observe everything else diligently, as in the first year.

c. 9. WHAT MUST HE OBSERVE IN THE REMAINING FOUR YEARS?

Then four years remain, in each of which he is to fast three periods of forty days. The first is before Easter, with the rest of the Christians, abstaining from wine, mead, honeyed beer, cheese, and fat fishes. The second, before the nativity of St. John; if anything remains of the forty days, let him fulfil it after the mass of St. John. The third, before the Nativity of the Lord, he is to fast as mentioned above. During the four abovementioned years, he may make use of whatever he wishes on Tuesday, Thursday, and Saturday; he may also redeem Monday and Wednesday for the price mentioned earlier. In every way, he is to keep Friday at bread and water, and may never redeem it. When he has fulfilled these things, let him receive sacred communion.

c. 10. ON ONE WHO HAS COMMITTED HOMICIDE VOLUNTARILY.

From the Council of Ancyra.

Those who have committed homicide voluntarily are to submit themselves to penance perpetually, but they are to attain completion only near the end of their lives.

c. 11. ON THE SAME MATTER.

From the Council of Paris.

If anyone has committed homicide willingly, and not while resisting a violent person, but used force and killed an innocent person who was simply going by, there is to be no communion at all with such a one, yet in such a manner that, if he has done penance, the viaticum of communion is not to be denied to him at the end of his life.

c. 12. ON HOMICIDES.

From the Council of Agde.

We have also adjudged that homicides and false witnesses are to be removed from ecclesiastical communion, unless they have washed away by the satisfaction of penance the crimes which they committed.

c. 13. ON THE SAME MATTER.

From the Council of Nantes.

If anyone has killed a man voluntarily and by plotting, he is to submit himself to the yoke of penance. And if it is established that this was done publicly, and he is a layman, he is to be removed from the communion of prayers for five years. After five years, he is to be received only into the communion of prayers, but he is not to make an offering, nor to touch the body of the Lord. After remaining in such a state for fourteen years, then he is to be received into full communion with offerings.

c. 14. ON THE SAME MATTER.
From the same.

In Exodus, the Lord says of homicides: "If a man kill his neighbour on set purpose and by lying in wait for him, you shall take him away from my altar, that he may die (Ex. 21:14)."

c. 15. ON HOMICIDES NOT COMMITTED WILLINGLY.
From the Council of Ancyra.

As for homicides not committed willingly, an earlier rule directed that completion be attained after seven years of penance, but a second rule directed that a term of five years be completed.

c. 16. ON THE SAME MATTER.
From the letter of Rabanus to Bishop Heribaldus.

For as to those who did not kill men willingly, we read that God through his law-giver designated cities of refuge, by fleeing to which they would save themselves from the avenger of their neighbour's blood and would not die (cf. Jos. 20:1–6). Hence, it is written in Deuteronomy: "This shall be the law regarding the homicide whose life is to be spared: He who struck his neighbour unknowingly, and who is proved to have had no hate against him yesterday or the day before, but had simply gone with him into the woods to cut down trees, and, during the cutting of the tree, the axe escaped his hand, or the blade fell off the handle and struck and killed his friend. This man is to flee to one of the aforementioned cities and live (Deut. 19:4–5)."

c. 17. ON THE SAME MATTER.
From the Council of Worms, c. 5.

It often happens that, while one cuts down a tree out of need, another comes by and is caught under it. Concerning this, if it has happened by the will or negligence of the one who was cutting down the tree, then he must submit to penance entirely as a homicide. But if it has happened neither by his desire but by carelessness, nor even with his knowledge – but, while perhaps he was attending to a necessary task, the other has unexpectedly come below the tree and has been crushed under it – then, the one cutting down the tree is not treated as a homicide.

c. 18. ON THE SAME MATTER.
From the Council of Tribur.

If two brothers are cutting trees in a wood and, as the fall of the tree approaches, one brother says to the other, "Beware," and the second, in flight, is caught under the falling tree and is killed, the brother who remains alive is to be adjudged innocent of his brother's blood.

c. 19. ON THE SAME MATTER.
From the same.

If a mother placed her infant near a fireplace, and some man placed water in a pot and, when the water boiled over, the child was killed, the mother is to do penance for her negligence and the man is to be safe.

c. 20. ON THE SAME MATTER.
From the same.

As for homicides not committed willingly, it is to remain within the bishop's judgment as to what yoke of penance they who committed them shall be subject.

c. 21. ON THE SAME MATTER.
From the same.

If a man has not killed his own child willingly, let him to penance as for a homicide not committed willingly.

c. 22. ON THE SAME MATTER.
From the Council of Nantes.

If anyone perpetrated a homicide by chance, and not willingly, let him do penance at bread and water for forty days. After these are completed, he is to be separated from the prayer of the faithful for two years; he is neither to receive communion, nor to make the offering. After those two years, he is to be received into the communion of prayer, but is not to make an offering, nor to receive communion. After five years, he is to be received into full communion. Abstinence from foods is to remain at the discretion of the priest.

c. 23. HE WHO HAS KILLED A MAN IN A FEUD.
From a Penitential, c. 14.

He who has killed a man to avenge his brother or other relatives is to do penance for one year and, for the next two years, he is to observe three forty-day fasts and the weekdays prescribed by law, that is, Monday, Wednesday, and Friday.

c. 24. ALSO.
From the same.

He who has killed a man suddenly in wrath, a fight, or drunkenness, is to do penance for four years.

c. 25. ON THE SAME MATTER.
From the same.

If any free man, at his lord's command, killed a slave, he is to do penance for forty days. And if any free man, at his lord's command, killed an innocent man, he is to do penance for one year and, for a further two years, he is to observe three forty-day fasts and the weekdays prescribed by law.

c. 26. OF THOSE WHO KILL THEIR SLAVES WITHOUT JUDICIAL PROCESS.
From the Council of Agde, c. 26.

If anyone has killed his own slave without the knowledge of a judge, he shall cleanse the guilt of the blood with a two-year excommunication.

c. 27. ON PARRICIDES AND FRATRICIDES.
From the Council of Mainz.

We establish that parricides and fratricides persevere in praying for the Lord's clemency before the doors of the church for a whole year. At the completion of the year, they are to be introduced into the church, but are to stand among the hearers until the period of a year is completed. When these things have been done, if the fruit of penance is evident in them, let them share in the body and blood of the Lord, lest they become obdurate in despair. They are not to eat meat for all the days of their lives, and they are to fast until the ninth hour every day, excepting feast-days and Sundays. They are to abstain from wine, mead, and honeyed beer for three days each week. They must not dare to bear arms, unless against the pagans. And wherever they wish to go, they must do so without a vehicle and proceed on their own feet. But we place it in the bishops' discretion to be able to extend or shorten the time of this penance, in accordance with their manner of life. If they have wives, they are not to be separated from them. But if they do not have them, and they are not able to remain continent, let them take lawful women to marriage, lest they be seen to fall into the pit of fornication. But if the end of their life should come about before they complete the course of the said two years, let the viaticum not be denied to them.

c. 28. ON THE SAME MATTER.
From another Council of Mainz, c. 20.

How detestable a crime is parricide, the Lord has shown by his judgment between Cain and his brother Abel (cf. Gen. 4:11–15). But because in modern times, exiled parricides wander through different places and pursue various vices and the enticements of gluttony, it seems better to us that they should remain in one place and chastise themselves by a strict penance, if perhaps they are to merit to receive from the Lord's goodness indulgence for their crime.

C. 29. THAT ARMS AND MARRIAGE BE FORBIDDEN TO PARRICIDES.
From the same.

Indeed, neither will it be licit for them to receive further the belt of military service, or to be united in marriage, because the sacred canons do not allow them this.

C. 30. OF HIM WHO KILLS A MAN WHO IS DOING PUBLIC PENANCE.
From the Capitularies, bk. 3, c. 17.

He who has killed a man doing public penance is to pay our ban threefold as composition, and he is to pay the wergild to his relatives.

C. 31. OF HIM WHO KILLS A MAN IN A CHURCH.
From the same book, c. 13.

If anyone, for a slight cause or for none at all, has killed a man in a church, he is to make composition for the life. But if they had been fighting outside, and one of them fled the other in the church, and there killed him while defending himself, and if he has no witnesses to the deed, let him swear with twelve lawful witnesses that he killed the other while defending himself; afterwards let him pay 600 shillings on behalf of the church which he polluted by that homicide, and in addition he is to be compelled to pay our ban. As for the one who was killed, let him lie without composition, and then let the killer accept the penance which, according to canonical judgment, is suitable for the crime which he committed. If someone's slave has done these things, let him be examined by the ordeal of boiling water as to whether he did this willingly or in his own defense. If his hand is burned, let him be killed; but if it is not, his lord is to pay to the church the wergild for the dead man, or, if he prefers, he is to hand the slave over to the same church. As for a slave attached to a church, to the fisc, or to a benefice, we will that, for one time, the wergild be paid in composition for him; for the second time, the slave is to be handed over for punishment. Yet, the inheritance of a free man who has been condemned to death for such a crime is to go to his lawful heirs. If this sort of homicide has been committed in the porch of a church, whose door has been consecrated with the relics of the saints, a similar composition and emendation is to be made. But if it is not consecrated, let composition be paid in the same way as a crime which is committed in violation of a church's sanctity.

c. 32. ON THE INJURIES OF PRIESTS OR CLERICS.
From the same, c. 14.

For the shedding of blood done with a club in a church, if he was a priest, threefold composition is to be paid, two parts of which are to go to the same priest and one part to the church as a fine, and, in addition, our ban. Similarly, in the case of a deacon, threefold composition is to be paid according to his composition, along with our ban. As for a subdeacon and a cleric of whatever order, threefold payment is to be made according to his composition, and, in addition, our ban.

c. 33. OF A BLOW.

Similarly, for a blow without the shedding of blood affecting a cleric of whatever order, threefold composition is to be paid, and, in addition, our ban. And anyone who does not have the resources to pay the church is to give himself in service to the same church until he satisfies the whole debt.

c. 34. IF ANYONE HAS ROBBED A CLERIC.
From the Council of Tribur.

That, if any deeds have been perpetrated against the clerics themselves or the churches, that is, if anyone has robbed or wounded a cleric, or has caused some injury, or has seized or withheld the tithes of a church, if the matter has not already been punished worthily by the secular power, let the bishop summon those malefactors to his synod and worthily correct them. If they have contemned to come, let them be excommunicated.

c. 35. IF ANYONE HAS WHIPPED A CLERIC.
From the same.

If anyone has whipped a cleric, or debilitated or harmed him in any way, let him do penance canonically and make correction according to the law, in accordance with what is written in the Capitulary.

c. 36. ON THE SAME MATTER.
From the Council of Toledo.

If any of the powerful men has despoiled a cleric or a religious, and the bishop has commanded him to appear and be heard, and he has been in contempt, let writings immediately be sent mutually to all the bishops of the province, and whomsoever they may reach, that he be held excommunicate until he is heard and makes restitution for things not his own.

c. 37. ON FIGHTING AND HOMICIDE IN THE CHURCHYARD OF A CHURCH.
From the Council of Tribur.

If anyone fights or commits a homicide in the porch of a church, whatever amends are to be offered for violating its sanctity are to be paid at the altar of him whose church it is.

c. 38. ON FIGHTING IN CHURCH.
From the same.

If anyone has struck a cleric in a church with a club or sword, so that blood is shed, or from a blow without shedding of blood, let composition be paid according to what is written in the Capitulary, that is, threefold according to his composition.

c. 39. THAT LAYMEN NOT TAKE ANY PORTION OF THE POSSESSIONS OF THEIR DYING PRIESTS.
From the same, c. 2.

It was also reported to the holy Synod that some laymen act wickedly against their priests so that they claim shares for themselves in the possessions of dying priests, as if they were their slaves. By canonical authority, we forbid this to be done henceforth, but, just as they were made free men in order to receive their degree and perform the divine office, so nothing is to be required from them apart from the divine office. They are to usurp nothing for themselves from the personal property of the priests, but the priests may do whatever seems best to them with two parts of it, while leaving a third part to the churches which they serve, in accordance with the commands of the canons.

c. 40. ON THE COMPOSITION OF A PRIEST, IF HE HAS BEEN KILLED.
From the same.

If a priest has been wounded or cut down, but has escaped death, the whole composition is to go to the priest. But if he is dead, the composition is to be divided into three portions: that is, one for the altar which the priest served, the second for the bishop, the third is to be paid to the relatives of the priest.

c. 41. ON THE SAME MATTER.
From bk. 2 of the Capitularies, c. 48.

Murdered priests are to be made atonement for to the bishop to whose parish he pertains, according to the Capitulary of the glorious Charles, our parent, namely, in such manner that the bishop bestow half of such a priest's wergild to the uses of the church over which the priest presided and justly distribute the other half in alms on his own behalf, because no one seems to us a closer heir to him than the one who joined him to the Lord.

C. 42. ON THE ONE WHO KILLED A PRIEST.
From the Council of Worms.

He who has killed a priest voluntarily is not to eat meat, nor to drink wine, for all the days of his life. He is to fast until vespers, except on feast-days and Sundays; he is not to bear arms, or ride a horse. He is not to enter a church for five years, but is to stand at the doors of the church. After five years, he is to enter the church, yet without communicating, but he is to stand or sit with the hearers. When the course of twelve years has been completed, permission to receive communion is to be granted to him, as also a remission as to horse-riding. But he is to persist in the other observances for three days each week in order to merit a more perfect purification.

C. 43. ON THE SAME MATTER.
From the Council of Mainz, c. 24.

He who has killed a priest: Let a penance of twelve years be imposed on him according to the canons; or if he should deny it, and he is free, let him swear with twelve others; but if he is a slave, let him purge himself on twelve burning ploughshares. One convicted of such a crime is to put aside the knightly belt for the rest of his life, and he is to lose his wife.

C. 44. ON ONE WHO HAS KILLED A DEMOTED PRIEST.
From the same Council.

It has been announced to us that some men were brutally killed who said that they had formerly been priests and afterwards, having been demoted and doing penance for their sins, passing through different places, sought the suffrages of the saints. We deny every ecclesiastical communion to this sort of killers, until they perform worthy penance for their crime according to the judgment of the bishops.

C. 45. ON THE HOMICIDES OF CLERICS.
From the Capitularies, bk. 3, c. 25.

He who has killed a subdeacon is to pay 300 shillings as composition; a deacon, 400; a priest, 600, a bishop, 900; a monk, he is to pay 400 as composition.

c. 46. IF ANY ORDAINED PERSON HAS COMMITTED A HOMICIDE.
From a Penitential.

If any bishop, or any ordained person, has committed a homicide, he is to do penance for ten years, three of them at bread and water.

c. 47. IF ANYONE HAS CONSENTED OR COUNSELLED THAT A MAN BE KILLED.
From the same.

If anyone has consented to and given counsel that a homicide be committed, and it has been done, he is to do penance for seven years. But if it has not been done, he is to do penance for three years.

c. 48. IF ANYONE HAS KILLED HIS BLOOD-KIN OR SUPERIOR.
From the same.

If anyone has killed his neighbour and blood-kin, he is to do penance for ten years. Likewise, if anyone has slain his superior and lord by guile.

c. 49. ON THE SAME MATTER.
From the sayings of the deacon Ferrandus.

They ruinously deceive themselves, who hold that they alone are homicides who kill a man with their own hands, and not rather those by whose counsel, fraud, and exhortation men are killed. Indeed, the Jews never killed the Lord by their own hands, as it is written: "It is not lawful for us to put any man to death (Jn. 18:31)." But yet, the Lord's death is imputed to them because they killed him with their tongue, saying: "Crucify, crucify him (Jn. 19:15)." So it was that one Evangelist says that the Lord was crucified at the third hour (Mk. 15:25), another at the sixth (Lk. 23:44), because the Jews crucified him at the third hour with their tongue, and the soldiers at the sixth hour with their hands. Whoever betrays a man, then, kills him, as the Lord says: "He who has delivered me to you has the greater sin (Jn. 19:11)." Hence the Psalmist: "The sons of men, whose teeth are weapons and arrows, and their tongue a sharp sword (Ps. 56:5)." Let them subject themselves to penance, then, by whose counsel blood is shed, if they wish to deserve mercy.

c. 50. ON THOSE WHO TREAT AS NOTHING THE HOMICIDE PERPETRATED IN WAR.
From the letter of Rabanus to Heribaldus, bishop of Auxerre, regarding the battle fought at Fontenay.

But some excuse homicide recently perpetrated in the course of the sedition and battle of our princes, as if it were not necessary for each one of them to do penance because it was carried out at the command of their princes, and so was decided by God's judgment. Indeed, we know that God's judgment is always just and worthy of no reproof. Yet, it is incumbent on those who desire to defend this nefarious slaughter to consider whether they are able to excuse themselves as free of guilt before God's eyes, as it were, who out of avarice, which is the root of all evils and is compared to the service to idols, and for the favour of their temporal lords contemned their eternal Lord and spurned his commandments, committing homicide not by chance, but on set purpose. Hence, it is written in Exodus: "If a man kill his neighbour on set purpose and by lying in wait for him, you shall take him away from my altar that he may die (Ex. 21:14)." And in Deuteronomy: "But if someone who hates his neighbour plots against his life and, rising up, strikes him and he dies, and then flees to one of the aforesaid cities, then the elders of that city shall send and take him from his place of refuge, and hand him over to the next of kin of him whose blood was shed, and he is to die. You shall have no mercy on him (Deut. 19:11–13)." Hence, who is to say that he is not guilty whom the Lord has judged worthy of death? How is he not an opponent of God's law, who contends that what God has commanded is void? But between these things it is to be known that there is a great difference between a lawful prince and a seditious tyrant.

c. 51. ON THE SAME MATTER.
From a Penitential.

If anyone has killed a man in a public war, he is to do penance for forty days.

c. 52. ON A CLERIC WHO HAS KILLED HIS NEIGHBOUR.
From the same.

If a cleric has committed homicide and has killed his neighbour in premeditated hate, he is to do penance for seven years as an exile.

c. 53. ON PARRICIDES.
From a Penitential.

If anyone has perpetrated this crime, some adjudged that they ought to do penance for seven years or for fourteen; others, until the end of life, like Cain, who committed similar things.

c. 54. ON ONE WHO HAS CRIPPLED A MAN.
From the same.

He who has crippled or maimed a man is to pay the medical expenses, compensate him for the harm, do his work for him until the latter is healed, and do penance for half a year. If he does not have the resources to make restitution, he is to do penance for a year.

c. 55. ON MUTILATIONS OF LIMBS.
From the Council of Mainz, c. 6.

It is not licit for those by whom the Lord's sacraments are handled to pursue a judgment of blood. And so, such an excess is earnestly to be forbidden, lest, seized by the movements of indiscreet presumption, they presume to judge by their own sentence that which must be punished by death, or personally inflict mutilations on any persons, or command them to be inflicted. If anyone, unmindful of these precepts, should have done any such thing either upon the servants of his church, or upon any other persons, he is to be deprived of the honour of the order granted to him and of his place, confined in a prison of perpetual condemnation. Yet, communion is not to be denied to such a one as he exits this life, by the mercy of the Lord.

c. 56. WHAT DISCRETION THERE MUST BE IN THE RULERS OF CHURCHES, LEST THEY SUFFER THE STIGMA OF HOMICIDE FOR THEIR IRREGULAR DISCIPLINE.

Since, according to the pronouncement of an ancient precept, benevolence is more effective toward those to be corrected than severity, more encouragement than anger and more charity than power is to be applied.

c. 57. ON PARRICIDE.
From the Theodosian law, bk. IX.

If anyone should kill his father, mother, sister, son, daughter, or other near relations, any other kind of torment shall be removed, and a leathern sack, called a *culleus*, shall be made. When he is placed in it, snakes are to be enclosed with him, and, if the sea is not close by, he shall be thrown into any stream, so that one condemned to such a penalty may never obtain burial.

c. 58. ON A MISTRESS WHO KILLS HER MAIDSERVANT.
From the Council of Elvira.

If any mistress, burning with jealous anger, has killed her maidservant so that, within three days, she gives up her soul in torment, because it may be uncertain whether she has killed intentionally or by chance; if intentionally, it has pleased that she be admitted to communion after seven years, if she has done lawful penance, and after five years if by chance.

c. 59. IF A SLAVE IS KILLED BY HIS MASTER WHILE HE IS BEING CHASTISED WITH WHIPS.
From the Theodosian law.

If a slave has died while the master is punishing a fault, the master is not bound by the guilt of homicide, because one is guilty of homicide when he is convicted of having willed to kill. But correction is not termed a crime.

c. 60. ON THE CRUSHING OF INFANTS.
From the Council of Mainz.

If someone has crushed carelessly his infant child, or suffocated it by the weight of clothing, and this was done after baptism, he is to do penance at bread and water, vegetables and legumes, for forty days, and he is to abstain from his wife. Afterwards, he is to do penance for three years on the weekdays prescribed by law, and he is to observe three forty-day fasts each year. But if the infant was crushed before baptism, he is to do penance for the next forty days as above. But afterwards, he is to fulfil the rest for five years.

c. 61. IF AN INFANT DIES UNBAPTIZED THROUGH ITS MOTHER'S NEGLIGENCE.
From the letter of Rabanus to the rural bishop Reginbaldus.

As for infants who are found dead next to their father and mother, and it is not apparent whether the infant was suffocated or killed by the father or the mother, or whether it died by a natural death, the parents must not thereby feel secure and be without penance; nevertheless, there is to be a consideration of mercy in those cases, where not will, but chance, was the cause of death. But if it is no secret that they were its killers, they must know that they were gravely delinquent, which is proved in the Council of Ancyra. Some adjudge that penance of such a person must be for three years, of which one is to be at bread and water, and they are to keep themselves from all lust in the time of their penance.

A woman who gives birth, and whose child has died unbaptized through negligence, is to do penance for one year, and she is never to be without some penance. But if through the negligence of the priest, etc.; find it in the earlier book, c. 130, From a Penitential, c. 17.

c. 62. ON WOMEN WHO KILL THEIR OFFSPRING.
From the Council of Ancyra.

As for women who fornicate and kill their offspring, or who act upon themselves so that they cast out what they have conceived in their uterus, an ancient decision removes them from the Church until the end of their life. But we now decide more humanely that a period of ten years be granted to them according to the prescribed degrees of penance.

c. 63. ON THE SAME MATTER.
From the Council of Lérida.

As for those who have striven to kill what they had wickedly conceived, made, or brought forth from adultery, or which they attacked in the womb of the mothers with some potions, to the adulterer of either sex, that is, to the father or mother, communion may be given after the passage of seven years, but in such a way that they remain tearful and humbled for their whole lives.

c. 64. ON THE SAME MATTER.
From the Council of Elvira.

If a woman has conceived by adultery during an absence of her husband, and after her crime she killed it, it pleased that communion be given to her only just at the end because she twinned her heinous act.

c. 65. IF A WOMAN HAS CAST OUT HER FOETUS.
From a Penitential.

If any woman, before forty days, has willingly destroyed her foetus in the womb, she is to do penance for one year. But if she killed it after forty days, she is to do penance for three years. But if she destroyed it after it was ensouled, she is to do penance as if a homicide. But it makes a great difference whether a poor woman did so because of the difficulty of bringing it up, or it is by reason of fornication, and she did it in order to hide her misdeed.

c. 66. IF A WOMAN HAS KILLED HER SON OR DAUGHTER WILFULLY.
From the same.

If a woman has wilfully killed her son or daughter, she is to do penance for ten years for the homicide.

c. 67. ON THE SAME MATTER.
From the Council of Rouen.

It has come to the notice of the holy Council that there are some women who, having conceived from fornication and fearing that the shameful deed which they committed secretly become manifest, killed the children which they had borne and covered them with a mass of earth, or threw them into the water. How nefarious a deed is this, the canons of the Councils of Ancyra, Elvira, and Lérida attest. They decree that communion is to be given to these women only just at the end of their lives. But treating them more humanely, it pleased that such women be received to communion after a penance of ten years.

C. 68. THAT THE CHILDREN OF ADULTERY BE EXPOSED BEFORE THE DOOR OF THE CHURCH.
From the same.

Therefore, because, at the devil's persuasion and with the delight and consent of the fragile flesh, many times such things are perpetrated, we, desiring somehow to heal another woman from a death-dealing potion, lest her crime be twinned, namely, of homicide and adultery, counsel that each priest announce publicly in his congregation that, if any woman has been secretly corrupted and has conceived and borne offspring, she is not, at the urging of the devil, to kill her son or daughter. By whatever ingenuity she can devise, she is to have the child brought before the doors of the church and deposited there so that, delivered to the priest on the next day, it may be taken and brought up by one of the faithful. In such way, she shall avoid the guilt of homicide and, even worse, of parricide, for the person who kills a son or daughter is in every way guilty of parricide.

C. 69. ON EXPOSED INFANTS.
From the Theodosian law, bk. 5, c. 7.

Whoever has taken up a recently born child with the knowledge of its father, mother, or lord, and has brought it up by his own effort, let it be in the power of the one who has taken it up whether he wishes the one whom he has raised to be freeborn or a slave.

C. 70. ON THE SAME MATTER.
From the same.

He who, for the sake of mercy, has taken up an exposed boy or girl with the knowledge of its master or patron, will retain dominion over the child, but only if the bishop or clerics have signed an attestation of his taking the child. No one will afterwards be able to call such a child his own, whom it is proved had cast it to its death.

C. 71. ON THE SAME MATTER.
From the same.

If anyone has reared an infant from birth, he is to have the power to keep and possess it. Certainly, if the master or father should wish to have the child back, either he is to give to the person who reared it a slave of the same value, or the foster-father is to receive the price the child so reared is worth.

c. 72. ON HOMICIDES.
From the Council of Tours.

There is to be no communion at all with homicides, until their crimes have been washed away by penitential confession.

c. 73. ON THOSE WHO KILL THEIR WIVES.
From the Council of Mainz.

If a husband has killed his wife, or a wife her husband, the judgment over them shall be the same, as the Lord says: "Do not respect the person of the poor, nor honour the countenance of the mighty (Lev. 19:15)." And after a few words: "Hear the little as well as the great: neither shall you respect any man's person, because it is the judgment of God (Deut. 1:17)." And so, each of them, in an action for this sort of crime, if either denied it, is to be examined by an equal judgment.

c. 74. ON THE SAME MATTER.
From the Capitularies, bk. 3, c. 89.

As it is forbidden in the Lord's law, so no homicides are to be done in our fatherland, either for the sake of vengeance, or avarice, or robbery. And wherever they are found, they are to be punished by our judges according to the law by our mandate. And a man is not to be killed other than at the command of the law.

c. 75. ON THE SAME MATTER.
From the same.

Whoever has abandoned his wife, or killed her without law, or cause, or certain proof, and has taken another wife, is to set aside his weapons and do public penance; if he should prove contumacious, he is to be seized by the count, bound in irons, and kept in custody, until the matter may be brought to our notice.

c. 76. ON THE FIGHT OF TWO MEN, WHICH OUR PEOPLE CALL *CHAMP*, WHICH IS CUSTOMARY TO BE WAGED FOR THE CHARGE OF ADULTERY.
From the letter of Pope Nicholas to King Charles.

But we do not accept single combat in law, which we do not find was commanded; although we have read that some entered into it, as sacred history reveals of holy David and Goliath (1 Sam. 17), yet divine authority nowhere else approved that it should be received as a law, since those who pursue it and the like appear only to tempt God.

c. 77. ON THE SAME MATTER.
From the same letter.

As we have learned from the report of many, King Lothar is preparing to hold an assembly and plans to subject Queen Theutberga to his own examination and judgment. And if he should be able to show by deceits of his own counterfeiting that she was not his lawful wife, he wishes to separate her wholly from himself. But if not, he is willing to admit her as his wife, but then to accuse her of being an adulteress, and, for this, compel his man and the man of Theutberga to single combat; if the man of the same queen falls, he intends to kill her without delay. We believe that the greatness of your Prudence already realizes how much these things are contrary to every law of God.

c. 78. ON PARRICIDES.
From the Capitularies.

Whoever, for the sake of cupidity for goods, has killed his father or mother, brother or sister, or nephew, or other relative, the inheritance of the one killed is to go to the lawful heirs, but the inheritance of the killer is to be paid into the fisc. As for the killer himself, at the bishop's order, he is to be subjected to public penance.

c. 79. ON THOSE WHO ARE BOUND IN CHAINS.
From the same.

That mongers and tramps, who go wandering through this land without any law, are not to be allowed to wander about to deceive men, as neither are those who, bound and wrapped in chains, say that it has been enjoined upon them by a priest that they go about wandering and fleeing through the country. It seems better to us that they remain in one place, working and serving and having patience, according to what may have been enjoined on them canonically.

c. 80. ON RESTRAINING FEUDS.

If anyone has committed a homicide under the compulsion of some necessity, the count within whose administration the matter was perpetrated is to have them make composition and to pacify the feud by an oath. If one of the parties should be unwilling to consent to him in this, that is, either the one who committed the homicide, or the one who ought to receive the composition, let him cause the one who objects to come into our presence, so that we may send him into exile for a period pleasing to us, until he is there chastised and no longer dares to be disobedient to his count, and does not cause greater harm.

c. 81. ON A WOMAN WHO HAS KILLED A MAN BY SORCERY.
From a Penitential, c. 15.

If a woman has killed others by a sorcerous art, that is, by a potion or some other device, she is to do penance for seven years. If she is poor, let her do penance for three years.

c. 82. ON THE SAME MATTER.
From the Council of Elvira.

If anyone kills another by sorcery, because he would not have been able to commit such a horrible crime without idolatry, he is not to be given communion even at the end.

c. 83. ON THE SAME MATTER.
As above.

If anyone has destroyed another by his sorcery, let him do penance for seven years and give many alms.

c. 84. ON THE SAME MATTER.

If a wife kills her husband with poison for the sake of fornication, or causes him to perish by means of any art, because she has killed her lord and consort, she is to do penance for ten years.

c. 85. ON ONE WHO KILLED ANOTHER.
From the Roman law, Sentences of Paul, bk. 5, c. 25.

But he who kills some man is sometimes absolved, and he who does not kill is held or condemned as if a homicide. Indeed, it is each one's intention, and not the deed, which is to be punished. Thus, he who wished to kill another and was unable to do so because of some chance circumstance is to be punished as a homicide. And he who by chance and imprudently kills a man by throwing a javelin is absolved.

c. 86. ON THOSE WHO PERSUADE MEN TO KILL.
From the same.

Those who commission a killing, that is, who command or persuade men to kill, are to be punished in the same manner as homicides.

c. 87. ON ONE WHO HAS CASTRATED A MAN.
From the same.

He who has castrated a man for the sake of lust or trade, and has handed him over to be castrated, whether he is a slave or a free man, is to be punished capitally.

c. 88. ON THE SAME MATTER.
As above.

If anyone, for the sake of satisfying lust, or out of premeditated hate that no offspring be born of someone, has done something to a man or a woman, or has given some drink, so that they cannot generate or conceive, he is to be regarded as a homicide.

We have set out all this from the Roman law so that the priest may gather from the law the manner of penance in such transgressions. Indeed, canonical authority for the most part agrees with Roman law.

c. 89. ON THOSE WHO ARE CIRCUMCISED.
From the same law, c. 24.

Roman citizens who, in accordance with the Jewish rite, allow themselves or their slaves to be circumcised are to lose their goods and to be transported to an island; the physicians are to be punished capitally.

c. 90. IF A JEW CIRCUMCISES A SLAVE OF ANOTHER NATION.
From the same.

If Jews have circumcised purchased slaves of another nation, they are either sent into exile, or punished capitally.

c. 91. ON THOSE WHO KILL THEMSELVES.
From the Council of Braga, c. 15.

It has pleased that, in the case of those who inflict death on themselves, either by a sword, or poison, or by throwing themselves down a precipice, or by hanging, or in any other manner, no commemoration is to be made for them at the offering, nor are their corpses to be brought to burial with psalms. Indeed, because of ignorance, many take it upon themselves to do this. It has pleased us that the same be done with regard to those who are punished for their crimes.

c. 92. ON THOSE WHO ARE HANGED FROM GIBBETS.
From the Council of Mainz.

It has been asked by some of the brethren, regarding those who, after making their confession to God, are hanged from gibbets for their crimes, whether their corpses should be brought to the churches, and whether or not offerings are to be made and masses celebrated for them? To whom we respond: If, according to the canonical mandate, communion is to be given to all who at the end make a pure confession of their sins and worthily repent, why should it not be given to those who pay the extreme penalty for their sins? For it is written: "The Lord does not judge twice in the same matter (cf. Nahum 1:9 LXX)."

c. 93. ON THE SAME MATTER.
From the Council of Tribur.

As for thieves and brigands, if they are killed in the course of theft and plunder, it has seemed fit that there is to be no prayer for them. If they are caught or wounded, and they have confessed to a priest or deacon, we do not deny them communion.

c. 94. ON ONE WHO HAS KILLED A JEW OR A PAGAN OUT OF CUPIDITY.
From the Council of Mainz.

One who, out of premeditated hate or on account of cupidity, has killed a Jew or a pagan must fittingly do penance as a homicide because it is not a slight fault that has been committed. Indeed, ancient people were instructed not to wage war even on foreign nations, unless they had rejected the offered peace.

c. 95. IF SOMEONE KILLS A MAN IN A FIT OF INSANITY.
From the same.

If someone should return to sound mind who, while insane, has killed another, a lighter penance is to be imposed on him than on one who committed such a thing while of sound mind. Although a penance is to be imposed on the former, yet, since his infirmity, even if perhaps hidden, is believed to have been the cause of the sin, it is so much lighter than that of one who kills another while sound, so great is known to be the difference between the sound and the insane, the rational and the irrational.

c. 96. IF SEVERAL PERSONS HAVE KILLED ONE MAN.
From the Council of Mainz.

If four or five men, or even more, have fought with one man, and he has died from the wounds inflicted by them, whichever of them caused a wound is to be adjudged a homicide according to the statutes of the canons.

c. 97. ON ONE WHO IS ACCUSED OF HOMICIDE, AND IT CANNOT BE PROVED.
From the same.

Where it can be established that a man has perpetrated a homicide, according to canonical authority, a worthy judgment of penance is to be inflicted upon him. But if it cannot be proved by manifest indicia that he is a homicide, nor is he willing to confess, he is to be reserved to the judgment of almighty God, to whom all hidden things are manifest. Yet, he is to be told that he is unworthy of the

Church's communion, until he has confessed the crime which he has perpetrated and struggles to free himself from this crime by confession and worthy penance.

HENCEFORTH ON ADULTERIES AND FORNICATIONS.

C. 98. FROM THE COUNCIL OF ANCYRA.

If any man's wife is adulterous, or if he himself has committed adultery, it is fitting that he achieve perfection by a penance of seven years according to the original degrees [of penance].

C. 99. OF ONE WHO, EVEN AS HE HAS A WIFE, KEEPS A CONCUBINE.
From the Council of Toledo.

He who, even as he has a wife, has kept a concubine is not to receive communion. But one who does not have a wife and keeps a concubine as a wife is not to be refused communion, so long as he is satisfied with union with one woman, whether a wife or a concubine, as it pleases him. But otherwise, so long as he lives, he is to be cast out until he ceases and returns to penance.

C. 100. ON REPUDIATION.
From the letter of Pope Innocent.

Your Dilection asked also concerning those who, after repudiation, joined themselves to others in marriage; it is manifest that they are adulterers on both sides. Even though their marriage appears to be dissolved, those who, while the wife is still alive, rushed to another union cannot but be regarded as adulterers in so far as even those persons with whom they become joined are seen as having committed adultery, according to what we read in the Gospel: "Whoever has dismissed his wife, and taken another woman, commits adultery (cf. Mk. 10:11)"; hence, all of them are to abstain from the communion of the faithful.

C. 101. ON WOMEN WHO ABANDON THEIR HUSBANDS.
From the Council of Elvira.

Also, women who have abandoned their husbands for no preceding cause, and joined with someone else, are not to receive communion even at the end.

C. 102. ON AN ADULTEROUS HUSBAND.
As above.

As for a woman of the faithful who has abandoned her adulterous husband, who was also of the faithful, and marries another man, she is forbidden to do so.

But if she has done so, she is not to receive communion until the one whom she has abandoned has left this world, unless the necessity of illness compel that she be given it.

c. 103. ON DIVORCE.
From the African Council.

It has pleased that, according to the discipline of the Gospel and the Apostles, neither the man dismissed by his wife, nor the woman dismissed by her husband, be joined to another, but so remain, or become reconciled. If they contemn this, they are to be reduced to penance, in which case it is to be asked that an imperial law be promulgated.

c. 104. ON THE SAME MATTER.
From the sayings of Augustine on the Lord's Sermon on the Mount.

The Apostle Paul says: "But to them who are joined in marriage, not I but the Lord commands, that the wife depart not from her husband. And if she depart, that she remain unmarried, or be reconciled to her husband (1 Cor. 7:10–11)." It may happen that she depart for a reason which the Lord has allowed. Or if the woman is allowed to dismiss her husband even apart from the cause of fornication, what shall we answer as to what he says next: "And let not the husband put away his wife?" Why has he not added: except for cause of fornication, which the Lord allows? Except because he wishes a similar form to be understood, that if he dismiss his wife (which is permitted for the cause of fornication), he is to remain without a wife, or be reconciled to his wife? (And after a few words:) Indeed, the Lord allowed dismissal of a wife because of fornication. But he did not command what he allowed.

c. 105. ON THE SAME MATTER.
From the Capitularies, bk. 1, c. 43.

That neither a wife dismissed by her husband is to take another husband while her husband lives, nor is the husband to take another wife while his first wife lives.

c. 106. ON LAWFUL MARRIAGES.
From the sayings of St. Jerome.

We read in the Scriptures that there are three lawful marriages. The first lawful marriage is when a chaste virgin, in her virginity, is endowed lawfully to a man. Second, a virgin is seized by a man within the city, and she is joined to him by force (cf. Deut. 22:23–29); if her father should will it, this man will endow her as much as the father will judge, and he shall pay the price of her purity. But if she had a suitor before she was seized, she shall be given to him. Third, after the said daughter has been taken, if it is not the will of the father, he shall take her from the said man and give her to another, and he shall endow her, and she shall be lawful to him. But the first is preferred to these two. A fourth kind of lawful marriage is also added. When his wife has died, it is lawful for him to take another, but not one who has been repudiated or who is espoused to a man. The woman may do likewise. Paul manifestly teaches this, saying: "Because a woman is subordinate to a husband she is bound to her husband by law while he lives (Rom. 7:2)," and the rest. A fifth is added: When either the husband or the wife, with the other's consent, takes up the religious life, it is licit for the other to make a new marriage, but [to] a girl or a boy.

C. 107. THIS AUTHORITY, OR SO WE BELIEVE, THE COUNCIL FOLLOWED, WHICH GATHERED AT COMPIÈGNE IN THE TIMES OF KING PEPIN, IN WHICH WE READ IT WAS DECREED AS FOLLOWS, AT C. 16:

If any man has dismissed his wife and, for the sake of religion, has given her license to serve God in a monastery and receive the veil, as we said, for the Lord's sake, her husband, if he wishes, may take a lawful wife. A woman may do likewise.

But this sentence is informed by canonical and apostolic documents, as was shown above. But we are also informed by the decrees of Pope Nicholas, who writes as follows to King Lothar:

C. 108. IF A MARRIED PERSON WISHES TO ABANDON THE WORLD.
From the letter of Nicholas.

Accordingly, attend vigilantly and, having seen to it with the greatest care to cherish and love your wife, Theutberga, as your own flesh, do not consent by any agreement to her parting from you. Hence, if she wishes to go away from you, stop her – indeed, correct her – and strive to recall her from such an intention in every way. But if she seeks a separation out of love of purity, and insists on the dissolution of the conjugal union, it is certain that, as the Apostle says, a wife has no power over her own body, but her husband does (1 Cor. 7:4). But if you too run eagerly after purity and wish to dissolve your union for the sake of religion, we grant it only if it is done without deceit. For although it is written: "What God has joined, let not man put asunder (Mt. 19:6)," yet it is God who sunders, and not man, when marriages are dissolved by the consent of both parties out of consideration for divine love. Hence, if you now wish this, we permit it with a ready spirit and quickly grant our assent, but we forbid your mutual separation to be done otherwise.

C. 109. ON THE SAME MATTER.

From the sayings of Bishop Basil.

If any married man wishes to convert to monastic life, he is not to be received, unless first he is absolved by his wife, who herself professes chastity. If she should marry another through incontinence while her husband is still alive, she would undoubtedly be an adulteress. Nor is a husband's conversion to religious life received before God, if its consequence is the prostitution of the conjugal bond. Then do such people follow Christ without fault after leaving the world, if they have with equal will the consent of chastity.

C. 110. ON THOSE WHO DISMISS THEIR SPOUSES WITHOUT ECCLESIASTICAL JUDGMENT.

From the Council of Agde.

Those secular men, who set aside, or have set aside, the conjugal fellowship in the absence of any of the more serious faults, and without putting forward for proof any causes of separation, set aside their marriages so that they may proceed to unlawful things or to those that pertain to others. If they have cast aside their wives before stating the cause of separation before the bishop of the same province, and before their wives are condemned in judgment, they are to be excluded from the communion of the Church and from the assembly of holy people, because they stain the faith of marriage.

C. 111. THAT ANY CONTROVERSY WHICH HAS BEGUN TO BE PURSUED BEFORE AN ECCLESIASTICAL JUDGMENT IS NEVER TO PASS TO A SECULAR JUDGMENT.

From the Capitularies.

It has been established that any controversies which have begun to be pursued by ecclesiastical authority and judgment never pass to a secular judgment in order to be litigated there anew, but that they be determined by the ecclesiastical provisions. Indeed, it is not licit to appeal to other judges from those judges which the common consent has chosen, unless there be a greater authority according to the canonical norm. But if a cause has been first ventilated at a secular judgment, that is, at the count's plea, let it be ended according to the world's law, saving the privilege of ecclesiastical law.

C. 112. ON THE SAME MATTER.
From the letter of Pope Nicholas to King Charles.

Queen Theutberga has written to us that she wishes to be absolved from her royal dignity and marital union, desiring to be content only with private life. We have written to her that this cannot be done otherwise than if her husband, Lothar, should choose the same life. (And after a few words:) As to the previous controversy, Theutberga must not be called on to make a new response. What has once been well-defined, and deliberated with the interposition of oaths, is not to be reopened by any repetition (unless perhaps where there is greater authority).

C. 113. ON ECCLESIASTICAL JUDGMENT.

Furthermore, because she seeks the Church's refuge and always asks for ecclesiastical judgment, she must not be submitted to a secular judgment. But hereafter, since we were called on as judge by each of the parties, that is, by both the king and the queen, and we have pursued the controversy of both of them, it is not fitting to have recourse to any other judges regarding this matter since, according to the sacred canons, it is not licit to appeal from the judges which the common consent has chosen. Where appeal is allowed, it is only licit to do so where there is a greater authority. But since there is no greater authority than that of the Apostolic See, which has pursued the case of both parties, we do not know that it is licit for anyone to judge its judgment or reconsider its sentence.

C. 114. THAT NO ONE IS TO PRESUME TO RENEW A CAUSE ALREADY JUDGED.
From the Capitularies, bk. 3, c. 31.

If anyone has presumed to raise again in court a cause already judged, and he is convicted there by witnesses, he must either pay fifteen shillings as composition, or he is to receive fifteen blows from the judges (*scabini*) who had already judged the cause.

C. 115. THAT A WOMAN CHARGED WITH ADULTERY, IF SHE MUST ENTER INTO A LEGAL CONTEST WITH HER HUSBAND, MUST BE RESTORED TO HER OWN CONTROL FOR A TIME.
From the letter of Pope Nicholas.

Moreover, whether the judicial case is to be heard with regard to the marriage bond, or to the crime of adultery, no reason allows that Theutberga can enter the dispute with Lothar, or enter the legal contest as to the controversy, unless she has first been returned for a time to her control and has freely joined her blood relatives. And so, a place is also to be provided for her among them in which she may have no fear of the violence of the multitude, and in which it will not be difficult to produce witnesses, or the other persons which are required in these sorts of controversies by the holy canons and the venerable Roman laws. We have said these things in order to show what sort of legal conflict Lothar asserts that he is able to engage in. He troubles her person every day to her innermost being; he grinds her down when he pleases, summons her to judgment when he pleases, and locks her up in cloisters, and when she is brought out, unless she admit what he has commanded, etc. It is necessary, then, that she be entrusted to her own liberty and freed from all the power and oppression of the one with whom the conflict is entered, and make free use of her own resources; and it is fitting for her to reject suspect persons as she desires to prove that she is innocent of the charges against her.

C. 116. THAT A BISHOP'S SENTENCE IS NOT TO BE RE-EXAMINED.
From the Roman law.

Emperor Constantine says: Whatever has been determined by the sentence of the bishops is to be regarded as holy and venerable, nor is it licit for a matter to be re-examined further which the sentence of the bishops has decided.

C. 117. IF ANY WOMAN HAS TAKEN COUNSEL WITH OTHERS REGARDING HER HUSBAND'S DEATH.
From the Council that was held at Verberie in the times of King Pepin, c. 6.

If any woman has taken counsel with others regarding the death of her husband, and the same husband has killed her man in defending himself, if he can prove it, he can (as it seems to us) dismiss that wife and, if he should wish, he can take another. As for the scheming woman herself, she is to be subject to penance and remain without hope of marriage.

C. 118. ON THE FREEBORN MAN WHO HAD TAKEN ANOTHER'S MAIDSERVANT.
From the same, c. 7.

If any freeborn man takes another's maidservant as his wife, and believes that she is freeborn, and afterwards she is reduced to servile condition, if he can redeem her from her servitude, let him do so; if he cannot, let him marry another, if he should wish. A freeborn woman can do likewise as regards another's slave.

C. 119. IF A SLAVE HAS A MAIDSERVANT AS HIS CONCUBINE.
From the same, c. 8.

If a slave has a maidservant as his concubine, if it pleases, after dismissing her, he may take an equal maidservant of his master.

c. 120. ON A FREEDMAN WHO KEPT HIS MASTER'S MAIDSERVANT.
From the same.

If a slave, having received his freedom from his master, afterwards committed adultery with his master's maidservant, if the master wishes it, and whether or not he himself wills it, he shall have her as his wife.

c. 121. IF A SLAVE AND A MAIDSERVANT ARE SEPARATED BY REASON OF A SALE.
From the same.

If a slave and a maidservant have been separated by reason of a sale, they are to be admonished to remain so, if we cannot marry them.

But the Roman law appears to treat far better of this matter:

c. 122. ON THE SAME MATTER.
In the Roman law, c. 25.

Since it is unjust that children be separated from their parents and wives from their husbands, in the partition of patrimonies, whether those of the lords of the fisc or private persons, whenever possession has come to anyone, it must be especially observed that slaves who were together, that is, a wife with her husband and children, belong to one person, on whom rests the responsibility of making the exchange, with substitutes provided for them. It must be the special care of officials to ensure that a separation cannot at all occur. It seems that the same must also be observed in purchase and sale, that when someone has purchased a husband, he purchase also the wife, unless perhaps she is someone else's maidservant. For this reason, the law commands and forbids that no slave, whether a private person's, or a church's, or the fisc's, ever marry someone else's maidservant; similarly, a maidservant must never marry another's slave; if either does so, such a marriage is to be held as void, and is to be deemed adultery.

c. 123. IF A HUSBAND, UNDER THE COMPULSION OF A CERTAIN NECESSITY, HAS FLED THE DUCHY.
From the Council as above.

If anyone, under the compulsion of unavoidable necessity, has fled to another duchy or province, or has followed his superior, to whom he cannot break the faith and fidelity that he promised, and his wife, while she is able and can, because of love of her parents and possessions, is not willing to follow him, throughout the whole time while her husband, whom she has been unwilling to follow, lives, she is to remain ever unmarried. But as for the one who remains in another country under the compulsion of necessity, if he does not hope ever to return to his own country and is unable to practice continence, he may take another wife, yet with penance.

c. 124. OF ONE WHO ALLOWED HIS WIFE TO BE VEILED.
From the same, c. 22.

He who allowed his wife to be veiled is not to take another.

c. 125. IF A WOMAN TAKES THE VEIL WITHOUT HER HUSBAND'S LICENSE.
From the decree at Compiègne.

If a woman placed the veil on her head without her husband's license, the husband may receive her again in marriage, if it pleases him.

c. 126. OF A MAN WHO TOOK A WIFE IN ANOTHER PROVINCE.
From the same, c. 9.

A Frankish man received a benefice from his superior in another province and took his vassal with him; afterwards, that superior died there, and the said vassal remained there. Another man received that benefice, and, in order that he might more securely have the same vassal, he gave to him a woman from that benefice, and the vassal had her for a time. Because that superior acted harshly against him, the vassal left his wife and returned to the kinsmen of his dead superior, and he took a wife there. It was decided that he may have the one whom he took afterwards.

c. 127. ON A VIOLATED VIRGIN.
From the same, c. 10.

If someone has taken a wife and, finding her contaminated, abandoned her, and took another, it has been established that he return entirely to his earlier wife, because it may very well be that he, too, when he took her, was not himself a virgin, nor is a wife bound by her husband's law until she is joined to her husband. As for the one whom he took afterwards, she may marry whomever she pleases.

c. 128. THAT THE INSANE ARE NOT TO BE JOINED IN MARRIAGE.
From the Roman law.

Neither an insane man nor an insane woman can contract marriage; but if it has already been contracted, it is not dissolved.

c. 129. IF THEY CONTRACTED MARRIAGE WHILE HEALTHY.
From the same.

As for those who contracted marriage while in health, and then to one of them has come dementia, insanity, or some other illness, the marriages of such cannot be dissolved because of this infirmity. The same is true of those who are blinded or maimed by their enemies.

C. 130. IF SOMEONE'S WIFE HAS COMMITTED ADULTERY.
From the Council of Nantes, c. 21.

If someone's wife has committed adultery, and this has been learned and made known by the husband, let him dismiss his wife, if he wishes, because of fornication; as for her, let her do public penance for seven years. But the husband, while she lives, is not to take another wife. If he wishes to become reconciled with the adulteress, he has license to do so, yet in such a way that he do equal penance with her and, when the penance is complete, after seven years, each of them may receive communion. A similar form will be followed in the case of a woman, if her husband has committed adultery against her.

C. 131. IF THOSE NOT JOINED IN MARRIAGE HAVE COMMITTED FORNICATION.
From the same, c. 22.

If a woman without a husband or a man without a wife have committed fornication, let them do penance for three years.

C. 132. IF AN UNMARRIED PERSON AND A MARRIED PERSON HAVE COMMITTED ADULTERY.
From the same.

If a man who has no wife has committed adultery with another's wife, or if some woman who has no husband has done so with another's husband, as said above, the one who has violated the pact of marriage is to do penance for seven years. The one who is not bound by the law of marriage is to do penance for five years. Indeed, an equal penance is not to be given to those for whom the embrace of their spouses might have sufficed to satisfy their lust, and to those who, pressed by the ardour of lust and lacking a spouse, fell into fornication.

C. 133. ON THE SAME MATTER.
From a Penitential.

If someone who lacks a wife has polluted himself with another's wife, he is to do penance for two years. The same is to be observed concerning women.

C. 134. IF A MARRIED MAN HAS KEPT HIS OWN MAIDSERVANT.

If a married man has kept his own maidservant, let him do penance for one year, and for three forty-day fasts and the weekdays prescribed by law for a second year, and let him first abstain from his wife for three months. As for the maidservant, if she suffered force, let her do penance for forty days; if she consented, for three forty-day fasts in a year and the weekdays prescribed by law.

c. 135. IF A LAYMAN HAS FORNICATED WITH A LAYWOMAN.
From the same.

If a layman with a laywoman, that is, they are both free from the law of marriage, they are to do penance for three years. And the more often and the more negligently they have committed those sins, so much the more are time and severity to be added to their penance.

c. 136. OF HIM WHO HAS A WIFE AND HAS FREQUENTLY COMMITTED FORNICATION.
From the Council of Elvira.

If any of the faithful has a wife and has committed adultery not once, but often, he is to be approached when in danger of death. If he promises that he will desist, communion is to be given to him. If he is restored [to communion] and again commits adultery, it pleased that there be no further deceit of others as to the communion of peace.

c. 137. ON ONE WHO HAS LAPSED ONCE.
From the same Council.

If someone who perhaps has a wife has lapsed once, it pleased that he do penance for five years for this matter and so be reconciled, unless the necessity of illness urges that communion be given before the time. This is also to be observed regarding women.

c. 138. WHY HUSBANDS DO NOT REMAIN IN COMMUNION WITH THEIR ADULTEROUS WIVES.
From the letter of Pope Innocent.

It is desired to be known why husbands who receive communion do not come together with their adulterous wives, whereas, to the contrary, wives are seen to remain in fellowship with adulterous husbands. On this matter the Christian religion condemns adultery by an equal reason in both sexes. But wives do not easily accuse their husbands of adultery, and hidden crimes are not punished. Husbands, on the other hand, have been more freely accustomed to bring their adulterous wives before the priests, and so, once their crime is revealed, communion is denied to the wives. But for so long as the husbands' offense remains hidden, one is not easily excommunicated as a result of suspicions. But he shall be removed, if his crime is detected. For although the cause is equal, while proof is unavailable, the reason for punishment rests.

c. 139. IF A WIFE COMMITTED ADULTERY WITH HER HUSBAND'S KNOWLEDGE.
From the Council of Elvira.

If a wife has committed adultery with her husband's knowledge, it pleased that communion not be given to him even at the end. But if he abandoned her, let him receive communion after ten years.

c. 140. IF ONE HAS COMMITTED ADULTERY WITH A JEWESS OR A PAGAN WOMAN.
From the same.

If one of the faithful who has a wife has committed adultery with a Jewess or a pagan woman, he is to kept away from communion. But if someone else has married her, after doing lawful penance for five years, he may be joined in the Lord's communion.

c. 141. ON PROCURING.
From the same.

It pleased that if a woman or parent, or any woman of the faithful has acted as a procuress, for selling another's body or her own, she is not to receive communion even at the end.

c. 142. THAT A JEW NOT TAKE A CHRISTIAN WIFE.
From the Theodosian law, bk. 9.

A Jew is not to take a Christian wife, nor a Christian a Jewish one. If anyone has done this, let it be punished as an adultery at anyone's accusation.

c. 143. ON ADULTERERS.
From the same book, c. 4.

In a case of adultery, no one is to accuse a woman unrelated to him, but the relatives to whose knowledge it pertains, that is, her full brother, her half-brother, her uncle, or her cousin. Yet, before the accusation, the others may obtain forgiveness by satisfaction, if the accused agrees.

c. 144. ON HUSBANDS WHO ACCUSE.
From the same.

Husbands, indeed, are allowed to accuse even on suspicion.

c. 145. THAT A HOUSEHOLD MAY BE DISTRAINED CONCERNING AN ADULTERY.
From the same.

Concerning the adultery of their wives, it is permitted for husbands to investigate by torture of either household, that is, of their own and of their wife's, so long as, at the time when it is said to have been committed, these same slaves are proven to have been present or in the same house. Likewise, if the husband complains that his adulterous wife had been preparing his own death. Likewise, an investigation by torture of either household may be carried out, if the husband had been preparing his wife's death for any reason.

C. 146. IF A FREEBORN WOMAN JOINED HERSELF TO HER OWN SLAVE.
From the same, c. 6.

If any freeborn woman has secretly joined herself to her own slave, she is to be punished capitally. Also, a slave who has been convicted of adultery with his mistress is to be burned by fire. It is licit even for slaves to make an accusation of this crime and, if they have proved it, they are to receive their freedom; if not, they are to be punished. The woman's inheritance is to be given to her children, if they were conceived from her husband, or to those kinsmen succeeding by law.

C. 147. WHEN IT IS PERMITTED FOR A WIFE TO BE KILLED.
Sentences of Paul, bk. 2, c. 27.

A husband may kill a wife caught in adultery only if he catches the adultery at home.

C. 148. ON ONE GUILTY OF PANDERING.
From the same.

It has pleased to consider guilty of pandering the man who did not immediately dismiss his wife caught in adultery.

C. 149. ON THE SAME MATTER.
As above.

In a cause of adultery, if it was manifest, the requested delay cannot be granted.

C. 150. ON LAY VIRGINS.
From the Council of Elvira.

Virgins who did not preserve their virginity, if they have taken as husbands those who violated them, since they violated only their nuptials, are to be reconciled after a penance of one year. If they knew other men, since they committed adultery, they are to do penance for five years, and so have access to communion.

c. 151. ON THOSE WHO BREACH THE FAITH OF ESPOUSALS.
From the same.

If any parents have broken the faith of espousals, they are to abstain [from communion] for three years. Yet, if the espoused themselves were caught in a grave crime, the parents will be excused.

c. 152. ON BLESSING A BRIDE.
From the Council of Carthage.

When a bridegroom and bride are blessed by a priest, they are to be presented by their parents or attendants (*paranymphi*); when they receive the blessing, out of reverence for it, they are to remain in virginity for that night.

c. 153. THAT NO ONE TAKE A WOMAN ESPOUSED TO ANOTHER.
From the letter of Siricius.

You asked about conjugal violation, whether a man may take in marriage a girl espoused to another man. We forbid in all ways that it be done, because, if that blessing which the priest says over the woman about to marry is violated by any transgression, it is like sacrilege before the faithful.

c. 154. ON RAVISHED ESPOUSED GIRLS.
From the Council of Ancyra.

It has pleased that espoused girls, who are afterwards carried off by others, are to be retrieved and returned to those to whom they had been already espoused, even if it is established that violence was inflicted on them by their ravishers.

c. 155. ON THE SAME MATTER.
From the Capitularies, bk. 1, c. 99.

It pleased and was established by the sacred assembly that a ravisher be punished by public penance. As for the ravished woman, if the man to whom she is espoused is unwilling to receive her and if she had not consented to the same crime, license to marry another is not to be denied. But if she consented, she will be subject to the same penalty. And if they should presume to join together afterwards, both are to be anathematized.

c. 156. ON THE SAME MATTER.
From the Council of Meaux, c. 68.

As to those who ravish those espoused to others, the ancient and synodal sentence is to be observed, if perhaps such an event is known to be found in the

Church, that pontiffs have the right to treat it more humanely for the sake of what is due to well-being and religion, as canonical authority (if we may use the expression) teaches, because the earlier decision, it is said, treated it more harshly, but the later one more humanely. Yet in no way, that we sink to the broadest indulgence, is the taker of another man's espoused to be allowed to go without public penance and without paying a lawful fine as composition to that man. If he should be unwilling to obey this, he is to be anathematized without any opposition. As for his supporters, they are to do penance by the bishop's decree according to the manner of their guilt. But if (which we do not wish!) someone from an ecclesiastical degree manifestly shows himself a consenter to or an intermediary in such nuptials, he is to be removed from his degree. And if he is assailed by plausible suspicions in the matter, let him purge himself canonically.

C. 157. ON THOSE NOT ESPOUSED.

From the Capitularies, bk. 1, c. 98.

As for ravished girls who are not yet espoused, in the Council of Chalcedon, it is written that "the holy Synod decreed that those who ravish girls under the name of living together, as also those who aid or abet the ravishers, if they are clerics, must fall from their degree; if they are laymen, they are to be anathematized." By these words, it is given to be understood how the authors of such an evil are to be condemned, when their accomplices and abettors are struck by such an anathema, and, in accordance with canonical authority, they may in no way claim for themselves by right in lawful marriage the women they have ravished.

ON THE RAVISHERS OF VIRGINS AND WIDOWS.

From the Council of Meaux.

The ravishers of virgins or widows, even if afterwards with the consent of their parents, etc. (Seek it above, in the first booklet, on the ordination of clerics, c. 428.)

C. 158. ON THE SAME MATTER.

From the same, c. 65.

But if, when this constitution has been promulgated in everyone's hearing, they have not yet taken the women whom they ravished to marriage with the consent of their parents under the aforementioned title of espousal or endowment, they are to be separated from their union and subjected to public penance. But the ravished women are to be returned to their parents lawfully. After the public penance has been completed, if age and incontinence require it, they may be joined in lawful marriage with the consent of both parties. For in these matters, we do not establish a rule, but, to use the words of Leo the Great, we assess what is more tolerable. And if one of the spouses has died, the one who did public penance and has survived is not to presume to marry again, unless perhaps the bishop has decided to grant some indulgence in order to be able to remove a graver offense.

c. 159. ON THE SAME MATTER.
From the same, c. 66.

As for those who henceforth presume to ravish virgins or widows, according to the synodical decision of Blessed Gregory, they and their accomplices are to be anathematized, and the ravishers are to remain without hope of marriage in perpetuity.

c. 160. ON THE SAME MATTER.
From the letter of Pope Symmachus.

Therefore, because of the enormity of such a crime, we detest the ravishers of widows or virgins, and we pursue even more vehemently those who have striven to join in marriage with sacred virgins, whether these are willing or unwilling. Because of the atrocity of such a nefarious crime, we command that they are to be suspended from communion.

c. 161. ON THOSE WHO RAVISH NUNS.
From the aforementioned Council, c. 67.

Those who ravish nuns, virgins, or widows and, in the course of their crime, even take them in marriage are to be subjected to public penance. The women themselves are to be confined in suitable places of penance and are to be compelled to return to the habit of religion. Both are to remain forever without hope of marital union. But if (far be it!) they presume to repeat their marriages, they are to be subject to a harsher vengeance and to be compelled more forcefully. If perhaps they refuse to obey salutary admonitions, let them be anathematized.

c. 162. ON THE SAME MATTER.
From the letter of Pope Gregory.

It has reached us that a most evil man, by diabolical instinct, has persuaded a woman consecrated to God to leave the monastery; after being once recalled away from that man, that same very evil man once more drew her out of the monastery by an iniquitous persuasion and now keeps her with himself unchastely. We will that, by the authority of your episcopate, she be recalled and confined in the monastery.

c. 163. ON VIRGINS CONSECRATED TO GOD IF THEY COMMITTED ADULTERY.
From the letter of Pope Gelasius.

We have become aware that certain persons temerariously join themselves to consecrated virgins and, after their intention had been declared, they join in incestuous and sacrilegious unions. It is equitable that these people be immediately cast out of holy communion and, unless by public and private penance, they are not to be received. But the viaticum is not to be denied to those about to leave the world, if they have repented.

c. 164. ON THE SAME MATTER.
From the letter of Pope Siricius.

As for those unchaste and detestable persons, namely, monks and nuns who, setting aside the intention of holiness, joined themselves by an unlawful and sacrilegious contagion, we command that they be expelled from monastic communities and ecclesial assemblies. Confined in their places of correction, bemoaning such a crime with long lamentation, let them be consumed by the purificatory fire of penance so that it may be possible, at least when they are at death's door, for them to be aided by reason of mercy alone with the grace of communion.

c. 165. THAT THE BISHOP GO INTO THE MONASTERY OF MONKS OR GIRLS.
From the Council of Rouen.

That a bishop is to enter frequently the monastery of monks and nuns, and, residing in a religious community of men and of women, he is to discuss diligently their life and manner of living with grave and religious persons, and he is to endeavour to correct it, if he finds anything worthy of reproof. He is also to investigate subtly the purity of the nuns, and if one of them is found who, neglecting her intention of chastity, joins shamelessly with some cleric or layman, she is to be corrected bitterly with blows and is to be confined in private custody, where she may repent worthily of the evil she has committed. By the authority of the holy canons, he is also to forbid that any layman or cleric enter their cloisters and private habitations, as also priests, except only for mass. After the completion of mass, they are to return to their churches. Furthermore, he is to denounce to all, publicly and privately, what a wicked sin it is to presume to violate a bride of Christ. Indeed, if he is held to be guilty who violates a man's bride, how much more is he made guilty of treason who corrupts the bride of almighty God?

c. 166. THAT THE ABBESS NOT GO OUT OF THE MONASTERY.
From the Council of Mainz, c. 16.

An abbess is never to go out of her monastery, unless by the license of her bishop, or unless perhaps if she is compelled by royal command. And if ever she is outside, she is to take the greatest care of the nuns she brings with her that no occasion of sin is presented to them.

c. 167. WHAT NUNS MUST DO.
From the same.

Nuns established in a monastery are to apply themselves to reading and singing, and they are to celebrate the canonical hours solemnly together. All of them, apart from those detained by illness, are to sleep in the dormitory, and every day they are to come to the chapter and the evening assemblies (*collationes*). They are to observe with diligence the rule established for them by the holy Fathers.

c. 168. ON THE SAFEGUARDING OF NUNS.
From the Council of Seville.

This safeguarding is to be observed with regard to all, that they be far from the private space of virgins, nor are they to have familiar permission to come any closer than the vestibule, nor is the man who presides over them to speak alone with one of them, but under the witness of two or three sisters and in such way that the approach is rare and the speech brief.

c. 169. THAT CLERICS OR THE CONTINENT ARE NOT TO APPROACH VIRGINS.
From the Council of Carthage.

That clerics and the continent are not to approach widows or virgins, except by the command or permission of the bishops or the priests; and they are not to do this alone, not even bishops or priests, but where clerics are present or some grave Christians.

c. 170. ALSO, ON CORRUPTED NUNS.
From the letter of Pope Innocent.

Those who marry in Christ spiritually, if afterwards they marry publicly or become corrupted secretly, are not to be admitted to do penance, unless he with whom she joined herself has departed this world. Indeed, if this rationale is observed in the case of humankind, namely, that any woman who has married another man while her husband is alive is treated as an adulteress and is not granted permission to do penance unless one of them has died, how much more is it to be held of her who first joined herself to the immortal Bridegroom and afterwards passed to human nuptials?

c. 171. ON SECULAR WIDOWS AND NUNS.
From the Council of Meaux, c. 71.

That those women who appear to be nuns living under the veil of religion, but live rather among pleasures, are accounted as dead in God's eyes as they go wandering through the provinces, meddlesome and full of gossip. If they are accused of serving lust and the other desires of the flesh, and this can be manifestly detected, let them be compelled by episcopal authority and royal power to reside under religious watchfulness in such places where, if they do worthy penance, they may even achieve fruitful penance. But if this cannot be manifestly detected, let them be compelled to purge before the Church in a canonical way the ill fame of their reputation. Let them be compelled by episcopal decree and the royal power to live more religiously henceforth and to dwell in monasteries. Indeed, of such as these, the Apostle says: "These, when they have grown wanton against Christ, wish to marry (cf. 1 Tim. 5:11)."

c. 172. CONCERNING WIDOWS, THE APOSTLE SAYS:

Instruct the widows to be without reproach. Let a widow no less than sixty be chosen who has a name for good works if she has brought up children, etc. Avoid younger widows; when they have grown wanton against Christ, they wish to marry, incurring condemnation because they made void their first faith, and idly they wander from house to house, and not only idle but meddlesome and full of gossip, saying what it is not fitting to say. So, I would have the younger women marry and bear children and have households to manage and give no occasion to our adversary to speak ill. For already there are some who have turned aside to follow Satan (cf. 1 Tim. 5:7–15).

c. 173. ON THE SAME MATTER.
From the Roman law of the Novels of the blessed Majorian.

We are deeply troubled by the obstinacy of widows, who have borne no children and condemn their own fertility and the restoration of their family by rejecting a repetition of marriage. As may be gathered, they choose a solitary life and freedom of living, not out of love of religion and chastity, but of power and lasciviousness. Either the feigned religion of the persons attempting to seduce them or adroit legacy hunters applaud with favour at their every practice of license. Recalling such women to the path of a more honourable life, we establish that a woman of forty, left destitute by her husband's death and still able to bear children, is to marry within five years. At the expiry of the five years, if she persists in widowhood, she is immediately to share her wealth with her kinsmen; or if these perhaps are lacking, she is to share her marriage portion with the fisc.

C. 174. AS ABOVE.
From the Council of Nantes.

Since the Apostle says: "Women are to be silent in church, for it is not permitted for them to speak; indeed, it is unseemly for a woman to speak in church (cf. 1 Cor. 14:34–35)," it seems odd that some mere women, against the divine and human laws, acting with a shamelessly impudent attitude, unceasingly attend general pleas and public meetings. They disturb, rather than dispose of, the business of the kingdom and what is useful to the commonwealth, since it is indecent and worthy of reproof even among barbarian nations for women to discuss the causes of men. They usurp to themselves senatorial authority in the public assembly as if they resided at court, they who ought to dispute regarding their wool-works and textiles and women's matters in the women's quarters. This disgraceful presumption is to be ascribed more to their supporters than to the women themselves. Hence, because the divine laws speak against it, as was shown above, and the human ones likewise forbid the same thing, women must pursue nothing in public other than their own cause. For the Theodosian law says: "Women are for no reason to have the power to pursue further causes other than their own, and they should know that another's cause must not be pursued by them." Hence, by canonical authority, we forbid that any nun, virgin, or widow approach the general assemblies, unless she is summoned by the prince or by her bishop, and unless perhaps the reason of her own need impels her, and this too with the license of her bishop.

C. 175. WHEN VIRGINS ARE TO BE VEILED.
From the African Council.

That virgins are not to be veiled before their twenty-fifth year, unless perhaps by need of endangered virginal chastity, and, as Pope Gelasius says, they are not to be consecrated at any time other than Epiphany, and in the octave of Easter, and on the feasts of the Apostles, unless in pressing danger of death.

C. 176. THAT WIDOWS (*VIRGINES*) NOT BE VEILED.
Gelasius.

None of the pontiffs is to attempt to veil widows.

c. 177. ON THE SAME MATTER.
From the Council of Tribur.

Those virgins who, before their twelfth year and without the knowledge of their guardians, placed the sacred veil on their heads, if their guardians consented by remaining silent for a year and a day, are to remain in their holy intention. But if the guardians, in the aforesaid year and a day, made a claim for them, assent is to be given to their petition, unless, perhaps touched by the fear of God, the virgins persevere in the habit of religion with their license.

c. 178. ON THE SAME MATTER.
From the same Council.

The holy Synod decreed that widows who, of their own free will, receive from the altar the veil of sacred religious life are to remain in the same intention. Indeed, we decree it not to be right that, once they have consecrated themselves to the Lord under the veil and made offerings among the veiled, they again be allowed to lie to the Holy Spirit.

c. 179. ON THE SAME MATTER.
Pope Zacharias, c. 7.

That no one is to dare to steal a virgin or widow as his wife, except for the one who had espoused her. If anyone, with daring boldness, has presumed to do this, let him be anathema.

c. 180. ALSO, ON NUNS.
From the same Council.

The Synod grants that, if a nun, with her abbess' license, has decided to pass to, and remain in, another monastery for the gain of her soul, she may do so. But if she has sought another place in order to flee from discipline, she is to be compelled to return.

c. 181. ON CONCUBINES.
From the letter of Pope Leo.

Not every woman joined to a man is that man's wife, as not every son is his father's heir. And so, a wife is one thing, a concubine another, just as a maidservant is one thing, and a free woman another. Hence, to cast a maidservant out of the marital bed and to take a wife of certain free birth is not the duplication of marriage, but the advance of decency. For it is not in doubt that a woman has no part in marriage, with whom it is clear there was no nuptial mystery, unless perhaps that woman is seen to have been freed, lawfully endowed, and rendered honourable by public marriage.

c. 182. THAT WHEN HUSBANDS RETURN FROM CAPTIVITY, THEIR WIVES ARE TO RETURN TO THEM.

From the letter of Leo.

That women who married other men when their husbands were captured and taken into captivity and who believed them to be dead must rejoin their first husbands at their return from captivity so that that which each used to have lawfully is restored, and each receives what is his own, and the nuptial pacts are made whole again.

c. 183. ON THE SAME MATTER.

From the same.

That he is not proved to be at fault who is seen to have taken in marriage the wife of one who was captured. And if the men who have returned from captivity are not offended by the intemperance of their wives, and wish to receive them in marriage, let them have free faculty to do so. And if the women are so captured by love of their later husbands as to refuse to return to their earlier husbands, they are to be deprived of ecclesiastical communion.

c. 184. ON THE INCESTUOUS.

From the Council of Lérida, c. 4.

As for those who stain themselves by the pollution of incest, it has pleased that, for so long as they persevere in this detestable and unlawful carnal intercourse, they are to be admitted in church only until the dismissal of the catechumens; with these, as the Apostle commanded, it shall not even be lawful for any Christian to take food (1 Cor. 5:11).

c. 185. ON THE SAME MATTER.

From the Council of Toledo.

We also judge it salubrious to warn that anyone of the faithful is not to desire to join to himself in marriage a woman who is a close blood relative until he knows the lines of relationship and family succession, because it is written: "No man shall approach her who is blood kin to him, to uncover her shame (Lev. 18:6)."

c. 186. ON THE SAME MATTER.

From the Council of Agde.

As for incestuous unions, we reserve absolutely nothing of forgiveness, except when they heal the adultery by separation. And we adjudge these to be: If any man, by carnal joining, has polluted his brother's widow, who was formerly his sister; if any man has taken to wife a sister of his brother's wife, a stepmother, a cousin, the widow or daughter of a maternal uncle, the daughter of a paternal uncle, or his own stepdaughter. As for those to whom an unlawful union is forbidden, they shall have the freedom (that is, the power) to enter a better (that is, a lawful) marriage after they have done penance.

c. 187. ON THE SAME MATTER.
From the Roman Council.

Pope Gregory said: If any man has married God's handmaid, that is, a nun, let him be anathema. If any man has married his spiritual godmother, let him be anathema. If anyone has married his brother's wife, let him be anathema. If any man has married his granddaughter, let him be anathema. If any man has married his stepmother or daughter-in-law, let him be anathema. If any man has married his cousin, let him be anathema. If any man has married a woman from his own kin, or whom a kinsman had had to wife, let him be anathema. If any man has stolen a widow to be his wife, or anyone consenting to this, let him be anathema. If any man has stolen a virgin to be his wife, unless he had espoused her, or anyone consenting to this, let him be anathema. And with regard to all these things, the whole Council replied three times: Amen.

c. 188. ON JUDITH.
From the Council at Koblenz. Charles to Louis.

Baldwin has stolen as his wife our daughter Judith, a widow who, according to divine and human laws, was under ecclesiastical protection and the royal guardianship. After lawful judgment, the bishops of our kingdom excommunicated him according to the sacred canons and the pronouncement of Pope St. Gregory, who says: "If any man has stolen a widow to be his wife, or anyone consenting to this, let him be anathema."

c. 189. ON WOMEN WHO LOSE THEIR HUSBANDS.
From the Capitularies, bk. 1, c. 96.

As to women who lose their husbands, it pleases that they not veil themselves as ill-advisedly as formerly, but wait for thirty days after the death of their husbands. After the thirtieth day, let them choose what they ought to choose with the counsel of their bishop, or, if the bishop is absent, with the counsel of other religious priests and of their friends. Petitioned by the sacred assembly that those who do public penance, and women who lose their husbands, be protected by our authority until they deliberate what to do, we decreed that chapters be drafted specially as to these matters and inserted among the chapters of worldly law.

c. 190. ON THE SAME MATTER.
From the Capitularies, bk. 4, c. 16

Whoever has joined with a widow, whether she is willing or unwilling, within the first thirty days of widowhood is to make composition for sixty shillings. And if he took her unwilling, he is to make composition to her for her law and not to touch her further.

c. 191. ONE WHO HAS KILLED A MAN WHO WAS DOING PUBLIC PENANCE.
From the same, c. 17.

Whoever has killed a man who was doing public penance is to pay our ban threefold as composition, and he is to pay the man's wergild to his kinsmen.

c. 192. ALSO, ON INCESTS.
From the Council of Orléans.

That a brother is not to take over the marriage bed of his deceased brother, nor is anyone who has lost his wife to dare to join with her sister.

c. 193. ON THE VIOLATION OF A SPOUSE'S SISTER.
From the Council of Ancyra.

A certain man who was espoused to a woman violated her sister and made her pregnant. Afterwards, he took the espoused woman to wife. But the one who had been violated killed herself by hanging. Those who knew of this are commanded to be received after a satisfaction of ten years in accordance with the established degrees of penance.

c. 194. ON A WOMAN WHO MARRIED TWO BROTHERS.
From the Council of Neocaesarea.

If a woman has married two brothers, she is to be cast out until death. But yet, at her end, because of mercy, communion may be granted to her. But if the man or the woman dies in such a union, penance will be difficult for the one who remains in life.

c. 195. ON THE SAME MATTER.
From the Council of Elvira.

If any man, after his wife's death, took her sister, and she was one of the faithful, it has pleased that she be kept from communion for five years, unless death threatens.

c. 196. ON THE SAME MATTER.
From the Council of Martin.

If any woman has married two brothers, or if any man two sisters, let them be severed from communion until death. For the sake of mercy, at their death, they may receive the viaticum.

c. 197. ON GODDAUGHTER AND GODMOTHER.
From the letter of Rabanus to Heribaldus, bishop of Auxerre.

As to your questions regarding whether the man who slept with his goddaughter, and the one who slept with his spiritual godmother, and the man who baptized his son while his wife received the child from the font, may afterwards remain in their marriages, we adjudged it entirely unlawful. For in the Council of Mainz, it is written: "No one is to receive his own son or daughter from the baptismal font, nor to take to wife his goddaughter or godmother, nor the woman whose son he held for confirmation before the bishop. Where this has been done, they are to be separated."

c. 198. IF ONE HAS TAKEN A WIDOW TO WIFE.
From the same.

If any man has married a widow, and then has committed fornication with his stepdaughter, or married two sisters, or if any woman married two brothers, or fornicated with father and son, we command that these joinings are to be anathematized and separated and the participants are never to be joined in marriage afterwards. This is to be done with great severity.

c. 199. ON ONE WHO POLLUTED HIS GODDAUGHTER.
As above.

How detestable and execrable a crime it is for any Christian to have intercourse with his goddaughter, St. Gregory attests in his Dialogues, where he reports that a certain man polluted his goddaughter. Because he neglected to do penance, he was immediately struck by a miserable illness and died. After he was buried, an invisible fire consumed not only his body, but his whole tomb.

c. 200. ALSO, ON INCESTS AND THEIR PENANCE.
From the Council of Mainz.

If any man has fornicated with two sisters, or his stepmother, or his sister, or his father's sister, or his mother's sister, or his paternal uncle's daughter, or his maternal uncle's daughter, or his father's sister's daughter, or his mother's sister's daughter, or his granddaughter, or his godmother, or the goddaughter whom he received at the font or held before the bishop (or if any woman has fornicated in a similar way), he is to abstain from entry into God's house for a year; during that same year, except on Sundays and feast-days, he is to use only bread, water, and salt. He is not to bear arms; he is to offer the kiss to no one; he is not at all to take the sacrifice, unless as viaticum. For the next six years, he may enter God's house, but he is to make no use of meat, wine, and beer, except on feast-days. But as to arms, the kiss, and the sacrifice, as it was written above. After this, for two years, when he eats meat, he is to contain himself from any drink that causes inebriation. And if he has a drink, he is not at all to eat meat, apart from the principal feast-days. As to arms, kiss, and sacrifice, let him retain the mentioned manner. From then until his death, except on the aforementioned feast-days, he is to abstain from meat; he is to keep the three days prescribed by law each week, and three forty-day fasts each year. As for arms, as it was said above, and he is never to enter into any marriage. This same penance is to be imposed on parricides, fratricides, or blood relatives, as also on those who freely and by fraud and avarice have killed a harmless man, which they call murder (*morchidum*).

C. 201. IN WHICH GENERATION THE FAITHFUL MAY JOIN.
From the letter of Rabanus to Bishop Humbert.

Also, as to marriage, or how consanguinity is to be honoured, the Lord speaks of it in Leviticus, saying: "No man shall approach her that is blood kin to him, to uncover her shame (Lev. 18:6)." Indeed, as the Lord wished to separate his people from the contaminations of the nations, first by a general term he forbade anyone from approaching a blood relative, lest he uncover her shame; then, he subdivided that generality into roughly twelve species, which yet do not proceed beyond the third or fourth generation. Hence, it happened, or so I reckon, that the lord Gregory declared when Augustine inquired as to the licitness of marriages joined in the third or fourth generation. Similarly, in the chapters of Theodore, archbishop of the English nation, which he wrote concerning necessary things, we found that it would be licit to marry in the third degree of blood relation according to the Greeks, in the fifth according to the Romans. Yet, the latter would not dissolve marriages done in the third degree, if they had been agreed to beforehand unknowingly, and equally [if] a man married someone from his kin or from his wife's kin after her death. As for this Theodore, he was born in Tarsus in Cilicia. Pope Vitellian ordained him as bishop in Rome and sent him to Britain. Thus, he had been fully instructed in the customs of both the Eastern and the Western Churches, nor could anything have escaped him as to the lawful observances of the Greeks and the Romans at that time, especially as he was perfectly instructed in both languages.

As for those more recent writings of the Roman pontiffs which state that the practice of marriage is to be deferred until the sixth or seventh generation, it is to be held that they took this more from human custom than from divine law. As for Isidore asserting in his Etymologies that there is to be abstention until the sixth generation of kinship, and then one may join in lawful marriage, I believe that he did this because he thought that the knowledge of consanguinity ought to be preserved for so long as one was able to recount the series of genealogies and bring them forth in a numbered order. And so, in order to renew the lineage and confirm the right of friendship, he allowed a return to marriage when the order of relationship ceased to be numbered. But it is to be considered above all that the censure of discipline be so tempered that the accumulation of sin may not be increased by immoderate correction. Indeed, we know that the same one who established in the Law that the principle of kinship be observed also instructed in the Gospel that the bond of marriage is not to be dissolved. For if, wherever something of proximity or consanguinity, no matter how distant, can be found among the married, the marriage is immediately dissolved, I fear that adultery and the crime of fornication may be multiplied. For when the fellowship of his partner is denied to a married adolescent or youth, nor is any solace extended to him by which he may preserve continence, burning with lust, by the instigation of the devil, he perhaps becomes corrupted by manifold fornication and so his soul is submerged into the abyss of eternal death. As you wished of my humble self, I have written to you what I think on this matter. Because of the fragility of the present time, I think it best to follow what Bishop Theodore pronounced definitively in his chapters, taking the middle path between Gregory and Isidore: that marriage be licit in the fifth generation, because divine law does not contradict this and the sayings of the holy Fathers do not forbid it. And if a joining was consummated in the fifth generation by the unknowing, it seems better to me, if the married man is not willing to practice continence, that he make satisfaction to God by the humiliation of penance.

C. 202. ON THE SAME MATTER.
Gregory to Augustine.

Hence, it is necessary that even the third or fourth generation of the faithful ought legally to be joined. As for the second that we mentioned, there must be absolute abstinence from it.

C. 203. ON THE SAME MATTER.
From the letter of Rabanus to the rural bishop Reginbaldus.

You asked what is to be done if a father and son, or two brothers, or a mother's brother and a nephew have fornicated with the same woman. It is manifest that this is to be punished with a heavy penalty because it is found to be a grave crime. For all adultery is forbidden where it is written: "You shall not commit adultery (Ex. 20:14)." How much more when with a kinswoman, or with the wife or concubine of a kinsman? Hence, it is written in Leviticus: "If any man commits adultery with another's wife, both adulterer and adulteress must die the death. He who has slept with his stepmother and with his daughter-in-law, and he who has married daughter and mother, and he who has taken his sister, they are to die the death (cf. Lev. 20:10–14, 17)." Indeed, if God commanded in the Law to avenge the shame of incest with a sentence of death, how shall an incestuous man avoid penance for his sin in the Gospel, where the highest justice lies? Hence the Apostle: "A man who, at the testimony of two or three witnesses, has made void the law of Moses dies without hope of mercy; how much more do you believe that he merits worse punishments who has trampled the Son of God under foot, and has reckoned unclean the blood of the covenant by which he was sanctified, and has mocked the Spirit of grace (Heb. 10:28–29)?" And so, Theodore adjudged that a man who has committed incest must do penance for twelve years; others have said fifteen, ten, or seven. Following in the footsteps of our ancient Fathers, temper the length of penance only for those who have done penance devoutly and with tears; the rest are to observe the defined time.

C. 204. OF ONE WHO MADE HIMSELF A SLAVE.
From the Council of Tribur, c. 11.

It has been related to the holy Synod that some freeborn man had married a freeborn wife and, after the procreation of children, for the sake of divorce, he made himself another man's slave. [It has been asked] whether he must necessarily keep his wife and, if he does, whether, according to the secular law, she must also be reduced to servitude. It has been adjudged that the wife is not at all to be dismissed, nor yet is she to be reduced to servitude because of Christ's law, since he made himself a slave without his wife's consent, whom she had taken as a free husband.

C. 205. ALSO, ON INCESTS.
From the same.

Also, it has been indicated that a certain man had violated a certain woman whom his brother afterwards took to wife. They established that the brother who had violated her and hid from his brother that she had been violated by him, because he twinned his sin, is to be chastised with a heavier penance, that it is fitting that such a marriage be dissolved, and that the woman never be given the power to marry while the brothers live, but out of mercy, the latter may be allowed marriage.

c. 206. IF ONE HAS SLEPT WITH THE DAUGHTER OF HIS MOTHER'S SISTER, ETC.
From the same.

Likewise, it was asked, if any man has slept with the daughter of his mother's sister or brother, or of his father's sister or brother, and if married, whether it is licit for him to make further use of his marriage or, if unmarried, to take a wife? As some statutes of our predecessors hold, it would be just if such men were to abstain forever from marriage. But by reason of human fragility, it has seemed best that such persons, after penance, are not to be deprived of marriage entirely; yet such an awful fornication is to be punished most harshly, as Pope St. Nicholas and other Roman pontiffs established, lest perhaps such people, in their despairing conscience, sin even more.

c. 207. ON THE SAME MATTER.
From the same.

To the bed of the husband, in the wife's absence, went the wife's sister; believing her to be his wife, he slept with her. As to this, it has seemed best to us that, if he has proved this by a true assurance that he committed this crime unknowing, let him do the penance which has been imposed on him and then be allowed to have his lawful marriage. But she is to be afflicted with a worthy punishment and be deprived of marriage in perpetuity.

c. 208. ON THE SAME MATTER.
From the same.

A certain man fornicated with a certain woman; afterwards, the man's son, ignorant of the father's deed, violated the same woman. When the father learned of this, he confessed as to himself and his son. They established that it would be better that legitimate marriages with worthy penance be allowed to those who have lapsed in this way, lest they fall into worse sins. But the fornicating woman is to be dealt with more heavily.

c. 209. ON THE SAME MATTER.
From the same.

If a man has fornicated with two sisters, and the one sister did not know that the other had previously been violated by the same man, or if the man did not know that she was the sister of the other whom he had previously violated, if they have done worthy penance, and if they are unable to remain continent, let marriages not be denied them after seven years. But if they were not ignorant, let them abstain from marriage until death.

c. 210. ON THE SAME MATTER.
From the same.

If a man has fornicated with two sisters, the man is to do penance for all the days of his life. But the sister who did not know about the other sister is to have license to marry.

c. 211. ON THE SAME MATTER.
From the same.

If a man has fornicated with a woman, and his brother unknowingly takes the same woman in marriage, the first brother, because he hid his crime from his brother, is to do penance and may marry after penance. But the woman is to do penance until death.

c. 212. ON THE SAME MATTER.
From the same.

If a brother has fornicated with a woman, and a second brother unknowingly slept with the same woman, the woman is to do penance all the days of her life; but after penance, the brother who had been unaware of the crime may marry, if he wishes.

c. 213. ON SEPARATION.
From the Council at Verberie in the times of Pepin.

In the third degree of consanguinity, they are separated. But if they are found joined in the fourth degree, we do not separate them, but decree penance for them. But, if it has not occurred yet, we do not give any power to marry in the fourth degree.

c. 214. ON THE SAME MATTER.
From the same.

If some man has intercourse with his stepdaughter, he can have neither the mother, nor the daughter; neither she nor he may join with anyone else at any time. And yet, his wife, if she so wills, and if she is unable to remain continent, if, after she knew that her husband had committed adultery with her daughter, she did not have carnal commerce with him, if she wishes, may marry another.

c. 215. ON THE SAME MATTER.
From the same.

If a man has slept with his stepmother, neither of them may come to marriage, but her husband can, if he wishes, marry another if he is unable to remain continent; it may be held similarly of one who sleeps with his stepdaughter, or with his wife's sister.

c. 216. ON THE SAME MATTER.
From the same.

One who has slept with two sisters, and one of the two was formerly his wife, is to have neither of them, nor are the adulterers themselves ever to be joined in marriage.

c. 217. ON THE SAME MATTER.
From the same.

If any man has slept with his brother's wife, adulterer and adulteress are to remain without hope of marriage all the days of their lives. But the one whose wife she was can, if he wishes, take another spouse.

c. 218. ON THE SAME MATTER.
From the same.

If any man has had intercourse with his son's espoused, and afterwards the son married her, the father is not afterwards to have a wife, nor the woman a husband; the son, who was ignorant of the father's crime, may take another wife.

c. 219. ON THE SAME MATTER.
From the same.

If any man has held his stepson or stepdaughter for confirmation before the bishop, he is to be separated from his wife and must never take another. Similarly, with a woman.

c. 220. ON THE SAME MATTER.
From the same.

If any man has fornicated with mother and daughter, while the mother did not know about the daughter, or the daughter about the mother, he is never to take a wife; but let the women, if they wish, take husbands. But if the women knew this, they must remain without husbands in perpetuity.

c. 221. ON THE SAME MATTER.
From the same.

Similarly, of two sisters, with one of whom he remained in the adultery while he married the other publicly; he is not to have his wife until the day of his death, and the one who did not know may take a husband.

c. 222. IF ONE FLEES BECAUSE OF A FEUD.

From the same.

If any men, because of a feud, flee to other countries, and leave their wives, neither they, nor their wives, may marry another.

c. 223. ALSO, ON INCESTS.

From the same.

If any man has committed incest with his kinswoman, he is to lose his personal property, if he has any; and if he is unwilling to emend himself, no one is to receive him at home, nor to give food to him. If he has done so, he must pay sixty shillings to the king as composition. And if he has no money and if he is free, he is to be sent to jail. If he is of servile status, he is to be flogged with many blows.

c. 224. ALSO, ON PARRICIDES.

From the Capitularies.

If a free man has killed his father or mother, a brother or a maternal uncle, he is to lose his inheritance. And if any man has committed adultery with his mother or sister or a father's sister, he is to lose his inheritance.

c. 225. ALSO, ON INCESTS.

From the Capitularies.

That bishops are to see to it that they investigate the incestuous. And if they are unwilling to repent, they are to be expelled from the Church until they return to penance. If they are unwilling to obey the priests, it is fitting that they be constrained by secular discipline.

c. 226. ON THE SAME MATTER.

From the Council of Mainz, c. 29.

If a man has taken a widow to wife, and afterwards has fornicated with his stepdaughter, or has sexual intercourse with two sisters, or if a woman with two brothers, or with father and son, or if a man has defiled his brother's widow, or granddaughter, or stepmother, or daughter-in-law, or cousin, or the daughter or widow or stepdaughter of his mother's brother, we instruct that they be separated and never join in marriage to another afterwards.

c. 227. ON THE SAME MATTER.

From the same.

We also forbid anyone henceforth to join in marriage in the fourth generation. Where this has been done after the prohibition, let it be separated.

c. 228. ON THE SAME MATTER.
From the Council of Worms.

If any man has committed fornication with two sisters, or if a woman with two brothers, or with those persons as to whom sacred Scripture forbids, and the person has done worthy penance and is unable to practice continence, it is to be licit for him or her to take a lawful wife or husband.

c. 229. IF ANY MAN HAS FORNICATED WITH HIS GODMOTHER.
From the same.

If any man has fornicated with his spiritual godmother, he is to be punished with anathema until worthy penance. Similarly, if he has fornicated with a girl whom he received at the sacred font, or one whom he held before the bishop. But if he has a lawful wife, he is not to dismiss her.

c. 230. ALSO, ON INCESTS.
From the same.

If any man has fornicated with his stepdaughter, after the dissolution of his marriage, he is to do penance, namely, he is to be suspended for a period of three years from the body and blood of the Lord; he is not to eat meat, nor to drink wine, and he is to fast every day, except for feast-days and Sundays. The same is to be observed concerning women who have lain in bed secretly with a father and his son, and those men who are aware that they have furtively polluted themselves with two sisters.

c. 231. THAT ILLICIT MARRIAGES ARE TO BE DISSOLVED WITH AN OATH.
From the Council of Tribur.

We will that those whose illicit marriages are to be dissolved confirm by oath that they will not share the same table nor live together under the same roof, or enjoy any familiar conversation, unless in public or in church. They are to divide the things which they had in common, lest any suspicion may arise and grow.

c. 232. THE OATH AS TO KINSHIP, HOW IT IS TO BE INVESTIGATED.

As to that kinship which they say exists between that man and this woman, his wife, whatever you know in regard to it or have heard imputed by your neighbours, or from your older relatives, you shall by no device nor out of regard for love, or fear, or reward, or kinship, hide it from your bishop or his envoy whom he had commanded to inquire into this, whenever he interrogates you in regard to this matter. So help you God, etc.

c. 233. ALSO, THE OTHERS.

That oath that this man made as to that kinship which is imputed between that man and his wife, that you shall observe it, insofar as you know or have heard. So help you God.

c. 234. OATH AS TO DIVORCE FOR INCEST.

That, from this day forward, by no device will you join with this woman, a blood relative of yours, named so-and so, who, against the law and right Christianity, until this day was your wife neither in marriage, nor in adultery or fornication; nor shall you drink and eat with her at one table, nor remain under one roof, except perhaps in church or in some other public place, where there may be no evil suspicion, that you speak together there before witnesses for a certain necessity. Nor will you take another wife, unless perhaps, after completing your penance, license be given to you by your bishop or his envoy. So help you God, and these relics of the saints.

c. 235. ATTESTATION TO JUDGMENT.

As to what has been imputed to me at this Synod, that I committed adultery or fornication together with this woman, I did not do it, nor acknowledge myself to be guilty of it, so help me God in this judgment of his.

c. 236. OATH AFTER PENANCE IS ASSIGNED FOR ACTS OF LUST.

From this day forward, you will not commit further adultery or fornication with this woman with whom you committed adultery or fornication for which you received discipline or penance, nor will you take her to wife, unless, after completing your penance, license be given to you by the bishop or his envoy. So help you God.

c. 237. OF A MAN WHO, WHILE HER HUSBAND WAS ALIVE, IS SAID TO BE ACCUSED OF HAVING COMMITTED ADULTERY WITH HIS WIFE.

From the Synod of Meaux.

He who, while her husband was alive, is accused of having committed adultery with his wife, and when the husband soon died, is known to have married her, is in every way to be subject to public penance. As to this same man, even after penance, if it is expedient, the aforesaid rule will be observed, unless perhaps the man, or the woman, is accused of having killed the dead husband, or kinship or any other criminal action is an impediment. If this should be proved, let them remain in perpetuity without hope of marriage and with penance. But if he denies that he ever committed adultery with the same woman while her husband lived, and neither of them is guilty of the aforesaid homicide, and neither of them can be convicted by approved witnesses, let them purge the rumour concerning their reputation at law and make use of the marriage they have entered, if no other reason, as we said, stands in the way.

c. 238. ON THE SAME MATTER.
From the Council of Tribur.

It has been related to the ears of the holy bishops that a man violated by rape another's wife, and he also gave an oath to the adulteress, while her husband was still alive, that, after her lawful husband's death, if he himself should still be alive, he would take her as his wife; which was done. We therefore forbid and anathematize such a marriage.

c. 239. ATTESTATION AS TO A HUSBAND'S OR WIFE'S DEATH.

As to the matter of which you stand accused in the presence of this bishop at this Synod, that by your deed or by your counsel your husband so-and-so, or your wife so-and-so, incurred death and lost his or her life, it is entirely not so, nor did you do anything against his or her life and limbs, nor counsel others, for which you would deservedly receive the remedies of penance according to an ecclesiastical judgment, or sustain death or some harm according to the world's law. So help you God in this judgment.

c. 240. OATH OR ATTESTATION AS TO AN IMPUTED HOMICIDE.

As to the matter that is imputed to you in the presence of your bishop, whose parishioner you are, that you, together with some other men, your followers, killed that man for this reason: that you might seize his goods and take his wife in marriage; in truth it is not so, nor did you, alone or with other men, kill that man, nor did you counsel others so that he might lose his life or limbs, nor have you done anything as to his death, for which you would deservedly receive penance, or sustain a feud, or pay some price. So help you God.

c. 241. OATH AS TO THE RECONCILIATION OF SPOUSES.

From this day forward, you shall keep this spouse of yours, named so-and-so, whom you had unjustly dismissed, as a husband by right ought to keep his wife in love and due discipline; nor shall you separate her from yourself by any wicked device, nor shall you take another while she lives. So help you God.

c. 242. THE WOMAN IS TO SWEAR AS FOLLOWS.

From now on, you shall keep and embrace this your husband, whom you had unjustly dismissed, and you will be subject and obedient to him in service and in love and in fear as a wife by right ought to be subject to her husband; nor shall you ever separate yourself from him, nor shall you join with another man in marriage or adultery while your husband lives. So help you God.

c. 243. OF THOSE WHO ARE JOINED IN MATRIMONY AND CANNOT HAVE INTERCOURSE.

From the letter of Rabanus to Bishop Heribaldus, c. 29.

You asked concerning those who are joined in matrimony, and yet cannot have intercourse, whether either of them may marry another; we answer not with authority, but on the basis of some men's statutes, in which it is written: "If a man and a woman have married, and afterwards the woman said of the man that he is unable to have intercourse with her, if she can prove by a just judgment that it is true, let her take another."

c. 244. ON THE SAME MATTER.

From the Council at Verberie, in the times of King Pepin, c. 17.

If any woman has proclaimed that her husband has never had intercourse with her, let them go out from there to the cross, and if it was true, let them be separated, and she may do what she wishes.

c. 245. ON THE SAME MATTER.

From the Council at Compiègne.

If any man has taken a wife and kept her for a time, and the woman says that he has not had intercourse with her, and the man says that he has done so, let it stand on the truth of the man because the husband is the head of the wife (cf. 1 Cor. 11:3).

c. 246. ON THE SAME MATTER.

From the Council of Tribur.

If a man has taken a wife and has been unable to have intercourse with her, and his brother secretly corrupted her and made her pregnant, let them be separated. After considering their feebleness, let mercy be shown to them as to marriage, only in the Lord (1 Cor. 7:39).

c. 247. ON THE FORNICATION OF DIFFERENT PERSONS.

From the Roman Penitential of Bishop Theodore and the priest Bede.

If an adolescent has sinned with a virgin, he is to do penance for a year. If once and by fortuitous chance, let his penance be lightened, yet let him do penance up to a full year. If a girl and an adolescent boy younger than twenty commit fornication, three forty-day fasts and the weekdays prescribed by law. If they are sentenced to human servitude for this sin, let them do penance for forty days. If a married man has fornicated with a virgin, let him do penance for two years in this way first of all: that he be continent with his wife, if his wife has consented to it; otherwise a mode of penance is to be assigned. If a layman has fornicated with a laywoman, let him do penance for three years, and the more often he has done so, the more time is to be added. A layman who stains himself with God's handmaiden is to do penance for two years. If he has engendered a child from her, let him do penance for three years. If he is not married, three forty-day fasts and the weekdays prescribed by law. Those who are canons and fornicate, one year; if frequently, two years. He who is in a degree is to do penance for three years. A monk without a degree or a canon with a degree, if they have fornicated with a lay girl, are to do penance for three years. If with a nun, they are to do penance for seven years. Monks with a degree committing fornication are to do penance for seven years. If a monk has taken a laywoman, let him do penance for three years, she for two, and the weekdays prescribed by law. If to the point of engendering a child, let him do penance for four years. If they have killed it, let him do penance for eight years. If a bishop has fornicated, let him do penance for eight years. Others adjudged twelve years; after three years, he may do penance more lightly. A priest fornicating with a girl, four years and three forty-day fasts in the course of the year, and Wednesdays and Fridays at bread and water. That if a bishop, priest, or deacon is caught in fornication, or perjury, or theft, he is to be deposed, but yet not deprived of communion, because "The Lord does not judge twice in the same matter (Nahum 1:9 LXX)."

c. 248. ALSO, ON INCESTS.

If an adolescent has taken his sister, he is to do penance for five years. If his mother, seven years. And, for so long as he lives, he is never to be without continence.

ALSO, OTHERS.

He who has fornicated with his mother is to do penance for fifteen years. He who has fornicated with his daughter or sister is to abstain from all meat for fifteen years. If a mother has fornicated with her young son, she is to abstain from meat for three years, and she is to fast until vespers one day each week. He who has intercourse with a mother and daughter, or with two sisters, or with the wife of his father or brother, or of a paternal or maternal uncle, or with his granddaughter or cousin, or those who are joined in the first, second, or third degree of consanguinity, we will to indicate to all these that they are to be separated, and, because of the recent establishment of the Church, to do penance for seven years: for the first three years, for three days each week, that is, Monday, Wednesday, and Friday, forty days before Easter, twenty days before the mass of St. John, twenty days before the Lord's Nativity. For the remaining four years, on Wednesday and Friday, and for fourteen nights before the mass of St. John and as many before the Nativity of the Lord. If he wishes to redeem himself, let him give one penny for each day, or the value of one penny. If he is poor, let him give half a penny.

C. 249. ON THE UNCLEANNESS OF BOYS.

Boys who mutually pollute each other with their hands are to do penance for forty days; if they are older, for one hundred days. Boys who defile each other between their thighs are to do penance for one hundred days; if they are older, for three forty-day fasts and the weekdays prescribed by law. A younger child pressed down by an older one is to do penance for seven days; if he consented, for twenty days. A boy who pollutes himself intentionally is to do penance for thirty days; but a youth is to do so for forty days.

C. 250. ON ABSTAINING DURING MENSTRUATION.

He who has had intercourse with a menstruating woman is to do penance for forty days. If any man has had intercourse with his wife from below, he is to do penance for forty days. If he has had intercourse from behind, for three years, because it is a sodomitical crime. Men fornicating between the thighs are to do penance for one year. If from behind, they are to do penance for three years. If they are boys, for two years.

C. 251. ON WOMEN.

A woman who, by whatever artifice, fornicates herself or with another woman is to do penance for three years. If a nun, by some device, fornicates with another nun, she is to do penance for seven years.

C. 252. ON AN ALLURING EMBRACE.

He who is polluted by the alluring embraces of a woman, or by a kiss, is to do penance for thirty days. He who touches shamelessly the flesh of the same woman is to do penance for three months. He who is polluted by obscene speech is to do penance for seven days. A priest, if he has kissed a woman through an unclean desire, is to do penance for twenty days. If he was befouled, he is to do penance for forty days. He who is polluted by a dream in church is to do penance for three days. He who was polluted willingly while asleep is to rise and sing the seven penitential psalms, and thirty psalms during the day. He who was willing to sin in his sleep, and did not become polluted, is to sing twenty-four psalms.

c. 253. ON CLERICS.

A cleric, if he has spilled his seed without touching, is to do penance for seven days. If he touches with his hand, he is to do penance for twenty days; if a deacon, for thirty days; if a priest, for four weeks. A priest, if he has spilled his seed by thoughts, is to do penance for seven days; a monk, likewise. He who has voluntarily spilled his seed in church, if he is a cleric, is to do penance for fourteen days; if a monk or deacon, for thirty days; if a priest, forty; if a bishop, for fifty days.

c. 254. ON FORNICATION WITH FOUR-FOOTED BEASTS.

He who sins with an animal, one year; some judge ten years, some seven, some three, some a hundred days.

ALSO.

If any cleric has fornicated with a four-footed beast, he is to do penance for two years; a subdeacon for three, a deacon and a monk for five, a priest for seven, a bishop for ten.

c. 255. ON SODOMITES.

As for one who has fornicated as a sodomite, some judged ten years, some seven, others one; boys, a hundred days.

ALSO.

Others judged that, if it has become a custom, a layman is to do penance for five years, a cleric seven, a subdeacon and monk eight, a deacon ten, a priest twelve, a bishop fourteen.

c. 256. ON THE SAME MATTER.

From the Council of Ancyra.

As for those who have turned, or turn to irrational [sexual] behaviour, all who have committed this crime before the age of twenty, after fifteen years spent in penance, may have the communion of prayer; after five years, that is, after twenty years, they may touch the sacraments of the offering. But all those who are older than twenty and have wives who have fallen into this sin are to do penance for twenty-five years and be received into the communion of prayer. And after five years, that is, after thirty years, then they may receive communion. If they have fallen after fifty, they may receive communion at the end of life.

c. 257. ON THE SAME MATTER.
From the same Council.

Those who have lived irrationally and have polluted others with the leprosy of an unjust crime, the holy Synod instructed that they pray among those who are disturbed by an unclean spirit.

c. 258. ON THE SAME MATTER.
From the Capitularies, bk. 1, c. 19.

If men are discovered who sin against nature with four-footed animals or with males, they are to be restrained by a harsh and strict penance. Therefore, bishops or priests, by whom the judgment of penance is enjoined, are to strive in every way to cut off this evil from the root.

c. 259. ON THE SAME MATTER.
From the sayings of St. Basil.

A cleric or a monk who pursues adolescents or children, or who is caught in a kiss or some other shameful occasion, is to be whipped publicly and lose his tonsure. When his hair has been shamefully shaved, his face is to be covered with spittle, and, bound with iron bonds, he is to be worn down in a prison cell for six months and fed three times a week at vespers with barley bread. Afterwards, for another six months, living in a segregated little courtyard under the custody of a spiritual elder, let him be intent on manual labour and prayer, subject to vigils and tears. He is to walk ever under the custody of two spiritual brothers, having henceforth no private speech or counsel together with young people.

c. 260. ON THE SAME MATTER.
From the sayings of Isidore.

If any of the younger men or any suspicious person has played with children, he is to be worn down by long penance.

c. 261. ON THE SAME MATTER.
As above.

If any brother is found playing with children, and having friendships with younger people, he is to be admonished three times to be mindful of decency and the fear of God. If he has not ceased, he is to be corrected most severely.

c. 262. ON THE SAME MATTER.
From the Theodosian law, bk. 9.

It is disgraceful to all to condemn the body of a man, made to look like a woman's, to suffer the semblance of an alien sex (for they appear to have no difference from women). You will expiate a crime of this sort with avenging flames in the sight of the people.

c. 263. ON THE COPULATION OF THE FAITHFUL.
From the Council of Worms.

In the copulation of the faithful, we do not define the number of generations, but we establish that it not be lawful for any Christian to take a wife from his blood kindred or relatives, for so long as the generation is remembered, known, or retained in memory.

We have summarized these matters concerning fornication of many kinds from diverse works, leaving it to the judgment of the priests to decree what is more salutary and useful in assigning penances.

c. 264. THAT NO ADULTERIES BE PERPETRATED IN THE HOUSES OF THE FAITHFUL.
From the Council of Meaux.

Let powerful men, and especially powerful women, see to it that adulteries, concubinary libidinousness, and incestuous relations do not thrive in their houses. And let them ensure that their priests, who go with them to chapel, practice such virtue that they cut off all vices in their houses, and compel all to retain and repeat the Lord's Prayer and the Creed, because parish priests and the bishops' ministers will strive to see to this among the lesser and less important persons.

c. 265. ON THE SAME MATTER.
From the Capitularies, bk. 3.

It has been reported to us that, in some places, bishops and counts receive securities from the incestuous and from those who do not give their tithes, and from priests for some faults, and they divide the money between themselves. We decree that this is entirely to be abolished, lest perhaps room be given to avarice.

HENCEFORTH ON THEFT AND RAPINE

C. 266. FROM A PENITENTIAL.

He who, seized by greed, has committed theft is to return what he stole and do penance for five years.

C. 267. ON THE SAME MATTER.
From the Roman law.

Ecclesiastical money taken by theft or rapine is to be repaid fourfold, secular money twofold.

C. 268. ON THE SAME MATTER.
From a Penitential.

He who has stolen frequently is to do penance for seven years.

C. 269. ON THE SAME MATTER.
From the same.

If anyone has committed capital theft, that is, has stolen four-footed animals, or broken into houses, let him do penance for seven years and return what he has stolen. But if anyone has stolen lesser things once or twice, let him return what he took and do penance for a year at bread and water. And if he cannot return it, let him do penance for three years. If anyone has violated a tomb, let him do penance for seven years, three of them at bread and water.

C. 270. ON THE SAME MATTER.
From the Council of Toledo.

If any cleric has been caught demolishing tombs, it is fitting that the one discovered in such a crime be removed from the clerical order and be set to penance for three years.

C. 271. ON THE SAME MATTER.
From the Council of Agde.

If any cleric has committed a theft against the church, a peregrine communion is to be given to him.

C. 272. ON THE SAME MATTER.
From the same.

If any cleric or monk has committed theft, which can rather be called sacrilege, we have adjudged it to be ordained that a younger one, guilty of such a crime, is to be beaten with rods and never receive an ecclesiastical office. But if one already ordained has been caught in this crime, he is to be deprived of the dignity of that office's name; because of the instability of his actions, let communion alone suffice for him after he has fulfilled the satisfaction of his penance.

c. 273. ON THE SAME MATTER.
From the sayings of Jerome on Titus.

A thief is judged such not only with regard to greater things, but also to lesser ones. Indeed, what is notable is not what has been taken by theft, but the mind of the thief. Similarly, in fornication, hence, fornication does not become something different if the woman is beautiful or deformed, slave or free, poor or rich; whatever the woman is like, fornication is the same. So also with theft: however much one has stolen, he incurs the crime of theft.

c. 274. ON THE SAME MATTER.
The sayings of Augustine.

The Lord said to Moses: "Each man is to ask his neighbour, and [each woman] her neighbour, for gold and silver vessels and for clothing (Ex. 11:2)," etc. No one is to believe he can take this as a precedent for despoiling his neighbour. For God commanded this, who knew what it was fitting for each one to suffer. Nor did the Israelites commit theft, but performed a service for God, who commanded it, in the same way in which a court officer kills one whom the judge has commanded to be killed. Indeed, if he does it of his own will, he is a homicide, even if he kills one whom he knows that the judge ought to have killed.

275. ON THE SAME MATTER.
Also, Augustine.

To steal something secretly is subject to punishment; it is much more punishable to snatch away something publicly. And so, to steal something from someone who does not wish it, whether it is done hiddenly or openly, has its own Commandment. For by the name of theft is properly understood all unlawful usurpation of another's goods. For He did not allow plunder who prohibited theft, but He willed that under the term theft plunder also be understood. For He openly signified the whole, whatever is stolen from a neighbour.

c. 276. ON THE SAME MATTER.
From a Penitential.

If anyone from the ministry of the Church had stolen anything in any way, he is to do penance for seven years.

c. 277. ON THE SAME MATTER.
From the Council of Worms.

It often happens that thefts are committed in monasteries. Hence, we establish that, when the same brethren must purge themselves of blame for such matters, mass be celebrated by the abbot, or by someone in the presence of the brethren and, at the end of the mass, all take communion with these words: "May the body of the Lord serve you for proof today."

c. 278. ON A CRIMINAL CAUSE.
From the same.

If a criminal cause, that is, homicide, or adultery, or witchcraft, is imputed to a bishop or priest, he must celebrate mass for each charge and say the Secret out loud and take communion, and show himself to be innocent of each of the charges imputed to him. If he should not do this, he is to be kept outside the bounds of the Church for five years.

c. 279. ON RAPINE AND VIOLENCE.
From a Capitulary.

Bishops are to keep briefly noted the sentences of evangelical, apostolic, and prophetic authority concerning rapine and violence, as also the canonical and apostolical decrees, and to read all these in public to all. The envoys sent out are also to make known to all the sentences of the law and of our predecessors and our own chapters on this matter. And bishops are to forbid depredations and rapine to all by the authority of God and of the bishops. Our envoys and counts are to see to it that they make this firm prohibition by our ban so that all may know that, if anyone has presumed to do such a thing, he will be sentenced by the bishop in accordance with the divine sentences, and be forced to emend in accordance with the laws and the royal chapters, and suffer a condign punishment in accordance with the judgment of our faithful subjects.

c. 280. ON THE SAME MATTER.
From the same.

If it should happen (far be it!) that such a one emerge who sets aside the fear of God, contemns ecclesiastical authority, and flees the royal power, let him know, whoever he may be, that, according to canonical authority, he shall be made a stranger from the company of all Christians and from the fellowship of Holy Church in heaven and on earth; and by the royal power and the common agreement of the faithful subjects of the kingdom, he shall be pursued as an enemy of God and a devastator of the kingdom until he is driven out of the kingdom.

c. 281. ON THE SAME MATTER.
From the same.

If anyone has committed rapine within our kingdom, or has stolen anything with force from any of our faithful subjects or his man, he is to make threefold composition according to the laws with the one from whom he stole, and in addition he is to pay our ban. Afterwards, he is to be brought before us by the count so that, locked up in strict custody at our pleasure, he may suffer punishment. Indeed, if he acted publicly, let him do penance for it according to the provisions of the holy canons. If secretly, let him do penance at the counsel of the priests because thieves, as the Apostle says, unless they have done true penance, shall not possess the kingdom of God (cf. 1 Cor. 6:10). But those who have stolen something from the goods of churches are to be judged more severely for it, because the theft of sacred things is a sacrilege, and he is called sacrilegious who has stolen something from there. Indeed, such persons are to be firmly noted and kept out of the bounds of the Holy Church of God until they make satisfaction to the church which they harmed.

c. 282. ON THE SAME MATTER.
As above.

Let the grasping hear what the Lord says through Isaiah: "The spoil of the poor is in your house (Is. 3:14)." And through the Apostle: "Nor those who commit rapine, nor homicides, nor adulterers shall possess the kingdom of God (cf. 1 Cor. 6:10)." Let them understand from this what and how great a sin is rapine, which the holy Apostle compared to adultery and homicide. Also, the same Apostle says: "If any man is a fornicator, or an adulterer, or an extortioner, or a homicide, with such a one it is not licit for a Christian even to eat before satisfaction (cf. 1 Cor. 5:11)." And the blessed Apostle John forbids greeting such a man, saying: "Neither say hail to him, nor receive him into your house. Indeed, one who says hail to him shares in his wicked works (2 Jn. 1:10–11)." Let them hear what is written in the Council of Toledo: "If any of the more powerful men has despoiled a cleric or a poor man" (find it above, c. 36, where it speaks of homicides). Let robbers and plunderers of ecclesiastical things hear what St. Anacletus, ordained by the Apostle Peter, says:

c. 283. ON THE SAME MATTER.
Anacletus.

Whoever steals anything from his father, he says, is a homicide's accomplice. Without doubt, God is our Father, who created us. But the Church is our mother, who gave birth to us spiritually in baptism. Hence, he who takes, plunders, or defrauds the money of Christ from the Church is a homicide, and is regarded as a homicide in the sight of God. Indeed, he who has stolen the things of the Church commits sacrilege and is to be judged as such.

c. 284. ON THE SAME MATTER.
Also, Urban, pope and martyr, says.

The goods and resources of the Church are called oblations because they are offered to the Lord, and they are the vows of the faithful, and the wages of sins, and the patrimonies of the poor. If anyone has stolen those things, he incurs the condemnation of Ananias and Saphira (cf. Act. 5); and it is fitting to hand such a one over to Satan so that his spirit may be saved on the day of the Lord (cf. 1 Cor. 5:5).

c. 285. ON THE SAME MATTER.
Also, Pope Lucius.

We anathematize and by apostolic authority expel from the bounds of Holy Church and condemn plunderers of the Church's goods and resources, and we adjudge them to be sacrilegious. And not only them, but also all who give their consent to them, because not only those who act are judged guilty, but also those who give their consent.

c. 286. ON THE SAME MATTER.

Augustine says that whoever steals and plunders anything from the Church is compared to the traitor Judas.

c. 287. ON THE SAME MATTER.
Written in the canons.

If anyone wishes to take away or give the offerings of a church outside the church without the knowledge of the bishop or of him to whom these functions have been committed, let him be anathema.

c. 288. ON THE SAME MATTER.
From the Council of Meaux, c. 61.

They are known as despoilers of ecclesiastical possessions not only who retain those same things against authority, but also those who devastate them cruelly; some even in various collaborations despoil the resources of the Church and rob them of their rents, and afflict, waste, and oppress mercilessly the poor, neighbours, and those in the surrounding area. Since, according to the Apostle, extortioners are excluded from the kingdom of God (cf. 1 Cor. 6:10), these people are to make satisfaction with public penance for their criminal and public sin. If they are unwilling to do this and are not exhorted or forced by royal power, let that terrible sentence of the Apostle be issued against them which says: "If anyone who is counted among the brethren is an extortioner, no one is to presume to take bread with such a one (cf. 1 Cor. 5:11)," because it is iniquitous and sacrilegious, as Pope Symmachus says, and as Blessed Gregory after him writes to the subdeacon Sabinus: It is even against the laws, if anyone, by the efforts of a depraved will, has striven to retain to his own profit whatever is bequeathed to venerable places. According to the statutes of the canons, as one guilty of sacrilege, he must be kept from all ecclesiastical communion until he sees to it that he corrects by a worthy satisfaction what he has set aside.

c. 289. ON THOSE WHO BREAK INTO SACRED PLACES.
From the same.

That those who break into monasteries, and places dedicated to God, and churches, and take away from there what is deposited there or anything else, and who not only dishonour priests and ecclesiastical men, but also afflict them in various ways, are to be subject to a canonical sentence and excommunicated as guilty of sacrilege.

c. 290. HOW THE BISHOP IS TO CALL PLUNDERERS TO THE SYNOD.
As above.

The bishop in whose parish someone lives who has plundered something shall call that person once, twice, and a third time, if it is necessary, by his summons through his priest, to emendation or composition, and to penance, so that he may satisfy God and the Church, which he harmed. But if the man despised and contemned his summons and most salubrious invitation, let the bishop strike him with his pastoral staff, that is, by a sentence of excommunication, that he may be severed from the communion of Holy Church and all Christians until suitable satisfaction and worthy emendation. The same bishop is to make this excommunication known to the man's superior, and to all his fellow bishops, lest they receive him before worthy satisfaction.

c. 291. ON THOSE WHO ARE ANOTHER'S PARISHIONERS.
From the same.

But as for those who have a benefice or inheritance within a parish, and are another bishop's parishioners, and while they travel from place to place, carry out robbery and depredations, it has pleased us and our faithful subjects that they be excommunicated, nor are they to leave the parish before they have worthily corrected what they perpetrated. Their excommunication is to be signified to their superior and to their own bishop, lest they receive them before they make restitution to that place where they committed the robbery and make full correction.

c. 292. ON THE SAME MATTER.
As above.

It has pleased us and our faithful subjects, for the common utility and pressing necessity, that none of the bishops bear it badly, if another bishop has excommunicated his parishioner by reason of his having committed such plunder.

c. 293. ON THE SAME MATTER.
From the same.

If someone has treated royal power and episcopal authority as nothing, and while so rebellious he was killed in the course of rapine, no one is to declare a feud against any of our faithful subjects, who killed him, nor is he to make any composition for his death.

c. 294. IF A BISHOP DOES NOT EXCOMMUNICATE PLUNDERERS.
From the Council at Pîtres.

According to the seventh chapter of the second Council of Toledo, if the bishop, to whom those men who do such things against God and the peace of the Church are known to pertain, has delayed summoning or excommunicating them for any gift or favour or out of negligence, either to take them under his control as they return or cast them out of the Church as contemners, he is to be regarded as excommunicate from the fellowship of the rest until a sentence of their condemnation or emendation is promulgated by him. Indeed, unless we all struggle jointly so that justice may be preserved in all things, neither the king as father of the fatherland, nor the bishops as the people's propitiators and reconcilers, nor we who are called Christians by our share in Christ's name, truly are in the sight of God what we are called by human speech.

c. 295. ALSO, ON THE RAPACIOUS.
From the Council of Mainz.

Anyone who, inflated with contemptuous pride, renders the house of God contemptible, and has treated dishonourably, or has presumed to breach, or has committed with temerarious daring arson or devastation against possessions consecrated to God and established in God's honour under the defence of royal immunity, is to be cut off from the communion of all the faithful as a usurper and violator of God's Church, which is the house of the living God. It is also fitting that he feel the indignation of the lord king, whose benevolence he has contemned and whose constitution he has violated.

c. 296. THAT BISHOPS MUST PROTECT AND DEFEND THE PEOPLE.
From the Council of Toledo.

Bishops must not avoid the care imposed on them of protecting and defending their people. Hence, when they see that judges and powerful persons are oppressors of the poor, they are first to reprove them by their priestly admonition; if they contemn to be emended, they are to make known their insolence to the royal ears, so that the royal power may restrain from wickedness those whom the priestly admonition does not bend to justice.

c. 297. ALSO, ON MALEFACTORS.
From the Council of Tribur, c. 8.

Some have complained of some malefactors whose wickedness is so great that they do not heed the admonition of the priests, contemn the episcopal ban, disdain to come to the synod to which they have been summoned three or four times, and when they are finally excommunicated, they treat it as nothing. Concerning such persons, it is provided also in the Capitulary that they must be brought to the royal cognizance. And it pleased the devout King Arnulf, together with the holy Synod, that any of those who, after due excommunication, give such little weight to God and Christianity are to be pursued by the secular power and, if they are killed, they are to lie without composition.

c. 298. ON THE SAME MATTER.
From the Council at Soissons.

It was also granted by the most devout prince Charles that any of the incestuous and other lost ones who flee the examination of bishops are to be brought to their presence by the public judges, lest the failure to punish vices feed the enticement to sin.

c. 299. ON THE SAME MATTER.
From the Council at Lorris, in the country of Angers, in the year 844, sixth Indiction, in the month of October, c. 1.

If anyone is found to be a public prevaricator of the divine law, or a contemner of the just and reasonable ecclesiastical judgments for his manifest crimes, and an opponent of the constitutions of the holy Fathers, and if he has delayed obeying episcopal summons, he is to be anathematized.

c. 300. ON THE SAME MATTER.
From the same, c. 2.

If anyone is proven to have acted deceitfully, cunningly, and perniciously against the royal dignity, unless he has made the most condign satisfaction, he is to be anathematized.

c. 301. ON THE SAME MATTER.
From the same, c. 3.

Royal power, according to the Apostle, comes from no one else than God (cf. Rom. 13:1–6). If anyone, in a contumacious and puffed-up spirit, has presumed to oppose or resist it, and has been unwilling to obey its reasonable and just commands according to God and ecclesiastical authority and the civil law, let him be anathematized.

c. 302. ON THE SAME MATTER.
As above, c. 4.

Whosoever, burning with the fires of pride or vexed by their own impudence, have violated with their own hands those things which have been defined unanimously for the tranquility of Holy Mother Church and the priestly rigour, it pleases that they all be anathematized.

c. 303. IF A MAN IS ACCUSED AND HAS DENIED IT.
From the Council of Tribur.

A man who is noble or freeborn, if he is accused in synod and denies it, and if they know that he is faithful, is to purge himself by oath. But if he had been caught in theft or perjury, he is not to be admitted to the oath, but (like one who is not freeborn) he is to purge himself with boiling water and red-hot iron.

c. 304. THAT NO ONE USURP ANOTHER'S PARISH.
From the letter of Pope Callixtus.

No one is to usurp another's boundaries, nor presume to judge or excommunicate another's parishioner, because such a judgment or excommunication will not be approved, nor will it have any force, since no one will be bound or condemned by the sentence of any other judge than his own. No primate or metropolitan is to usurp a Church or parish of a diocesan bishop or presume to excommunicate or judge anyone from his parish without the counsel or judgment of the same bishop, but let him observe what has been established by the Apostles, the Fathers, and our predecessors and confirmed by us.

c. 305. ON THE SAME MATTER.
Also, from the same letter.

If any metropolitan bishop, except for what pertains to his own parish, has attempted to do anything elsewhere without the counsel and will of all the bishops in the same province, he shall be subject to the loss of his degree, and whatever he has done shall be held to be null and void.

c. 306. THAT NO ONE EXCOMMUNICATE ANOTHER'S PARISHIONER.
From the letter of Pope Zephyrinus.

No one is to be judged in absentia because human and divine laws forbid this. And the sentence pronounced by a judge not his own is not to be binding on any of them, that is, of the accused, because even the laws of the world instruct that this be done.

c. 307. ON THE SAME MATTER.
From the Theodosian law.

In the causes of private persons such a rule (*ratio*) is to be observed that no one be bound by the sentence of a judge other than his own.

c. 308. ON THE SAME MATTER.
From the same.

No one is to be heard at all who has wished to divide the bringing forward of his cause before two judges.

c. 309. ON THE SAME MATTER.
From the Capitularies.

That none of the bishops sever a sinning man from the Church and the Christian religion or communion until, in accordance with the evangelical precept, he has admonished the man to return to correction and penance. If the man has remained incorrigible, let the bishop make it known to the royal power, so that he may be constrained. If he is not corrected even in this way, then he is to be severed from ecclesiastical communion according to the canonical laws.

c. 310. ON THE SAME MATTER.
In the Synod of Meaux, c. 55.

That none of the bishops is to deprive anyone of ecclesiastical communion without a certain and manifest cause of sin. Without the consent of the archbishop and fellow bishops, he is not to impose any anathema even when an evangelical summons has been made, except where canonical authority instructs, because the anathema is an eternal condemnation of death, and must not be imposed except for a mortal crime, and on him who cannot otherwise be corrected.

C. 311. THAT A BISHOP NOT EXCOMMUNICATE ANYONE QUICKLY AND MOVED BY ANGER.

From the letter of Pope Evaristus.

Almighty God, in order to restrain us from the precipitous issuing of a sentence, even though all things are naked and open to his eyes, yet did not wish to punish the reported evils of Sodom before he had known manifestly the things that were reported. Hence, He says: "I shall go down and see whether they have indeed done the report that has reached me; whether or not it is so, so that I may know (Gen. 18:21)." By His example, we are admonished lest we be ever precipitous in issuing a sentence, or to judge in any way temerariously and without diligence what we have not in any way examined.

C. 312. ON THE SAME MATTER.

From the sayings of Gregory.

Blessed Job says: "The cause which I did not know, I investigated most diligently (Job 29:16)." Rulers of Churches, and those who pronounce public judgments, are to be especially careful that, in issuing sentences, they are not precipitous because of fickleness or anger. After having the causes diligently discussed, when the matter which was heretofore unknown has become fully clear, then the divine and human law is to be examined, and definitive sentence is to be pronounced in accordance with what is established in such law without acception of persons. That is why Moses always brought the complaints of the people to the Lord in the tabernacle, and he set out judgments in accordance with what the Lord commanded (Ex. 33:7–11), truly instructing us that we issue sentences of condemnation or justification not out of our own heart, but from the divine precept.

C. 313. ON THE SAME MATTER.

From the Theodosian law, bk. 2, c. 18.

When a judge has begun to hear a cause, he is to receive patiently the assertions or responses of the litigants, and he is to enquire into all things by a full examination. He is not to be willing to face the litigants with his sentence until all things have been carried out and the litigants have nothing else to propose for discussion or controversy. It is fitting there be frequent questioning lest anything remain unexamined.

c. 314. THAT NO ONE MAY FORGIVE THAT WHICH SOMEONE SINS AGAINST THE LORD.
From the sayings of St. Jerome.

It is to be noted that the Lord says: "If your brother has sinned against you (Mt. 18:15)." It is one thing to sin against us, another to sin against God. If someone has sinned against us, we have the power to forgive him. But if someone has sinned against God, it is not subject to our discretion. Indeed, it is written: "If man does wrong to man, God may be placated with regard to him; but if he has sinned against God, who shall pray for him (1 Sam. 2:25)?" We, on the contrary, are kind and merciful with regard to God's injury, and, as if it were in our power to decide God's will, with impunity we forgive an offense against God without a suitable punishment of penance. And yet, we do not suffer anything to pass without punishment that is done against us, were it only an injurious word lightly spoken. Let us then remit, for the sake of God, what is done against us; as for what is done against God, since, according to the constitution of the holy Fathers, we cannot remit it, let us punish it according to canonical authority.

HENCEFORTH ON PERJURY.

c. 315. FROM THE CAPITULARIES.

We have it written in God's law: "You shall not commit perjury in my name, nor defile the name of your God, nor take the name of your God in vain (Lev. 19:12; Ex. 20:7)." And so, all are to be admonished to guard diligently against perjury, not only at the altar and over the relics of the saints, but also in common speech. Also, beware lest anyone honour gold more than the altar, lest the Lord say to him: "Fool, which is greater, the gold, or the altar that sanctifies the gold (Mt. 23:17)?"

c. 316. ON THE SAME MATTER.
Also.

It also seems decent to us that he who dares to swear on holy things is to do it while fasting and with all honesty and fear of God, and that children, who have not reached the age of reason, not be compelled to swear. He who has once committed perjury is not afterwards to be a witness, nor assent to an oath, nor be an oath swearer in his own cause or another's.

c. 317. ON THE SAME MATTER.
From the Capitularies, bk. 3, c. 8.

That fidelity not be promised by oath to anyone other than ourselves and to each one's proper superior for that superior's utility and our own, except for those oaths which are justly owed by one to another according to law.

c. 318. ON THE SAME MATTER.
From the same, c. 10.

As to perjurers, that they are to be warned and not to be admitted to an oath as witnesses before they are examined. And if they cannot be examined otherwise, they are to be separated from each other and investigated severally, and it is not to be licit for the accuser alone to choose witnesses in the absence of the opposing party. And no one at all is to be admitted to the oath or as a witness, unless he is fasting. And they are to be chosen from the same district or nearby hundreds. And if anyone has been convicted of perjury, let him lose his hand or redeem it.

c. 319. ON THE SAME MATTER.
From the same, c. 58.

That the oaths which have been promised at the palace be performed in the palace. And if the men who are to swear have refused to come, they are to be compelled to come by the lord's command, or written order, or seal.

c. 320. ON THE SAME MATTER.
From bk. 4, c. 26.

Where it has been the custom anciently, and where the court is held, there the oaths are to be sworn.

c. 321. THAT A BISHOP NOT SWEAR ON SACRED OBJECTS.
From the Council of Meaux, c. 37.

That no bishop henceforth presume to swear on sacred objects, which the holy patriarchs asked for and did for the sake of the mystery. Indeed, faith is kept not in the doubt and malice of the one requiring such things, but in unfeigned charity. If anyone has presumed to transgress this with bold daring, in whatever way he may have been enticed, he shall be subject to the loss of his degree.

c. 322. ALSO, ON PERJURY.
From the same, c. 38.

That it is to be announced with greater care to all how detestable and hateful to God is the multiplicity of oaths and the confusion of perjuries by which many souls of the faithful are known to be lost in this whole kingdom. So great is this evil that, at the shrines of martyrs, where the illnesses of many are healed, there perjurers, even if they are not manifestly seen to be possessed, are seized by demons at God's just judgment. And as St. Gregory says: "To the bodies of these, the ill come and are cured, while perjurers come and are possessed by a demon."

c. 323. AT WHAT TIME OATHS ARE TO BE SWORN.
From the Council at Pîtres.

Together with the consent and counsel of our faithful subjects, we establish that, from the day on which an oath is accepted, after forty days and forty nights, that is, on the forty-second day or after six weeks, on the same weekday, the one who accepted that oath must swear lawfully in the established places. And if that day should fall within Lent, let no one presume to swear. And if anyone has presumed to do so, let him make composition for our ban and do penance for it according to the episcopal judgment. We instruct that Lent itself is to be kept from the beginning of the fast with the Wednesday included until Monday after the octave of Easter.

c. 324. THAT OATHS NOT BE SWORN ON THE WEDNESDAY BEFORE LENT.
From the Council at Saint-Médard.

That our envoys are to announce firmly to the counts and all ministers of the state by our word that from Wednesday before the beginning of Lent until after the octave of Easter they are not to presume to hold a public court, except as to concord and peace, nor is anyone to swear.

c. 325. ON THE SAME MATTER.
Also.

Likewise, they are to observe this also from the Wednesday before the Lord's Nativity until after the consecrated days, as also on the fasts of the Ember Days, and on the Rogation Days. Also, no one is to hold a plea or swear an oath on a Sunday.

c. 326. ON A CLERIC, IF HE HAS PERJURED HIMSELF.
From the Council of Orléans.

If any cleric has sworn an oath, and afterwards by the evidence of things it is detected that he perjured himself, he is to be punished with excommunication for a period of two years.

c. 327. ON THOSE WHO BIND THEMSELVES BY OATH NOT TO RETURN TO PEACE.
From the Council of Lérida.

He who has bound himself by oath not to return to peace in any way is to be severed from the communion of the body and blood of the Lord for one year for his perjury; he is to make satisfaction for his crime with alms and fasts. Let him hasten to come quickly to that charity, which covers a multitude of sins (1 Pt. 4:8).

c. 328. ALSO, ON PERJURY.

From the sayings of Jerome.

Herod promised with an oath that he would grant to the dancing girl whatever she would ask of him (cf. Mt. 14:1–12). If he says that he did it because of the oath he had sworn, would he have done it or not if she had asked him for the death of his father and mother? Hence, what he would have repudiated with regard to his own, he ought to have rejected also with regard to the prophet.

c. 329. ON THE SAME MATTER.

From the sayings of the priest Bede.

If perhaps it has happened that we have sworn something incautiously, whose observance might make for a worse outcome, we know that we ought to change it by a more salubrious counsel; if necessity presses, we ought rather to perjure ourselves than to fall into some graver crime for the sake of avoiding [a breach of] the oath.

c. 330. ON THE SAME MATTER.

From a Penitential.

Whoever knowingly commits perjury is to do penance for seven years, and afterwards he may receive communion.

c. 331. FROM A PENITENTIAL.

As above.

If anyone has perjured himself, he is no longer to be admitted to the oath.

c. 332. ON THE SAME MATTER.

From the same.

If someone suspects that he is being induced to commit perjury, and yet he consents to swear, he is to do penance for two years.

c. 333. ON THE SAME MATTER.

From the same.

If anyone has committed perjury out of greed, he is to sell all his possessions and distribute the income to the poor and, entering a monastery, he is to submit himself to the yoke of penance.

c. 334. ON THE SAME MATTER.
As above.

If anyone has committed perjury, laymen are to do penance for three years, clerics for five years, subdeacons for six, deacons for eight, priests for ten, bishops for twelve years.

c. 335. ON THE SAME MATTER.
From the same.

If one knowingly commits perjury under compulsion from his lord, he is to do penance for three forty-day fasts and the weekdays prescribed by law.

c. 336. ON THE SAME MATTER.
From the same.

One who perjures himself on a bishop's or priest's hand, or on a consecrated cross, is to do penance for three years

c. 337. ON THE SAME MATTER.
From the same.

But if he does so on an unconsecrated cross, he is to do penance for one year. If he does so on the hand of a man, among the Greeks, this is of no consequence. But he who has been misled and has perjured himself in ignorance, and afterwards comes to know it, let him do penance for three forty-day fasts.

c. 338. ON THE SAME MATTER.
From the same.

If anyone commits perjury under compulsion to redeem his own life, or for any other cause of necessity, he is to do penance for three forty-day fasts. But others judge that he ought to do penance for three years, one of which on bread and water.

c. 339. ON FALSE WITNESS.
From the Council of Orléans.

If any cleric has committed theft, or has given false testimony, since these are capital crimes, he is to be allowed communion, but to be demoted from his order.

c. 340. ON THE SAME MATTER.
From the Capitularies, bk. 4, c. 22.

If anyone has a dispute with another for any cause, and witnesses have been produced in judgment against him, if he suspects that they are false, it is to be licit for him to bring forward against them other and better witnesses whom he can. If the two parties so disagree among themselves that each is wholly unwilling to yield to the other, let two be chosen from among them to fight in the field with shields and clubs; and the right hand of the champion who is defeated is to be cut off because of the perjury. But the other false witnesses may redeem their hands; two parts of this are to be paid to the one who suffered calumny, the third part for a fine. And this in a secular cause. But in ecclesiastical ones, where it is a secular matter on one side and an ecclesiastical matter on the other side, the same mode is to be observed. But where it is an ecclesiastical matter on both sides, and the rectors are not able to make peace, their advocates are to pursue their causes in court before the count. But the witnesses must be from the same county.

c. 341. ON THE SAME MATTER.
As above, c. 32.

The best man in a district or city is to be taken as witness, and the one against whom he is to give testimony may not impute any crime to him.

c. 342. ON THE SAME MATTER.
From the same, c. 52

That witnesses be not led to give testimony by a bribe, and no one is to give testimony, except while he is fasting. And that witnesses, before they swear, be examined separately as to what they wish to say regarding the matter as to which they are to give testimony.

c. 343. ON THE SAME MATTER.
From the Capitularies, tit. 14.

Anyone who has been proven to have knowingly induced witnesses to commit perjury is to be brought to the palace with sureties, where we may consider with our faithful subjects what is to be done regarding such persons. But it shall fall to the bishops to deliberate regarding penance.

c. 344. ON THE SAME MATTER.
From the Council of Agde.

It pleased that those who have been convicted of having falsely charged their brothers with capital crimes are not to communicate until the end, unless they have repented with worthy satisfaction.

c. 345. ON THE SAME MATTER.
From the Council of Elvira.

If anyone has charged a bishop, priest, or deacon with false crimes, and has been unable to prove them, communion is not to be given to him even at the end.

c. 346. ON THE SAME MATTER.
From the Council of Seville.

If any cleric has been convicted of false witness, he is to be adjudged guilty of a capital crime.

c. 347. ON THE SAME MATTER.
From the Council of Agde.

That a bishop is to excommunicate the accusers of their brothers; if they emend this vice, he may receive them to communion, but not among the clergy.

c. 348. ON THE SAME MATTER.
From the Council of Elvira.

A false witness shall be kept away [from communion], as it is a crime. Yet, if the crime which he charged was not subject to the death penalty, and he has proven that he kept quiet for a long time, he is to be kept away for a period of two years. But if he did not prove it in an assembly of clerics, it pleased that he be kept away for five years.

c. 349. ON THE SAME MATTER.
From the Council of Agde.

False witnesses are to be removed from ecclesiastical communion, unless they have washed away the crimes they have committed by the satisfaction of penance.

c. 350. AS ABOVE.

False witnesses are to know that, if false witness were not a capital crime, the Lord in the Gospel would never have numbered it among the principal crimes. For he says: "From the heart proceed homicides, adulteries, thefts, false testimonies (Mt. 15:19)." And so, a false witness is to do penance and be excommunicated like an adulterer, or a thief, or a homicide.

c. 351. ON ONE WHO HAS STOLEN A MAN.
From the letter of Bishop Rabanus to the rural bishop Reginbaldus.

You asked first what is to be done concerning him who has solicited and stolen a Christian man and has brought him for sale to a pagan nation. At that time, I answered that such a man seemed to me to incur the crime of homicide upon himself. And afterwards, reading the divine law, I found in Deuteronomy (Deut. 19:21) that a homicide ought to render a soul for a soul, an eye for an eye, a tooth for a tooth, etc. And again: "If any man be found to have solicited his brother of the children of Israel, and to have sold him, taking a price, he is to be put to death (Deut.

24:7)." Hence, it appears to me that, just as an equal sentence is established in the divine law for the homicide and for the thief who sells a man, so also, by canonical authority, he is to be punished in an equal manner who sold his brother by stealing and soliciting as one who has unjustly killed his neighbour, that is, a Christian man.

C. 352. ON THE SAME MATTER.
From the Theodosian law, bk. 9.

Those who have thievingly abducted the children of others and transferred them elsewhere, whether they be freeborn or slave, are to be punished by death.

C. 353. ON THE SAME MATTER.
From the same.

It is fitting to observe diligently that it not be licit for any Jew to have a Christian slave, nor is he to presume to transfer him to his own law.

ON ENCHANTERS, MAGICIANS, AND SOOTHSAYERS.

C. 354. FROM THE COUNCIL OF ANCYRA.

Those who seek out divinations and follow them according to the custom of the gentiles, or introduce such men into their houses for the sake of obtaining or averting something by a malefic art, are to lie under the rule of five years, according to the defined degrees of penance.

C. 355. ON THE SAME MATTER.
From the Council of Braga.

If anyone, following the custom of the pagans, has introduced diviners and soothsayers into his house, as if to expel evil outside, or to discover enchantments, he is to do penance for five years.

C. 356. ON THE SAME MATTER.
From the decrees of Pope Gregory.

If anyone has paid heed to fortune-tellers, diviners, or enchanters, or has made use of phylacteries, let him be anathema.

C. 357. ON THE SAME MATTER.
From the Council of Carthage.

He who devotes himself to auguries and incantations is to be severed from the assembly of the Church. Similarly for him who adheres to Jewish superstitions and the observance of days.

c. 358. ON THE SAME MATTER.
Pope Gregory.

It has reached us that you have pursued some enchanters and soothsayers; know that your solicitude and zeal have been entirely welcome to us. And so, let it remain your effort to seek carefully and correct by strict punishment any such enemies of Christ whom you find.

c. 359. ON THE SAME MATTER.
From the Council of Toledo.

If any bishop, priest, or deacon, or anyone from a clerical order, has been found to consult magicians, diviners, fortune-tellers or soothsayers, or sorcerers, or those who profess any art of this kind, he is to be deposed from the honour of his dignity, receive the punishment of a monastery, and there give himself to perpetual penance, so that he may expiate the crime of sacrilege which he has committed.

c. 360. ON THE SAME MATTER.
From the Roman law.

Magicians, or enchanters, or the bringers of storms, or those who trouble the minds of men by the invocation of demons, are to be punished by every kind of punishment.

c. 361. ON THE SAME MATTER.
From the same.

He who, out of curiosity regarding future events, has consulted an invoker of demons, or the diviners they call fortune-tellers, or the haruspex who collects auguries, is to be punished capitally.

c. 362. ON THE SAME MATTER.
Also.

Those who have celebrated the night sacrifices of demons, or by incantations have invoked demons, are to be punished capitally.

c. 363. ON THE SAME MATTER.
From a Penitential.

Those who devote themselves to auguries or divinations are to do penance for five years. The bringers of storms are to do penance for seven years.

c. 364. ON THE SAME MATTER.

If a woman has done diabolical divinations or enchantments, she is to do penance for one year, or for three forty-day fasts, or for forty days, according to the quality of the wrong.

c. 365. ON THE SAME MATTER.
From the same.

Those who have paid heed to auguries, or those lots falsely called of the saints or divinations, or of any writings whatsoever, or have made or fulfilled vows to a tree, or to a stone, or to any thing whatever, except to the Church, are all to be excommunicated. If they come to penance, clerics are to do penance for three years, lay persons for a year and a half.

c. 366. AS ABOVE.
From the Council of Nantes.

Bishops and their ministers must struggle with the greatest effort to root out and burn those trees consecrated to demons which the people worship and hold in such great veneration, so that they dare to cut neither a branch nor a twig from them. Also, the stones which those deceived by the tricks of demons venerate in ruined and forested places, and at which they make and fulfil vows, are to be entirely dug up and cast into such places where they can never be venerated by their worshippers. And let it be announced to all how great a crime idolatry is, and he who venerates and worships such things, as if denying his God and renouncing Christianity, is to receive such a penance for this as if he had adored idols. And let it be forbidden to all to make a vow there, or to bring a candle or some other gift asking for their health anywhere other than in church to the Lord their God. For it is written: "Make your vows and render them to the Lord your God (Ps. 75:12)." We know how many things the Lord threatened through the prophets to his people of old, those who sacrificed in groves and made offerings in high places. If anyone has transgressed these things, he has lost his faith, and he is worse than an infidel. And so, he is to be cut off from the fellowship of Holy Church in every way and, unless he has repented worthily, he is not to be received.

c. 367. ON THE SAME MATTER.
Rabanus.

As to those who sacrifice to demons, we have the constitutions of Bishop Theodore in which it is written: "Those who make offerings to demons to the least degree are to do penance for a year; those who sacrifice to a great degree are to do penance for ten years."

c. 368. ON THE SAME MATTER.
From the same.

If any woman places her child on the roof, or in the oven, for the healing of fevers, she is to do penance for seven years. He who causes grains to burn where a man has died for the health of the living and of the house is to do penance for five years.

C. 369. ON MENSTRUAL BLOOD.
Rabanus to Heribaldus.

As to those regarding whom you questioned us – that is, the woman who mixed her menstrual blood with food or drink and gave it to her husband to eat, or the one who drank her husband's semen in a drink, or her who burned a man's skull with fire and gave it to her husband for him to avoid illness – with what penance they are to be punished, as it seems to us, they are to be punished with the same sentence as magicians and fortune-tellers who are known to have practiced the magical art.

C. 370. ON THE SAME MATTER.
From the Council of Ancyra.

A woman, if she has fornicated with another woman, is to do penance for three years. That woman is to do a similar penance who mixes her husband's semen into his food so that he may love her more.

C. 371. ON THE WOMEN WHO SAY THAT THEY GO RIDING WITH DEMONS AT NIGHTTIME.
As above.

Bishops and the ministers of bishops must strive with all their might to entirely uproot from their parishes the pernicious magical art of soothsaying invented by the devil; if they have found any man or woman who adheres to this kind of crime, they are to cast such a shamefully dishonoured person from their parishes. For the Apostle says: "A man who is a heretic, after the first and second admonition, avoid, knowing that such a one is subverted (Tit. 3:10–11)." They are subverted and held captive by the devil who, after abandoning their Creator, seek the devil's aids. And so Holy Church must be cleansed of such a plague. It is also not to be passed over that some wicked women, having turned back toward Satan and seduced by the illusions and phantasms of the demons, believe and profess that, at nighttime, they ride about on some beasts with Diana, the goddess of the pagans, and a numberless multitude of other women, and that they cross the distance of many lands in the silence of the dead of night, and that they obey her commands as their mistress, and that they are called to her service on certain nights. If only these women had perished alone in their perfidy and not drawn many with them to the destruction of infidelity! Indeed, a numberless multitude, deceived by this false opinion, believe these things to be true and, so believing, turn away from right faith and fall back into the error of the pagans, as they adjudge that something of divinity or sacredness exists apart from the one God. For this reason, priests throughout the churches entrusted to them must preach with all zeal to the people so that they may know these things to be entirely false and that it is not from a divine spirit, but from a malignant one, that such phantasms are imposed on the minds of infidels. Indeed, Satan himself, who transfigures himself into an angel of light (2 Cor. 11:14), when he has seized the mind of some little woman and made her subject to himself through infidelity and unbelief, transforms himself on the spot into the appearance and likenesses of diverse persons; in dreams, he deludes the mind which he holds captive, showing now happy events, now sad ones, now known persons, now unknown ones, and leads it through devious ways. Even though her spirit alone experiences this, the faithless mind imagines that these things happen not in the spirit, but in the body. Indeed, who is not led outside himself in dreams and night visions, and sees many things in sleep which he had never seen while awake? Who is so dull and foolish as to think that these things, which happen in spirit alone, happen also in the body when the Prophet Ezekiel saw visions of the Lord in spirit, and not in the body? And the Apostle John saw and heard the signs of the Apocalypse in spirit, not in the body, as he himself says: "And immediately I was in the spirit (Apoc. 4:2)." And Paul does not dare to say that he was caught up in the body (2 Cor. 12:1–6). And so, it is to be publicly announced to all that he who believes these and similar things has lost his faith, and he who does not have right faith in God belongs not to God, but to the one in whom he believes, that is, to the devil. Indeed, of our Lord, it is written: "All things were made through Him (Jn. 1:3)." Therefore, anyone who believes that anything can be made, or any creature be changed for the better or the worse, or be transformed into another species or likeness, by anyone other than the Creator who has made all things and through whom all things are made, is undoubtedly an infidel.

c. 372. ON THE OBSERVANCE OF MONTHS AND DAYS.
From the sayings of Ambrose.

The Apostle says: "You observe days and months, times and years. I fear that I laboured in vain among you (Gal. 4:10–11)." They observe days who say, for example, that tomorrow is not good for travel, that something must not be begun after tomorrow, and so they are often greatly deceived. They venerate the months who consider carefully the course of the moon, saying: Tools are not to be made on the seventh day of the new moon; it is not fitting to bring a purchased slave home on the ninth day of the new moon. And by these things, adversities tend to occur more easily. They observe the times who say: Today is the beginning of spring, and so it is a holiday. The day after tomorrow is the feast of Vulcan. And again: It is unlucky, and it is not licit to go into the house. They observe the years when they say that a new year begins on the Kalends of January, as if the years were not completed each day. This superstition must be far from God's servants.

c. 373. ON THE SAME MATTER.
From the Council of Braga.

It is not licit for Christians to observe the traditions of the gentiles, and to observe or venerate the elements, or the course of the moon or stars, or to consider the vain deceit of signs for the building of a house, for the planting of crops or trees, or for the joining of marriages. For it is written: "All whatsoever you do in word or in work, do all in the name of the Lord Jesus Christ, giving thanks to God (Col. 3:17)."

c. 374. ON THE GATHERING OF HERBS.
From the same.

It is not licit to keep some observances and incantations in the gathering of medicinal herbs, unless only with the divine Creed, or the Lord's Prayer, so that God and our Lord be honoured.

c. 375. ON WOMEN'S WOOL-WORKING.
From the same.

It is not licit for Christian women to observe vanities in their wool-working, but let them invoke God as their helper, who granted to them the wisdom of weaving.

c. 376. ON DEAD ANIMALS.
From a Penitential.

He who eats unclean flesh, or the meat of dead animals or of animals torn by beasts, is to do penance for forty days; if someone eats by the necessity of hunger, he is to do a much lighter penance. He who knowingly eats what has been obtained by fraud, rapine, or theft, if he is poor, is to do penance for seven days; if powerful, for forty days. As for the infirm, if knowingly, they are to do penance for fifteen days. He who eats and drinks something contaminated by a domestic animal, that is, by a dog or a cat, is to do penance for two days.

c. 377. ON A LIQUID.
From the same.

He who has given to another a liquid in which a mouse or weasel was found dead, if he is a layman, is to do penance for seven days. But if they are in a monastery, let him sing 200 psalms. He who comes to know afterwards that he drank such a drink is to sing the psalter.

c. 378. ON BLOOD.

If anyone has eaten the blood of any animal, he is to do penance for forty days.

c. 379. ALSO, THAT NO ONE IS TO EAT BLOOD.

The faithful are to be admonished that no one presume to eat blood. For we read that, in the beginning, when license to eat meat was given to man by God, the blood was forbidden. Indeed, the Lord says to Noah and his sons: "Everything that moves and lives shall be food for you, saving that flesh with blood you shall not eat. For I will require the blood of your lives at the hand of every beast, and at the hand of man (cf. Gen. 9:3–5)." Which is not only forbidden very often in the old Law, but also in the New Testament, as the Apostles write with great deliberation to the primitive Church of the gentiles to abstain themselves from the contaminations of idols, fornication, things strangled, and from blood (Act. 15:20). Expounding this, Jerome says: "And according to the letter, these precepts are suitable for every Christian, that he not eat a dead animal, whether birds or cattle, whose blood has never been spilled." A letter sent by the Apostles from Jerusalem admonishes that these things are to be necessarily observed (Act. 15:29). So also what is caught by a beast, because it is similarly suffocated. And from blood, that is, it is not to be eaten with its blood. If these things, then, were written as sufficient for salvation to those coming from the life of gentiles for the rudiments of faith and in view of the inveterate custom of paganism, what transgressor will slight them? At the same time, this too is to be considered, that what is strangled and blood are compared to idolatry and fornication. Hence, let it be announced to all how wicked a deed it is to eat blood, since it is compared to idols and fornication. If anyone has violated these precepts of the Lord and of the Apostles, he is to be suspended from ecclesiastical communion until he repents worthily.

c. 380. ON THOSE IN DISCORD.
From the Council of Carthage.

The offerings of brothers who are at variance are to be received neither in the sacristy, nor in the treasury.

c. 381. ON THE SAME MATTER.
From the Council of Agde.

It has also pleased that (as often happens) those who have been in discord because of hate or long dispute among themselves, and have not been able to be called back to peace because of long-standing obstinacy, be expelled from the Church's assembly by a most just excommunication.

c. 382. ON THE SAME MATTER.
From the sayings of Isidore.

If anyone is quarrelsome and litigious, and disagreeable because of hate, until he return to concord, he is to be alien from the assembly and fellowship of the Church, as the canons command.

c. 383. ON THE SAME MATTER.

If anyone who holds someone else in hate is not willing to return to peace, as the holy Fathers established, he is to be excommunicated at bread and water and to be severed from the Church.

c. 384. ON THE SAME MATTER.
From the Council of Carthage.

If not the fear of God, then let the Synod reconcile bishops who disagree.

c. 385. ON THE SAME MATTER.
From the same.

The bishop is to see to it that he exhort brethren who are at variance, whether they are clerics or laymen, to peace rather than to judgment.

c. 386. ON THE JUDGMENT OF GOD.

If anyone eats, or drinks, or carries something on his person by which he thinks that he can pervert God's judgment, and this has been proved, he is to be struck down with the same sentence as are magicians, fortune-tellers, and enchanters, that is, he is to be punished with a penance of seven or five years.

c. 387. ON THE OFFERINGS OF THE DECEASED.
From the Council of Vaison.

Those who retain the offerings of the deceased and delay in giving them to the churches are to be cast out from the Church as faithless people.

c. 388. ON THE SAME MATTER.
From the same.

If any persons steal the offerings of others, they are to be admonished to restore what they have taken fraudulently. But if they are unwilling to return them, until they do so, as the holy Synod has established, they are to be severed from the fellowship of the Church.

c. 389. ON THE SAME MATTER.
From the Council of Agde.

Clerics or secular persons, who have presumed to retain their parents' offerings, donations, or testamentary bequests, or who have believed that they ought to take away what they themselves have donated to churches or monasteries, are to be excluded from churches as killers of the poor, until they make restitution.

c. 390. ON COMMUNION.
From the same.

If any cleric has wilfully caused harm to a church, he is to make restitution from his own resources and be deprived of communion. If anyone has sung diabolical verses over the dead at nighttime, etc. (Seek it in the first booklet, c. 398.)

c. 391. THAT THE PRINCIPAL FESTIVITIES BE CELEBRATED IN THE CITIES.
From the Council of Agde.

Seculars who do not communicate at the Lord's Nativity, Easter, and Pentecost are not to be believed to be Catholics, nor to be received among Catholics. (Seek it in the first booklet, c. 195.)

c. 392. ON THE SAME MATTER.
From the Council of Orléans.

That it is not licit for any of the citizens to celebrate in the countryside the solemnities of Easter, the Lord's Nativity, or Pentecost, unless illness is proved to have prevented him.

c. 393. ON THE SAME MATTER.
From the Council of Elvira.

If anyone who dwells in the city has not come to church for three Sundays, he is to be excommunicated until he appears to be corrected.

c. 394. ON THE SAME MATTER.
From the Council of Agde.

That citizens who, at the feasts of Easter, the Lord's Nativity, or Pentecost, have neglected to be present in their cities with the bishops for the sake of receiving communion or the blessing, those who have neglected this are to be deprived of communion for three years.

c. 395. ON THE TITHINGMEN TO BE SENT THROUGH THE PARISHES.
From the Council of Rouen.

That the people be admonished in every way to come to vespers, night vigils, and mass on Sundays and feast-days; and that in cities and settlements truthful and God-fearing men are to be established as tithingmen who may admonish the idle and the negligent to hasten to God's service without delay; and that the same tithingmen are to be bound by oath that, for no intervening cause, namely, of love, fear, or kinship, or reward, will they remain silent regarding the negligent and the transgressors, or fail to make manifest their faults to their priests. It will pertain to the priests, with divine zeal and love, so to correct their vices with due discipline as they do not wish to receive a sentence of just condemnation for the errors of others. And feast-days are to be celebrated with due honour and without servile work from vespers to vespers.

c. 396. ON THE EXCOMMUNICATE.
From the sayings of Cassian.

If anyone has been suspended from prayer for his own fault, no one is to have license to pray or speak with him before he is reconciled. Indeed, anyone who has presumed with inconsiderate pity to join with him in prayer and speech before he is received by the superior incurs the same condemnation.

c. 397. ON THE SAME MATTER.
Also, Isidore.

It is not licit for anyone to pray, or to speak, or to eat with an excommunicate.

c. 398. AS ABOVE.

If any brother, openly or hiddenly, has spoken with an excommunicate, he immediately contracts with him the shared penalty of excommunication.

c. 399. ON THE SAME MATTER.
From the sayings of Bishop Fructuosus.

No one is to speak with an excommunicate, neither to encourage him by any compassion or commiseration, nor to presume to support him to contradiction or pride.

c. 400. ON THE SAME MATTER.
From the Rule of St. Benedict.

If anyone in any manner has associated with an excommunicated brother, or has sent him a message, let him incur a similar punishment of excommunication.

c. 401. ON THE SAME MATTER.
Also.

But that brother who is guilty of a weightier fault is to be suspended both from the table and from the oratory. Let no one associate with him in fellowship or in speech.

c. 402. ON THE SAME MATTER.
From the Council of Antioch.

It is not licit to communicate with excommunicates, nor with those who meet in houses, avoiding the prayers in church; we are to pray together. If any member of the clergy has been caught communicating with excommunicates, even he is to be deprived of communion.

c. 403. ON THE SAME MATTER.
From the Canons of the Apostles.

If anyone has prayed with an excommunicate, even within a house, he is to be deprived of communion.

c. 404. ON THE SAME MATTER.
From the Council of Nicaea.

As to those who are deprived by bishops of communion, whether from the clergy, or from the order of the laity, let the regular provision obtain that persons who are cast out not be received by others. And yet inquiry should be made lest the person be seen to have been excluded from communion from pusillanimity, or contentiousness, or any other flaw on the bishop's part.

c. 405. ON THE SAME MATTER.
From the Council of Antioch.

If anyone has been deprived of communion by his own bishop, he is not to be received by other bishops before he is reconciled with his own bishop.

c. 406. ON THE SAME MATTER.
From the Canon of the Apostles.

If anyone has prayed together with a condemned cleric as if with a cleric, he is to be condemned.

c. 407. ON THOSE CONDEMNED BY A SYNOD.
From the Council of Antioch.

If any bishop who has been condemned by a synod, or a priest or deacon by his bishop, shall have dared to carry out any part of the ministry, it is not to be licit for them in any way to have hope of restoration in another synod, or opportunity of making satisfaction.

C. 408. ON THE SAME MATTER.
From the Council of Carthage.

Also, it has pleased the whole Council that, if he who has been excommunicated for his own negligence, whether he is a bishop or a cleric, has presumed to communicate in the time of his excommunication and before a hearing, he is to be adjudged to have pronounced a sentence of condemnation against himself.

C. 409. IF A BISHOP WISHES TO BANISH A CLERIC FROM THE CHURCH.
From the Council of Sardica.

If a bishop wishes to banish a cleric of his from the Church, provision is to be made that an innocent person is not condemned, and so he is to have the power to appeal to neighbouring bishops, and his cause is to be heard and treated diligently, because it is not fitting that audience be denied to one who asks for it. Let the bishop bear it patiently that his sentence be either approved or emended.

C. 410. AS ABOVE.
In the Canons of the Apostles.

If any bishop, priest, or deacon justly deposed for certain crimes has dared to exercise the ministry formerly committed to him, such a one is to be wholly cut off from the Church.

C. 411. ON AN ACCUSED PRIEST.
From the Council of Rouen.

That no bishop remove an accused priest from the office of mass, unless he has failed to come to state his case, after being summoned by letter, on the appointed day, that is, within the space of a month. And if he has not come after a second month, then he is to be suspended from the office, until he gives an account of himself. Indeed, if laymen are not excommunicated canonically, unless they have been summoned and admonished three times, it seems unworthy that priests, who are of greater order and dignity, be denied what the ecclesiastical rule indulgently allows to laymen. Indeed, the removal of a priest from office is to be held equivalent to the cessation from the Church's communion for a layman, for priests are removed from the service of the altar for the same reasons for which laymen are excommunicated. (See c. 290.)

C. 412. HOW A BISHOP IS TO EXCOMMUNICATE THE FAITHLESS.
As above.

A bishop, when he has decided to excommunicate or anathematize some faithless person for certain and manifest crimes, after the reading of the Gospel, is to address clergy and people as follows.

ALLOCUTION.

Your Charity knows, my brethren, that a certain man named N., at the persuasion of the devil, has set aside the Christian promise which he made at his baptism, has turned toward Satan in apostasy, whom he had renounced and all his works, and does not fear to waste and plunder the Lord's vineyard, that is, his Church, and oppresses violently and kills the poor of Christ, whom He redeemed with His precious blood, and steals their goods. Whence, because he ought to have been a son of this Church of ours (over which, by God's authority, we preside), because he was reborn in it by water and the Holy Spirit, and he was numbered among the adoptive sons of God, though now, by imitating the devil, he has become a son of the devil, we were concerned lest, by our pastoral negligence, any of the sheep entrusted to us perish, for which we would be compelled to give an account at the fearful Judgment before the prince of shepherds, our Lord Jesus Christ, as he himself threatens us terrifyingly, saying: "If you have not denounced his iniquity to the wicked man, I will require his blood from your hand (cf. Ez. 3:18)." And so, we sent to him our priest and letters of admonition, once, twice, and a third time, inviting him canonically to emendation and satisfaction and penance, correcting him with paternal affection. But he (what sorrow to say it!), as the devil hardens his heart, spurned our salutary admonitions; persevering in the malice in which he had begun and puffed up in a spirit of pride, he disdains to make satisfaction to the Church of God, which he has harmed. Regarding such transgressors and violators of the holy religion and peace which Christ gave and left to his disciples, we have precepts from the Lord and the Apostles by which we are instructed as to what we must do as to prevaricators of this sort. For the Lord says in the Gospel: "If your brother has sinned against you, correct him (cf. Mt. 18:15)." Brothers, whoever sins against Holy Church sins against each of us. Indeed, if Holy Church is one body, and the head of this body is Christ, each of us is a member one of the other. And when one member suffers, all members suffer with him (cf. 1 Cor. 12:16); undoubtedly he sins against us who harms our members. Hence, the Lord commands that a brother, that is, a Christian, who sins against us is first to be corrected privately, then to be reproved before witnesses; finally, he is to be summoned publicly before the assembly of the Church. If he contemns these three admonitions and pious corrections and despises to make satisfaction, then, [the Lord] says, "Hereafter let him be to you as a heathen," that is, as a gentile and a pagan, so that he is no longer treated as a Christian, but as a pagan (cf. Mt. 18:15–17). And in another place, regarding a member that has become separated from the body and severed from the bond of charity and scandalizes the whole body, the Lord commands that it be cut off and cast out, saying: "If your eye, or hand, or foot scandalizes you, tear it out and cast it away from you (Mt. 18:8)." And the Apostle says: "Remove the evildoer from your midst (1 Cor. 5:13)." And again: "If the unbeliever departs, let him depart (1 Cor. 7:15)." And in another place, he excludes the grasping from the kingdom of God, saying: "Nor extortioners shall possess the kingdom of God (1 Cor. 6:10)." And elsewhere: "If anyone who is named a brother and is a fornicator, or an adulterer, or a homicide, or an extortioner, you must not even eat with him (cf. 1 Cor. 5:11)." And John, the most beloved disciple of Christ, forbids that such a nefarious man be even greeted, saying: "Neither say hail to him, nor receive him into your house. Indeed, one who says hail to him shares in his wicked works (cf. 2 Jn. 1:10–11)." And so, in fulfilment of the precepts of the Lord and the Apostles, let us with the sword of excommunication cut off from the body of the Church the putrid member that cannot be healed and does not respond to medicine, lest the other members of the body be infected by such a pestiferous illness as by a poison.

c. 413. EXCOMMUNICATION.

Hence, because he has contemned our admonitions and repeated exhortations; because he has despised to come to emendation and penance after being summoned three times in accordance with the Lord's precept; because he has not yet acknowledged nor confessed his guilt, nor sent a representative to us, who are examining his cause (since he is our parishioner), asking for forgiveness; because he perseveres in the malice in which he had begun with the devil hardening his heart, and in accordance with what the Apostle says: According to his hardness and impenitent heart he stores up wrath for himself on the day of wrath (cf. Rom. 2:5), therefore, by the judgment of almighty God, Father, Son, and Holy Spirit, and of Blessed Peter, prince of the Apostles, and of all the saints, as also by our own humble authority, and by the power conferred on us by God of binding and loosing in heaven and on earth, we sever him with all his accomplices, partners and supporters from the reception of the precious body and blood of the Lord and from the fellowship of all Christians, and we exclude him from the bounds of Holy Mother Church in heaven and on earth, and we decree him to be excommunicate and anathematized, and we judge him to have been condemned with the devil and his angels and all reprobates in the eternal fire, unless perhaps he frees himself from the snares of the devil and returns to emendation and penance, and makes satisfaction to the Church of God, which he has harmed. And let all answer a third time, "Amen," or, "So be it," or "Let him be anathema."

Twelve priests are to surround the bishop, and to hold burning candles in their hands, which, at the conclusion of the anathema or excommunication, they are to cast on the ground and trample under their feet. After these things, the bishop is to explain the excommunication in common words to the people so that all may understand how terribly damned he is, and that they may know that from that hour forward he is not to be treated as a Christian, but as a pagan, and that anyone who communicates with him as if he were a Christian, or has eaten or drunk with him, or has kissed him, or has spoken familiarly with him, unless perhaps to encourage him to return to satisfaction and penance, is undoubtedly similarly excommunicated. Afterwards, letters are to be sent to priests throughout the parishes, containing the mode of excommunication. In them, it is to be commanded that, on all Sundays after the reading of the Gospel, they announce publicly the same excommunication to the people entrusted to them, lest anyone communicate with the excommunicate out of ignorance. It is fitting, too, that the same excommunication be made known to other bishops. Indeed, the Council of Toledo instructs that writings circulate among all the bishops of the province whomsoever they can reach so that he is heard to be excommunicated. The excommunication must also be made known to his superior.

C. 414. ALSO, ANOTHER ALLOCUTION OF EXCOMMUNICATION.

You have heard, most beloved, how many and how horrible deeds of depravity and iniquity that man has not feared to perpetrate at the instigation of the devil, and how, by apostasy and with a profane mind, he has withdrawn from the worship of the whole Christian religion. You have heard how he was summoned canonically to make satisfaction, but he delayed coming, and how frequently he was admonished to free himself from the snares of the devil, by which he was held bound, but, hardening the ears of his heart, he contemned to hear our most salutary admonitions. Regarding such a contumacious brother, who refuses to accept ecclesiastical correction, the Lord says in the Gospel: "If he will not listen to the Church, let him be to you as a heathen and a publican (Mt. 18:17)," that is, he is no longer to be counted among the Christians, but among the pagans. Hence, Paul, following the teaching of his Master, reproves the Corinthians because they had communion with the criminous and the wicked, and he says: "And you are puffed up and have not rather mourned: that he might be taken away from among you (1 Cor. 5:2)," that is, that a man who committed such a crime be separated from your fellowship. And he adds: "For I myself, though absent in body, but present in spirit, have already passed judgment, as if present, on the man who has acted thus, in the name of our Lord Jesus Christ, you being gathered together and with my spirit, by the power of my Lord Jesus: to hand over such a person to Satan, for the destruction of the flesh (1 Cor. 5:3–5)." And after a few words: "I wrote to you not to keep company with fornicators (1 Cor. 5:9)." And he adds immediately: "If anyone who is named a brother," that is, a Christian, "is a fornicator, or an extortioner, you must not even eat with him (cf. 1 Cor. 5:11)." And elsewhere: "Remove the evildoer from your midst (1 Cor. 5:13)." And: "If the unbeliever departs, let him depart (1 Cor. 7:15)." For one ill sheep contaminates the whole flock, and a little yeast corrupts the whole dough (Gal. 5:9), and often one putrid member infects the whole body. And so, let such a pernicious plague be removed by its roots from the body of the Church.

c. 415. EXCOMMUNICATION.

Instructed by the precepts of the Lord and the Apostles, by the judgment of God the Father, and of his Son, our Lord Jesus Christ, and of the Holy Spirit, and in virtue of the authority and power granted by God to the Apostles and to the successors of the Apostles, together with you, we exclude the said very bad man from the bounds of Holy Mother Church, and we sever him from all Christian fellowship and communion, and we decree him to be severed for all eternity, that is, in the present world and in the future one. No Christian is to greet him or presume to kiss him. No priest is to dare to say mass with him, or to give to him the most holy body and blood of the Lord. No one is to join with him in any partnership or business. And if anyone has associated himself with or participated in his malignant works, he is to know that he is struck by a similar anathema, except for those who join with him in order to call him back from error and call him to satisfaction, unless perhaps he has reconsidered and, by the inspiration of God's grace, he has turned to the remedy of penance and, by a worthy emendation, has made humble satisfaction to God's Church, which he has harmed.

c. 416. ALSO, ANOTHER AND MORE FEARFUL EXCOMMUNICATION.

Following the canonical institutes and the examples of the holy Fathers, in the name of the Father and the Son and by the power of the Holy Spirit, as also by the authority conferred on bishops through Peter, prince of the Apostles, we sever from the womb of Holy Mother Church and condemn by the anathema of perpetual curse, violators of God's churches, namely thieves, brigands, and homicides. May they be cursed in the city and cursed in the country. May their barn be cursed, and their remains be cursed, and the fruit of their womb be cursed, and the fruit of their land be cursed. May they be cursed as they go out, and cursed as they come in. May they be cursed in the house and fugitives in the field. May all those curses come over them which the Lord threatened through Moses to send over the people that transgressed against the divine law. May they be anathema maranatha, that is, may they perish at the second coming of the Lord. No Christian is to greet them. No priest is to presume to celebrate mass or to give holy communion to them. Let them be buried with a donkey's burial (cf. Jer. 22:19), and may they be on a dung-heap on the surface of the earth. And just as these candles are cast out of our hands and extinguished today, so may their light be extinguished for all eternity, unless perhaps they reconsider and make satisfaction by emendation and worthy penance to God's Church, which they have harmed.

C. 417. BRIEF EXCOMMUNICATION.

Following the canonical institutes and the examples of the holy Fathers, by the authority of God and the judgment of the Holy Spirit, we cast those violators of God's churches out of the bosom of Holy Mother Church and the fellowship of all Christianity, until they reconsider and make satisfaction to God's Church.

C. 418. HOW A BISHOP MAY RECONCILE OR RECEIVE AN EXCOMMUNICATE.

When someone who has been excommunicated or anathematized, led by repentance, seeks forgiveness, and promises correction, the bishop who excommunicated him is to come before the doors of the church, and twelve priests with him, who are to stand around him on both sides. Those to whom injury or harm was done are also to be present. There, according to human and divine laws, it is fitting that the harm done be remedied or, if it has already been remedied, this is to be proved by their testimony. Then the bishop is to ask whether he is willing to accept penance in accordance with what the canons prescribe for the wrongs committed. And if he prostrates himself on the ground, seeks forgiveness, confesses his guilt, implores penance, and promises precautions as to the future, then the bishop, taking him by the right hand, is to bring him into the church and restore him to Christian communion and fellowship. After these things, let the bishop enjoin penance on him according to the manner of his guilt, and send letters throughout his parish so that all may know that he has been received into Christian fellowship. Let him also make this known to all the other bishops. But no bishop is to presume to excommunicate or reconcile another's parishioner without the knowledge or consent of the proper bishop.

c. 419. ON ONE WHO DISHONOURS HIS FATHER OR MOTHER.
From the Council of Rouen.

If anyone strikes his father or mother, or curses them, since he has committed capital crimes, he is to do public penance for them as for graver sins. Indeed, the Lord says: "He that curses his father, or mother, shall die the death (Ex. 21:17)." Indeed, one whom the Lord adjudges to be worthy of death must undoubtedly be held to be a homicide and must do penance as a homicide.

c. 420. ON OXHERDS AND SWINEHERDS.
As above.

Priests must admonish the people subject to them that, at least on Sundays and other feast-days, they make or allow to come to mass the oxherds, swineherds, or other shepherds who remain continuously in the fields, or in the woods, and so live in the fashion of beasts, for Christ redeemed even these by his precious blood. If they neglect to do this, without doubt let them know that they will have to render an account for their souls. For the Lord, at his coming into this world, did not choose orators and the nobler sort, but recruited fishermen and the unlettered as his disciples, so that he might show in deed what he himself affirms in the Gospel with his words, when he says: "What is highly esteemed among men is an abomination in God's sight (Lk. 16:15)." And without violation of deeper understanding, the birth of our Redeemer was announced by an angel to shepherds first of all.

c. 421. WHAT PRIESTS MUST DO ON SUNDAYS.
From the Council of Nantes.

That on Sundays and feast-days, the priests, before they celebrate mass, are to question the people whether another's parishioner is in the church who, contemning his own priest, wishes to hear mass there. If they have found any such, they are to cast him out of the church immediately and compel him to return to his own parish. Similarly, let them ask whether there are any persons feuding who have an implacable dispute between them; if any are found, let them be reconciled immediately. If they are unwilling to accept peace, they are to be cast out of the church until they return to charity. Indeed, we cannot offer a gift or offering at the altar, unless first we are reconciled with our brother. When these things have been done, the priests may properly carry out the solemnities of mass.

C. 422. ON ONE WHO REMAINS SILENT AS TO HIS BROTHER'S SIN.
From a Penitential.

He who has been silent about a sin of his brother which is unto death and has not corrected him, or reported it to God's Church so that he might be corrected, is to do penance for as long as he consented.

As regards confession, penance, tithes, drunkenness, and vomiting after the Eucharist, it has been stated in the first booklet above.

C. 423. ON THE POOR, HOW THEY ARE TO BE FED.
From the Council of Tours.

That each city is to feed its poor and needy with suitable food according to its ability, and both the neighbouring priests and the citizens are each to nourish their poor; this is to be done so that the poor themselves do not wander through other cities.

C. 424. ON THE SAME MATTER.
From the Capitularies, bk. 1, c. 118.

As for the mendicants who course through our fatherlands, we will that each of our faithful subjects nourish his poor from his benefice or his household, and not allow the poor to go begging elsewhere. And where such are found who can work with their hands and do not do so, no one is to presume to give anything to them.

C. 425. OF ONE WHO GIVES SLIGHT WEIGHT TO THE BAN OF THE BISHOP OR PRIEST.

Whoever in his pride has given slight weight to the ban or excommunication of his bishop or priest, such a one is to be entirely uprooted from the Church. For the Lord says to Moses: "The soul that transgresses the Lord's mandate through pride shall perish from among his people (Num. 15:30)." Hence, the Lord in the Gospel: "He that despises you despises me (Lk. 10:16)." And Moses says to the contumacious: "Your murmuring is not against me, but against the Lord (Ex. 16:8)." And Dathan and Abiron were swallowed up alive because they rose up against the same Moses and spurned his mandate (cf. Num. 16). And so, such a wrong is to be punished most gravely.

C. 426. ON A PRIEST WHO HAS BEEN DEMOTED.
From the Capitularies, tit. 10.

If any priest has been demoted by his bishop, or has been suspended from office for certain crimes, and he, through contempt and pride, has presumed to carry out anything of the ministry forbidden to him, and has perdured in his initial presumption after being corrected by his bishop, then he is to be excommunicated in every way and to be expelled from the Church. Whoever shall have knowingly communicated with him is to know that he is similarly excommunicated. It is to be observed similarly concerning all excommunicated clerics, laymen and women. If anyone should contemn all these things, and the bishop is unable to correct him, he is to be condemned to exile by the king's judgment.

c. 427. THAT NO ONE DENY HOSPITALITY TO A TRAVELLER.
From the Council at the palace of Verneuil.

It has pleased us and our faithful subjects that priests admonish their parishioners to be hospitable and to deny a place of rest to no traveller. And in order that all occasion for robbery be taken away, they are not to sell anything dearer to travellers than they could sell it for at the market. If they wish to sell it dearer, let the travellers report this to the priest and, at his command, let them sell to travellers with humanity.

c. 428. ON THE SAME MATTER.
From the same Capitulary.

That all occasion for robbery may be taken away, we will that priests, who must extend a good example of charity to all, be hospitable, in accordance with the precept of the Lord and the Apostles and show humanity to travellers, because some people so pleased God through their hospitality that they received angels as guests. And on the day of Judgment, the Lord will say to his chosen ones: "I was a stranger, and you received me (Mt. 25:35)." And Job says: "My door was always open to the traveller (Job 31:32)."

c. 429. ON ONE WHO DISHONOURS A PRIEST.
As above.

If anyone dishonours his priest, insulting him by word or deed, he is to be kept away from the bounds of the Church until he makes satisfaction by worthy penance. For the Apostle says: "Let priests who rule well be deemed worthy of double honour (1 Tim. 5:17)." Also, he says elsewhere: "Obey those who have charge of you, and be subject to them (Heb. 13:17)," etc.

c. 430. ON GODFATHERS OR GODSONS.
From the Capitularies, bk. 2.

We command that each godfather or all kin instruct their spiritual children in a Catholic manner.

c. 431. ON THE SAME MATTER.
From the same, c. 44.

That parents instruct their children most diligently, and the godparents do so with those whom they receive from the font, the former because they generated them and they were given to them by God, and the latter because they stood surety for them.

c. 432. IF ANYONE OPPOSES A BISHOP AS TO THE FLOGGING OF SLAVES WITH RODS FOR CRIMES.
From the Council at Saint-Médard.

That our envoys announce to all throughout the several parishes, as was agreed at the Synod, that, if a bishop or the ministers of bishops, with discretion and for no undue reason, flogged tenants with rods for their crimes to strike fear in others so that the criminous themselves may be corrected or so that the unwilling may do penance lest they perish eternally, if the superiors of the said tenants took it badly and wished to exact some vengeance for it, or if they presumed to contend that the same tenants are not be disciplined, let them know that they are to make composition for our ban and, together with ecclesiastical excommunication, they will bear our harshest punishment.

c. 433. ON FOREIGNERS WHO ARE UNJUSTLY REDUCED TO SERVITUDE.
From the Council of Charles the Younger and Lothar at Valenciennes, c. 10.

As for the foreigners who, because of the oppression of the Northmen or the Britons, have fled to the parts of these kingdoms, your lords established that they are not to suffer any violence, oppression or exaction from any minister of the commonwealth, but that it is to be licit for them to ask for safe conduct until, with the return of peace, they return to their own places, or their lords receive them. But no one is to dare to enslave them for having remained with some person in the capacity of a hireling, nor to exact a tax or tribute. If anyone of the commonwealth's ministers, or anyone else, has been found to act or to have acted against this precept of piety, he is to make composition for our ban for it.

c. 434. AS ABOVE.

It has come to the hearing of the priests that, in our regions, fugitives, who, having lost all their goods, scarcely avoided the hands of the pagans, are being unjustly oppressed by some people in our realms and are reduced to servitude, against divine and human laws, since the Lord says through the Prophet: "Do not oppress a stranger in this place, and I shall make my dwelling with you (cf. Jer. 7:6–7)." And again: "You shall not molest a stranger (Ex. 22:21)," and many others similar to these. Hence, such persons are to be corrected severely, and the foreigners are to be taken out of their hands, according to what is written: "Who delivers the poor from the hand of them that are stronger than he (Ps. 34:10)," etc. Indeed, foreigners among their brethren, that is, Christians, are to be hirelings, not slaves. If they are reduced to servitude, what profit has it been to them to flee the hands of the pagans, since then they have not fled the yoke of captivity and harsh servitude? And so, the piety of priests must struggle against this cruelty lest the divine wrath consume Christian people for such great malice.

C. 435. THAT THE MEASURES BE JUST.
From the Capitulary at Pîtres.

That the counts and all the ministers of the commonwealth and the rest of our faithful subjects see to it that the peck be just and the sextary equitable, according to sacred Scripture and the chapters of our predecessors, in cities, villages, and vills for buying and selling, and that they take the standard measure from our palace according to the ancient custom. And if it is imputed to someone that he adulterated the measure, if he is a free man, either he is to purge himself by oath according to his law, or, if he is found guilty, he is to pay our ban, and what he wished to sell by an unjust measure is to be seized by the ministers of the commonwealth. But if this has been imputed to a tenant or slave, let him examine himself for it by the judgment of God or, if he is convicted, he is to lose the thing, that is, that whose measure he has adulterated; furthermore, he is to be flogged with rods on his bare skin. And whether he is slave or free, after legal correction, he is to receive the episcopal judgment because he acted against God's prohibition. For He says: "Let the bushel be just, and the sextary equal (Lev. 19:36)." And elsewhere: "Diverse measures the Lord hates (Prov. 20:10)." And also: "He did not give his money at usury (Ps. 14:5)." This sin is reckoned among those capital sins regarding which the Apostle says (1 Cor. 5:11), that it is not licit for a Christian even to eat with him who commits them. Likewise, throughout the cities, villages and markets, the commonwealth's ministers are to see to it that those who sell bread and meat for a fee and wine by the sextary are not able to adulterate their measure; but as many loaves measurable by a just measure as the bishops and abbots in each city receive from their bakers, so many loaves measurable by a just measure they are to have made by the bakers who make bread for sale. If they have been found to adulterate the measure or to diminish it, they are to suffer harm and be flogged with rods. As for the men to whom it has been committed to see to it that the measures are not diminished, if they have been convicted of perjury for having sworn that they would not consent to this, they are to be punished according to law and either lose their hand, or redeem it, or suffer grave harm, and afterwards they are to accept public penance from the bishop for their perjury.

C. 436. ON THE SAME MATTER.
From the Capitularies, bk. 3, c. 90.

That all have equal measures and equal weights, whether in the cities or in the monasteries, to give or to take mutually, as we are commanded in the Lord's Law.

C. 437. ON CONSPIRACIES.
From the Council of Chalcedon.

The crime of plotting or conspiring is entirely forbidden even by foreign laws. Much more is it suitable to admonish that this not be done in God's Church. Hence, if any clerics or monks have been found conspiring or banding together, or hatching plots against their bishops or clerics, they shall be wholly cast out of their degree.

C. 438. ON THE SAME MATTER.
From the Capitularies, bk. 1, tit. 29.

Neither clerics nor monks are to engage in conspiracy or plots against their shepherd.

C. 439. ON THE SAME MATTER.
From the Council at Pîtres.

Just as the holy 630 pontiffs of the Council of Chalcedon forbade the practice of conspiracy, and as other Councils of bishops prohibited the doing of such pernicious things, so we bishops, too, by the authority of God and of the sacred canons, forbid such things because those who do such things, by the judgment of those who already reign in heaven with God, are severed both from the heavenly Church and from the fellowship of Christians, unless by worthy fruits of penance they return to such a point that they may be reunited with Holy Church.

C. 440. ON THE SAME MATTER.
From the Capitularies, bk. 3, c. 9.

Those who have presumed to commit conspiracies, and who have affirmed any conspiracy by their oath, are to be judged in a threefold manner. First, that wherever some evil has been perpetrated in this way, the authors of the deed be killed. But those who have aided them are to flog each other and to cut off each other's noses. But where no evil has been perpetrated, they are similarly to flog each other and cut off each other's hair. But if a conspiracy has been done by their right hands, if they are free men, either they are to swear with suitable oath-takers or, if they cannot do this, they are to make composition for their law. But if they are of servile state, they are to be flogged.

C. 441. ON CONFRATERNITIES OR ASSOCIATIONS.
From the Council of Nantes.

As for the gatherings or confraternities, which they call associations, as we admonished orally, so now we expressly instruct in writing that it be done only insofar as is right for authority and utility and pertains to the salvation of the soul. But let no one, neither priest, nor faithful in our parish, dare to go beyond this: that is, in every service of religion, namely for the offering, lights, mutual prayers, the burial of the dead, alms-giving, and the other offices of piety. But as for those meals and banquets, which divine authority forbids, where excessive drinking, undue exactions, shameful and vain pleasures and fights are accustomed to occur, often even, as we have experienced, to the point of homicides, hates, and dissensions, these we entirely forbid in such manner that whoever has presumed to act against this decree, if he is a priest or any cleric, is to be deprived of his degree; if a lay man or woman, he or she is to be severed from the Church until satisfaction. But as for the gathering of such brethren, if it is necessary that they come together, or if perhaps one of them has a dispute against his peer which needs to be reconciled, and this cannot happen without the gathering of priests and the rest, after performing those things which are God's and are fitting for the Christian religion, and after due admonitions, if it should happen that all come together for the restoring of true charity and mutual fraternal consolation, we allow such gatherings to take place in such manner that, with the observance of modesty and temperance, sobriety and the concord of peace, as befits brethren, all be done to the edification of fraternity and the praise and glory of God and with the giving of thanks. And let that which the Saviour says be kept firmly in mind: "And take heed lest perhaps your hearts be overcharged with intemperance and drunkenness (Lk. 21:34)." Those who wish it may receive blessed bread from the priest; and breaking only bread, with each taking a single drink, they are not to presume to touch anything more. And so, each may return to his own affairs with the Lord's blessing.

C. 442. THAT IF A PRIEST HAS DIED, A NEIGHBOURING PRIEST IS NEVER TO OBTAIN HIS CHURCH AT THE DISPOSAL OF A SECULAR LORD.
From the same.

That, if any priest has died, the neighbouring priest is not to obtain that church at the disposal of a secular lord by any petition or gift, because the title itself was previously established; not even a chapel without consulting the bishop. If he has done so, he is to receive a definite sentence issued against him, just as canonical authority decreed concerning a bishop that, if he lusted after a greater city out of ambition, he is to lose the one which he held and is never to obtain the one which he attempted to usurp.

C. 443. OF THE LIQUID INTO WHICH A MOUSE HAS FALLEN.
From a Penitential.

If a mouse has fallen into a liquid, let it be removed from it, and let [the liquid] be sprinkled with holy water and consumed. But if the mouse was found dead in it, let all that liquid be thrown away. But if the quantity of that liquid is great, let it be purged and sprinkled with holy water and consumed, if it is necessary. If a dead mouse is found in flour, or in curdled milk, or in honey, let what is around the mouse be thrown out, but the rest may be consumed.

C. 444. IF ANYONE HAS VIOLATED A TOMB, ETC.
As above.

If anyone has violated a tomb, he is to do penance for seven years, three of which at bread and water. If anyone has made amulets, which is detestable, he is to do penance for three years, one of which at bread and water. If anyone has eaten carrion or something sacrificed to idols, he is to fast for twelve weeks. If anyone has wilfully cut off one of his own limbs, he is to do penance for three years, one of which at bread and water. If anyone has exacted usury from anywhere whatsoever, he is to do similar penance. If anyone has invaded or taken another's goods unjustly by violence or by any wicked device, he is to do similar penance. If anyone has sold some man unjustly, likewise. If anyone has wilfully set on fire another's threshing-floor or house, he is to do similar penance. If anyone has struck another in anger, and has shed his blood, or made him disabled, he is to do penance for forty days at bread and water.

C. 445. IF ANYONE HAS DIED WHILE EXCOMMUNICATE.

If anyone has died excommunicate, who has already made his confession, and did not come to meet the priest, but death forestalled him at home or on the road, let his relatives make offering for him at the altar and pay the ransom for captives. If anyone has stolen food or clothing because of necessity, or an animal because of hunger or nakedness, he is to do penance for four weeks; if he has made restitution, he is not to be compelled to fast.

c. 446. ON THE PRICE OF REDEMPTION.
From a Penitential.

If anyone perhaps cannot fast, and has the wherewithal by which he can redeem the obligation, if he is rich, he is to give twenty shillings for seven weeks. If he does not have the resources to be able to give so much, he is to give ten shillings. But if he is very poor, he is to give three shillings. Let no one be troubled that we commanded the payment of twenty shillings or less because, if he is rich, it is easier for him to give twenty shillings, than it is for the poor to give three. But let each one attend to whom they are to give them, whether for the ransom of captives, or on the holy altar, or to the servants of God, or to the poor in alms.

c. 447. WHAT IS TO BE DONE FOR ONE MONTH.
As above.

For one month during which he ought to do penance at bread and water, let him sing 1,200 psalms on his knees, but if not on his knees, let him sing 1,680 psalms. And on each day, if he wishes, and he cannot abstain, he may eat at sext, except on Wednesday and Friday, when he is to fast until nones. He is not to consume meat and wine, but he may take the rest.

c. 448. WHAT FOR ONE WEEK.

For one week, let him sing 300 psalms on his knees, or sing them in order in one place.

c. 449. WHAT FOR ONE YEAR.
Also.

But he who does not know the psalms, and who cannot fast, for one year during which he must fast at bread and water, is to give twenty-six shillings in alms, and each week he is to fast one day until nones, that is, on Wednesday, and on another day, that is, on Friday, until vespers. During three forty-day fasts, let him estimate how much he consumes and give in alms half that value.

c. 450. ALSO, ON THE PRICE OF ONE YEAR.

During the first year, some allowed four three-day fasts, others twelve three-day fasts, that is, once each month. Some said [they should] spend these three-day periods engaging in flagellations and vigils for the three days.

c. 451. ON THE PRICE OF ONE DAY.

The price of one day, that is, alms for two or three poor persons, or one penny. Others prescribed the whole psalter in summer, but fifty psalms in spring, winter, or fall; others said twelve wounds or blows.

c. 452. ALSO, ON THE REDEMPTION OF ONE DAY.

Let the one who can fulfil what is written in the Penitential give thanks to God. But to him who could not fulfil it, we give counsel by God's mercy: First, for one day at bread and water, let him sing fifty psalms on his knees, or sing seventy of them standing in one place, or give one penny, or feed three poor persons. Some say fifty blows or fifty psalms for one day in the fall, a hundred blows or fifty psalms for one day in spring or winter, one psalter or a hundred blows for one day in summer.

c. 453. ALSO, ON THE REDEMPTION OF THREE YEARS.

Let him who cannot do penance as we said above in the first year distribute twenty-six shillings in alms. In the second year, twenty shillings. In the third year, eighteen shillings. This makes sixty-four shillings. But powerful men are to do for their faults what Zacchaeus did, for he said to Jesus: "Behold, Lord, the half of my goods I give to the poor; and if I have stolen anything unjustly, I restore it fourfold (Lk. 19:8)." And let him free some of his slaves, and ransom captives, and forgive from his heart those who sin against him. And he who has committed illicit acts is to abstain even from licit ones, and he must afflict his body with fasts, vigils, and frequent prayers. Indeed, joyful flesh draws us to guilt, while an afflicted flesh leads back to forgiveness.

c. 454. HOW WE MAY PERFORM A PENANCE OF SEVEN YEARS IN ONE YEAR.
From the sayings of St. Boniface, bishop.

One three-day fast for thirty days and the singing of 120 psalms. For one day, fifty psalms and five "Our Father." For three days, one psalter and fifteen "Our Father." Also, for one day, "Blessed are those who are undefiled" three times and "Have mercy on me, God," six, and let him prostrate himself to the ground seventy times, and each time let him say the "Our Father." Also, if he does not know the psalms, for one day, he is to prostrate himself to the ground one hundred times, and each time he is to say, "Have mercy on me, God," and "Lord, forgive my sins." The singing of one mass can redeem twelve days; ten masses, four months; twenty masses, eight months; thirty masses, twelve months. For one week, 300 psalms are to be sung while kneeling. Let him who does not know the psalms and cannot fast estimate how much he consumes each day and give half the value in alms.

See, we have set out in order the different opinions of the different Fathers as to the remedies of sins and the lightening of penance, leaving it to the judgment of the prudent priest to decree what is more salubrious and useful for the soul of the penitent.

HERE ENDS THE SECOND BOOK

Appendices

The appendices that follow were produced by unspecified persons at disparate and unspecified times in the course of the tenth century. The decision to include them in the translation is moved by the thought that they might be considered as evidence of three critical readings of Regino's work in the decades following the completion of his work. All three reveal that later readers found the work engaging and useful enough to take the time to improve it according to their own reading of needs, times, and circumstances.

Appendix One

C. 1. ON FORGERIES AND DOUBTFUL NARRATIVES.
From bk. 1 of the Capitularies.

Forgeries and doubtful narratives, or those which are entirely contrary to the Catholic faith, such as that very bad and false letter which they say to have fallen from heaven in Jerusalem, are neither to be believed nor read, but to be burned.

C. 2. ON PREPARING THE ALTAR LINENS.
From the same.

That priests are to make it known to the women in their parishes that they are to prepare the linens to cover the altars.

C. 3. ON THOSE WHO ARE STOPPED FROM THE FORNICATION WHICH THEY INTENDED.
From the Council of Neocaesarea.

If any man lusting after a woman intended to lie with her, and his plan does not come to fulfilment, it is evident that he has been freed by God's grace.

C. 4. A LAYMAN WHO REJECTS HIS WIFE IS TO BE DEPRIVED OF COMMUNION.
From the Canons of the Apostles.

If any layman, rejecting his own wife, has taken another or one dismissed by another man, he is to be deprived of communion.

C. 5. ON THOSE WHO ABANDON MARITAL INTERCOURSE AS IF IT WERE A SIN.
From the Council of Gangra.

If any woman, abandoning her husband, wishes to go away out of an abhorrence for marriage, let her be anathema.

c. 6. ON WOMEN WHO USE MALE CLOTHING.
From the same.

If any woman assumes male attire instead of the usual female dress, let her be anathema.

c. 7. ON THOSE WHO DESPISE THEIR CHILDREN UNDER THE PRETEXT OF CHRISTIANITY.
From the same.

If anyone abandons his children and does not look after them, but neglects them by reason of continence, let him be anathematized.

c. 8. ON THOSE WHO FAST ON SUNDAY.
From the same.

If anyone, for the sake of continence, fasts on Sunday, let him be anathematized.

c. 9. ON THOSE WHO DETEST PEOPLE WHO EAT MEAT.
From the same.

If anyone condemns another who is religious and faithful for eating meat, apart from blood (that is, without blood) or what is sacrificed to idols or what has been strangled, let him be anathema.

c. 10. THE COMMEMORATIONS OF MARTYRS ARE NOT TO BE DONE ON FAST DAYS.
From the Council of Laodicea.

It is not to be fitting for the birthdays of the martyrs to be celebrated in Lent, but it is meet for their holy commemoration to be done on Saturdays and Sundays.

c. 11. THAT IF SLAVES OF THE FISC HAVE BUILT CHURCHES, THIS MUST REMAIN FIRM.
From the Council of Toledo.

If any of the slaves of the fisc have perhaps built churches and endowed them from their poverty, let the bishop see to it that, at his petition, this is confirmed by royal authority.

c. 12. THAT THE POSSESSED BE EXORCISED EVERY DAY.
From the Council of Carthage.

Every day, exorcists are to impose hands on the possessed.

c. 13. ON FEEDING THE POSSESSED.
From the same.

Daily food is to be administered by the exorcists to the possessed who sit in God's house.

c. 14. ON SLAVES WHO FLEE TO THE CHURCH.
From the Council of Orléans.

As for a slave who has fled to a church for any fault, if he has received an oath from his master regarding the committed fault, he is to be compelled to return to his master's service immediately. After the oath has been given and he is delivered to his master, if he has suffered any punishment for the same fault, his master is to be held a stranger from the communion of Catholics because of his contempt for the Church and breach of faith.

c. 15. HOW THE NAMES OF THE FAITHFUL ARE TO BE RECITED AT THE CELEBRATION OF MASS.
From the letter of Innocent.

As for the names to be recited, let this be observed, that first the offerings of those who offer are commended, and then the names of those whose offerings they are are to be named within the sacred mysteries of mass.

c. 16. THAT, AS ON FRIDAY, SO THERE BE FASTING ALSO ON SATURDAY.
From the same letter.

That on Saturday there ought to be fasting a most evident reason shows. For if we celebrate on Sunday for the sake of the venerable resurrection of our Lord Jesus Christ, and not only at Easter but throughout each circle of seven days we repeat the image of that day, and if we fast on Friday for the Passion of the Lord, we must not omit Saturday, because it is seen to be clearly bounded between the sadness and joy of that time. It is entirely certain that the Apostles, on those two days, were in mourning and hid for fear of the Jews. Hence, as there is to be fasting on Friday, so also on Saturday, because both those days show sadness, as Sunday does joy.

c. 17. AS ABOVE.

As for the fasts prescribed by law, that is, Wednesday and Friday, they are not to be omitted, unless there is some great necessity, because on Wednesday Judas pondered the Lord's betrayal, and on Friday the Lord was crucified. It follows that anyone who does not fast on these days will be seen to betray the Saviour with the traitor, or crucify him with his crucifiers.

c. 18. THAT PRISONERS BE VISITED ON SUNDAYS BY OFFICIALS OF THE CHURCH.
From the Council of Orléans.

For the sake of mercy, we have decided it to be equitable to observe that, as the guilty are consigned to prison for any faults, they be sought out on Sundays by the one set over the Church so that the needs of those so bound may be mercifully relieved according to the Lord's commandment, and suitable nourishment may be provided from the Church's household.

C. 19. A WOMAN IS NOT TO DARE TO TEACH MEN IN AN ASSEMBLY NOR PRESUME TO BAPTIZE.

From the Council of Carthage.

A woman, however learned and holy she may be, must not presume to teach men in an assembly. Similarly, neither must she baptize.

C. 20. ON THOSE WHO FLEE TO A CHURCH, THAT THEY NOT BE TAKEN OUT.

From the Council of Orléans.

It is not fitting that those who have fled to a church be taken out, but let their masters persuade them to leave after promising forgiveness. If the latter inflict some punishment on those who exit the church, they are to be held as excommunicates as enemies of the Church.

C. 21. ON THE ACCUSED AND THE ACCUSERS.

Furthermore, in regard to every ecclesiastical order, it is to be observed in every way that no one at all presume to indict with an accusation any of the brethren in a conciliar or synodal assembly, unless first he has signed with his own hand in writing in an orderly manner the crime being charged and the reason for litigation, and has presented it to the bishop or the sacred synod so that the disputes of the litigants might be settled justly and canonically. As Roman authority attests, it is not licit for anyone to be made a defendant nor to be brought to judgment unless the accusation has been made known, because, just as a penalty binds the one convicted of a crime, so also the accuser, if he fails to prove what he has charged.

C. 22. ON THE SAME MATTER.

From the Council at Saint-Médard.

Hincmar, archbishop of Reims, said to his accusers: What is your petition, brothers? They said: We petition for mercy to be granted to us by your Paternity as to the administration of the ecclesiastical orders to which we were formerly promoted by the lord Ebbo, and have been suspended by your authority. Archbishop Hincmar said: Do you have a bill of complaint or an application for redress, as ecclesiastical tradition requires? But they answered that they had no bill at hand. Archbishop Hincmar said: The authority of ecclesiastical laws is such that they always require a written document in causes of actions, so that anyone who approaches the sacred font is commanded to give his name. Anyone who is promoted to the highest priesthood is elected by a decree strengthened by the signatures of all. Anyone who is ordained is commanded to receive letters from those who ordained him, and anyone who is separated from ecclesiastical fellowship because of some excess is readmitted or expelled by a written bill. Anyone who is accused, or excommunicated, or reconciled, is commanded to be accused or reconciled in writing. And to such an extent is writing required in all such things that, as Blessed Gregory writes in his letter of admonition to the defender John, citing from the Roman laws: "A sentence which is not presented in writing does not even deserve to have the name of sentence." Hence, brothers and sons, it is necessary, according to ecclesiastical authority, that you submit your complaint in writing confirmed by your signatures and present it to the sacred Synod so that you may be answered suitably and canonically. Then the same brethren wrote a bill, signed their names to it, and gave it to Bishop Hincmar, who then presided over the Synod together with Wenilo, archbishop of Sens, and Amalric, likewise archbishop of Tours, in the presence of the glorious King Charles.

c. 23. ON THE SAME MATTER.
From the Roman law.

In both a civil and a criminal matter, a statement written in the hand of the accuser is to precede the accusation.

c. 24. ON THE SAME MATTER.
From the same law.

Whoever indicts another on some charge as to a capital crime is not to be heard by the judges before he has attested by his signature that he will undergo a similar punishment as the one with which he threatens the accused.

c. 25. ALSO, AS ABOVE.

In criminal causes or accusations no one is to accuse by mandate; but he who brings in a criminal charge shall accuse in person after presenting a written accusation. Judges are to be punished, and their office staff is to be condemned, if they believed that someone should be subject to questioning, if a written accusation has not first been submitted.

c. 26. ON THE SAME MATTER.
From the same.

No one is made criminous before a written accusation. When the written accusation has been made in an orderly fashion, then the accused is to be seized by the judge and to be handed into custody with the accuser.

c. 27. ON THOSE WHO HAVE DONE SOME INJURY OR DISHONOUR TO A BISHOP.
From bk. 6 of the Capitularies of King Charles, c. 99.

If anyone has done some injury or unjust dishonour to a bishop, he is to make composition for his life, and all the possessions which he appears to have are to be handed over to the Church over which the bishop is known to preside, and our ban is to be paid threefold, that is, sixty shillings, or he is always to be placed in the service of our fisc until he is able to redeem himself threefold according to his wergild. Truly, Holy Church consists of its priests. Hence, they are to be struck with a great penalty who have done an injury to the bishops or the other priests or exposed them to contumely. For detraction against priests extends to Christ, whose place they hold in the Church by delegation.

c. 28. WHAT PENANCE IS TO BE IMPOSED ON THOSE WHO KILL A THIEF OR A ROBBER.

If a thief or robber, captured while he steals, can be seized without being killed and yet he is killed, because they are created in the image of God and baptized in His name, let their killers not enter a church for forty days. Wearing woolen dress, let those placed under interdict abstain from food and drink, along with their marriage-bed, sword, and horse-riding. On Tuesdays, Thursdays, and Saturdays, they may by turns make temperate use of some kinds of legumes or herbs, and apples and small fishes, with some middling ale. But if it is proven by truthful witnesses that they had killed those members of the devil without premeditated hate while preserving themselves and their goods, by way of indulgence, let them abstain for forty days from church, meat, wine, and marriage, giving large alms. And if he is a priest, he is not to be deposed; yet, let him do penance all the days of his life.

c. 29. ON THE VARIED HARASSMENT OF PRIESTS.
From the Council of Orléans, c. 8.

It has been reported to the holy Synod that many harassments are inflicted very often by wicked Christians on Christ's priests and on other clerics of a lesser degree. Hence, it has seemed best to the holy Council, lest such things occur henceforth, to strike them with a spiritual weapon so that, if anyone has inflicted some injury or calumny on a cleric, he is to be cast out of the bounds of Holy Church until worthy satisfaction.

c. 30. FROM THE COUNCIL OF ROUEN.

[At this place in the manuscript seven lines of writing have been erased so that nothing can be educed from it.]

c. 31. ON FREEBORN CLERICS.
From the Register, part 1, to Amos, bishop of Jerusalem.

Since we trust that your Fraternity loves the statutes of the canons and the vigour of discipline, we have taken care to command you to enquire into this matter: that freeborn clerics of a more capacious and sharper intelligence are often forbidden by the envy of their bishops from moving to places which are perceived to be more excellent in knowledge and learning when they seek to do so for the sake of learning and for the utility of the Church and their own need. The latter bring forward against them c. 20 of the Council of Chalcedon, where it is stated: "It is not fitting for clerics ministering in a Church to be established in the Church of another city," disregarding by the obfuscation of envy the words that follow, where those are excepted who have moved to another Church from necessity. But he is gripped by great necessity who is fettered by hunger; and he who is constrained by the injury of ignorance has need to be restored by the instruction of knowledge. Hence, the distinction must be drawn cautiously by a bishop between the fugitive and the studious so that the former may not find a place to lurk, but the latter not face an obstacle to change to a better place and to go from virtue to virtue and may rather be raised up by the help of that charity which never fails (cf. 1 Cor. 13:8). Hence, if they have been running the course piously and justly on the right way of life thus far, we adjudged that permission not be denied to them to seek places which are more perfect for the sake of religion.

c. 32. ON HATE AGAINST A BROTHER.

If anyone has hated his brother unjustly, God severs such a one from his kingdom and withdraws him from heaven, because hate is neither removed by suffering, nor expiated by martyrdom, nor erased by the shedding of blood. To be spoken of disparagingly by another out of hate, for the sake of one's own interest, is more against nature than death, than suffering, or the other evils of this sort.

c. 33. ST. GREGORY.

St. Paul the Apostle says: "Let him who sins emend by penance (cf. 2 Cor. 12:21)," that is, with fasts, vigils, and alms. The one whom a delighted flesh drew to fault, an afflicted flesh draws back to forgiveness.

c. 34. ST. AUGUSTINE SAYS:

There is no sure penance apart from the hatred of sin and the love of God. You must repent in such manner that what used to be sweet in your life begins to taste bitter to your spirit.

c. 35. ALSO, AUGUSTINE, ON HATRED.

It is a great and wonderful sentence that, just as there is a man's love for his own life so that he perishes, there is hate that he may not perish. If you have loved badly, then you have hated. If you have hated well, then you have loved. Happy are they who have hated [their life] while guarding [it] lest they lose [it] by loving [it].

c. 36. POPE GREGORY ON LAPSED PRIESTS.

As to lapsed priests, or any others of the clergy, we desire that you observe this, that in dealing with their property, you remain free from any contamination. But seek out the poorest monasteries which adhere to the Rule and which know how to live according to God, and hand the lapsed over to penance in these monasteries, and let the property of the lapsed go to the benefit of the place in which they are given over to penance, so that those who bear the care of their correction may have the support of their goods. But if they have relatives, let their goods be given to their legitimate relatives, yet in such a way that support for those who have been handed over for penance be sufficiently provided. But if any members of an ecclesiastical household, whether priests or laymen, or monks, or clerics, or any others, shall have lapsed, we will that they be handed over to penance, but that their goods not be withdrawn from the Church's right. Yet let them receive for their own use enough to support them during their penance, lest, if left destitute, they should be burdensome to the places to which they have been handed over. If any have relatives on a [Church] estate, their goods are to be handed over to them, so that they may be preserved with them for the Church.

Moreover, let no lord, by virtue of external power, inflict violence upon the priests, but with excellent consideration for the sake of Him, whose servants they are, so rule over them as also to show them due reverence. For in holy writ priests are sometimes called gods, and sometimes angels. Indeed, through Moses, it is said of him who is about to be led to swear an oath: "Bring him to the gods (cf. Ex. 22:8)," that is, to the priests. And again: "You shall not speak ill of the gods (Ex. 22:28)." And the Prophet says: "The priest's lips keep knowledge, and they seek the law from his mouth; for he is the angel of the Lord of hosts (Mal. 2:7)." Why, then, would it be strange, if your Piety were to deign to honour those to whom even God himself in His own Word gives honour, calling them angels or even gods? Ecclesiastical history also testifies that, when accusations against bishops had been presented to the Emperor Constantine of pious memory, he accepted the bills of accusation, but, calling together the bishops who had been accused, in their sight he burned the bills which he had received, saying: You are gods, constituted by the true God. Go and settle your causes among you, because it is not worthy that we should judge gods. In ancient times there were emperors in the republic, who knew not the true God, but worshipped gods of wood and stone, and yet they paid the greatest honour to their priests.

So it is that, except for crimes, Gregory deposed none of the priests; instead, venially according to the quality of their wrongs, he deprived them of communion.

And so, if sometimes something had to be discussed regarding the crimes of priests, Gregory proceeded with the greatest constraint and great caution, examining the measure of each charge, and he promulgated his sentence more with difficulty than with ease, saying: While all matters need care in investigating the truth, yet those which pertain to deposition from the priestly degree are to be scrutinized more strictly. In these, what is at stake is not so much humble decisions as an opposition to the divine blessing. Indeed, it is a very heavy and indecent thing that a sure sentence be issued regarding a doubtful matter.

c. 37. LEST THE LORD'S PRIESTS BE COMPELLED TO SWEAR AS THE MULTITUDE IS ACCUSTOMED TO DOING.

Pope Cornelius, in a letter to Rufus, an Eastern bishop.

We have never known an oath to be previously exacted from the highest priests, or from the other orders for right faith, nor have we found that they swore voluntarily. Hence, especially St. James the Apostle speaks forbidding the oath and says: "But above all, my brethren, do not swear (Jas. 5:12)." Dearest brethren, the Lord himself forbids these things, that is, not to swear, not to require oaths other than for right faith. All the Apostles, the holy men who preceded us, those who presided over this holy, universal, and apostolic Church before us, the Prophets and the other holy doctors spread to preach throughout the world, forbid these things, forbid oaths.

c. 38. TESTIMONY AS TO AN ECCLESIASTICAL CONTROVERSY.

[Council of Mainz, c. 6.]

That every controversy as to ecclesiastical matters, according to the divine law, is to be settled by two or three witnesses, the Lord [attests,] saying: "Do not let one stand against another, but let every assertion stand by the mouth of two or three witnesses (cf. Deut. 19:15; Mt. 18:16)." Likewise, concerning the separation of spouses, let three truthful men testify as to this, if seven cannot be found.

c. 39. ON THE LAMING OF AN INFANT.

[Council of Tribur, c. 33.]

A physician was careless in the treatment of an infant and made him lame. It is asked whether such a one could merit a position in the clergy. And it seemed that, if he showed other good progress, a debility of this kind ought not to stop him from a position.

c. 40. ON THE TONSURE OF CLERICS AFTER A WIFE'S DISMISSAL.
[Council of Tribur, c. 27.]

If a cleric has set aside his tonsure and taken a wife, and he is without a position, and was not handed over to a monastery by his parents, if he is allowed to have a wife, he must be compelled to be tonsured again, and not dare to neglect his tonsure in the course of his life. But one whom his progenitors have handed over to a monastery, and who has begun to sing and read in the Church, cannot take a wife, nor desert the monastery. If he has gone away, he is to be brought back; if he has set aside his tonsure, he is to be tonsured again; if he has wrongfully taken a wife, he is to be compelled to set her aside.

c. 41. ON THE VEILING OF GIRLS.
[Council of Tribur, c. 24.]

If a girl, before her twelfth year of age, has freely taken up the sacred veil, her parents or guardians can immediately render this deed void, if they wish. But if they should consent by disregarding it for a year and a day, neither they nor she can change this subsequently. But if, at a later age, a girl or boy should choose to serve God, the parents have no power to prohibit it.

c. 42. ON LAYMEN WHO PLUNDER THE WEALTH OF DYING PRIESTS.

It has also been reported to the holy Synod that some laymen act basely against their priests so that they claim for themselves portions of the wealth of dying priests as if from the wealth of their peasants. Hence, we forbid that this be done further, but as they were made free men to receive their degree and perform the divine office, so nothing is to be required from them other than the divine office. Let them claim nothing for themselves from the personal property of priests, but with two parts of it, let priests do whatever they please; a third part, according to the mandates of the canons, they are to leave to the churches which they serve.

c. 43. ON THE MANSE AND TITHES.

Also, it has been ordered in the Capitulary that they must not do any service, apart from the ecclesiastical one, for the manse of the church, for the tithes, for the offerings of the faithful, or for the houses or porches situated near the church. If they have anything more, let them provide service to their [secular] superiors for it.

c. 44. THAT NO ONE OF A SERVILE CONDITION BE PROMOTED TO THE CLERGY.

That no one of a servile condition be promoted to the sacred degrees, unless first they have received their lawful freedom from their own masters. The charter of this freedom is to be read publicly from the ambo before the ordination and, if no one objects, he shall be properly consecrated. Furthermore, if they afterwards fall from their degree, they are to be of the same condition as they were before their degree.

c. 45. WHAT PRIESTS AND OTHER CLERICS MUST FULFIL.
From a canonical letter.

That none of the bishops, priests, or deacons, or even of the clerics, have it in their power to sell the possessions of a church, nor to give them to any of their relatives. Whoever may have done this, with all speed, having paid back the value, will return them to the sacred places to which they pertain. But if anyone, contemning this provision, should presume to do this, he must leave his own possessions to that same church and he himself is to be cast out, because it is congruent with divine reason that those who receive churches to rule do not do so to disperse them. Similarly, they are to have no power to alienate or sell in any way; indeed, without the consent of their bishop, they may not appoint vicars or leave [their church] to their children. As we have adjudged above, whoever has presumed to do this, if he has property of his own, is to make restitution for the same amount. If he does not have it, he is to be stripped of all that he has and cast out. As for the things themselves, they are to revert to the church whose possessions they are.

c. 46. FROM THE COUNCIL OF MEAUX, C. 21.

If a priest who had nothing of his own when he was promoted to the ecclesiastical order afterwards has bought properties, it is to be investigated to whose right they belong, because they ought to belong to the church. Indeed, each priest is to leave to his church those things which he acquired after the day of his consecration. If he has acquired possessions under another's name, and has built structures there, or placed things there which pertained to the church, this wicked deed is done against the decrees of the canons because it is sacrilege and is recognized to be a crime equal to that of Judas, a thief who stole the sacred offerings.

c. 47. ON WOMEN WHO TOOK THE HABIT OF RELIGION IN THEIR OWN HOUSES, IF AFTERWARDS THEY CHOSE MARRIAGE, WHAT IS TO BE DONE.

As for widows and girls who, in their own houses, have changed into the habit of religion, either on their parents' initiative or their own, if afterwards they propose to marry against the institutes of the Fathers or the precepts of the canons, they are to be suspended from communion for so long as they do not emend what they have perpetrated illicitly. If they should neglect to do so, they are to be severed in perpetuity from the communion or the table of all Christians.

c. 48. LETTER OF THE BLESSED POPE GREGORY SENT TO ARCHBISHOP BONIFACE IN WHICH, AMONG OTHER THINGS, THE FOLLOWING DECREE CONCERNING WIDOWS IS READ:

Your Dilection has sought our advice regarding widows who have withdrawn from their intention of widowhood; I believe you know, dearest brother, that, unless they are converted, they were once condemned by the holy Apostle (1 Tim. 5:11–12) and many holy Fathers. We also decree by our apostolic authority that they are to be condemned, and to be kept from the communion of the faithful and the bounds of the Church, until they obey their bishops and, willing or unwilling, return to the good which they had begun. Concerning virgins not veiled, if they should go astray, we have a decree of our predecessor Innocent of sainted memory, in the following terms: "As for those who have not yet been covered with the sacred veil, and yet have pretended that they would ever remain of virginal intent, even if they were not veiled, if they have married, they are to do penance for a time, because the role of their bridegroom was held by the Lord. For if even among men it is by no means the common practice for a contract made in good faith to be dissolved, how much more is this kind of promise, which binds one to God, not to be dissolved without some punishment," etc. Indeed, if virgins not yet veiled are punished in this way by public penance, and are excluded from the company of the faithful until satisfaction, how much more are widows, who are of more perfect age and maturer wisdom and counsel, and who were very accustomed to the society of men, and who allowed themselves to be veiled and have taken the habit of religion, and then have apostatized and returned to their former vomit, to be kept until satisfaction by us and all the faithful from the bounds of the Church and the company of the faithful and even to be placed in jail! Did they not, according to the blessed Apostle Paul, hand a man of this sort over to Satan so that his spirit might be saved in the day of the Lord (1 Cor. 5:5)? Of such, the Lord also speaks through Moses, saying: "Take the evil away from your midst (Deut. 13:5)." Of them also, he says through the Prophet: "The just shall rejoice when he shall see the revenge: he shall wash his hands in the blood of the sinner (Ps. 57:11)." Of such, and of those like them, and of those who lend their consent to them, because not only those who do, but also those who lend their consent to the doers, are guilty (Rom. 1:32), the Lord speaks through the same Prophet David and says: "You saw a thief and ran with him: and with adulterers you were a partaker (Ps. 49:18)." And there are many other texts similar to these. Such persons, then, are indubitably shown to be adulterous because, having abandoned their immortal Spouse, they have returned to their former life like dogs to their vomit; they have become unlawful apostates and, by joining with mortal men, are polluting themselves by a sacrilegious union. According to the same Apostle Paul, because they have set aside their intention of widowhood and have presumed to break the faith which they had pledged to God, and have transgressed against their first faith (cf. 1 Tim. 5:12), these women are to be condemned by us. As has been already said, they are to be banished from the bounds of the Church and the company of the faithful until satisfaction by you and the rest of the men of our order, that is, by each in his own diocese.

C. 49. THAT CLERICS NOT JOIN IN FAMILIARITY WITH WIDOWS.
From the Council of Carthage, c. 102.

It pertains to the guilt of the bishop or of the priest who presides over a parish if, for the sake of sustaining their present life, younger widows or nuns are made subject to the familiarity of clerics.

C. 50. ON WIDOWS WHO ARE SUPPORTED FROM THE STIPENDS OF THE CHURCH.
From the same, c. 103.

Widows, who are supported by a stipend from the Church, are to be so assiduous in God's work that they aid the Church by their merits and prayers.

C. 51. ON WIDOWS WHO TRANSGRESS AGAINST THEIR PROFESSED CONTINENCE.
From the same, c. 104.

Since the reward of chastity is good, it is to be preserved with greater observance and attention. Any widows, even if they are still in the years of their minority and have been widowed by their husband at an immature age, if they have devoted themselves to God, and have cast aside the lay habit and have taken on the religious habit with the bishop and the Church as witnesses, and if afterwards they have passed to worldly nuptials, according to the Apostle Paul, they shall have damnation because they have dared to make void the faith of chastity which they had vowed to God (1 Tim. 5:12). Such persons are to be severed from the communion of Christians, nor are they to share even a meal with Christians. For if adulterous wives are guilty of a crime against their husbands, how much more shall these widows who vowed a religious life to God be marked with the crime of adultery, if they have corrupted with a libidinous will the devotion which they offered to God freely and passed into a second marriage? Even if they had been carried off by someone's violent attack, but afterwards consented to remain in a marriage with their ravisher or violent husband because of the delights of lust, they are to be held guilty by the condemnation expressed above. Of such, the Apostle says: "When they have grown wanton, they wish to marry: having damnation, because they have made void their first faith (1 Tim. 5:11–12)."

c. 52. ON WOMEN WHO HAVE PROFESSED WIDOWHOOD BEFORE THE BISHOP.
From the Council of Orange, c. 20.

The profession to preserve widowhood made before the bishop in the sacristy, with the imposition of the widow's habit by the bishop, is not to be violated. A woman who abandons such a profession, or her ravisher, is deservedly to be condemned.

c. 53. ON VIRGINS YOUNGER THAN TWENTY-FIVE WHO ARE VEILED UNDER THE COMPULSION OF NECESSITY.
From the eighth Council of Carthage in Africa, c. 26.

Also, it pleased that if any of the bishops has veiled a virgin before the age of twenty-five years by necessity of a threat to virginal purity, when either a suitor or ravisher is feared, or even if she has been pricked by some anxiety about the danger of death, lest she die unveiled, or because her parents or those to whom her care pertains require it, no obstacle shall arise for him from the Council provision regarding this number of years.

c. 54. THAT IT IS NOT TO BE LICIT FOR A WOMAN TO SET ASIDE THE HOLY VEIL WHICH SHE HAS ACCEPTED.

In whatever way a woman, with her husband giving his permission canonically, or after his death, has received the holy veil on her head, whether freely or unwillingly, she is to remain in it forever and not set it aside.

c. 55. ON THOSE WHO RECEIVE THE BODY AND BLOOD OF THE LORD.

"Whosoever shall eat this bread, or drink the chalice of the Lord unworthily shall be guilty of the body and of the blood of the Lord (1 Cor. 11:27)." "Unworthily," or immoderately, or in a disorderly manner. "Guilty," that is, he who has despised such a great mystery as a vile thing is worthy of condemnation by the sacrifice itself. It is written: "Everyone who is clean shall eat of it. The soul that sinned, as unclean, shall be cut off from among his people (Lev. 7:19–20)." "Unworthily," as the Lord says: "If you stand before the altar, and there you remember (Mt. 5:23)," etc. First, the conscience is to be examined as to whether it reproves us with regard to that; and so, we must make an offering or receive communion. Some say: He calls back from the holy [sacrifice] not the unworthy, but the one who receives unworthily. For if a worthy one is held back for approaching unworthily, how much more one who cannot receive worthily? Hence, it is fitting for those who are full of vices to cease from their vices, that they may receive the holy body of the Lord in a holy manner. "Let him prove" (1 Cor. 11:28), that is, let him ask whether he is worthy. For he who eats is made twice guilty, namely for his presumption and for his sin. "Not discerning" (1 Cor. 11:29), that is, not distinguishing it from other foods. Hence, since so great is the wound of sin and the onset of illness that the medicine of the body and blood of the Lord is to be delayed, each one must remove himself from the altar to do penance by the authority of the bishop, and by the same authority be reconciled. For this is to receive unworthily the body and blood of the Lord: if one receives it at a time when one ought to be doing penance. For when the holy and religious bishops, acceptable to God, enter under God's roof, then the Lord himself enters there through them, as if receiving God. And when you make use of the bread of life and the cup, when you eat and drink the blood of the Lord, then the Lord enters under your roof. But where He enters unworthily, there He enters to the judgment of the one who receives Him.

C. 56. IF A BISHOP DIES, WHAT IS TO BE OBSERVED REGARDING THE PROPERTY OF A CHURCH.

From the Council of Lérida of eight bishops, held in the year 584 of the era.

The ancient authority of the canons has never been silent regarding the matter as to which we are deciding to make salutary provision, but has instructed with a clear and binding decree that, whenever the pontiff of any Church has died, no one is to rush in indiscriminately, according to his own pleasure, to plunder those things which the dying man has left, or to turn his house upside down. But the priest who is present at the time of the funeral must provide with diligent circumspection all things that pertain to utility and preservation. Yet, what is worse, this decree is known to be violated by many clerics, so that, when a bishop dies, setting aside all affection and disregarding all severity of discipline, they monstrously seize and take away the things found in the pontiff's house. It has now pleased that all among us keep the whole tenor of this decree or constitution by this further judgment, that, when a bishop has died or while he is still on his deathbed, no cleric of any order, office, or degree presume to take anything from the house or from the useful implements that are known to pertain to the house, that is, let him not attempt to seize any ecclesiastical good, whether movable or immovable, concealing nothing, taking nothing away, stealing nothing by theft or by force or by fraud. But the one to whom the house is entrusted, having joined to himself with the advice of the clergy one or two of the most faithful men, must preserve all things until the coming of the successor bishop and supply the customary sustenance to those clerics who are found in the household. The successor bishop must use those things which he has received in accordance with the provisions of the deceased or as God inspired him with those whom he knows have faithfully complied with the discipline and charity of his predecessor. But if henceforth any cleric of whatever order, for whatever reason, as has been said above, is proven to have stolen or perhaps to have withheld fraudulently anything from the house of the Church or from any of its resources, he is to be condemned as guilty of sacrilege by a more far-reaching anathema, so that he may scarcely be granted even the peregrine communion. It is indeed hard that those who are known to have laboured long in the Lord's service in the company of the bishop of the first See be afflicted to any extent by the disrespect of those who are known to be unlawful possessors of their goods or looking after their own advantages having done no work for them.

C. 57. ON ACCUSED PRIESTS, AS ALSO ON THE OPTIMATES OF THE PALACE AND OFFICERS (*GARDINGI*), UNDER WHAT GUARANTEE OF JUSTICE IT IS FITTING THAT THEY BE EXAMINED.

From the Council of Toledo 13, tit. 2.

By a submission made at our second conference, a lamentable matter was presented to our assembly which must be removed by the weight of a synodal judgment as it causes immense harm and ruin to the people. Indeed, in past times, we have seen and much bemoaned that many have fallen from the office of the palatine order, whom a forced confession cast down from their honour and whom an immutable judgment by the decree of kings subjected to death or to perpetual infamy. The mind of our pious prince, intending to abolish this unbearable evil and horrible wrong of impiety, has introduced the matter for reconsideration by the general judgment of all the bishops and instructed that the practice be stopped by the avenging authority of the synodal power. Hence, issuing a pronouncement which is congruent with his devotion, we decreed in common that no one henceforth from any degree of the palatine order or from the assembly of holy religion be kept from the honour of his order or the service of the royal house by the cunning of royal subtlety or the instigation of profane power, or the effort of the malicious will of some men, without manifest and evident proof of his guilt. He is not to be bound in chains, he is not to be subjected to questioning, he is not to suffer any sort of torture or whipping, he is not to be deprived of his possessions, he is not to be placed in jail, nor is he to be driven by any unjust pretexts applied from all sides in order to extract from him a forced, secret, or fraudulent confession. Rather, the one who is accused will retain the degree of his order, and he will feel none of the harm from the articles listed above; having been brought to a public trial of the priests, lords, and officials (*gardingi*) and investigated with the greatest justice, if he is guilty, let him receive the lawful punishments for the proven guilt; if he is innocent, let him be seen to have been proved such by the judgment of all. As for those, however, who it is known live in such places from which prejudicial flight is suspected, or those who must be guarded with greater diligence in order to avoid troubling the country, it will be fitting for these to remain under free custody, without any harm of chains or injury. In this way, setting aside all fear, they are to be held under diligent and circumspect custody so that the time at which it is fitting for them to be judged in no way be delayed fraudulently, for if they are separated too long from their wives and relations, as also from their possessions, it may appear that they made their confession unwillingly. Even if such a confession has been made, it will not at all be valid, but according to the order set out above, that alone will be accepted as true which is known from his own mouth and is approved in the general judgment. A similar order shall be observed with regard to other freeborn persons, who do not hold palatine office, and yet are seen to bear the title of the dignity of free birth. Even if, for the least faults, as is customary, they are beaten by the prince with the blows of whips, yet they will not thereby lose their reputation or be deprived of the things that are due to them. If a charge is made against them as to the crime of infidelity, they are to be judged in accordance with the same order as set out above. We trust that this synodal decree has been promulgated by the divine Spirit. If any king henceforth either temerariously neglects to observe it, or maliciously chooses to transgress it, so that any of the mentioned persons is condemned otherwise than is set out above, or is killed as the result of an intrigue maliciously brought against him, or deposed and deprived of his place in his order, then let such a king, together with those who took delight in consenting to him, having been struck with a perpetual anathema in the sight of the most high God the Father, and of his only-begotten Son, and of the Holy Spirit, be sentenced to be burned by the divine and eternal flames. Furthermore, whatever has been done against this rule of our sentence as to anyone's person, or whatever has been adjudged as to the goods of the accused person, is to have no force by which a person judged otherwise than we have decreed either lose the dignity of his reputation or be deprived of the income of his property. Yet, by these and other such provisions, the power of domestic correction is not taken away from the princes. Indeed, especially regarding those laymen who are not bound by the offence of infidelity, but who are either torpid in the conduct of their service, or who are found to be snappish or rather negligent in the actions entrusted to them, it will be lawful for the prince to correct such persons without any dishonour to them, either by loss of goods or change of service, and to put more pleasing persons in their place.

c. 58. LEST ANYONE BE CONDEMNED WITHOUT A LAWFUL ACCUSER.
From the Council of Toledo 6, tit. 11.

It is worthy that the life of the innocent be not tainted by the pernicious action of their accusers; and so, if someone is incriminated by anyone, the accused is not to be punished before the accuser presents himself, and the pronouncements of the laws and canons are sought so that, if the person is found unworthy to accuse, no judgment is to be made as to his accusation, unless where the cause touches upon the head of the royal majesty. Once they, namely the priests who have been accused, are freed from enmity, from alien snares, from lies, freed from all sorts of shame and villainy, then how they are to be convicted or defended is stated by the Apostle Paul to Timothy, saying: "Against a priest, do not receive an accusation unless under two or three witnesses. Reprove one who sins in the presence of all that the rest also may have fear (1 Tim. 5:19–20)." The Lord in the Gospel says to the Jews: "And in your law it is written that the testimony of two men is true (Jn. 8:17)." As to the accusers of clerics, it is found sufficiently in the canons, and especially in the Council of Carthage, that the faith and manner of life of the accuser be investigated: "But if priests and deacons have been accused, their own bishop having convened a lawful number of colleagues from neighbouring places whom those accused asked of him, six of them including himself in the case of a priest, three in the case of a deacon, are to examine their causes."

Appendix Two

C. 1. THAT OFFERINGS NOT BE MADE ELSEWHERE THAN IN CHURCH.
[Council of Gangra, c. 7.]

If anyone wishes to receive or give the offerings of the Church without the knowledge of the bishop or of him to whom such offices have been entrusted and is not willing to act with their counsel, let him be anathema.

C. 2. AGAINST THOSE WHO SAY THAT ST. GREGORY, ROMAN POPE, AT THE REQUEST OF AUGUSTINE, BISHOP OF CANTERBURY, ISSUED A RESCRIPT THAT MARRIAGES CONTRACTED IN THE FOURTH DEGREE OF CONSANGUINITY WERE NOT TO BE DISSOLVED.
Excerpt from the Life of St. Gregory, bk. 2, c. 37.

Gregory, Roman pope, asked by Augustine, bishop of the English nation, up to which generation the faithful ought to marry, issued a rescript by way of dispensation: A certain earthly law in the Roman state permits that the son and daughter of a brother or sister, or of two full brothers or two sisters, unite. But we have learned from experience that the offspring of such a marriage cannot flourish. And so, it is necessary that the faithful lawfully ought to marry each other in the fourth or sixth generation. But in the second, which we have mentioned, there must be complete abstention. But after a long time, Gregory was asked by Felix, bishop of Messina in Sicily, whether he had written to Augustine that the marriages of the English contracted within the fourth generation should not be dissolved; among other things, Gregory, humblest of fathers, offered the following explanation: Know that what I wrote to Augustine, bishop of the English nation and your student, about the degree of consanguinity, as you will remember, was meant not generally, but specifically for him and that nation of the English, which had recently come to the faith, lest it recede from the good which it had begun out of fear of the more austere requirements. And the whole Roman city is my witness in this. Neither did I write these mandates to them with the intention that, once they have become solidly and firmly rooted in the faith, they should not be separated, if they were found within their kin, or that they should marry within the line of affinity, that is, until the seventh generation. But while they still remain neophytes, it is necessary first to teach them repeatedly about what things are unlawful, and to instruct them by words and examples, and to remove reasonably and faithfully whatever they may later do of these things. In accordance with the Apostle, who says: "I gave you milk, not meat (1 Cor. 3:2)," we mercifully allowed them to maintain these things for now, not their posterity, lest, as we have said, the good which was planted, weakly rooted as it is, be uprooted, but might become somewhat firm and preserved until its perfection. Hence, I, John, saw to it that these things were briefly recounted so that those who by occasion of the new dispensation contract illicit marriages may see that that most learned man did not approve generally of unions in the fourth degree, but only permitted them temporarily by way of indulgence.

C. 3. THAT PRIESTS AND DEACONS ARE NOT TO BE DEPOSED BY A SINGLE BISHOP.
From the Council of Toledo, c. 13.

We learned that a certain Fratiganus, a priest of the Church of Cordoba, was once unjustly deposed by his bishop and, although innocent, was condemned to exile. Restoring him again to his order, we have again decreed against our own presumption that, according to the synodal decision of the ancient Fathers, none of us is to dare to depose any priest or deacon without the inquiry of a council. Indeed, it is the bishop alone who can give honour to priests and ministers; but he alone cannot take it away. Assuredly, a priest cannot be condemned by one alone, nor be stripped of the privileges of his dignity by the judgment of one alone, but what the canon has instructed concerning these matters is to be decided by the warrant of the synodal tribunal.

C. 4. THAT ABBOTS BE SUBJECT TO BISHOPS, AND ON WANDERING MONKS.
From the Council of Orléans, c. 15.

For the sake of the humility of religion, abbots are to be in the bishops' power, and if they have done anything outside the Rule, they are to be corrected by the bishops; they are to convene once a year by summons in a place chosen by the bishop. But monks are to be subject to abbots in all obedience and devotion. And if any one of them should prove undevout by contumacy and has presumed to wander here and there or to have any possessions of his own, let all that he has acquired be taken away by the abbots, according to the Rule, for the benefit of the monastery. As for the wanderers themselves, wherever they may be found, with the bishop's help, let them be recalled under custody as runaways. And let that abbot who has not disciplined such persons by punishment according to the Rule, or who has received another's monk, know that he will be found guilty.

c. 5. ON THE DISTINCTION OF POWER THAT BISHOPS CAN HAVE IN MONASTERIES.
From the Council of Toledo IV, c. 51.

It has been reported to the present Council that monks are rendered subject to servile work at episcopal command, and that the rights of monasteries are usurped by an unlawful presumption against what is established in the canons so that what belongs to the monastery is almost made their possession, and an illustrious portion of Christ is reduced to shame and servitude. Hence, we admonish those who preside over the Churches that they no longer presume to do such things, but that bishops claim for themselves in a monastery only that which the canons instruct, that is, to advise abbots as to a holy manner of life and to put in place the other offices, and to correct what is done apart from the Rule. If any have presumed to do to the monks what the canons forbid, or if they have striven to usurp anything from the monastery's possessions, a sentence of excommunication will not be lacking for those who henceforth do not refrain from illicit acts.

6. ON THOSE WHOM THEIR PARENTS HAVE CONSIGNED TO CLERICAL OFFICE FROM THEIR INFANCY, IF AFTERWARDS THEY HAVE THE INTENT TO MARRY.
From the Council of Toledo, c. 119.

Concerning those whom the will of their parents dedicated to the divine ministries from their earliest infancy, we establish this to be observed: that, as soon as they have been tonsured or admitted to the ministry of lectors, they are to be educated by one set over them in a house belonging to the Church in the presence of the bishop. Yet, they are to retain their freedom of choice as to where they choose to give themselves to the clerical office. But when they have completed their eighteenth year, their wish concerning the possibility of marriage is to be explored by the bishop in the presence of the whole clergy and people. If, at God's inspiration, the grace of chastity should please them and they promise to preserve their chastity without the need for marriage, then, as people who desire the very narrow life, let them become subject to the very light yoke of the Lord. First, let them have the ministry of the subdiaconate, which, after proof of their profession, they may receive after their twentieth year. If they reach their twenty-fifth year without incurring guilt or offense, they can be promoted to the diaconate, so long as it has been fully established by the bishop that they can knowledgeably fulfil this office.

c. 7. THAT A DEACON NOT BE ORDAINED BEFORE THE AGE OF TWENTY-FIVE, NOR A PRIEST BEFORE THAT OF THIRTY.

From the Council of Arles III, c. 1.

Because what was established by the ancient Fathers regarding the ordination of clerics is known not to be entirely observed as it ought, lest perhaps the Lord's priests be troubled by importunate and inordinate requests and be compelled to transgress those instructions that have so often been given, they pronounce definitively that it be observed among themselves that none of the bishops presume to ordain a deacon who has not reached the age of twenty-five. No layman is to receive the honour of the episcopacy or of the priesthood before a conversion of life or before the age of thirty.

c. 8. THAT PENITENTS AND THOSE WHO HAVE BEEN MARRIED TWICE AND THE HUSBANDS OF DIVORCED WIVES NOT BE ORDAINED.

From the same, c. 3.

No one is to dare to ordain in the said honours a penitent, a twice-married, or the husbands of those who were previously married. And although the provisions of almost all the canons already confirm this, yet, lest the importunity of petitioners (as we have already said) or an iniquitous suggestion steal upon any of the bishops, it has been necessary that the Lord's bishops should now be willing to impose a stricter rule upon themselves. And so, whoever should, from this day on, presume to ordain a cleric in violation of what has been set out above, from the day on which this can be proved against him, is not to dare to say mass for an entire year. If anyone should refuse to observe this provision and, acting against the consent of his brethren, presume to celebrate mass, he is to know himself separated from the love of all the brethren. For it is suitable that he should feel the severity of ecclesiastical discipline, who has despised to observe provisions so frequently and healthfully instituted by the holy Fathers.

c. 9. AT WHAT AGE DEACONS ARE TO BE ORDAINED.

From the Council of Agde, c. 16.

But a bishop is not to entrust the blessing of the diaconate to those younger than twenty-five. Even if married young men have consented to be ordained, the will of their wives is also to be investigated so that, having separated their sleeping quarters and made a profession of religion, after they have equally converted, they may be ordained.

c. 10. AT WHAT AGE BISHOPS OR PRIESTS ARE TO BE CONSECRATED.

From the same, c. 17.

None of the metropolitans is to presume to ordain a priest or bishop before his thirtieth year, that is, before he has reached the age of complete manhood, lest they incur blame through some error because of their age (which sometimes happens).

c. 11. ON THE LAWFUL AGE FOR ORDAINING PRIESTS.

From the canons of ancient Eastern Fathers, c. 20.

If someone has not completed the thirtieth year of his age, he is not in any way to be ordained a priest, even if he is very worthy, because the Lord himself was baptized in his thirtieth year, and so he began to teach. It is fitting, then, that the one who is to be ordained also be kept until this legitimate age.

c. 12. ON THE ORDINATION OF BISHOPS.

From the Council of Toledo IV, c. 19.

A pernicious custom is not to be passed over in silence which, transgressing the statutes of the ancients, has troubled the whole order of the Church. While some aspire to the episcopate out of ambition, others take on the pontificate by offering gifts, yet others, unworthy to do so, have come to the honour of the highest sacred order while implicated in crimes or devoted to secular military service, something of necessity had to be established regarding their case and their removal. But lest very great disturbance arise in the Church, setting aside what was done in the past, henceforth, we believe it necessary in accordance with the rules of the canons to list those who are not to be promoted to the priesthood, namely: those who are detected in some crime, or are stained with the mark of infamy, or have confessed that they committed some wrongs by public penance, or have fallen into heresy, or are known to have been baptized or re-baptized in heresy, or have mutilated themselves, or are known to have something missing either naturally by a defect of their members or by amputation, or have entered into a union with a second wife, or have married several times, or have married a widow or a woman abandoned by her husband, or have been husbands of women who were not virgins, or have concubines for the purpose of fornication, or are bound by a servile condition, or are recent converts or laymen, or are not known, or are devoted to secular military service, or are bound by obligations to a court, or do not know their letters, or have not reached the age of thirty, or have not proceeded through the ecclesiastical degrees, or seek the honour by reason of ambition, or attempt to obtain the honour by gifts, or are chosen for the episcopate by their predecessors. But neither shall he henceforth be a bishop whom neither the clergy nor the people of his own city have chosen and whom the authority of the metropolitan or the consent of the bishops in the province did not seek out. And so, whoever is henceforth nominated for the episcopal order and, upon being investigated as to the matters aforesaid, is found to be guilty of none of them, and is of an approved manner of life and doctrine, then, according to the synodal or decretal provisions, with the consent of all clerics or citizens, he shall be consecrated to the episcopacy on a Sunday by all the bishops in the province, or at least by three of them, with the absent ones expressing their consent by letter, and even more by the authority or presence of the one who is established in the metropolitan see. A bishop is to be consecrated with the bishops of his province at a time chosen by the metropolitan, but nowhere other than in the metropolitan city, with the bishops of the province gathering there. But if anyone unworthy henceforth strives to aspire to the episcopal degree against the aforementioned prohibitions of the canons, he and those who ordain him shall be subject to the loss of the honour which they have acquired.

C. 13. THAT WIDOWS NOT BE VEILED.
From the general decrees of Pope Gelasius.

None of the bishops is to attempt to veil widows, since neither divine authority grants such a thing, nor the provision of the canons warrants it. Hence, this is by no means to be carried out, and ecclesiastical protections shall be brought against them so that nothing unlawful may be done.

C. 14. THAT, AS HAS BEEN SAID ABOVE, WIDOWS ARE NOT TO BE VEILED. BUT IF, WITH A CHANGED INTENTION, THEY TRAMPLE UPON THEIR PROFESSION OF CONTINENCE, THEY ARE TO RENDER AN ACCOUNT FOR THEMSELVES TO GOD.
Cap. 21 of the same.

We have spoken at sufficient length above about widows who are not to be veiled with any blessing. If, by their own will and with a changeable mind, they have trampled on the promised chastity of their first marriage, it will be their dangerous concern by what satisfaction they ought to placate God, because, according to the Apostle, they made void their first faith (1 Tim. 5:12). For just as, if they were perhaps unable to practice continence, according to the Apostle, they were not at all forbidden to marry (1 Cor. 7:9), in the same way, having deliberated with themselves, they were bound to keep the faith of chastity which they had vowed to God. We must not ensnare such women, but only set before them the exhortations of an eternal reward and the punishments of the divine judgment, so that our conscience may be free and their right intention may render an account of itself to God. Warning is to be taken from what the Apostle Paul says of their morals and actions (1 Tim. 5:12). We pass over a plainer exposition lest their unstable sex seem not so much to be deterred as to be incited.

c. 15. ON WIDOWS WHO TRANSGRESS AGAINST THEIR PROFESSED CONTINENCE.
Council of Carthage IV, in Africa, held by 214 bishops, in the year of the era 436.

Since the reward of chastity is good, it is to be preserved with greater observance and attention. Any widows, even if they are still in the years of their minority and have been widowed by their husband at an immature age, if they have devoted themselves to God, and have cast aside the lay habit and have taken on the religious habit with the bishop and the Church as witnesses, and if afterwards they have passed to worldly nuptials, according to the Apostle Paul, they shall have damnation because they have dared to make void the faith of chastity which they had vowed to God (1 Tim. 5:12). Such persons are to be severed from the communion of Christians, nor are they to share even a meal with Christians. For if adulterous wives are guilty of a crime against their husbands, how much more shall widows who vowed a religious life to God be marked with the crime of adultery if they have corrupted with a libidinous will the devotion which they offered to God freely and passed into a second marriage? Even if they had been carried off by someone's violent attack, but afterwards consented to remain in a marriage with their ravisher or violent husband because of the delights of lust, they are to be held guilty by the condemnation expressed above. Of such, the Apostle says: "When they have grown wanton, they wish to marry: having damnation, because they have made void their first faith (1 Tim. 5:11–12)." I, Aurelius, bishop of the Church of Carthage, attest by my signature. Donatianus, of the first see of Thelepte.

c. 16. ON WOMEN WHO HAVE PROFESSED WIDOWHOOD BEFORE THE BISHOP.
Council of Orange, held by 14 bishops, in the year of the era 477, tit. 1, c. 27.

The promise to preserve widowhood made before the bishop in the sacristy, with the imposition by the bishop of the widow's habit, is not to be violated. A woman who abandons such a promise, or her ravisher, is deservedly to be condemned.

c. 17. HERE BEGIN THE CHAPTERS WHICH THE HOLY SYNOD CONFECTED IN GOD'S NAME IN THE CITY OF TOLEDO, C. 10.

For the consideration of chastity, which ought to increase most greatly with this Council's encouragement, with the consent of our glorious lord King Reccared, this holy Council affirms that those widows whom it may please to observe chastity are in no way to be forced to enter into marriage again. But if, before the profession of continence, they have chosen to marry, let them marry whom they have wished to have as husbands by their own will. A similar condition is to be observed as to virgins, that they not be compelled to take husbands apart from their parents' or their own will. But if anyone has impeded the intention of chastity of a widow or a virgin, let him be kept apart from holy communion and the bounds of the Church.

c. 18. ON SACRED MEN AND WOMEN TRANSGRESSING AGAINST THEIR SACRED INTENT.
Council of Toledo.

The downward course is from the will, and nature is an imitator of the vices. For that reason, any man or woman who has once put on a habit or has freely taken up the religious habit, or if a man or a woman has been dedicated to the company of the Church, or she has been placed in a female monastery, let the transgressor of either sex be compelled to return to their intended state of life unwilling, so that the man is tonsured and the girl enters the monastery. But if they intend to continue as deserters with someone's patronage, they are so to be held as outsiders from the assembly of Christians by a priestly sentence that they are to have no common place whatever. As for widows too who desert their profession or habit, the universal Synod has already established that they are to be condemned by the preceding sentence.

c. 19. THAT WIDOWS OR VIRGINS WHO HAVE PROFESSED CONTINENCE NOT MARRY.
Also, the same Pope Gelasius to the Sicilian bishops.

Nor do we suffer those widows to pass into marriage who remained in a long-lasting observance of a religious intention. Similarly, we forbid virgins to marry who happen to have come of age after several years in monasteries.

c. 20. ON THOSE WHO HAVE TAKEN IN MARRIAGE VEILED WOMEN CONSECRATED TO GOD.
[Council of Tribur] c. 23.

If any man has taken in marriage a woman consecrated with the sacred veil, and after the vow to God, they join in incestuous and sacrilegious unions, it is equitable that, as we read in the constitutions of Pope Gelasius, c. 20, these people be immediately cast out of holy communion and, unless by public and approved penance, they are not to be received. But, if they do penance, the viaticum is not to be denied to those about to leave the world. In the Council of Chalcedon, c. 16: "Those who perpetrate this are to be excommunicate; if they confess, let mercy be granted to them by the bishop's authority." Also, in the letter of Pope Siricius, c. 6: "As for women who have been veiled and consecrated to God, if, setting aside their intention of holiness, they have secretly joined themselves in a sacrilegious contagion or freely and publicly given birth to children from unlawful intercourse, we command that these unchaste and detestable persons be expelled from monastic communities and ecclesial assemblies. Confined in their places of correction, they are to bemoan such a crime with constant lamentation." Hence, by the Lord's word and canonical authority, in this holy Synod we command that they be completely separated and be bound by oath not to cohabit further under the same roof, nor to engage in familiar conversation, unless in church or in public, or to have anything in common from which a suspicion of wanton desire or the scandal of a lustful deed may justly arise. If there are things to be divided between them, let them divide them and each make provision for what belongs to each.

c. 21. ON VEILED WIDOWS.
Pope Gelasius.

None of the pontiffs is to attempt to veil widows, as was established in the decrees of Pope Gelasius, c. 13, because neither divine authority, nor the provision of the canons prescribed this. If she has professed continence by her own will, as we read in c. 21 of the same Gelasius, let her intention render an account of itself to God because, according to the Apostle, if she was not able to remain continent, she was in no way forbidden to marry (1 Cor. 7:8–9); once she has so deliberated with herself, she must keep the promise of chastity which she has made to God. With the support of the Fathers' authority, in this holy Council, we freely adjudge and decree that, if she has freely taken on the veil, although not a consecrated one, and she has made the offering to God in the church with the veiled women, willing or not, she must henceforth wear the nun's habit, even if she should wish to confirm by oath that she so took the veil on the ground and condition that she could lay it down again.

c. 22. ON VEILED WIDOWS.
From the African Council, c. 89.

A widow who has placed the sacred veil upon her head, has prayed in the church among the other veiled women, and has offered the oblation with them, and has professed to remain in the same habit, vowing never to set aside the veil of religion, is not to presume to abandon the observance of religion. We desire your Holiness to be well in Christ.

c. 23. ON THE MAN WHO HAS ENTERED A MONASTERY AGAINST HIS WIFE'S WILL, THAT, EVEN IF HE HAS BEEN TONSURED, HE MUST ABSOLUTELY BE RETURNED TO HIS WIFE.

From the Register, part 1, c. 180, to Adrian, notary of Palermo.

Agathosa, the bearer of these presents, has complained that her husband, against her will, has become a monk in the monastery of Abbot Urbicus. Since this undoubtedly touches on the abbot's guilty jealousy, we command your Experience to look into the matter with diligent inquiry, lest he perhaps has entered the monastery with her consent, or that she herself promised to change [her manner of life]. If this should be the case, let him provide for him to remain in the monastery, and compel her to act in accordance with her promise. But if neither of these is the case, and you do not discover that the aforesaid woman committed any crime of fornication (for which it is lawful for a husband to leave his wife), then, lest his entry into religious life might become an occasion of perdition to the wife left in the world, we will that you, without allowing any excuse, must by all means restore her husband to her, even if he has been already tonsured. For although the law of the world prescribes that, for the sake of entry into religious life, a marriage may be dissolved even if a spouse is unwilling, yet the divine law does not allow this to be done. Indeed, except for the cause of fornication, it does not allow a man to abandon his wife for any reason. After the husband and wife have been made one body (cf. 1 Cor. 6:16) by marital copulation, such a body cannot in part enter monastic life, and in part remain in the world.

c. 24. A BISHOP MUST LAY DOWN HIS HONOUR, IF HE HAD A CONCUBINE AT THE TIME WHEN HE WAS ESTABLISHED IN A SACRED ORDER.

From a letter of St. Gregory, c. 43.

He writes to Andrew, bishop of Taranto, saying: Anyone who is conscious of his crime will look upon the tribunal of the eternal Judge with security, if he now strives to placate it with worthy penance. It has come to our knowledge with manifest truth that you had a concubine, about whom an uncongenial suspicion has arisen among some people. But since in ambiguous matters judgment must not be absolute, we have chosen to entrust the matter to your own conscience. If, then, you remember having been defiled by carnal intercourse after being established in the sacred order, you must resign the honour of the episcopacy and not presume in any way to approach its administration, knowing that you will minister to the danger of your soul, and that, without doubt, you will have to render an account to our God if, while conscious of this crime, you should choose to remain in the order in which you are, hiding the truth.

c. 25. ON THE RAVISHING OF VIRGINS.

In the year of the Incarnation of the Lord 952, Indiction 9, it was established in Frankfurt by the most glorious King Otto, in the fifteenth year of his reign, with the consent of the bishops, counts, and many other faithful subjects, and by the authority of the canons of the holy Fathers, as also by the decrees there set out of the Capitularies of preceding kings, that no oppression or ravishment of virgins or widows be done by any men, and that those who ravish them under the title of living with them, as those also who cooperate or connive with the ravishers, if any of them are clerics, they are to fall from their degree; but if they are laymen, they are to be anathematized, and the ravishers are to remain in perpetuity without hope of marriage. If after such things they presume to join with each other, both are to be anathematized.

c. 26. AS ABOVE.

It was also found before the said king that no abbey which has its own election may be given to a monastery or to anyone as his own. But those which lack their own election may be made subject by the king's gift and privilege to another monastery which is established under his protection (*mundiburdium*).

c. 27. ON CHRIST'S MINISTRY.

"If any man minister to me, let him follow me." With what fruit, with what reward, with what prize? "And where I am," He says, "there shall also my minister be (Jn. 12:26)." Let Him be loved freely and let the reward for ministering to Him be to be with Him. Where will it be well without Him, and when will it possibly be bad to be with Him? Listen as He speaks more explicitly: "If any man minister to me, him will my Father honour (Jn 12:26)." With what honour, if not that of being with His Son? For that which He says again and again: "Where I am, there shall also my minister be" is understood to have been expounded when He says: "Him will my Father honour." Indeed, what greater honour may an adoptive child receive than to be where the only Son is, not made equal in His divinity, but associated with Him in His eternity? But we ought rather to ask ourselves what it is to minister to Christ, a work for which such a great reward is promised. Indeed, if we understood ministering to Christ to consist in the preparation of the things necessary for the body, in cooking or setting out His supper, or mixing His drink and giving it to Him, this is what they did who were able to be in His physical presence, such as Mary and Martha when Lazarus too was one of those at table with Him. But in this sense, Judas, condemned to perdition, also ministered to Him. For he kept the purse, and although he most wickedly stole from it (cf. Jn. 12:6), yet the preparation of necessary things was also done through him. Hence, when the Lord said to him: "That which you do, do it quickly," some thought that the Lord had commanded him to prepare what was necessary for the feast-day or to give something to the poor (cf. Jn. 13:27–29). And so, it was not at all of such ministers that the Lord said: "Where I am, there shall also my minister be. If any man minister to me, him will my Father honour," for we see that Judas, who ministered in this way, was reprobated rather than honoured. Why, then, do we seek elsewhere what it means to minister to Christ, and not recognize it from these very words? For when He said: "If any man minister to me, let him follow me," he wished it to be understood as if He were saying: If a man does not follow me, he does not minister to me. Hence, they minister to Christ who seek not their own interest, but that of Jesus Christ (cf. Phil. 2:21). "They follow me," then, means that they walk my ways, not their own, as it is written elsewhere: "He who says that he abides in Christ, ought himself also to walk even as he walked (1 Jn. 2:6)." If he gives bread to the hungry, he must do so out of mercy, not out of vanity, with the left hand not knowing what the right hand does (cf. Mt. 6:3), that is, so that the intention of cupidity be far from the act of charity. He who ministers in this way ministers to Christ, and it will be rightly said to him: "What you have done to the least of these, you have done it to me (Mt. 25:40)," who does for Christ not only works of bodily mercy, but any good deeds. And these will be good because "the end of the law is Christ to the righteousness of anyone who believes (Rom. 10:4)," even to that work of great charity which consists in laying down one's life for one's brothers, because this, too, He will say to His members: "What you have done for these, you have done for me." With regard to such a deed, He deigned to make and call Himself a minister, when He said: "Just as the Son of man came not to be ministered to, but to minister, and to lay down his life for many (Mt. 20:28)." Hence, it follows that each one is a minister of Christ for those same reasons for which Christ is a minister. Similarly, the Father will honour him who ministers to Christ by that great honour of being with His Son, nor will his happiness ever fail. And so, brethren, when you hear the Lord saying: "Where I am, there shall also my minister be," do not think only of good bishops and clerics. You, too, in your own small way, minister to Christ by living well, giving alms, preaching His name and doctrine to those to whom you are able. And let each father of a household also know by this title that he ought to extend paternal affection to his own household; for the sake of Christ and eternal life, let him admonish, teach, exhort, correct them all; let him extend benevolence and exercise discipline. In this way, he exercises within his own household an ecclesiastical office, and in some way an episcopal one, ministering to Christ, and he will be with Him for all eternity. Indeed, many of your number have ministered that highest ministry of martyrdom; many who were not bishops, nor clerics, but youths and virgins, the elder with the younger, many married men and women, many fathers and mothers of families, ministering to Christ, even lay down their lives in martyrdom, and since the Father honours such, they received the brightest crowns.

c. 28. ON CLERICS WHO DESIRE THE MONASTIC PURPOSE.
From the Council of Toledo, c. 50.

Clerics, who seek the monastic purpose and desire to follow a better life: It is fitting that free entry into monasteries be granted to them by a bishop; the resolve of those who strive to pass to the desire for contemplation is not to be forbidden.

c. 29. FROM THE LETTER OF THE BLESSED POPE GREGORY SENT TO ARCHBISHOP BONIFACE, IN WHICH, AMONG OTHER THINGS, WE READ THE FOLLOWING DECREE AS TO WIDOWS.

Your Dilection has sought our advice regarding widows who have withdrawn from the intention of widowhood; I believe you know, dearest brother, that, unless they are deflected, they were once condemned by St. Paul (1 Tim. 5:11–12) and many holy Fathers. We also decree by our apostolic authority that they are to be condemned, and to be kept from the communion of the faithful and the bounds of the Church, until they obey their bishops and, willing or unwilling, return to the good which they had begun. Concerning virgins or those not veiled, if they should go astray, we have a decree of our predecessor Pope Innocent of sainted memory in the following terms: "As for those who have not yet been covered with the sacred veil, and yet have pretended that they would ever remain of virginal intent, even if they were not veiled, if they have married, they are to do penance for a time, because the role of their bridegroom was held by the Lord. For if even among men it is by no means a common practice for a contract made in good faith to be dissolved, how much more is this kind of promise, which has bound one to God, not to be dissolved without some punishment?" etc. Indeed, if virgins not yet veiled are punished in this way by public penance, and are excluded from the company of the faithful until satisfaction, how much more are widows, who are of more perfect age and maturer wisdom and counsel and who were very accustomed to the society of men, and who allowed themselves to be veiled and have taken the habit of religion, and then have apostatized and returned to their former vomit, to be kept until satisfaction by us and all the faithful from the bounds of the Church and the company of the faithful and even to be placed in jail! Did they not, according to the blessed Apostle Paul, hand a man of this sort over to Satan so that his spirit might be saved in the day of the Lord

(1 Cor. 5:5)? Of such, the Lord also speaks through Moses, saying: "Take the evil away from your midst (Deut. 13:5)." Of them also, he says through the Prophet: "The just shall rejoice when he shall see the revenge: he shall wash his hands in the blood of the sinner (Ps. 57:11)." Of such, and of those like them, and of those who lend their consent to them, because not only those who do, but also those who lend their consent to the doers, are guilty (cf. Rom. 1:32), the Lord speaks through the same Prophet David and says: "You saw a thief and ran with him: and with adulterers you were a partaker (Ps. 49:18)." And there are many other texts similar to these. Such persons, then, are indubitably shown to be adulterous because, after abandoning their immortal Spouse, they have returned to their former life like dogs to their vomit; they have become apostates and, by joining themselves with mortal men, are polluting themselves by an illicit and sacrilegious union. According to the same Apostle Paul, because they have set aside their intention of widowhood and have presumed to break the faith which they had pledged to God, and have transgressed against their first faith (cf. 1 Tim. 5:12), these women are to be condemned by us. As has been already said, they are to be banished from the bounds of the Church and the company of the faithful until satisfaction by you and the rest of the men of our order, that is, by each in his own diocese. We command that all the faithful abstain from the fellowship and society of such persons in every way. In addition to these things, it also pleased that, for so long as they persevere in that detestable, illicit, and sacrilegious sharing of the flesh, no Christian other than those whom their own bishop has commanded to do so for the sake of correction communicate with them with regard to anything, or go into the house in which they are, since with such as these, as the aforementioned holy Apostle instructed, it is not lawful for any of the faithful even to take food (1 Cor. 5:5). If anyone should presume to attempt or boldly do any of these things, he is to be struck with an equal sentence of excommunication with them.

C. 30. OF THE WIDOW WHO IMPOSED A VEIL ON HERSELF FOR A TIME UNDER THE GUISE OF RELIGION.

Cap. 5.

Nicholas, bishop, servant of the servants of God, to our most reverend and holy fellow brother Adalwinus, archbishop of the holy Church of Salzburg. You posed a question concerning a woman who, after her husband's death, placed a sacred veil over her head and under the said veil feigned being a nun, but afterwards she married again. Because, by her bad faith, she wished to trouble the ecclesiastical rule and did not lawfully persevere in her vow, it seems good to me that she do penance for her nefarious foolery and return to that which she promised and began in the sacred ministry. For if we consent that anyone feign, as they wish, all ecclesiastical sacraments and not perform them truly, the whole Church order is troubled, the rights of the Catholic faith are not certain, and the sacred canons are not duly observed. For what use was it to Simon Magus that he feigned receiving sacred baptism and that he would remain a Christian? When the Apostle discovered his fraud, that which would happen to him was stated, for the Apostle said: "Take your money with you to perdition, for your heart is not right before God. Do penance for this baseness of yours and pray to God, in hope of forgiveness for this thought of your heart, for I see that you are in the gall of bitterness and in the bond of iniquity (Act. 8:20–23)." If such people do not return to their senses, we decree they be struck by the spiritual sword, for it is not meet to lie to the Holy Spirit, and, as Ananias and Sapphira lied, they immediately perished (cf. Act. 5:1–10).

C. 31. ON PENITENT MEN, WIDOWS, AND VIRGINS WHO DESIST FROM PENANCE AND BECOME LAITY, OR CHANGE THEIR HABIT, OR JOIN IN MARRIAGE.
Council of Toledo IV, c. 55.

Any of the seculars who tonsured themselves while receiving penance and transgressing have become laymen again are to be apprehended by their bishop and recalled to the penance from which they withdrew. If any of these cannot be recalled by force, nor return after admonition, as truly apostates, they are to be condemned by a sentence of anathema before the Church. Not otherwise also those who were tonsured by their parents, or by their own free will vowed themselves to religion after the loss of their parents, and afterwards took up a secular habit; the same are also to be apprehended by the bishop and recalled to the practice of religion after first doing penance. If they refuse to return, as truly apostates, they are to be subjected to a sentence of anathema. This form shall also be observed with regard to consecrated widows and virgins, and to penitent women, who wore the habit of a nun, and afterwards either changed their habit, or passed into marriage.

C. 32. ON THE DISTINCTION BETWEEN SECULAR AND RELIGIOUS WIDOWS.
Also, from the same, c. 56.

There are two kinds of widows, secular and religious. Secular widows are those who, still having the intent to marry, have not set aside their lay habit. The religious ones are those who, having already set aside their secular habit, appeared in religious garb in the sight of the bishop or of the Church. If the latter pass into marriage, according to the Apostle, they will not be without condemnation because, having first vowed themselves to God, afterwards they cast aside their intention of chastity (1 Tim. 5:11).

C. 33. A WOMAN WHO CAST ASIDE HER RELIGIOUS HABIT IS TO BE COMPELLED TO RETURN TO IT AND TO BE ENCLOSED IN A MONASTERY.

From the Register of Gregory, to Vitalian, bishop of Siponto.

If you had known how to be a guardian of the religious habit or a bishop, then it would not have been allowed with you there for the daughter of Tullian, the general of glorious memory, to cast aside her religious clothes and revert to worldly dress, nor to send us a perverse letter. But because you are pressed down by excessive sloth and torpor, to your dishonour this still unpunished unlawfulness has been committed. Indeed, if, as we have said, you had been careful, news of the punishment of this most depraved woman ought to have reached us before that of the offence did. Accordingly, since you are so slothful and so negligent that, unless you have experienced canonical punishment yourself, you do not know how to be responsible for the correction and discipline of others, if it please the Lord, at an appropriate time, we shall show you what care you ought to exercise. Upon receipt of these writings, wake up and, once awake, at least carry out what you have deferred until now under the pressure of your fecklessness. Let it be your urgent business, together with Sergius, our defender, to apprehend the said woman and, immediately and without any excuse, not only recall her to the habit which she has evilly despised, but thrust her in a monastery, where she may be very strictly held. Show toward her all care so that, from your correction, she may understand how nefarious her deeds are. If it should happen in this matter (which we do not believe) that any layman attempt to resist you by any means, suspend him from participation in the most holy communion and act promptly to report back to us, so that, if he does not gather by his own reflection how execrable his presumption is, he may know it by the quality of his correction. In all these things, see to it that you show yourself to be so prudent and vigilant that your negligence will not double your fault, but your care may somewhat diminish it.

C. 34. ON THE SAME MATTER.

Gregory, to Sergius, our defender.

If you were a man, or if you had any rigour, you ought to have been such a guardian of regular discipline that you would have corrected with punishment those deeds that are being illicitly committed there before news of them reached us. But as excessive foolishness makes you negligent, not only are we offended by such matters, but we are also called upon to punish your sloth as well. Setting aside every delay and excuse, hurry, together with our brother and fellow bishop Vitalian, to apprehend the daughter of Tullian, the general of glorious memory, who has cast aside the religious clothes, which she had freely taken on, and disgraced herself with lay dress. Recall her to her religious habit and send her to a monastery, where she may be very strictly kept, nor allow her detention to be eased at all until you receive new instructions in writing from us. For if you should prove in any way negligent or slow in this matter, know that you shall be punished so severely that you may know from the sharpness of the punishment what you have failed to learn on your own, because, as we have said, if you had had the intelligence of a man, you ought to have known before the things which you are now commanded to do and the levying of a punishment from you.

c. 35. WHAT IS TO BE DONE REGARDING WOMEN WHO CHANGED INTO RELIGIOUS HABIT IN THEIR OWN HOUSES, IF AFTERWARDS THEY CHOSE MARRIAGE.
Council of Toledo IV, c. 57.

As for widows and girls who, in their own houses, have changed into the habit of religion, either on their parents' or their own initiative, if afterwards they desire to marry against the ordinances of the Fathers or the precepts of the canons, both spouses are to be suspended from communion until they emend what they have perpetrated illicitly. If they should fail to emend, they are to be severed in perpetuity from the communion or the table of all Christians.

c. 36. THAT ECCLESIASTICAL CUSTOM IS TO BE OBSERVED AS IF IT WERE LAW.
Among the sermons of our holy Father Basil to the blessed Amphilochius on the Holy Spirit, c. 27.

Among the customs of ecclesiastical institutions, some we have received in writing, others mysteriously by apostolic tradition through confirmed successions. And that these have equal power and the same effect of piety who would doubt who is even only a little versed in the sacred Scriptures? If we attempted to esteem as nothing the customs of the Church not handed down in writing by the Fathers, it will be clearly established to those who consider it how much harm this would inflict on religion. Indeed, to begin with, which written document taught the faithful to sign themselves with the sign of the Cross of salvation? And which compilation has left the words of the extended prayer over the bread and the chalice, or of consecration? For not only do we say in the Secret of the mass that which is contained in the Gospels and the Apostle, but we also add many other things, as if endowing these consummate mysteries with greater force. Which form of letters taught us to turn toward the East in prayer? We bless the font of baptism with the oil of unction. In addition to this, we immerse three times those whom we baptize, anoint with oil and teach in words the renunciation of Satan and his angels. From where do we receive these and many others of the same kind, if not from the secret and mystical tradition of the Fathers, which, as is the custom of the Church, are observed as to the mysteries with a more reverential diligence in silence than those made public in writing.

C. 37. ALSO, C. 29.

The day fails me, if I were to undertake to explain the several customs of the Church. What more? Who taught us in writing the very confession of faith, of believing in the Father, the Son, and the Holy Spirit, except that the piety of faith afterwards imitates the handing down of baptism, and as we are baptized, so we believe? What writing has instructed us to pray while standing on feast-days, but do not do so on non-festive days? Hence, if the practice of the Church, by a mystical observance, piously keeps so many things that are not handed down in writing, I adjudge it not to be absurd, but rather apostolic, also to keep firmly those traditions which are not written down. The Apostle says: "I praise you that in all things you are mindful of me, and keep my traditions as I have delivered them to you (1 Cor. 11:2)." And the other one: "Hold the traditions which you have learned, whether by word or by our letter (2 Thess. 2:15)." Hence, although every word stands in the mouth of two or three witnesses (cf. Mt. 18:16), we have preferred to rely on many examples by which it may appear more persuasively to the learned that the observance of ecclesiastical custom introduced by our ancestors is to be held as if it were law.

Appendix Three

C. 1. FROM THE COUNCIL OF TOLEDO.

Concerning the Jews, the holy Synod taught this: that henceforth no force is to be brought to bear on anyone to believe. "For God is merciful to whom he wills and hardens the heart of whom he wills (Rom. 9:18)." Indeed, such ones are not to be saved if unwilling, but willing, so that the form of justice is kept whole. Just as man perished by obeying the serpent with his own will of discretion, so too each man is saved by believing, when called by God's grace and the conversion of his own mind. And so, it follows that they are to be persuaded, and absolutely not compelled, to convert, not by force, but by the free exercise of discretion. As for those who have already been compelled to come to Christianity (as was done in the time of the most religious prince Sisebut), because it is clear that, sharing in the divine sacraments, they have received the grace of baptism, have been anointed with chrism, and have been partakers of the body and blood of the Lord, it is fitting that they be compelled to retain the faith which they took up, even if by force or necessity, lest the faith which they took up be thought vile and contemptible.

C. 2. FROM THE COUNCIL OF TOLEDO.

Nothing is presumed by audacious temerity against the established order, nor those things which are esteemed with the highest veneration or are fulfilled with even the least touch of presumption, since to this end alone are those things which have been commanded to be done known to be interrupted: lest by the onset of illness their nature be deprived of the strength of salvation. And so, thought is given not only to human fragility, but provision is also abundantly made for the honour of God's mysteries, while care is solicitously taken that they are kept from the risk of harm. Hence, we have judged it to be fitting that, when the holy mysteries are being consecrated by the priests at the time of the mass, if some event of illness should occur, by which the mystery of consecration, already begun, cannot be completed, it is permitted for a bishop or priest instead to complete the consecration of the office already begun. For nothing else is suitable for supplementing the mysteries once commenced than the complete blessing of a priest, whether he be the one who came first, or the one who follows, since they will not be seen to be perfect, unless they be completed by the order of perfection. And since we are all one in Christ, diversity [of persons] forms nothing contrary where the unity of faith makes manifest the efficacy of a happy conclusion. Moreover, clerics of any order are not to doubt that this provision applies and is granted also to them, and so, as has been said, others may freely take the place of those who have precedence over them for the sake of completion. But lest that which is granted in aid of a weakness of nature should be turned into ruinous presumption, no one is to presume to say mass after food or drink, however small the quantity taken, and no minister or priest at all is to leave incomplete any offices which he has begun, without the evident onset of affliction. If anyone should temerariously presume to do these things, he shall sustain a sentence of excommunication.

C. 3. FROM THE COUNCIL OF TOLEDO.

Until now, the effect of weak enforcement has sometimes rendered nugatory an honourable legal edict, while something is ignorantly regarded as dissoluble which is bound by the authority of an indissoluble confirmation. Therefore, it is becoming that whatever unsuitable thing has occurred from uncertainty be clearly cast out, in order that henceforth nothing remain that is in doubt. And so, if one or both parents gave to their children of either sex at any stage of their minority the due dress for religion or the tonsure of religion, or if the parents were unwilling or unaware when the children received it, if they did not immediately disavow that it be seen on their children but, either before themselves, or before the Church, and publicly in the community, they have permitted the said children to have such things, it shall not ever be at all lawful for those children to revert to secular habit. If they are convicted of at some time having had the tonsure and religious dress, they are to be immediately recalled to the observance and habit of religion, and are to be compelled to devote themselves to this holy practice under severe constraint. As for parents, permission for them to consign their children to the religious life cannot extend beyond the tenth year of the children's age; but afterwards, it shall be lawful for the children to take on the religious life either with the agreement of their parents, or by the solitary vow of their own devotion. Whoever should be found to have transgressed either by taking away the tonsure, or by wearing secular dress, shall receive the punishment of excommunication, and remain forever in a religious community.

c. 4. FROM THE COUNCIL OF TOLEDO.

It often happens that matters which pertain to the holy statutes are not fulfilled because of the sloth of some people. Accordingly, because it is known what dignity is to be observed from the canons in the burial rites of a dying bishop by the tradition of ancient custom, we only add this, that if, in accordance with the statutes of the Council of Valencia, any of the bishops, admonished to come to the burial of the body of a deceased bishop, delays doing so because of a slothful will, at the summons of the clerics and with the bishops' compliance, before the synod or before the metropolitan bishop, for the space of one year he is to have no license of doing mass or receiving communion. As for the priests and others who held a greater place of honour in the same Church whose bishop has died, if they are found to have been tardy in extending all care to the burial rites of the bishop once he was dead, or in summoning a bishop while he lay dying, or are proved to have neglected it for whatever vexation of spirit, they are to be sent to do penance in monasteries for one whole year.

c. 5. FROM THE COUNCIL OF TOLEDO.

The Prophet's speech announces woe to those who do the Lord's work fraudulently and slothfully (cf. Jer. 48:10); if they incur woe who do the Lord's work negligently, what punishment shall they deserve who withdraw the observance of the divine service from the altars of Christ with the intervention of malice? We are speaking of those who, confounded by the deceit of an obstinate mind when some spur of fraternal quarrels has pricked them, seized there and then by an insane boldness, strip the altars, take off the sacred cloths, remove the lights and, with the intervention of malice, withdraw the observance of the divine sacrifices. Because they are unable to avenge themselves against men, what is worse, they inflict an injury on God. Hence, if someone incurs the guilt of homicide for hating his brother, what penalty shall he merit for such contempt of God? Indeed, as the text divinely admonishes, if a man has sinned against a man, God may be placated. But if someone has sinned against God, who shall plead for him (cf. 1 Sam. 2:25)? And so, that sentence of the Lord by which the malice of priests is punished will easily apply to the excesses of such priests, for He says: "Those who honour me I shall honour; but those who despise me shall be despised (cf. 1 Sam. 2:30)." Any priest or minister, then, who henceforth, moved by reason of some sorrow or bitterness, either has presumed to strip the divine altar of its sacred cloths, or has dressed it in some other mourning clothes, or even has taken away from God's temple the customary service of sacred lights and has commanded these to be extinguished, or has brought any sort of grievance into God's temple and, what is worse, has given occasion by which the usual offices are absent from the Lord's temples, or the offering of the singular sacrifice is seen to be defrauded in any way, if the satisfaction of true penance before the metropolitan has not first purged him, let him know that, in accordance with the higher sentence of the Lord, he is consigned to perpetual shame and deprived of the dignity and honour of his rank. Undoubtedly, in this sentence of punishment are not included those persons who happened to do these things fearing the contamination of sacred orders, or the subversion of holy faith, or in the course of hostile attack or siege, or even in fear of the sentence of divine judgments, since in the deed of these is declared more the humility that placates God than the deceit of inner spite.

c. 6. DECREE OF POPE CELESTINE, C. 16.

We have learned, dearest brothers, that some have been ordained as bishops who were not prepared by any ecclesiastical orders for the glory of such dignity. He acknowledges that he has done this by usurpation, against the decrees of the Fathers, although the episcopate ought to be reached through those orders by which it has most frequently been enjoined so that those who have been admitted to the lesser offices may be made more firm for the greater ones. For whoever desires to be a teacher must first be a disciple, so that he may teach what he has learned; every institution of life confirms itself by this rationale to reach its proper end. Someone who has not made any effort at letters cannot be a teacher of letters. Someone who has not progressed through the several terms of military service cannot reach the order of veteran. Is the priesthood alone, I ask, more despised among such occupations that what is fulfilled with greater difficulty is granted with greater ease? But it is not enough now to ordain laymen, which no order allows to be done, but some are even ordained whose crimes are thoroughly known throughout almost all the provinces. Indeed, in a report sent to us from the Eastern parts, Daniel has been accused of abominable abuses by the whole monastery of virgins of which he had charge, and many shameful deeds have been brought against him by many. He has been sought in some part of the earth in which he skulks so that, if he trusts in his own innocence, he ought not to avoid the judgment which has been sought against him. Letters sent to the bishop of Arles through our subdeacon Fortunatus to bring him before the episcopal judgment are contained in our daybook, copies of which we have also sent to you. He, who is burdened with so many testimonies and struck with so many charges of crimes, having, as it is said, become polluted by incest with consecrated virgins, is alleged to have been ordained a bishop. At the very time when he was summoned by our letters to state his case, he crept into the pontifical dignity. Far be such injury from the sacred title! It is more probable that the one who ordained lost this dignity in giving it than that the one ordained received it. He shall share in his conviction who believed that he should join such a person to himself by conferring the pontifical dignity. Indeed, anyone who would ordain such persons shows what sort of person he is himself. These things now having been brought before you, and since there are several of you who are knowledgeable as to the statutes of the Apostolic See, let your Fraternities, gathered together at our exhortations and having considered these matters for a time with us, make haste to bring all things back to the norm of discipline.

C. 7. FROM THE DECREES OF POPE CELESTINE, C. 18.

A bishop is not to be given to the unwilling. The consent and desire of the clergy, people, and religious order are to be sought. Another may then be chosen from another Church, if no one suitable can be found (which we do not believe will happen) from the clergy of the city whose bishop is to be ordained. Indeed, the latter must first be rejected as unsuitable in order for any from other Churches to be deservedly preferred. Let each have the fruits of his service in the Church in which he has spent his life in all the offices. Let no one in any way creep into the offices of others, nor dare to claim for himself another's due reward. Let the clergy have the power to resist, if they see themselves burdened, and let them not fear to reject those whom they know are being imposed on them improperly. If not their due reward, they must have free judgment about the man who is to rule them.

C. 8. FROM THE DECREES OF POPE CELESTINE, C. 20.

Celestine, to all the bishops established throughout Apulia and Calabria. It is not to be lawful for any priest to be ignorant of the canons or to do anything which may contravene the rules of the Fathers. What worthy matter will we preserve if the norm of the enacted decretals is breached at someone's request when license is allowed to the people?

C. 9. FROM THE DECREES OF POPE CELESTINE, C. 21.

We have heard that some cities, devoid of their rulers, wish to seek their bishops from among the laity and believe such a glorious office to be so vile as to think we can confer it on those who have been serving not God, but the world. Not only do they badly judge their clerics, in whose contempt they do this, but they also think very badly of us, whom they believe are capable of doing it. They would never dare to think this way, if the opinion of some persons there did not lend their consent to them and connive at it. Thus, those things which have been very frequently decreed are of no profit when this is ignored, as if nothing had ever been written in this regard. Of what profit will it be for clerics to have served in their several offices and to have spent their whole life in the Lord's encampments, if those who are to be set over them are sought from among the laity? The latter, who have been busy with worldly affairs and know nothing of the ecclesiastical order, by a preposterous leap and with immoderate cupidity, desire to jump up into another man's honour and, trampling all reverence for ecclesiastical discipline, to pass into another manner of life. Dearest brothers, we who have charge of the rudder of our law (*ius*), that is, of the canons, of necessity must stand in the way of such persons. By these letters, we admonish your Fraternity that no one is to admit any layman to the clerical order, nor to suffer it to be done, as a result of which he would deceive that layman and give rise to causes against himself by which he would be guilty against the established decretals.

C. 10. FROM THE DECREES OF POPE CELESTINE, C. 22.

The people are to be taught, not followed; if they do not know what is lawful and what is not, we must admonish them, and not offer to them our consent. Hence, whoever should attempt to do what is forbidden will know that the censure of the Apostolic See will not at all be lacking. For whatever we do not correct by the sole authority of admonition, we must necessarily punish with a severity that fits the rules. And we wish this to be known throughout all the Churches which lack their own rulers, that no one, having perhaps been flattered, should delude himself with vain hope. Given on the twelfth day before the Kalends of August, in the consulate of Florentinus and Dionysius.

C. 11. FROM THE COUNCIL OF GANGRA, C. 2.

If anyone condemns another who is religious and faithful for eating meat, although he abstains from blood and animals sacrificed to idols or strangled, as if he were without hope on account of such partaking, let him be anathema.

C. 12. FROM THE COUNCIL OF GANGRA, C. 4.

If anyone discriminates against a married priest on the grounds that it is not fitting to partake of the oblation administered by him, let him be anathema.

C. 13. FROM THE COUNCIL OF GANGRA, C. 6.

If anyone holds assemblies outside of a church, and, despising the Church, has wished to usurp the things that are the Church's, without the priest's agreement in accordance with his bishop's decree, let him be anathema.

c. 14. FROM THE COUNCIL OF GANGRA, 17.

If any woman has for the sake of divine worship, as she believes, cut off her hair, which God gave her as a reminder of her subjection, as if dissolving the commandment of obedience, let her be anathema.

c. 15. FROM THE DECREE OF BISHOP HILARY.

Furthermore, brothers, new and unheard seeds of perversities (as has come to us by a sure report in letters sent from Spain) are arising in some places. In short, some think the episcopate, which is not given for anything other than preceding merits, is not a divine gift but a hereditary right and so believe that, in the same way as transitory and mortal things, so too the office of bishop can be bequeathed by right of legacy or testament. For many bishops, when they are at death's door, are reported to specify others by name for their position, namely, so that lawful election is not awaited, but the pleasure of the deceased is taken for the assent of the people. Consider how grave this is! And so, if it please you, let us also take away generally this license from Churches lest (which is shameful to say) anyone think he owes something which is God's to some man. In order that what has been reported to us may also come to your notice, let the writings of our Spanish brothers and fellow bishops be read. Paul the notary read them aloud.

c. 16. FROM THE DECREE OF BISHOP ANASTASIUS, C. 7.

May the most sacred heart of your Serenity know that, according to the custom of the Catholic Church, no taint of defect from Acacius's name attaches to any of those whom he baptized or whom, in accordance with the form of the canons, he ordained priests or deacons, by which perhaps the grace of the sacrament conferred by an evil one may seem less certain. For even baptism which (far be it from the Church!) is conferred by an adulterer or by a thief comes to the receiver an unspotted gift because that voice which issued from the dove casts out all mark of human pollution by declaring and saying: "This is the one who baptizes in the Spirit and fire (cf. Lk. 3:16; Mt. 3:11)." For if the rays of that visible sun, although they pass through the foulest of places, suffer no contamination by the contact, how much more is the power of that Sun which made the visible one entirely undiminished by the unworthiness of His ministers. For although Judas committed sacrilege and theft, all the acts which he performed among the Apostles by reason of the dignity entrusted to him were benefits conveyed through an unworthy one and suffered no detriment because of it. The Lord himself declared it by the clearest assertion in saying: "The scribes and Pharisees sit in the chair of Moses; do whatever they enjoin upon you (Mt. 23:2–3)."

Thus, whatever any minister in the Church, in accordance with his own office, is seen to perform for the betterment of men, all of this [is also seen] to be embraced by the fulfilling effect of the divinity. So it is that Paul, through whom Christ speaks, affirms: "I planted, Apollo watered, but God gave the increase. Therefore, neither he who plants nor he who waters is anything, but only God who gives the increase (1 Cor. 3:6–7)." Thus, God does not ask who, or what kind of person, preaches, but what he preaches so that he affirms that even the envious preach Christ well (cf. Phil. 1:15). By the same infirmity, the devil himself was cast down, and yet he did not cease to preach because of this.

C. 17. FROM THE DECREE OF BISHOP ANASTASIUS, C. 8.

Therefore, even this one, whose name we declare must be kept unspoken, by evilly administering good things, harmed himself alone. The inviolable sacrament, given through him to others, kept the wholeness of its power. It is the overanxious suspicion of some which extends itself so far as to imagine that, after the published judgment of Pope Felix, Acacius performed without efficacy the sacraments he usurped, and accordingly to fear for those who received the mysteries that were passed down, whether in consecration or in baptism, lest the divine gifts be seen to be without effect. Let them remember also with regard to this that what was said earlier likewise prevails, because having been condemned he did not do this without usurpation of the priesthood. In this case, the guilty person did not cause harm to the mysteries that retain their power nor also to others. Indeed, to him pertains what David's trumpet sings out: "But God shall break the heads of his enemies: the hairy crown of them that walk on in their sins (Ps. 67:22)." For pride always brings about its own ruin, not that of others. The entire authority of the heavenly Scriptures attests to this, as is also said by the Holy Spirit through the Prophet: "He that works pride shall not dwell in the midst of my house (Ps. 100:7)." Hence, when someone who is condemned claims for himself the title of priest, the swelling of pride is inflicted on his own head. It is not the people, thirsting for the gift in the mysteries, who are excluded, but that soul alone which had sinned was properly guilty by a just judgment, as the frequent instruction of the Scriptures attests. Hence, removing all strivings and wiles of men placed in this still present fragility, according to our prayers, by your imperial authority, offer to our God the one, Catholic, and apostolic Church, because it is in this thing alone in which you can triumph without end not only on earth, but also in heaven. Subscription: May almighty God preserve your kingdom and well-being by his perpetual protection, most glorious and clement ever Augustus.

c. 18. ON A CHURCH'S CANTORS.
From the Council of Laodicea, c. 15.

That it is no longer to be fitting for others to ascend the pulpit and sing in church apart from those who are the regular cantors and sing from a book.

c. 19. FROM THE COUNCIL OF LAODICEA, C. 24.

That it is not to be fitting for those dedicated to the sacred mystery, from the priests to the deacons, and the rest of the ecclesiastical order, that is, subdeacons, lectors, cantors, exorcists, and doorkeepers, as also those who are among the continent and the monks, to enter taverns.

c. 20. FROM THE COUNCIL OF LAODICEA, C. 40.

That it is not to be fitting that bishops who have been called to a synod entirely refuse to attend, but to go immediately and teach or be taught what is useful for the correction of the Church or of other things. He who has refused will call himself to account, unless perhaps he cannot go because of illness.

c. 21. FROM THE COUNCIL OF LAODICEA, C. 50.

That it is not to be fitting to stop the fast on the Thursday of the last week of Lent, and to pass through all of Lent without veneration; it would be more meet that all of Lent be venerated with a strict fast.

c. 22. FROM THE COUNCIL OF LAODICEA, C. 51.

That it is not to be fitting for the birthdays of the martyrs to be celebrated in Lent, but it is meet for their holy commemoration to be done on Saturdays and Sundays.

c. 23. FROM THE AFRICAN COUNCIL, C. 54.

It has pleased that the prayers which were approved in the Council, whether prefaces, or commendations, or laying on of hands, be celebrated by all. Nor let other ones be uttered against the faith, but only those are to be said which have been discussed with those who are more prudent.

c. 24. FROM THE AFRICAN COUNCIL, C. 76.

Also, it has pleased that any bishops, who neglect to win over for Catholic unity places which pertain to their see, are to be summoned by diligent neighbouring bishops, so that they may not delay to act in the matter. If they have not done so within six months from the day of their summons, let the places pertain to whomever is able to convert them. But if the one to whom the places seemed to pertain should be able to prove that the other bishop's negligence had been preferred by the heretics, so that they might continue there with impunity, and his own diligence had been obstructed in such a way that his more solicitous care might be avoided, when the judging bishops come to know this, then those places are to be returned to that bishop's see. If the bishops between whom the cause exists are of different provinces, that primate is to assign judges in whose province the place in contention is. If they have chosen neighbouring judges by common consent, either one is to be chosen, or three; if they choose three, the sentence of all, or of two of them, is to be followed.

C. 25. FROM THE AFRICAN COUNCIL, C. 78.

If a bishop in mother sees has been negligent toward the heretics, let him be summoned by the diligent neighbouring bishops, and let his negligence be shown to him so that he may not excuse himself. If within six months from the day on which he is summoned, if a writ of execution occurred in his province, and he has not seen to it to bring them back to Catholic unity, there is to be no communion with him until he fulfils this. But if an executor does not come to those places, let this not be ascribed to the bishop.

C. 26. THAT LAYMEN WHO CONTEMN THE CANONS BE EXCOMMUNICATED, AND CLERICS WHO DO SO BE DEPRIVED OF THEIR HONOUR.

From the Council of Carthage, c. 15.

Bishop Gratus said: According to the statutes of the Council and the pronouncement of my Insignificance, it pleases that all matters be brought to conclusion. All the items that have been designated and set out are to retain their sentences, even without which I believe you to hold that the impiety of rebaptism, which has been condemned at many Councils by our Fathers and by tradition, must be punished. I believe that these matters also received their determination at our Council. But it is necessary that the other things, which have been done or said or included above, or which are found to have been written by other Councils according to law, be kept. If anyone transgressed and has broken these statutes or has regarded them as to be held as null, if he is a layman, he is to be deprived of communion, if a cleric, of his honour. Bishop Gratus said: It remains only that all that has pleased us and which, with your consent, has been written down you now also affirm by your signature. They all said: The writings of this Council attest that we have consented, and that consent will be declared by our signature. And they signed.

c. 27. FROM THE COUNCIL OF CARTHAGE, C. 7.

Felix, bishop of Selemsela, said: But I submit to your Holiness that those who are expelled from the Church for their crimes have dared either to approach the imperial court or to rush to civil courts, or, if perhaps a bishop or a cleric of whatever people, to test the bounds of the Catholic Church; what do you think regarding these persons? Epigonius, bishop of Bulla Regia, said: If any bishop in the Catholic communion has incited a man of this sort with vain blandishments, let him know that he has become as corrupt as such rejects, having passed into their fellowship. Bishop Genethlius said: Hence, our brothers and fellow bishops rightly submit that, if those who have been expelled from the Church by merit of their crimes are received into communion by some bishop or cleric, the latter are also to be found equally guilty with the former. It was said by all: It pleases all.

c. 28. FROM THE COUNCIL OF CARTHAGE, C. 16.

That bishops are not to read the books of the gentiles; as for those of the heretics, they may do so in accordance with need or time.

c. 29. FROM THE COUNCIL OF CARTHAGE, C. 26.

A bishop is to strive to encourage dissident brothers, whether clerics or lay, more to peace than to judgment.

c. 30. FROM THE COUNCIL OF CARTHAGE, C. 98.

Laymen are not to dare to teach in the presence of clerics, unless with their approval.

c. 31. FROM THE COUNCIL OF CARTHAGE, C. 7.

It is not licit for any infamous and sacrilegious person to testify against a good Christian (however lowly and servile the latter may be) at any time in any lawsuit, nor to sue a Christian by action or accusation on any matter.

c. 32. FROM THE COUNCIL OF CARTHAGE, C. 13.

The persons of accusers must be such whose faith, associations, and worthy manner of life are without reproof and who lack all suspicion, for even in our present time, at the Synod of Nicaea, these and several other things have been decreed because of the wiles of wicked men.

c. 33. FROM THE COUNCIL OF CARTHAGE, C. 5.

If anyone has charged any bishop, priest, or deacon with false crimes, and has been unable to prove them, communion is not to be given to him even at the end.

c. 34. FROM THE COUNCIL OF CARTHAGE, C. 8.

That if anyone has robbed another person, and has not made restitution at the bishop's admonition, he is to be excommunicated.

c. 35. FROM THE COUNCIL OF CARTHAGE, C. 8.

It is not licit for the emperor or for any preserver of piety to presume anything against the divine mandates.

c. 36. FROM THE COUNCIL OF CARTHAGE, C. 18.

An unjust judgment or an unjust decision ordained by judges through fear of or by command of any king is not to have any validity.

c. 37. FROM THE COUNCIL HELD AT VALENCIA, C. 84.

Anyone who is among the penitents, however good he may be, is not to be ordained a cleric. If this should happen due to the bishop's ignorance, he is to be deposed from the clergy for not having revealed at the time of ordination that he was a penitent. But if the bishop ordained him knowingly, the bishop himself is to be deprived at least of the power of ordaining, if not of his episcopate.

c. 38. FROM THE DECREES OF POPE MARCELLINUS, C. 4.

Hence, it is not licit for the emperor or for any preserver of piety to presume anything against the divine mandates, nor to do anything which is opposed to the evangelical, prophetical, or apostolic rules. Indeed, an unjust judgment or an unjust decision ordained by judges through fear of or by command of any king is not to have any validity, nor will anything stand which is done against evangelical, prophetical, or apostolic doctrine and a constitution of theirs or the holy Fathers, and whatever has been done by infidels or heretics shall be entirely quashed.

c. 39. FROM THE DECREES OF POPE PIUS.

If anyone has presumed to usurp for himself the possessions of the Church and to persecute the very clerics and priests of the Lord, let such a one be held as sacrilegious and be adjudged guilty of sacrilege. Indeed, we have heard that those who do this persecute the Lord's clerics and priests, so as to add evil to evil and become worse, not understanding that the Church of God consists in its priests and grows into the temple of God. Just as he is guilty of sacrilege who devastates God's Church and despoils and invades its goods and donations, so also he who attacks its priests is adjudged guilty of sacrilege. Desire eagerly the better gifts, brothers, and do not do such things since not only those who do such things are guilty of this crime, but also they who give their consent to those who do them.

C. 40. FROM THE DECREES OF POPE CLEMENT, C. 84.

And so, it is to be diligently observed that, when the law of God is read, it not be read or taught according to one's own understanding. For there are many things in the divine Scriptures which can be drawn to that sense which each one presumptuously presumes for himself, but it is not fitting to do this. For you must not seek an alien or extraneous sense which you extrinsically adulterate, or confirm it in any way by the authority of the Scriptures, but seize the sense of truth from the Scriptures themselves. And so, it is necessary to learn the meaning of the Scriptures from someone who keeps it according to the truth handed down to him by our predecessors, so that he may assert with competence what he has received rightly. Indeed, when someone has received from the divine Scriptures the whole and firm rule of truth, it will not be absurd if he adds something for the exposition of true doctrine from the common erudition and the liberal studies which he perhaps acquired in childhood, but in such a way that, when he has learned true things, he set aside the false and feigned ones. Indeed, even for young people, length of life is uncertain, even as it is not all uncertain for the aged. It is not to be doubted that, however long it may be believed to be, it is short.

C. 41. FROM THE DECREES OF POPE PIUS, C. 3.

Indeed, what profit is it for someone not to be polluted by his own error, if he then gives his consent to one who errs? Undoubtedly, both he who sins and he who consents to one who errs fight against the commandments.

C. 42. FROM THE DECREES OF POPE ALEXANDER, C. 6.

Considering these forms of piety and avoiding the dangers for souls, together with all the Lord's bishops who have gathered with us in this sacred city and with all the members of this body, as we received from the blessed Apostles and the other holy Fathers and their successors, we decree and establish that all who go against the holy Fathers, or who manifestly strive to remove them and tear them to pieces, are infamous and are made alien from the bounds of the Church until satisfaction. For God so hates those who arm themselves against the Fathers, as attackers and destroyers of the Fathers, who are made infamous for their persecution of the Fathers, that it is not even licit to speak with those whom our highest doctors, as we call the bishops, oppose for their crimes. If so, how much more is it not licit to consent to or speak with those who attack them, lest they be found to be sharers in their crimes, since not only those who do, but also those who consent with those who do, are guilty? Hence, the blessed prince of the Apostles, Peter, at the ordination of our holy predecessor Clement, instructed the clergy and people in these terms: If Clement were to be inimical toward someone for his deeds, do not wait for him to tell you not to be friends with such a one. You must observe prudently and obey his will unswervingly and turn away from him whom you feel Clement opposes, nor speak with those with whom he does not speak, so that each of those who is at fault, while he desires to enjoy the friendship of all of you, may hurry more quickly to become reconciled with the one who presides over all and in this way return to salvation, as he begins to obey the admonitions of him who presides. But if someone is a friend to those to whom he is not a friend, and has spoken with those with whom he does not speak, he is one of those who wish to exterminate God's Church and, even as he appears to be with you in body, he is against you in mind and spirit; such a one is a worse enemy than those who are outside and are evidently your enemies. Such a one, through the appearance of friendship, does things which are inimical and scatters and devastates the Church.

c. 43. [COUNCIL OF ORLÉANS, C. 17.]

If an appeal has been made twice to the metropolitan by any bishop belonging to the same province in his own cause, and the metropolitan has deferred hearing him, let him have permission to pursue his business at the next synod; whatever may then have been established in justice by his fellow bishops is to be observed.

c. 44. ON A COMPLAINT BETWEEN A PRIEST AND A LAYMAN, C. 21.
[Council of Tribur.]

If any priest has a dispute as to a complaint against a layman, or a layman against a priest, it is to be determined at the bishop's direction without acceptation of persons. If it should be necessary, the layman is to bind himself by an oath; but the priest, instead of swearing an oath, is to be questioned "by the holy consecration," because priests are not to swear for a light cause. The hand which confects the body and blood of Christ is not to be polluted by an oath. Far be it, since the Lord in the Gospel says to his disciples (whose place we unworthily fill in Holy Church): "Do not swear oaths at all; let your speech be Yes, yes; No, no. For whatever goes beyond this is from evil (Mt. 5:34, 37)." He did not say: Whatever goes beyond this is evil, but it is from evil, that is, from an evil man by whose incredulity we are compelled to swear. Indeed, as we read in some homily of the blessed priest Bede: "If perhaps it has happened that we swore incautiously, namely, so that keeping what we swore will result in a worse outcome, we know that it is to be freely changed by a sounder counsel."

c. 45. IF A FREE MAN HAS MARRIED A FREEDWOMAN, HE WILL HENCEFORTH HAVE TO KEEP HER, C. 38.

[Council of Tribur.]

In the decrees of Pope Leo, c. 18, it is written: "Not every woman joined to a man is that man's wife, as not every son is his father's heir. For the bonds of marriage are lawful between the free born and between equals. And so, a wife is one thing, a concubine another, just as a maidservant is one thing, and a free woman another. Hence, if someone has given his daughter in marriage to a man who had a concubine, it is not to be taken as if he had given her to a married man, unless perhaps that woman has been rendered freeborn and is seen to have been lawfully endowed and rendered honourable by public marriage." Hence, following the authority of the Fathers, under the present list of this holy Council, we establish and freely adjudge that if a free man has lawfully taken to wife a freedwoman, that is, one who, by manumission and royal gift, has been made free from being a maidservant, he must keep her henceforth as if she had been engendered from a noble kin, excepting the cause of fornication, and so long as she lives, he is to take no other. As we have already said from the decrees of Pope Leo, she has been freed, lawfully endowed, and rendered honourable by public marriage, and so is no longer a concubine, but a wife acquired in accordance with the laws. This same law applies equally to freedwomen and freedmen.

c. 46. ON A FREEBORN WOMAN WHO MARRIES A SLAVE.

[Council of Compiègne, c. 5.]

If a freeborn woman marries a man of servile condition, knowing him to be a slave, let her keep him. The law shall be the same for man and woman.

c. 47. AT THE SYNOD OF ORLÉANS.

If an appeal has been made twice to the metropolitan by any bishop belonging to his province in his own cause, and the metropolitan has deferred hearing him, let him have permission to pursue his business at the next synod; whatever may then have been established by his fellow bishops is to be observed.

c. 48. AT THE SYNOD OF AGDE.

Neither is that to be omitted which greatly infests the faith of religion, that some clerics and laymen apply themselves to auguries and, under the name of a feigned religion, which they call the lots of the saints, profess the science of divination, or predict future events by the inspection of some writings. Whichever cleric or layman has been found to consult or teach such things is to be cast out of the Church.

c. 49. FROM SOMEONE'S CAPITULARY.

Thirdly, it is to be made known that, at the priest's salutations, the suitable responses be made, where not only the clerics and the priests dedicated to God are to offer the response, but the whole devout people is to answer with consonant voice.

c. 50. FROM THE SAME.

Sixth, these are necessary to priests for their learning, that is, a book of the sacraments, a lectionary, an antiphonary, an order of baptism (*baptisterium*), a book for calculating the date of Easter (*computus*), a canon of penance, a psalter, homilies suitable for all Sundays and feast-days throughout the year. If one of these should be lacking, even the name of priest will hardly be justified in him because those evangelical threats are very serious which say: "If one blind man allows another blind man to lead him, both fall into the ditch (Mt. 15:14)."

c. 51. FROM THE SAME.

Eighteenth, that none of the ordained or of those about to be ordained move from his parish to another, nor go on a pilgrimage to the thresholds of the Apostles for the sake of prayer, abandoning the care of his church, nor, having been suspended from communion, is he to be received by another to communion without the permission and prior knowledge of his bishop. If anyone has done so, such communion or ordination or migration is not at all valid. And it is to be announced to all the faithful that those who desire to go to the thresholds of the blessed for the sake of prayer are to confess their sins at home and so depart, because they are to be bound or loosed by their own bishop or priest, and not by a stranger.

c. 52. FROM THE SAME.

Twenty-fifth, that they announce to the people that they are sureties and sponsors of faith to those spiritual sons and daughters whom they receive at baptism, and that on their behalf they renounce the devil, to whom they were formerly subject. And so, until they have become adults and their sponsors have expounded and handed over to them the promise of their faith and the formula of renunciation, the sponsors are to have them in their providence, and what they had promised for them, they are to exact from them those same responses in their integrity.

c. 53. ON CLERICS WHO FEIGN BEING MONKS.

That clerics who, by habit and name, feign being monks, and they are not, are to be corrected and emended in every way so that they either be true monks, or true canons.

c. 54. THAT THE IMPOSITION OF HANDS IS TO BE DONE BY THE BISHOPS WHILE FASTING.

[Council of Paris, c. 33.]

That bishops are not to confer the Holy Spirit through the imposition of hands other than when fasting, excepting in the case of the infirm and those in danger of death. Just as at two seasons, namely, Easter and Pentecost, it is meet that baptism be celebrated by pontiffs who are fasting, so also the conferring of the Holy Spirit.

c. 55. [FROM A DECREE OF EMPEROR CHARLES.]

As for seeking information in tables and books, no one is to presume to cast lots in a psalter, or a gospel book, or other things, nor to do any divinations.

c. 56. FROM A DECREE OF EMPEROR CHARLES.

That they not baptize bells, nor hang papers on poles for the sake of [averting] hail.

c. 57.

The law of emperors is not above the law of God, but under it.

c. 58. HERE BEGINS THE ACCOUNT OF THE APOCRYPHAL BOOKS.

First, we profess that the Synod of Rimini, convoked by Constantius Caesar, son of Constantine, through the prefect Taurus, is from thenceforth and for all eternity, damned. Also, the Itinerary under the name of the Apostle Peter, which is called The Eight Books of St. Clement, is apocryphal. The Acts under the name of the Apostle Andrew, apocryphal. The Acts under the name of the Apostle Thomas, apocryphal. Another Act under the name of the Apostle Peter, apocryphal. The Acts under the name of the Apostle Philip, apocryphal. The Gospels under the name of Thaddaeus, apocryphal. The Gospels under the name of Barnabas, apocryphal. The Gospels under the name of the Apostle Peter, apocryphal. The Gospels under the name of Thomas, of which the Manicheans make use, apocryphal. The Gospels under the name of Bartholomew, apocryphal. The Gospels under the name of the Apostle Andrew, apocryphal. The Gospels which were forged by Lucian, apocryphal. The Gospels which were forged by Hesychius, apocryphal. The Book about the infancy of the Saviour, apocryphal. The Book about the birth of the Saviour and about Mary or the midwife, apocryphal. The book which is called The Shepherd, apocryphal. All books made by Leucius, a disciple of the devil, apocryphal. The book which is called Foundation, apocryphal. The book which is called Treasure; apocryphal. The book about the

Daughters of Adelgenensis, apocryphal. A Cento of verses concerning Christ, interleaved with Virgilian verses, apocryphal. The book which is called the Acts of Tecla and of Paul, apocryphal. The book which is called of Nepos, apocryphal. The book of Proverbs written by heretics and circulated under the name of St. Sixtus, apocryphal. The Revelation which is called of Paul, apocryphal. The Revelation which is called of Thomas, apocryphal. The Revelation which is called of Stephen, apocryphal. The book which is called the Passage of St. Mary, apocryphal. The book which is called the Penance of Adam, apocryphal. The book of Deogias the Giant, who is said by heretics to have fought with a dragon after the Flood, apocryphal. The book which is called the Testament of Job, apocryphal. The book which is called the Penance of Origen, apocryphal. The book which is called the Penance of St. Cyprian, apocryphal. The book which is called of Jamnes and Mambres, apocryphal. The book which is called the Lot of the Apostles, apocryphal. The book the Pastimes of the Apostle, apocryphal. The book which is called the Canons of the Apostles, apocryphal. The book Physiologus which was written by heretics and to which the name of blessed Ambrose has been affixed, apocryphal. The History of Eusebius Pamphili, apocryphal. The Works of Tertullian or Africanus, apocryphal. The Works of Postumianus and Gallus, apocryphal. The Works of Montanus, Priscilla, and Maximilla, apocryphal. All the works of Faustus the Manichean, apocryphal. The Works of the other Clement of Alexandria, apocryphal. The Works of Cassian, priest of the Gauls, apocryphal. The Works of Victorinus of Poitiers, apocryphal. All the works of Faustus of Riez, of the Gauls, apocryphal. The Works of Frumentius, apocryphal. The Epistle of Jesus to Abgar, apocryphal. The Epistle of Abgar to Jesus, apocryphal. The Passion of Cyricus and Julitta, apocryphal. The Passion of George, apocryphal. The writing which is called the Dispute of Solomon, apocryphal. All phylacteries, which were not compiled in the names of angels, as some pretend, but rather of demons, apocryphal. These and those works similar to them, which Simon Magus, Nicholas, Cerinthus, Marcion, Basilides, Ebion, Paul of Samosata, Photinus and Bonosus, who were found wanting for the same error, Montanus with all his depraved followers, Apollinaris, Valentinus or the Manichean, Faustus, Sabellius, Arius, Macedonius, Eunomius, Novatus, Sabbatius, Calistus, Donatus and Eustatius, Nibinianus, Pelagius, Julian of Eda, Caelestius, Maximian, Priscillian of Spain, Lampetius, Dioscorus, Eutyches, Peter and the other Peter, of whom the one defiled Alexandria and the other Antioch, Acacius of Constantinople with his associates, and also all heresies which they themselves, their disciples, and schismatics have taught or copied and whose names we do not remember; not only are these works repudiated and cast out by the entire Roman Catholic Church, but we profess them, together with their authors and the followers of their authors, to be condemned forever under an indissoluble bond of anathema.

c. 59. THAT THOSE WHO RETAIN THE OFFERINGS OF THE DECEASED ARE TO BE EXCOMMUNICATED.
From the Council of Vaison, c. 188.

As for the condemnation of those who retain the offerings of the deceased and delay in giving them to the churches, they are to be cast out from the Church as faithless people. It is certain that this exacerbation of divine goodness reaches even to a weakening of the faith since they defraud the faithful departing from their bodies of the fulfilment of their vows and the poor of the consolation of food and their necessary sustenance. Such people are to have God's judgment as if killers of the needy and non-believers. Hence, one of the Fathers inserted this in his writings by a suitable sentence in which he says: "To steal something from a friend is theft; to defraud the Church is sacrilege."

c. 60. ALSO, FROM THE DECRETAL LETTER OF POPE CALLIXTUS DIRECTED TO ALL BISHOPS OF THE CITIES OF THE GAULS, C. 135.

Forbid the joinings of blood relations to be done, since both the divine and secular laws forbid them. For the divine laws not only cast out those who do this, and their issue, but also call them cursed. The laws of the world call such people infamous and exclude them from inheriting. But we, following our Fathers and walking in their footsteps, mark them with infamy, and adjudge them to be infamous, because they are spattered with the stains of infamy, nor must we receive those men or their accusers whom the laws of the world reject. And we call those blood relatives, whom the divine laws and the laws of the emperors of the Romans and of the Greeks call blood relatives, and receive in hereditary succession, and cannot exclude. For the joinings of such persons are neither legitimate, nor can be allowed to stand, but must be rejected. Hence, whoever has not been joined legitimately, or is known to have been married without title to dowry and without the priestly blessing, cannot at all make accusations of crime against priests or those joined lawfully, nor give testimony against them, because anyone polluted by the stain of incest is infamous and is not allowed to make accusation against the aforesaid. Hence, not only these are to be rejected and become infamous, but also all who give their consent to them.

c. 61. FROM THE DECREE OF POPE HILARY, C. 28.

As to bigamists, the question ought not even to have been raised, since the lesson of the Apostle is clear: "the husband of one wife (1 Tim. 3:2)" is to be admitted to the priesthood or to the clergy, and yet only if he took her as a virgin. For she who had a husband before, even though he has died, yet, if she afterwards joins with a cleric, the man who has taken her cannot be a cleric. It is warned in the Law that a priest cannot have a widow or a cast-off as his wife (Lev. 21:7).

c. 62. NO ONE IS TO BE AT THE SAME TIME ACCUSER, WITNESS, AND JUDGE.
From the African Council, c. 121.

No one should ever presume to be at once both accuser and judge or witness, for it is necessary that in every place of judgment four persons always be present, that is, elected judges, accusers, defenders, and witnesses.

c. 63. FROM THE AFRICAN COUNCIL, C. 131.

The same persons are not to be accusers and judges, but in an orderly way accusers, judges, witnesses, and accused are each to be severally in their own order. First, there is always to be a written accusation, so that a false accuser may receive retaliation, because no one is to be judged or condemned prior to a written accusation, since even secular laws retain these requirements. As to all these things, let true equality always be practiced, so that they may deserve by the truth of their deeds the recompense for their accusation, judgment, and testimony.

c. 64. TITLES FROM THE CORPUS OF THEODOSIUS, C. 22.

Anyone who does not believe that sins are forgiven in the Church, contemns the liberality of the divine gift, and closes his final day in this obstinacy of mind is guilty of the unforgivable sin against the Holy Spirit, in whom Christ remits sins. As to this very difficult question, in a certain little book written solely to this end, I disputed most clearly about it, insofar as I was able.

c. 65. FROM THE INSTITUTES OF CASSIAN, C. 252.

If anyone has been suspended from prayer for his own fault, no one is to have license to pray or speak with him before license is given to the supplicant by his superior. Indeed, anyone who has presumed with ill-considered pity to join with him in prayer and speech before he is received by his superior incurs the same condemnation, handing himself over willingly to Satan, to whom, according to the opinion of the Apostle, he had been consigned for the emendation of his crime. And in this he sins more gravely, who joins himself to the other, because, by giving him solace, he causes his heart to become more hardened and does not allow him to give thought to satisfaction and forgiveness for that for which he had been separated from prayer, but renders worse the delinquent's contumacy through the greater sin of pride.

c. 66. ALSO, ON THE SAME MATTER.
Bishop Basil, c. 253.

It shall not be licit for anyone to pray, or to speak, or to eat with an excommunicate.

c. 67. AS ABOVE.
Cap. 254.

If any brother, openly or hiddenly, has spoken or joined with an excommunicate, he is immediately to contract with him the shared penalty of excommunication.

c. 68. AS ABOVE.
Bishop Fructuosus, c. 256.

No one is to speak with an excommunicate, neither to encourage him by any compassion or commiseration, nor to presume to support him to defiance or pride.

c. 69. FROM THE COUNCIL OF ANTIOCH, C. 257.

It is not to be licit to communicate with excommunicates, nor to enter the houses and pray with those who do not participate in the prayer of the Church, nor for those who are excommunicated by one Church to be received in another. If it should appear that any of the bishops, or priests, or deacons, or even any of those who are retained in the canon communicates with the excommunicates, then he too must be deprived of communion as one who confounds the rules of the Church.

c. 70. FROM THE COUNCIL OF CARTHAGE, C. 32.

If anyone has resolved to do something which does not please God, he is to do penance according to the manner of his sin, and that which he has resolved temerariously and unjustly is to be revoked as void.

c. 71. FROM THE SAME COUNCIL, C. 38.

If anyone who has been offended is unwilling to become reconciled after the one who offended him has provided satisfaction, he is to be worn down with very strict fasts, until he accepts the satisfaction with a grateful spirit.

c. 72. FROM C. 46.

If anyone is unwilling to become reconciled to his brother, whom he holds in hate, he is to do penance at bread and water until he is reconciled to him.

c. 73. THAT THE CANONS NOWHERE COMMAND THAT ANOTHER SUCCEED ON ACCOUNT OF A BISHOP'S ILLNESS.

Cap. 158.

Your Dilection has written to me that our most pious lord has ordered a successor to be appointed to my most reverend brother John, bishop of Justiniana Prima, because of the ailment of the head from which he suffers, lest perhaps that city, while it lacks the jurisdiction of a bishop, be destroyed by its enemies (far be it!). And yet the canons nowhere command that a bishop succeed to another bishop because of illness, and it is wholly unjust that, if a bodily ailment attacks, the sick person should be deprived of his honour. Hence, this cannot be done by us, lest a sin come upon my soul because of his deposition. But it is to be suggested that, if he who is in charge is sick, such an administrator may be found for him who may manage all his concerns, and fill his place (without his being deposed) in the governing of the Church and in the safe-keeping of the city, so that neither may almighty God be offended, nor the city be found to be neglected. But if the same most reverend John perhaps, due to his illness, should petition that he must be freed of the honour of the episcopate, it is to be granted to him if he makes a request in writing. Otherwise, out of the fear of almighty God, we are entirely unable to do this. If he is unwilling to make this petition which is not pleasing to the most merciful God, whatever [the emperor] may command to be done is within his power, as he may provide; only do not allow us to be mixed up in such a deposition. But whatever he may do, if it is canonical, we bear it insofar as it is without our sin.

c. 74. THAT NO ONE'S ACCUSATION BE RECEIVED IN WRITING, BUT IN HIS OWN VOICE, BECAUSE NO ONE WHO IS ABSENT CAN BE JUDGED OR JUDGE.

Cap. 125.

The accusation of no person is to be received in writing, but in his own voice (if the person of the accuser is lawful and worthy), namely, in the presence of him whom he desires to accuse, because no one absent can be accused or accuse. Yet no man of the forementioned order can be accused, or must respond to his accusers, before he has been called by his primate in accordance with the rules and has occasion to defend or make inquiry in order to wash away his crimes.

Scriptural Index

References are to book and chapter or to appendix and chapter with appendices 1–3 being respectively designated as a–c.

Index of Names and Places

References are to book and chapter or to appendix and chapter with appendices 1–3 being respectively designated as a–c. Names in the Preface are indicated by pr.

Index of Subjects

References are to book and chapter or to appendix and chapter with appendices 1–3 being respectively designated as a–c; pr. designates the preface.